The Annotated Passover Haggadah

The Annotated Passover Haggadah

Edited by
Zev Garber
and
Kenneth Hanson

An Imprint of the
Global Center for Religious Research
1312 17™ Street • Suite 549
Denver, Colorado 80202

info@gcrr.org • gcrr.org

GCRR Press
An imprint of the Global Center for Religious Research
1312 17th Street Suite 549
Denver, CO 80202
www.gcrr.org

Copyright © 2021 by Zev Garber and Kenneth Hanson

DOI: 10.33929/GCRRPress.2021.02

All rights reserved. No part of this publication may be reproduced, stored in a retrieval system, or transmitted in any form or by any means, electronic, mechanical, photocopying, recording, or otherwise, without the prior permission of GCRR Press. For permissions, contact: info@gcrr.org.

Unless otherwise noted, Scripture quotations are from the English translation of the Torah © 1917, 1985 by the Jewish Publication Society; *Torah Nevi'im U-Khetuvim. The Holy Scriptures according to the Masoretic Text.* Philadelphia, PA: Jewish Publication Society of America, © 1917, 1945, 1955; Revised Standard Version of the Bible, copyright © 1946, 1952, and 1971 National Council of the Churches of Christ in the United States of America; *The New International Version.* Grand Rapids, MI: Zondervan, 1984, 2011; and *The Jewish Study Bible*, edited by Adele Berlin and Marc Zvi Brettler, Jewish Publication Society, TANACH Translation, Oxford University Press, 2014. Used by permission. All rights reserved worldwide.

Typesetting/Copyediting: Holly Lipovits
Cover Design: Darren M. Slade
Front Cover Image: Decorated initial-word panel from the Haggadah for Passover (the 'Sister Haggadah'), fourteenth century (British Library).

Library of Congress Cataloging-in-Publication Data

The annotated passover haggadah / edited by Zev Garber and Kenneth Hanson
p. cm.
ISBN (Paperback): 978-1-7362739-2-0
ISBN (eBook): 978-1-7362739-3-7
1. Haggadot—Texts. 2. Seder—Liturgy—Texts. 3. Judaism—Liturgy—Texts. 4. Haggadah. 5. Passover. I. Title.

BM674.643   .G373   2021

Contents

Editor's Note	viii
Reflections: Interpretation and the Passover Haggadah, An Invitation to Post-Biblical Historiosophy ZEV GARBER	1
Reflections: The Disappearing Deliverer, The Moses Enigma KENNETH HANSON	9
Luaḥ Ivri/Hebrew Calendar ZEV GARBER	15
Bedikat Chametz ZEV GARBER	31
`Eruv Tavshilin: "Mixing of [cooked] Dishes" ZEV GARBER	34
The Traditional Seder Table ZEV GARBER	36
Annotated Haggadah for Passover ZEV GARBER AND KENNETH HANSON	41
Excursus: The Moral Sense of the Ten Plagues ZEV GARBER	68
Excursus: Pidyon Ha-Ben ZEV GARBER	71
Excursus: The Image of Elijah KENNETH HANSON	99

Rabbinic Sages Index ... 125

Source Index ... 129

Supplementary Readings ... 134
    KENNETH HANSON

Eucharist and Seder: What Should the Simple Scholar Say? ... 144
    PETER ZAAS

Inserting Shoah at the Traditional Passover Seder:
Interpreting Anew the Five Cups, and What Would Jesus Say? ... 151
    ZEV GARBER

Sample Haggadot and Sedarim ... 159
    NATHAN HARPAZ

Romaniote and Judeo-Spanish (Ladino) Passover Haggadah:
Excerpts and Related Customs ... 176
    YITZCHAK KEREM

A Chassidisher Pesach: Passover Traditions and Insights
from Chassidic Perspectives ... 188
    DIANE MIZRAHI

Why is this Haggadah different? Haggadot in the
Non-orthodox Movements ... 211
    ANNETTE BOECKLER

Re-arranging Things at the Table for an Isolated and Peculiar
Jewish Community at the Bottom of the World ... 230
    NORMAN SIMMS

Select Haggadah and Exodus Topics ... 239
    WILLIAM KRIEGER

Exodus to Leviticus to Haggadah:
The Dynamism of Torahistic Law 248
    JONATHAN ARNOLD, ESQ.

The Memory of God and the Blindness of Humanity:
The Four Children 251
    LEONARD GREENSPOON

The Dawn of the Jewish Woman: Marginalization, Liberation,
and the Exodus 259
    ROBERTA SABBATH

Haggadah, Shoah, and the Exigency of the Holy 274
    DAVID PATTERSON

Passover, Holy Thursday, and Catholic Liturgy 289
    EUGENE FISHER

Setting Our Tables with Grace and Respect:
Reformed Table Talk for Post-Shoah Times 301
    HENRY KNIGHT

Manna and Matsa: Nourishment for the Soul 313
    SUSAN CM LUMIÈRE

Ziva: The Warrior of Light 327
    SUSAN GARBER

The Virtual Seder: 15 Nissan, 5780 341
    KENNETH HANSON

Contributors 345

Image Credits 351

Editor's Note

Zev Garber
Kenneth Hanson

About the Editors

The two editors of this work, both academics and scholars of Jewish life, culture, and literature represent two individual experiences with Passover tradition, one being of Orthodox background and the other a convert to the Jewish faith. Their lively collaboration is at the heart of what this volume represents, as it highlights an assortment of interactions with the essence and meaning of the festival, across multiple ethnic and religious boundaries.

The Institution of the Lord's Supper, a Passover Seder?

In November of 2018, a group of collegial scholars convened in Denver at a session of the National Association of Professors of Hebrew (NAPH) at the Society of Biblical Literature conference to treat the connections or disconnections between the Jewish Seder and Christian Communion. The convening panelist were Peter Zaas, from Siena College, Ken Hanson from The University of Central Florida, Zev Garber from Las Angeles Valley College, and respondent Charles Carpenter from Southwest Baptist Theological Seminary. Donald Kim, Southwestern Baptist Theological Seminary, chaired the session. The panel was entitled "The Institution of the Lord's Supper, a Passover Seder?" These collegial scholars responded to and from each other's vantage point, offering insights and opportunities for fruitful dialogue. Texts and abstracts by Hanson, Zaas, Garber and Carpenter are published on *The Bible and Interpretation* website and three of the articles by Hanson, Zaas, and Garber are reprinted in Supplementary Readings.

Respectful dialogue and vitriolic disagreement greeted the content and delivery of my "The Traditional Passover Seder: Interpreting anew the Four Questions and Five Cups What Would Jesus Say?" I suggested that in the main, the pageantry of the Passover Seder focuses on two periods of Jewish history: the biblical Exodus from Egypt and the rabbinic recalling of the account. Through ritual food, drink, and animated reading and interpretation, the participant travels with the Children of Israel as if "s/he came forth out of Egypt," and sits at the table of the Sages as they observe Passover in Jerusalem and Bnei Brak. Alas, the forty-year trek from wilderness into freedom succumbed in Jewish history into a long night's journey into exile. "Begin with disgrace and end with glory" (*m. Pesachim* 10.4). That is to say, talk openly and informatively about exilic degradation and destruction, so that, in contrast, the experience of Jewish freedom and triumph are cherished and appreciated. Thus, it is suggested, nay expected, that the greatest tragedy of the Jewish Night, the Shoah, be recounted on the night that accentuates Jewish birth and being. But for many Jews, it is not. How come?

Several questions arise for those who insert contemporary genocide in the midst of freedom. Where is the Shoah inserted, beginning, middle, or end of the Seder ceremony? Does not the message of Hell on Earth compromise the theme of redemption from Heaven? By reading the Shoah into the Haggadah, are we not turning Judeocide into a paschal sacrifice making it a biblical *holocaust* rather than a contemporary historical Shoah? Nonetheless, the "why" of the Shoah is unexplainable and may explain why it is inserted in the second part ("future") of the service.

The Four Cups at the Passover table represent the verbs of God's freedom in the biblical Exodus story (Exod 6: 6–8). Also, the Fifth Cup, the Cup of Elijah, is poured to overflowing and the door is opened and the "Pour Out Your Wrath" paragraph bellowed to the outside world. Why Shoah memory and the curse of Nations (pagan and monotheistic) at the Cup of Elijah, symbolic herald of messianic peace? What, if any, is the Shoah link to the Synoptic Last Supper which depicts Jesus proclaiming, "This is my body" (Luke 22:19) and "This is my blood of the covenant, which is poured out for many" (Mark 14:24; Matt 26:28)?

According to tradition of Rabbi Judah ben Bezalel, the Maharal of Prague (c. 1525–1609), one reads the "Great Hallel" with the Fifth Cup in hand, and in testimony to the passage, "Who remembered us in our low estate and has delivered us from our adversaries" (Ps 136: 23–24). So, in our day, drinking from the Cup of Elijah testifies "to the land (He gave) for a heritage unto Israel" (Ps 136: 21–22). Is there a link between Auschwitz and Jerusalem? Shoah and Church? Cause and effect or remembrance and not again?

After the session, Chair Donald Kim, was approached by an attendee who let him know how disappointed he was by the way the presenters acted in the room. Kim reports ("The Passover Seder or The Lord's Supper: What is at Stake?") that the individual was referring to Zev Garber, who had built up tension in the room because of his impassioned speech concerning the Passover Seder, especially regarding the five cups—

the last one being the cup of Elijah, a time of final justice. Garber was intense. He had Shoah on his mind. The Passover Seder is the remembrance of the great event of the Passover but also a way to look ahead to the final culminating day of deliverance, but the way forward has undergone much pain and suffering: "The Passover represents providential design in history—but Shoah evolved from history." The Seder deals directly with the pains and points to the future ahead for the Jews, whereas the Christian Lord's Supper commemorates Jesus' sacrifice with the elements representing the body and the blood. Jesus was having a Passover meal that culminated with the Lord's Supper, but the meal was *not* a Seder. If so then the Last Supper operative is a corrective exercise in remembering the blood Covenant of Christ *without* supersessionism, that is, *not* replacing the covenantal-faith trials and successes leading to the role of Yeshua` Ha-Mashiach. Kim summarizes that remembrance connects but does not equate the Last Supper and the Jewish Passover. Remembering the last meal between Jesus and his disciples is Christian commitment to and reenactment of the new covenant in the body, blood, and teaching of Jesus Christ. And Seder memory for the Jew recalls, reenacts, and recommits the Lord's salvific acts in pivotal memories of Jewish history.

Annotated Passover Haggadah

At the conclusion of our well-attended, emotive NAPH session on the Passover Seder and the Last Supper in Denver 2018 (see Iggeret 91, 25–29; http://vanhise.lss.wisc.edu/naph/?q=node/11, find link to Iggeret 91), panelist Peter Zaas suggested to me a follow-up Passover Haggada in the making. Unexpected tribute but overwhelming commitments prevented me from getting overtly excited at the time. Two years later inspired by a recently published monograph on *Judaism and Jesus* (Cambridge Scholars Publishing, 2020; with Ken Hanson) and completion of our "Pittsburgh Shabbat Massacre" papers by Garber-Hanson-Sabbath (NAPH session, 2019 AAR-SBL Annual Meeting, San Diego. Now published in Journal of Ecumenical Studies 55.3, Summer 2020), I decided to kick-start this venture. A prolong discussion with Ken Hanson confirmed this decision. Also, Ken accepted enthusiastically to serve as co-editor of this new Annotated Passover Haggadah (APH).

APH is parsed into two parts. Part One: Sefaria Haggadah, Hebrew-English text with appropriate religious directive and short paragraph commentary provided by the Editors. Obligatory Haggadah reading and participation is explained and directed in accordance with traditional standard of Passover Halakha. Part Two: Supplementary Readings from invited contributors are oriented to convey the Passover Story inside and outside the Seder service. In sum, a new innovative effort to teach, learn, and engage Judaism's story of People Freedom enacted at home, synagogue, and school. Go forth and *haggid/i/u haggadah*.

—Zev Garber

The annotated Haggadah presented here is intended to be unique, both in substance and appeal. It is unique although we have seen in recent years the proliferation of literally hundreds of fresh versions of the traditional "telling" of the Exodus from Egypt. The story is well-known and often repeated, beyond the Jewish world, having been immortalized in multiple religious traditions, as well as in cinematic film adaptations. The Haggadah of Orthodox tradition has been translated, elaborated, neutered, abbreviated, truncated, and all but exfoliated, to the extent that one may wonder what, yet another edition may possibly offer. The current volume nonetheless makes an important contribution, since, while preserving both the traditional Hebrew text, along with an equally traditional English translation, it provides important analytical, philosophical, and theological perspectives on the seminal event of Jewish consciousness, memory, and self-awareness.

It is, by design, academic in its approach, taking pains to offer the most meaningful commentary on long-overlooked sections of the text. Its two authors dredge deeply from their own backgrounds, one being an Orthodox Jew by heritage and the other a convert to Conservative Judaism. Equally, this volume brings forth contemporary reflections on the broader implications of the Exodus narrative, the liberation from bondage, and the stylistic intonations of the Haggadah, line by line. Important terminology and phraseology are highlighted and elaborated, in a manner which conveys serious understanding to scholars and lay people alike. It is, in short, serious, and scholarly yet accessible to a general readership.

From the opening *Kiddush*, explanatory notes reflect the eternal values and concepts communicated in the text, which is at once deeply Jewish, yet intrinsically universal, uniting an assortment of religious traditions across time and space, in the eternal shadow of the events which inexorably led across the Sea of Reeds and onward to Mount Sinai. Moreover, this Haggadah is intended, notwithstanding its scholarly rigor, for practical use in family and congregational settings, for those who wish, during this all-important night, to delve ever deeply into the narrative, to go beyond the mere repetition of an annual ritual into a more richly rewarding and profound experience.

Supplementing the careful commentary on individual passages, the authors include specific essays (excurses) dealing with important themes and concepts from an overarching, analytical perspective. From the nature of the ten plagues, to the redemption of the firstborn son, to the image of the prophet Elijah, the reader is taken on a journey deep into the essence of the great deliverance and its echoes across the generations of those who keep the tradition alive.

The "kosher meat" of this Haggadah is bookended with "standalone" interpretations, beginning with a post-biblical, theological interpretation of the course of history—"historiosophy." It highlights the literal, allegorical, typological, and moral sense of the Haggadah, in light of the evolving life of the Jewish community over the centuries. As the vicissitudes of Jewish experience have warranted, contemporary history has always been read into the Exodus narrative. The reader and participant in the Seder are encouraged to adopt the sequential steps of confrontation, analysis, interaction, and internalization. The Seder itself thereby becomes a learning device in the larger "hermeneutical circle." Additional reflections center on the figure of the great deliverer, Moses, who is conspicuously absent from the Haggadah. The fact that Moses, who is so central to the account in Exodus, has vanished from the traditional "telling" of the story is key in relating the ultimate message of Jewish monotheism. God alone, above and beyond any heroic personage, is the Master of History.

An explanatory section on the Hebrew calendar is next, being central to the Jewish notion of the sanctification of time. It is, moreover, important to understand the placement of Passover relative to the continuum of Jewish holidays within the yearly cycle. The adaptation of the traditional calendar to modern Israel, including the addition of Independence Day and Jerusalem Day, is also referenced.

The overall theme of this Haggadah is a celebration, not only of the deliverance from Egypt but of the widely disparate ways in which the Passover is observed by sundry traditions, worldwide. Going beyond the "normative" observance of the Passover Seder, this Haggadah breaks new ground in referencing the increasing interest among Christians and Messianic Jews in observing the Exodus from Egypt. While the theological concepts and doctrinal precepts among these disparate groups are beyond reconciliation, the fact that those who profess Christian faith have, in recent decades, come to appreciate and indeed celebrate the redemption of the Jewish people is at the very least noteworthy and due some level of consideration.

Bearing this in mind, several supplementary essays deal with an assortment of issues, such as the Last Supper of Jesus, its depiction in the Christian gospels and Pauline epistles, and its relation to the communal meal referenced in the Dead Sea Scrolls.

Additional contributions include:

- a discussion of the origin and development of the Christian Eucharist in light of the Passover Seder,

- a plea that the tragedy of the Shoah also be recalled on the night of Passover, and that Jewish belief and observance be recognized "without polemics" in Christian preaching and catechism,
- the Torah's "liberation from meaninglessness," and from a "merely material world,"
- the rootedness of the Christian Eucharist in Judaism and Jewish tradition, and,
- a call for Christians and Jews to engage in the mutual tolerance of each-others' religious traditions, especially in light of the Shoah, as they set their tables "with grace and respect."

Other articles deal with such topics as the Christian portrayal of the Last Supper in art, the way in which the Haggadah keeps the commandments of the Torah alive in present memory, and the four children at the Seder. An exploration of the roots of Chassidic Passover traditions includes the special place of women and femininity, and the *Seudat Mashiach*, the "Feast of the Messiah."

In keeping with the eclectic emphasis of this volume is an essay focusing on the customs of the Romaniote and Judeo-Greek Jews, whose unique Haggadah and Sephardic cuisine deserves our attention. Another deals with the observance of Passover in Hamilton, New Zealand. A final, "creative" section presents the reflections of a third-generation Jewish American, whose personal evolution ranged from an assimilated, secular upbringing to a culturally identified Jewish awareness. This is followed by a fictional story, revolving around a female character, and tracing the path of redemption, from the land of Goshen to the foot of Mt. Sinai, where Moses disappears into the mists to receive the tablets of the Law.

Fig. 1 Gustave Doré (1865), "Moses Showing the Ten Commandments"

Lastly, there is a description of perhaps the most unusual Passover season in history, brought on by the COVID-19 pandemic, as experienced in the spring of 2020. The many virtual Seders observed around the world at this time have underscored, more than ever, the unparalleled ability of the

Jewish people to adapt traditional observance considering whatever "plague" the blows of time and chance may have chosen to inflict. To be sure, the sanctified memory of this mighty deliverance, witnessed so long ago by the children of Israel, remains forever emblazoned in the Jewish soul. This being central to the day itself and its commemoration, the authors present this newly annotated Passover Haggadah.

—Kenneth Hanson

Reflections: Interpretation and the Passover Haggadah, An Invitation to Post-Biblical Historiosophy

Zev Garber

Interpreting the Passover Haggadah, a collection of documents on the deliverance of Israel from Egypt and considered authoritative by the Synagogue, is the problem of relating blocs of religious thought patterns to the fluid, constantly changing life of the Jewish community. It is a question of old forms and new challenges. In the history of the interpretation of these documents various hermeneutical methods have been employed. The following is a summary sketch of the more important ones.

I. Hermeneutics

What, then, can be said about the matter of how to approach the miraculous? After all, miracles are the fishbones that stick most pertinaciously in the skeptic's craw—not only because the religious conjure salvation by invoking them, but because they are flatly unbelievable and the skeptic has a suitcase-full of miracle stories that even the religious will agree are fraudulent. Although the issue does not lie at the heart of my project in this book, its position as a watershed problem is insured by the fact that it has both metaphysical and epistemological implications.

If miracles have occurred, then that surely implies something significant about the way the world is causally ordered and about what (or who) so orders it. Again, if there are or might be miracles, we must face questions about how they are to be identified: whether it is the proper business of science and historiography to do so, or whether other means must do it. And if the biblical miracle stories are false, then that may tell us something about the prospects, not only for Christian soteriology but also for assessment of the historical reliability of Scripture.

Literal

The text means just what is aid and nothing more. If a passage is not precisely clear, it can be made understandable by a comparison of the troublesome passage with other similar passages. For example, to fulfill the Mishnain requirement (*m. Pesaḥ.* 10.1,3 ff) that the Passover retelling must "begin with disgrace and end with glory," two separate paragraphs, one by Rav ("In the beginning our forefathers were idolaters"), and the other by Samuel ("We were Pharoah's slaves in Egypt"), are presented for the same purpose: to better explain a midrashic commentary of Deut 26: 5–8 ("A wandering Aramean was my father").

The separate responses themselves are reflections of historical developments. When Eretz Israel came under the sovereignty of the Ptolemies of Egypt (301–198 BCE) all references to Egypt's defeat and humiliation were cautiously avoided. Thus, we read in Samuel's reply that "we *were* slaves to Pharoah in Egypt," and this is followed by "the Lord brought us forth from there," and not "from Egypt" as expected. Similarly, when the Seleucids of Syria held control over Eretz Israel in the years 198–167 BCE, a pro-Seleucid sentiment was necessary. Thus, "Your fathers dwelt of old time beyond the river, even Terah, the father of Abraham…," is found in Rav's response.

Fig. 2 Hasmonean John Hyrcanus with Seleucid Antiochus VII

Allegorical

This hermeneutic assumes that the literal meaning of the text is neither the basic nor the "true" meaning. While the text may speak of an "A" in its literal story, it intends to call attention to a "B" which is another order of existence. Allegorical interpretation understands the literal figures, events, places, etc., within a text as ciphers—usually of extraordinary concepts which, for one reason or another, are not directly expressible in literal language. Sometimes the literal figures, etc., are understood as representations of larger entities. For example, the passage about the Four Sons/Children is "really" about the *masks* (sic) Jews wore in the Talmudic period and have worn in all ages up until today in their attempts at non-involvement in Jewish identity and Jewish destiny.

Another form of allegorical interpretation may best be described as mystical and esoteric. Here the text is understood as non-rational but not anti-rational whereby the divine draws one upward towards itself. The interpreter-reader is led to a unity with the divine reality which lies beyond the text. Thus, the intention of the text is not to impart information, no matter how lofty, but to bring one into communion with the divine reality, or to mediate an experience of the divine attribute of freedom. The Seder foods, rituals and commentary complement the text in this regard.

An illustration of an allegorical Passover ritual is *bedikat ḥamets*, the night before Passover search for leaven grain (specifically, wheat, barley, spelt, rye, oats, and their derivatives), which is biblically and rabbinically prohibited during the Passover week. Leaven grain ferments upon decomposition and this allegorically represents Man's rising inclination toward evil. The annual process of searching for *ḥamets* is a constant reminder for Man to search his/her everyday thoughts and deeds and resolve not to do evil but good. All are obligated to search for *ḥamets*, an indication that even the righteous are capable of transgression and wayward action. Also, as one obtains results in finding the pieces of ḥamets—the Lurianic school of Kabbalah suggests that ten pieces be found, corresponding to the ten *sefirot* or divine emanations—so that s/he improve her/his state by a solemn resolved to live in a cosmic unity with all that is around her/him, suggested by the presence at the Passover table of vegetable, animal, human and divine symbols.

Another example, the message of the hare-hunt scenes that are found in early Haggadahs is rather interesting, particularly since the allegory is so indirect. The problem of what sequence to follow when the Passover Seder was celebrated on Saturday night was solved through memorizing the order by way of an acronym, *YaKeNHaZ*. *YaKeNHaZ*, sometimes pronounced *YaKNeHaZ*, represented after the Sabbath (*ner*), the separation of the holiness of the Sabbath from weekdays (*Havdalah*), and thanksgiving for the festive season celebrated anew (*zeman*). To the Ashkenazi Jews, *YaKeNHaZ* sounded like the German-Yiddish *Jagenhaz*, "hare-hunt," which thereby was interpreted within the Passover message of freedom by understanding the hare as the Jewish People outsmarting its enemies, who are virtually illustrated as hunters with dogs and nets.

Typology

It was the hermeneutic method called typology that enabled the Sages to make use of the verses of Scriptures to read contemporary history into the Passover Haggadah. The verses serve as pointers toward a closer understanding of contemporary issues, e.g., "Go forth and learn what Laban, the Aramean, sought to do to Jacob our father; while Pharoah decreed death only for the male children, Laban sought to uproot all," is based on Gen 31:22–34, and especially Gen 32:24. The midrash reflects the trouble between the Seleucids (Syrian=Aram=Laban) and the Ptolomies (Egypt=Pharoah) over Eretz Israel. Passover is anti-Egyptian in outlook nevertheless some gesture was necessary for Jews living under benign Ptolemaic rule to placate their Egyptian rulers. Hence, the denunciation of Laban (read Seleucids) as a greater enemy of Jewish welfare and continuity.

Later, under Roman rule, "Laban the Aramean" is seen as Rome, through a play on the Hebrew consonants which spell "Rome" and "Aram," since Rome was then the threat in Eretz Israel against Jewish independence and freedom. Finally, in the course of Jewish history down to the present, in different places and times, "Laban the Aramean" has been interpreted as the threat (culturally, physically, spiritually) posed to Jewish survival by, e.g., the Church, Fascism, Russia, Arab nations, etc.

The Moral Sense of Haggadah

This hermeneutic concentrates on the use of certain passages to teach proper moral behavior and first became prominent in Jewish circles during the late Talmudic period when a consensus arose among rabbinical interpreters that the haggadic texts disclosed their meaning in a number of ways. Besides literal and allegorical hermeneutics, there was the method of interpreting scripture to get at its implications for ethical behavior. Through this method, one can save "embarrassing" traditional passages from deletion by the contemporary liberal-minded Jew, e.g., the Ten Plagues, especially the last, the killing of the Egyptian first-born, is not seen literally as the Torah commanding human slaughter but as a polemic against the gods of Egypt (cf. Exod 12:12b: "against the gods of Egypt, I will execute judgment," recited in the Haggadah and the key to understanding the plague narrative), suggesting that the way of God and Torah, however liberally interpreted, is the guarantor of Israel's survival and not Egypt's gods (read: diaspora assimilation, non-Jewish ways, etc.).

Similarly, the recitation of the "Pour out thy wrath" accompanying the Cup of Elijah need not be understood as an expression of vindictiveness toward he non-Jew but should rather be interpreted as invoking the Judge of all the Earth to deal justly with the nations of the world as He *continuously* does with Israel, so that the complete messianic fulfillment of the future, a brotherhood of man inspired by the Torah way, can be realized swiftly in our day. This is not poor theology, as some have claimed, but the authentic Jewish understanding of *Heilsgeschichte*, of the interdependence of mankind, and of dialogued between Israel and the nations conducted without politics, politeness, and paternalism and in the full power of the Jewish way, as seen, for example, in Genesis 17, Deuteronomy 32, Isaiah 2, and Micah 4.

In addition to the above, the continuous process of interpretation has produced other hermeneutical insights. It will continue to do so as long as the classical written tradition persists but cannot anticipate every possible new situation. It is for this reason that hermeneutical stances are needed to serve the interpreter as general principles for reaching decisions in concrete situations. The crucial problem in textual interpretation is to discover a suitable hermeneutic, one that is both fair to the original image and faithful to the contemporary ethic.

II. Historiograhy, Historiosophy

As the liturgy of the Seder night suggests, memory is an essential function of the Jewish consciousness. Yet, we often make the mistake of assuming that our stress on commemoration entails a commitment to the craft of the historian.

In recovering the past, Jewish memory has not traditionally been interested in history, as that term is currently defined. Since inception until modern times, Jews did not interest themselves in historiography. They did not see their literature as dealing with historical matters, nor did they collect "histories." They did not encourage techniques, theories, nor inspire principles of historical research and presentation; nor support methods of historical scholarship. The narrative presentation of history based on a critical examination, evaluation, and election of material from primary and secondary sources and subject to scholarly criteria are absent from Jewish classics. In a sentence, Jews, participants in history, wrote no "official" history. The one possible exception is Josephus, who lived in the first century, but as a Jewish apologist before Rome, he wrote not for Jews but on behalf of Jews.

Jews in pre-modern era did not look backwards with the aim of discovering facts. Rather they sought to derive paradigms from the sacred events of the past by which they can then interpret and respond to contemporary happenings. Paradigmatic and not pragmatic concern was the issue and emphasis. Jews dabbled in *historiosophy* (a philosophy of history) and not historiography. The biblical authors discuss life liberation, deliverance, and the Jewish People's continuous relationship with God. Running through this experience is an element of mystery stemming from God's penetration into history, limiting human knowledge and ethical conduct. The right and ethical life is to be attained by following creeds, rites, rituals, and appointed times—all of which enables each generation to reenact the pivotal moments in the life of the Jewish People.

The ambiguity of contemporary vicissitudes is illumined with reference to the paradigmatic categories of the past. Remembering the Exodus, for example, is not to ask which Pharoah, how many Israelites, and how a sea can split, but to think constructively and imaginatively about Freedom in the present and in the future. Responding to the destruction of

Jerusalem and the dispersion of the Jewish People, the Sages/Rabbis salvaged Judaism by placing it beyond time and history. They elevated Jewish values, practices, and thought beyond the daily course of events—determined by Gentiles—to a timeless plane.

After 70 CE Jews lived between the glories of the past and the messianic restoration to come. Contemporary events were noteworthy only insofar as they were foretold by past generations and/or gave clues about the coming redemption. In this context, Maimonides 'attitude towards history (*Commentary to Mishnah, Sanhedrin* 10:1) is typical, occupation with history is "a useless waste of time."

III. People and Land

We have suggested that the Passover Haggadah is non-historical but not anti-historical in foundation and tradition. Let us now confront the literature itself by looking at a selective theme in context: freedom from tyranny. In the biblical documents this is seen as the Exodus from Egypt (Diaspora) but for the *ba`al Haggadah* (redactor of the Haggadah), this concept extends to the liberation of the Land of Israel.

Mishnah *Pesaḥim* 10.4 specifically prescribes that the entire Deuteronomic confessional (Deut 26:5–10) of *Ḥag Habikkurim* (centrality of the Land) be recited but the *ba`al Haggadah* intentionally deletes the last two verses ("He brought us to this place and gave us this land. A land flowing with milk and honey. Wherefore I now bring the first fruits of the soil which you, O 'Lord, have given me.") due to the Land's subjugation to a foreign power (Rome).

The four cups of wine reflect the four verbs of freedom in Exod 6: 6–7:

> Wherefore say unto the children of Israel, I am the Lord, and *I will bring* you out from under the burdens of the Egyptians, and *I will deliver* you from their bondage, and *I redeem* you with an outstretched arm, and with great judgments, and *I will take* you to Me for a people, and I will be to you a God.

Yet a fifth verb mentioned in verse 8,

> *I will bring* you into the *land* concerning which I lifted up my hand to give it to Abraham, to Isaac, and to Jacob, I will give it to you for a heritage; I am the Lord.

is *passed over* (sic) due to the Realpolitik of Roman despotism in the Land.

Anti-Roman polemics are subtly conveyed in the Haggadah. Case in point, the post-70 question about the bitter herbs, in lieu of the pre-70 "meats" question ("Why on the night of Passover, roasted paschal lamb is eaten, and not stewed or boiled?") is clearly the present political situation despite the Exod 1:14 prooftext offered. Sentence in point, Deut 26:8 talks of the Exodus from Egypt with great terribleness (*MoRa'*) but the word suggests an appearance (*MaReH*) of God'a awe (*MoRa'*) equated to the defeat of Rome (*RoMaH*).

The paragraph about the five masters who recline together at Benei Berak talking about the departure from Egypt all night is a guise for discussing the liberatIon from Rome. The association of Rabbi Akiba with this Passover plot—he is one of the five—is historically sound since he was the major religious support for the Bar Kochba rebellion against Rome in 132 CE. A variant of this story is a tale told in *t. Pesaḥ* X.12 involving religious revolutionaries meeting in Lydda.

Moses and Joseph are not central in the Haggadah because their story is from off the Land of Israel. Likewise, the stories of persecution in the Middle Ages from Church and Mosque against *People and Land* is the *Sitz-im-Leben* of "Pour out thy wrath" passage. Finally, the challenging issue at the time of the Rabbis till our time, and every age in between, is how to "speedily lead the offshoots of thy stock/redeemed to Zion in joyous song" (next/this year in Jerusalem). Again, People and Land.

IV. Class Lesson

The counterpoint on the biblical (past) rabbinical (present) Passover message of freedom, that is, liberation of People and Land, is the role played by the Liberator who moves related but independent through passages of the Haggadah.

See, for example, the passages that speak of God and He alone, who redeems Israel and not messengers ("For I will go through the Land of Egypt in that night": I, and not an angel. "I will smite all the first-born in the land of Egypt": I, and not a serap. "And against all the gods of Egypt I will execute judgments": I, and not a messenger. "I am the Lord": I am He, and no other.) or messiahs (cf. the Sages 'opposition to Ben Zoma).

A deeper appreciation of the Haggadic hermeneutic devices develops if the professor in a class setting plays more of a passive role than is traditionally assigned to him/her. By encouraging the student to read the text as *p'shat* (literal meaning of text with special emphasis on its historical, literary, and linguistic features) and answer questions from context and prooftext, the professor is encouraging exegetical scholarship, which otherwise would not grow from the total lecture method that detaches the student from the material.

Take "Laban the Aramean," for example. In the Haggadah, we read: "Go forth and learn what Laban, the Aramean, sought to do to Jacob our father. While Pharoah decreed death for the male children (see Exod 1:16, 22), Laban sought to uproot (*la-`aKKoR*) all."

Now the prooftext (Deut 26:5) speaks of an Aramean who is a "wanderer"/ *'oBeD* (=Jacob) and not an Aramean who "would have destroyed"/ *'iBBeD* (= Laban). Furthermore, why is the crime of Laban (insider) worse than the aggravated offense of Pharoah (outsider)?

A possible explanation may be found in the statement about the Wicked Son/Child. About this child, we read: "S/He removes her/himself from the community, by denying the *`iKKaR*/ the Principle. That is, the Israelite or Jew who does not credit God (*`iKKaR*) as deliverer of Land and People, excommunicates oneself from the salvific message of Passover.

By plying the role of a class catalyst, the professor encourages the student to see the problems in the text and porooftext, including, the similarity of language by Laban and the Wicked Son/Child. Hopefully, the students experience the excitement of learning when they conclude that the Laban/Wicked Son/Child paradigm suggests that Israel's existence and destiny are shaped more by internal than external forces. Jewish self-hate, and not antisemitism, ultimately determines Israel's continuity and immortality.

V. Conclusion

In conclusion, let me suggest, that whatever hermeneutic is selected should take seriously the four sequential steps of the Learning process: initial *confrontation*, in which the interpreter experiences the idea, behavior, or object superficially; *analysis*, here the interpreter seriously probes the occasion or object in the light of previous experiences and knowledge; *interaction*, where the interpreter's reciprocal communication with others helps him/her benefit from their feelings, ideas, experiences, with the reality under discussion; and *internalization*, where, by turning the new experience and sharing of ideas upon him/herself, the interpreter reacts meaningfully to the new reality as it relates to him/her as an individual and as a member of society. The hermeneutic activity combines real life situations with inherited tradition and permits the interpreter to confront deep philosophical-religious ideas in a convincing application, since it nurtures sensitivity and empathy, which lead to ethical decision-making and moral development.

In discovering a suitable hermeneutic, the interpreter becomes a listener as well as an interrogator. The process of asking and listening constitutes a circle—the hermeneutical circle. It is in this fashion that the Seder institution originated, and the process of Haggadic interpretation has developed and proceeded down to the present day.

Reflections:
The Disappearing Deliverer, The Moses Enigma

Kenneth Hanson

According to the Biblical record, Israel's great deliverer, Moses, was able to unite twelve semi-nomadic tribes into the worship of a single deity. He managed to lead them in what some call a concerted "revolt" from slavery into freedom. The Exodus from Egypt amounted not only to a liberation from servitude; it was also the defining moment around which the tribal conglomerate known as Israel would become solidified as a national entity. Clearly, there is no single character more central to the narrative of the Exodus than Moses. Yet, when it comes to the "telling" of story, the Haggadah, Moses is strangely absent. He is the disappearing deliverer.

This is odd, since there is no biblical figure more revered in Jewish tradition than Moses, whose very name carries with it a high and exalted resonance. Renowned twentieth century Hasidic Rabbi Menachem Mendel Schneerson described Moses with kabbalistic imagery, as representing the "interiority of the Father [*pnimiyyut abba*]," who is the "interiority of the Ancient One [*pnimiyyut attiq*]." *Attiq* is identified as the highest aspect of *Keter* ["Crown"] and the lowest aspect of *Ein Sof* ["Without End"]. The messianic king is perceived as higher still ("in the aspect of the interiority of the Ancient One as it is in its place"), but Moses is characterized as "the first redeemer and the final redeemer."[1]

At the time of the composition of the Torah, it is doubtful that any ambiance of this sort was associated with Moses, but there was certainly an exponential blossoming of such imagery from the Torah's final redaction through the time of the early rabbinic *tannaim* and beyond. There even arose a tradition (perhaps in the Greek diaspora) that Moses had ascended alive

---

[1] M. M. Schneerson, *Torat Menahem: Hitwwa' aduyyot* 5717, Vol. 2 (Brooklyn, NY: Vaad Hanochos BLahak, 2001), 272. See also E. R. Wolfson, *Open Secret: Postmessianic Messianism and the Mystical Revision of Menachem Mendel Schneerson*, (New York: Columbia University Press, 2009), 367.

into heaven, notwithstanding the last chapter of the Torah, which asserts that he died on Mount Nebo. In Judaism Moses is of course hailed, as "our teacher" [*Rabbenu*] as well as the "lawgiver of Israel." However, during the Second Jewish Commonwealth we find yet more elevated views of Moses, as well as significant allusions to him (including messianic symbolism) in both Jewish and early Judeo-Christian literature. Again, how odd, that Moses is conspicuously truant from the Haggadah.

The Finger of God

Examining the text of the book of Exodus, it is when Moses returns to Pharaoh that he takes "center stage" in the narrative. The signs and wonders he performs are beyond what the magicians of Pharaoh are able to duplicate; yet it is made clear that they are by God's power, not Moses.' This is doubtless why, when recounting the ten plagues at the Passover Seder, each is vocalized, accompanied by the spilling of wine, but no mention is made of Moses.

The plagues in Egypt are brought about by what the magicians anthropomorphically call *etzbah Elohim* ("the finger of God," Exod 8:15). The expression is best understood as an attempt, given God's radical "otherness," to describe the deity in human terms. After all, the biblical worldview advances the notion that this God can be approached as a person, with whom one may reason, even argue. The same expression is repeated later in the book of Exodus, describing the two "tables of the testimony," written on stone by "the finger of God" (Exod 31:18). The Deuteronomist incorporates the same language into his own description of the stone tablets delivered to Moses on Mount Sinai (Deut. 9:10). Of course, the Hebrew text of Exodus is careful not to ascribe divinity to any human being, but the words "finger of God" allows for understanding Moses as the human conduit by which the divine presence is manifest.

By one estimation, it is Moses whose gravitas is worthy of the role of being God's personal "agent," in a sense the "hand" to which God's anthropomorphic finger is attached. We are told that his very choice of words could bring about the reign of God on earth—or not. Yosé the Galilean opined, with regard Moses' declaration at the Red Sea ("The Lord *shall reign* for ever and ever," Exod 15:18), that this manner of phrasing was regrettable. "Had Moses said 'The Lord *has reigned* for ever and ever,' the kingdom of heaven would have come about immediately."[2]

---

[2] See *Mekhilta* on Exod 15:18.

The Face of Moses

Other depictions of Moses in the book of Exodus further reinforce his exalted image. When he comes down from Mount Sinai holding the two tables of the law, we are told that, "Moses knew not that the skin of his face sent forth beams" (Exod 34:29, JPS 1917).[3] According to other translations, Moses' face "shone," "was ablaze with light," or "was radiant" (JPS, 1985), though the 1917 Jewish translation is arguably closer to the original Hebrew. From the verb *karan,* employed here, is derived the Hebrew noun, *keren,* which may be understood as a "ray" or "beam" (of light), but also as a "horn," or "antler." The expression *keren David* has been used in Jewish tradition to refer to the Messiah, recalling the prophet Samuel's "messianic" anointing of David, from a *keren shemen* "horn of oil" (1 Sam 16:13).

The Messiah to come will likewise be anointed with a horn of oil.[4] Saul, by contrast, was anointed, not from a *keren*, but a *pakh*, or mere "vial" of oil (1 Sam 10:1), prefiguring the fact that Saul was not to be God's true "anointed one." That designation would be reserved for the young Bethlehemite. The word *keren* also appears in Moses' instructions to make "horns" on the four corners of the altar (Exod 27:2), later alluded to as evocative of messianic redemption. In rabbinic literature Moses and Elijah are said to arrive jointly in the end of days. Moses and the Messiah are seen as companions of the *memra* (word) of God on the final Passover night.[5] The presence of Moses is also consistent with the ancient folkloric account (known as the Assumption of Moses) of his glorified ascent.

A Prophet Like Moses

Furthermore, the Deuteronomistic depiction of Moses was repeatedly alluded to by succeeding generations, who saw messianic overtones in one of his most important "prophetic" announcements. It is in the midst of Moses' address to the assembled Israelites that he discusses the portion of the priests and Levites and the avoidance of pagan customs, making the bold proclamation: "The Lord your God will raise up for you a prophet from among your own people, like myself; him shall you heed…" (Deut 18:15, JPS, 1985).[6] Some have speculated that Moses-like leaders may be found in the likes of Joshua, Gideon, Samuel, Elijah, and King Josiah, whose high

---

[3] וּמֹשֶׁה לֹא-יָדַע כִּי קָרַן עוֹר פָּנָיו

[4] See E. Frankel, B. P. Teutsch, *The Encyclopedia of Jewish Symbols* (Lanham, MD: Rowman & LIttlefield, 1992), 76.

[5] *Palestinian Targum on Exod* 12:42.

[6] Deut. 18:18 continues the theme, with God as the speaker: "I will raise them up a prophet for them from among their own people, like yourself: I will put My words in his mouth and he will speak to them all that I command him…" (JPS, 1985).

priest (Hilkiah) found the "Book of the Law" in the temple, and with whom the Deuteronomist writer/redactor is often associated.[7] It has even been argued that Josiah viewed himself in messianic terms.[8]

Indeed, the supposed personal connection between Moses and God was considered over time as being so intimate that during the Talmudic age, there was a perception that this union was all but absolute. The fourth generation Tanna Abba Saul went as far as to rearrange Moses' words of praise at the crossing of the Red Sea (Exod 15:2). Properly understood as "This is my God, and I will praise him" (זֶה אֵלִי וְאַנְוֵהוּ), Abba Saul rearranged the letters and read it as "This is my God, I and he" (זֶה אֵלִי אֲנִי וְהוּא). The intent of such a reading was certainly not to "deify" Moses, but it does a great deal to illuminate his subsequent image, as one who, together with God, carries out the divine will, and serves as an example to all who follow in his path. "Abba Saul said: Let us become like Him; as He is merciful and gracious, so be you merciful and gracious."[9]

Hashem vs. Heroics

Why, then, has Moses disappeared from the Haggadah of Passover? It is likely because, for the Jewish sages, the meaning of the Exodus far supersedes the exaltation of any narrative figure, including the great lawgiver himself. While it is difficult to avoid the powerful "aura" surrounding Moses, he nonetheless lacks a quality of holiness or divinity inherent in his personhood. This of course is not only consistent with Israelite monotheism; it is demanded by it. A simple reading of the text (on the level of *p'shat*) reveals the selection, elevation, and empowerment of Moses, in a fashion typical of an ancient Near Eastern ruler.[10] Unlike the Pharaoh, however, his exaltation will not result in his deification.

Instead, Moses must be subjugated to the greater message of the Exodus, and, in the final analysis, Hashem trumps heroics. Whereas the many pagan religions of the ancient world viewed the human condition as subject to the fickle laws of nature (represented by innumerable nature-

---

[7] See 2 Kings 22:8. It is argued that Mosaic typologies were scattered across the Deuteronomic history in such a way that at critical junctures a Moses-like leader arose, culminating in Josiah. See D. Allison, *The New Moses: A Matthean Typology* (Eugene, OR: Wipf & Stock, 1993), 49; R. Friedman, *Who Wrote the Bible?* (New York: Simon & Schuster, 2009), 101–16.

[8] See M. A. Sweeney, *King Josiah of Judah: The Lost Messiah of Israel* (Oxford: Oxford University Press, 2001), 315: "Josiah apparently saw himself as the king or Messiah of a reunified and restored kingdom of Israel centered around Jerusalem and the Temple…"

[9] *Mek.*, Shirata 3 on Exod 15:2.

[10] D. Mathews, *Royal Motifs in the Pentateuchal Portrayal of Moses* (London: T & T Clark, 2012), 144.

gods), at the foot of the holy mountain, when Moses brings down the tables of the Law, inscribed by the "finger of God," a powerful philosophic shift transpires. Human destiny is effectively separated from nature's vicious cycle, as surely as the image of Sinai is a symbol of radical "otherness." This people, Moses' people, have finally broken free from the fatalism and determinism which pervaded ancient near eastern religious systems. Life is progress, not repetition. This new "law of life" stressed the responsibility humans bear for their own destiny. What came forth from the mists of Sinai was the "subversive" idea that the human lot can be improved.

Moreover, the text of Exodus makes it clear that it is a single God, Israel's God, who has brought about this great emancipation. This represents a stark contrast with Egyptian royal literature, where the expression "mighty hand" is used synonymously with the person of the Pharaoh, and where the Pharaoh's deeds are described as being accomplished through his "outstretched arm."[11] The use of these terms in the book of Exodus (later repeated in the Haggadah) appears to represent a deliberate "borrowing" from the annals of Egypt in order to make a bold statement, that it is divine, not human agency, that lay at the root of this deliverance. It is not Moses who has won the victory, nor is he presented as a pharaonic potentate. Even when bringing down the ten devastating plagues upon Egypt, Moses is God's agent, but nothing more, and he acts only as an intermediary.

The Israelites themselves would refine and elevate the meaning of the Exodus. They would cast their deity as the God of transcendent compassion. The "I am" of Mount Horeb is the God who "will be there" (אֶהְיֶה אֲשֶׁר אֶהְיֶה). The pagan world, including the Egyptians, was accustomed to warrior divinities who vanquished their enemies, and on that level, it is unsurprising that the God of Israel would also be designated as the "God of armies." However, with the events surrounding the Passover, a unique, even revolutionary message arises in the ongoing narrative. Israel's God has taken the side of the oppressed and downtrodden Hebrew slaves. It is a theme brought forth in no other ancient literature, and it paves the way for a social ethic, which, during the centuries to follow, will become inextricable from Judaism itself.

In the end, the social ethic of Passover becomes fused with Jewish values across the landscape of history. It has in fact been said that our brightest dreams are Jewish, our deepest hopes, and our most profound words, including "progress," and the inherent dignity of the "individual." Such concepts, the "gifts of the Jews" to the world, are also the legacy of Passover, embodied in the Haggadah; for on this night, we celebrate a moment in time, leading to a future of freedom, bolstered by faith in the

---

[11] See J. Berman, *Ani Maamin: Biblical Criticism, Historical Truth, and the Thirteen Principles of Faith* (Jerusalem: Maggid Books, 2020).

human spirit and the values of universal justice.[12] It is a story worth repeating in every home, every year, throughout all time.

Bibliography

Allison, Dale C. *The New Moses: A Matthean Typology* (Eugene, OR: Wipf & Stock, 1993).

Berman, Joshua, *Ani Maamin: Biblical Criticism, Historical Truth, and the Thirteen Principles of Faith* (Jerusalem: Maggid Books, 2020).

Cahill, Thomas, *The Gifts of the Jews: How a Tribe of Desert Nomads Changed the Way Everyone Thinks and Feels* (New York: Anchor Books, 1998).

Frankel, Ellen, and Betsy Platkin Teutsch, *The Encyclopedia of Jewish Symbols* (Lanham, MD: Rowman & LIttlefield, 1992).

Friedman, Richard E., *Who Wrote the Bible?* (New York: Simon & Schuster, 2009).

Mathews, Danny, *Royal Motifs in the Pentateuchal Portrayal of Moses* (London: T & T Clark, 2012).

Schneerson, Menachem Mendel, *Torat Menahem: Hitwwa' aduyyot* 5717, Vol. 2 (Brooklyn, NY: Vaad Hanochos BLahak, 2001).

Sweeney, Marvin A., *King Josiah of Judah: The Lost Messiah of Israel* (Oxford: Oxford University Press, 2001).

Wolfson, Elliot R. *Open Secret: Postmessianic Messianism and the Mystical Revision of Menachem Mendel Schneerson*, (New York: Columbia University Press, 2009).

---

[12] See T. Cahill, *The Gifts of the Jews: How a Tribe of Desert Nomads Changed the Way Everyone Thinks and Feels* (New York: Anchor Books, 1998), 240–241.

Luaḥ Ivri/Hebrew Calendar

Zev Garber

Leviticus 23:1–8

א וַיְדַבֵּר יְהוָה, אֶל-מֹשֶׁה לֵּאמֹר.

1 And the LORD spoke unto Moses, saying:

ב דַּבֵּר אֶל-בְּנֵי יִשְׂרָאֵל, וְאָמַרְתָּ אֲלֵהֶם, מוֹעֲדֵי יְהוָה, אֲשֶׁר-תִּקְרְאוּ אֹתָם מִקְרָאֵי קֹדֶשׁ--אֵלֶּה הֵם, מוֹעֲדָי.

2 Speak unto the children of Israel and say unto them: The appointed seasons of the LORD, which ye shall proclaim to be holy convocations, even these are My appointed seasons.

ג שֵׁשֶׁת יָמִים, תֵּעָשֶׂה מְלָאכָה, וּבַיּוֹם הַשְּׁבִיעִי שַׁבַּת שַׁבָּתוֹן מִקְרָא-קֹדֶשׁ, כָּל-מְלָאכָה לֹא תַעֲשׂוּ: שַׁבָּת הִוא לַיהוָה, בְּכֹל מוֹשְׁבֹתֵיכֶם. {פ}

3 Six days shall work be done; but on the seventh day is a sabbath of solemn rest, a holy convocation; ye shall do no manner of work; it is a sabbath unto the LORD in all your dwellings. {P}

ד אֵלֶּה מוֹעֲדֵי יְהוָה, מִקְרָאֵי קֹדֶשׁ, אֲשֶׁר-תִּקְרְאוּ אֹתָם, בְּמוֹעֲדָם.

4 These are the appointed seasons of the LORD, even holy convocations, which ye shall proclaim in their appointed season.

ה בַּחֹדֶשׁ הָרִאשׁוֹן, בְּאַרְבָּעָה עָשָׂר לַחֹדֶשׁ--בֵּין הָעַרְבָּיִם: פֶּסַח, לַיהוָה.

5 In the first month, on the fourteenth day of the month at dusk, is the LORD'S Passover.

ו וּבַחֲמִשָּׁה עָשָׂר יוֹם לַחֹדֶשׁ הַזֶּה, חַג הַמַּצּוֹת לַיהוָה: שִׁבְעַת יָמִים, מַצּוֹת תֹּאכֵלוּ.

6 And on the fifteenth day of the same month is the feast of unleavened bread unto the LORD; seven days ye shall eat unleavened bread.

7 In the first day ye shall have a holy convocation; ye shall do no manner of servile work.

ז בַּיּוֹם, הָרִאשׁוֹן, מִקְרָא-קֹדֶשׁ, יִהְיֶה לָכֶם; כָּל-מְלֶאכֶת עֲבֹדָה, לֹא תַעֲשׂוּ.

8 And ye shall bring an offering made by fire unto the LORD seven days; in the seventh day is a holy convocation; ye shall do no manner of servile work. {P}

ח וְהִקְרַבְתֶּם אִשֶּׁה לַיהוָה, שִׁבְעַת יָמִים; בַּיּוֹם הַשְּׁבִיעִי מִקְרָא-קֹדֶשׁ, כָּל-מְלֶאכֶת עֲבֹדָה לֹא תַעֲשׂוּ. {פ}

9 And the LORD spoke unto Moses saying:

ט וַיְדַבֵּר יְהוָה, אֶל-מֹשֶׁה לֵּאמֹר.

10 Speak unto the children of Israel and say unto them: When ye are come into the land which I give unto you, and shall reap the harvest thereof, then ye shall bring the sheaf of the first fruits of your harvest unto the priest.

י דַּבֵּר אֶל-בְּנֵי יִשְׂרָאֵל, וְאָמַרְתָּ אֲלֵהֶם, כִּי-תָבֹאוּ אֶל-הָאָרֶץ אֲשֶׁר אֲנִי נֹתֵן לָכֶם, וּקְצַרְתֶּם אֶת-קְצִירָהּ--וַהֲבֵאתֶם אֶת-עֹמֶר רֵאשִׁית קְצִירְכֶם, אֶל-הַכֹּהֵן.

11 And he shall wave the sheaf before the LORD, to be accepted for you; on the morrow after the sabbath the priest shall wave it.

יא וְהֵנִיף אֶת-הָעֹמֶר לִפְנֵי יְהוָה, לִרְצֹנְכֶם; מִמָּחֳרַת, הַשַּׁבָּת, יְנִיפֶנּוּ, הַכֹּהֵן.

12 And in the day when ye wave the sheaf, ye shall offer a he-lamb without blemish of the first year for a burnt-offering unto the LORD.

יב וַעֲשִׂיתֶם, בְּיוֹם הֲנִיפְכֶם אֶת-הָעֹמֶר, כֶּבֶשׂ תָּמִים בֶּן-שְׁנָתוֹ לְעֹלָה, לַיהוָה.

13 And the meal-offering thereof shall be two tenth parts of an ephah of fine flour mingled with oil, an offering made by fire unto the LORD for a sweet savor; and the drink-offering thereof shall be of wine, the fourth part of a hin.

יג וּמִנְחָתוֹ שְׁנֵי עֶשְׂרֹנִים סֹלֶת בְּלוּלָה בַשֶּׁמֶן, אִשֶּׁה לַיהוָה--רֵיחַ נִיחֹחַ; וְנִסְכֹּה יַיִן, רְבִיעִת הַהִין.

יד וְלֶחֶם וְקָלִי וְכַרְמֶל לֹא תֹאכְלוּ, עַד-עֶצֶם הַיּוֹם הַזֶּה--עַד הֲבִיאֲכֶם, אֶת-קָרְבַּן אֱלֹהֵיכֶם: חֻקַּת עוֹלָם לְדֹרֹתֵיכֶם, בְּכֹל מֹשְׁבֹתֵיכֶם. {ס}	**14** And ye shall eat neither bread, nor parched corn, nor fresh ears, until this selfsame day, until ye have brought the offering of your God; it is a statute forever throughout your generations in all your dwellings. {S}
טו וּסְפַרְתֶּם לָכֶם, מִמָּחֳרַת הַשַּׁבָּת, מִיּוֹם הֲבִיאֲכֶם, אֶת-עֹמֶר הַתְּנוּפָה: שֶׁבַע שַׁבָּתוֹת, תְּמִימֹת תִּהְיֶינָה.	**15** And ye shall count unto you from the morrow after the day of rest, from the day that ye brought the sheaf of the waving; seven weeks shall there be complete;
טז עַד מִמָּחֳרַת הַשַּׁבָּת הַשְּׁבִיעִת, תִּסְפְּרוּ חֲמִשִּׁים יוֹם; וְהִקְרַבְתֶּם מִנְחָה חֲדָשָׁה, לַיהוָה.	**16** even unto the morrow after the seventh week shall ye number fifty days; and ye shall present a new meal-offering unto the LORD.
יז מִמּוֹשְׁבֹתֵיכֶם תָּבִיאוּ לֶחֶם תְּנוּפָה, שְׁתַּיִם שְׁנֵי עֶשְׂרֹנִים--סֹלֶת תִּהְיֶינָה, חָמֵץ תֵּאָפֶינָה: בִּכּוּרִים, לַיהוָה.	**17** Ye shall bring out of your dwellings two wave-loaves of two tenth parts of an ephah; they shall be of fine flour, they shall be baked with leaven, for first fruits unto the LORD.
יח וְהִקְרַבְתֶּם עַל-הַלֶּחֶם, שִׁבְעַת כְּבָשִׂים תְּמִימִם בְּנֵי שָׁנָה, וּפַר בֶּן-בָּקָר אֶחָד, וְאֵילִם שְׁנָיִם: יִהְיוּ עֹלָה, לַיהוָה, וּמִנְחָתָם וְנִסְכֵּיהֶם, אִשֵּׁה רֵיחַ-נִיחֹחַ לַיהוָה.	**18** And ye shall present with the bread seven lambs without blemish of the first year, and one young bullock, and two rams; they shall be a burnt-offering unto the LORD, with their meal-offering, and their drink-offerings, even an offering made by fire, of a sweet savor unto the LORD.
יט וַעֲשִׂיתֶם שְׂעִיר-עִזִּים אֶחָד, לְחַטָּאת; וּשְׁנֵי כְבָשִׂים בְּנֵי שָׁנָה, לְזֶבַח שְׁלָמִים.	**19** And ye shall offer one he-goat for a sin-offering, and two he-lambs of the first year for a sacrifice of peace-offerings.
כ וְהֵנִיף הַכֹּהֵן אֹתָם עַל לֶחֶם הַבִּכֻּרִים תְּנוּפָה, לִפְנֵי יְהוָה, עַל-שְׁנֵי, כְּבָשִׂים; קֹדֶשׁ יִהְיוּ לַיהוָה, לַכֹּהֵן.	**20** And the priest shall wave them with the bread of the first fruits for a wave-offering before the LORD, with the two lambs; they shall be holy to the LORD for the priest.

כא וּקְרָאתֶם בְּעֶצֶם הַיּוֹם הַזֶּה, מִקְרָא-קֹדֶשׁ יִהְיֶה לָכֶם--כָּל-מְלֶאכֶת עֲבֹדָה, לֹא תַעֲשׂוּ: חֻקַּת עוֹלָם בְּכָל-מוֹשְׁבֹתֵיכֶם, לְדֹרֹתֵיכֶם.

21 And ye shall make proclamation on the selfsame day; there shall be a holy convocation unto you; ye shall do no manner of servile work; it is a statute forever in all your dwellings throughout your generations.

כב וּבְקֻצְרְכֶם אֶת-קְצִיר אַרְצְכֶם, לֹא-תְכַלֶּה פְּאַת שָׂדְךָ בְּקֻצְרֶךָ, וְלֶקֶט קְצִירְךָ, לֹא תְלַקֵּט; לֶעָנִי וְלַגֵּר תַּעֲזֹב אֹתָם, אֲנִי יְהוָה אֱלֹהֵיכֶם. {פ}

22 And when ye reap the harvest of your land, thou shalt not wholly reap the corner of thy field, neither shalt thou gather the gleaning of thy harvest; thou shalt leave them for the poor, and for the stranger: I am the LORD your God. {P}

כג וַיְדַבֵּר יְהוָה, אֶל-מֹשֶׁה לֵּאמֹר.

23 And the LORD spoke unto Moses, saying:

כד דַּבֵּר אֶל-בְּנֵי יִשְׂרָאֵל, לֵאמֹר: בַּחֹדֶשׁ הַשְּׁבִיעִי בְּאֶחָד לַחֹדֶשׁ, יִהְיֶה לָכֶם שַׁבָּתוֹן--זִכְרוֹן תְּרוּעָה, מִקְרָא-קֹדֶשׁ.

24 Speak unto the children of Israel, saying: In the seventh month, in the first day of the month, shall be a solemn rest unto you, a memorial proclaimed with the blast of horns, a holy convocation.

כה כָּל-מְלֶאכֶת עֲבֹדָה, לֹא תַעֲשׂוּ; וְהִקְרַבְתֶּם אִשֶּׁה, לַיהוָה. {ס}

25 Ye shall do no manner of servile work; and ye shall bring an offering made by fire unto the LORD. {S}

כו וַיְדַבֵּר יְהוָה, אֶל-מֹשֶׁה לֵּאמֹר.

26 And the LORD spoke unto Moses, saying:

כז אַךְ בֶּעָשׂוֹר לַחֹדֶשׁ הַשְּׁבִיעִי הַזֶּה יוֹם הַכִּפֻּרִים הוּא, מִקְרָא-קֹדֶשׁ יִהְיֶה לָכֶם, וְעִנִּיתֶם, אֶת-נַפְשֹׁתֵיכֶם; וְהִקְרַבְתֶּם אִשֶּׁה, לַיהוָה.

27 Howbeit on the tenth day of this seventh month is the day of atonement; there shall be a holy convocation unto you, and ye shall afflict your souls; and ye shall bring an offering made by fire unto the LORD.

כח וְכָל-מְלָאכָה לֹא תַעֲשׂוּ, בְּעֶצֶם הַיּוֹם הַזֶּה: כִּי יוֹם כִּפֻּרִים, הוּא, לְכַפֵּר עֲלֵיכֶם, לִפְנֵי יְהוָה אֱלֹהֵיכֶם.

28 And ye shall do no manner of work in that same day; for it is a day of atonement, to make atonement for you before the LORD your God.

כט כִּי כָל-הַנֶּפֶשׁ אֲשֶׁר לֹא-תְעֻנֶּה, בְּעֶצֶם הַיּוֹם הַזֶּה--וְנִכְרְתָה, מֵעַמֶּיהָ.

29 For whatsoever soul it be that shall not be afflicted in that same day, he shall be cut off from his people.

ל וְכָל-הַנֶּפֶשׁ, אֲשֶׁר תַּעֲשֶׂה כָּל-מְלָאכָה, בְּעֶצֶם, הַיּוֹם הַזֶּה--וְהַאֲבַדְתִּי אֶת-הַנֶּפֶשׁ הַהִוא, מִקֶּרֶב עַמָּהּ.

30 And whatsoever soul it be that doeth any manner of work in that same day, that soul will I destroy from among his people.

לא כָּל-מְלָאכָה, לֹא תַעֲשׂוּ: חֻקַּת עוֹלָם לְדֹרֹתֵיכֶם, בְּכֹל מֹשְׁבֹתֵיכֶם.

31 Ye shall do no manner of work; it is a statute forever throughout your generations in all your dwellings.

לב שַׁבַּת שַׁבָּתוֹן הוּא לָכֶם, וְעִנִּיתֶם אֶת-נַפְשֹׁתֵיכֶם; בְּתִשְׁעָה לַחֹדֶשׁ, בָּעֶרֶב--מֵעֶרֶב עַד-עֶרֶב, תִּשְׁבְּתוּ שַׁבַּתְּכֶם. {פ}

32 It shall be unto you a sabbath of solemn rest, and ye shall afflict your souls; in the ninth day of the month at even, from even unto even, shall ye keep your sabbath. {P}

לג וַיְדַבֵּר יְהוָה, אֶל-מֹשֶׁה לֵּאמֹר.

33 And the LORD spoke unto Moses, saying:

לד דַּבֵּר אֶל-בְּנֵי יִשְׂרָאֵל, לֵאמֹר: בַּחֲמִשָּׁה עָשָׂר יוֹם, לַחֹדֶשׁ הַשְּׁבִיעִי הַזֶּה, חַג הַסֻּכּוֹת שִׁבְעַת יָמִים, לַיהוָה.

34 Speak unto the children of Israel, saying: On the fifteenth day of this seventh month is the feast of tabernacles for seven days unto the LORD.

לה בַּיּוֹם הָרִאשׁוֹן, מִקְרָא-קֹדֶשׁ; כָּל-מְלֶאכֶת עֲבֹדָה, לֹא תַעֲשׂוּ.

35 On the first day shall be a holy convocation; ye shall do no manner of servile work.

לו שִׁבְעַת יָמִים, תַּקְרִיבוּ אִשֶּׁה לַיהוָה; בַּיּוֹם הַשְּׁמִינִי מִקְרָא-קֹדֶשׁ יִהְיֶה לָכֶם וְהִקְרַבְתֶּם אִשֶּׁה לַיהוָה, עֲצֶרֶת הִוא--כָּל-מְלֶאכֶת עֲבֹדָה, לֹא תַעֲשׂוּ.	**36** Seven days ye shall bring an offering made by fire unto the LORD; on the eighth day shall be a holy convocation unto you; and ye shall bring an offering made by fire unto the LORD; it is a day of solemn assembly; ye shall do no manner of servile work.
לז אֵלֶּה מוֹעֲדֵי יְהוָה, אֲשֶׁר-תִּקְרְאוּ אֹתָם מִקְרָאֵי קֹדֶשׁ: לְהַקְרִיב אִשֶּׁה לַיהוָה, עֹלָה וּמִנְחָה זֶבַח וּנְסָכִים--דְּבַר-יוֹם בְּיוֹמוֹ.	**37** These are the appointed seasons of the LORD, which ye shall proclaim to be holy convocations, to bring an offering made by fire unto the LORD, a burnt-offering, and a meal-offering, a sacrifice, and drink-offerings, each on its own day;
לח מִלְּבַד, שַׁבְּתֹת יְהוָה; וּמִלְּבַד מַתְּנוֹתֵיכֶם, וּמִלְּבַד כָּל-נִדְרֵיכֶם וּמִלְּבַד כָּל-נִדְבֹתֵיכֶם, אֲשֶׁר תִּתְּנוּ, לַיהוָה.	**38** beside the sabbaths of the LORD, and beside your gifts, and beside all your vows, and beside all your freewill-offerings, which ye give unto the LORD.
לט אַךְ בַּחֲמִשָּׁה עָשָׂר יוֹם לַחֹדֶשׁ הַשְּׁבִיעִי, בְּאָסְפְּכֶם אֶת-תְּבוּאַת הָאָרֶץ, תָּחֹגּוּ אֶת-חַג-יְהוָה, שִׁבְעַת יָמִים; בַּיּוֹם הָרִאשׁוֹן שַׁבָּתוֹן, וּבַיּוֹם הַשְּׁמִינִי שַׁבָּתוֹן.	**39** Howbeit on the fifteenth day of the seventh month, when ye have gathered in the fruits of the land, ye shall keep the feast of the LORD seven days; on the first day shall be a solemn rest, and on the eighth day shall be a solemn rest.
מ וּלְקַחְתֶּם לָכֶם בַּיּוֹם הָרִאשׁוֹן, פְּרִי עֵץ הָדָר כַּפֹּת תְּמָרִים, וַעֲנַף עֵץ-עָבֹת, וְעַרְבֵי-נָחַל; וּשְׂמַחְתֶּם, לִפְנֵי יְהוָה אֱלֹהֵיכֶם--שִׁבְעַת יָמִים.	**40** And ye shall take you on the first day the fruit of goodly trees, branches of palm-trees, and boughs of thick trees, and willows of the brook, and ye shall rejoice before the LORD your God seven days.
מא וְחַגֹּתֶם אֹתוֹ חַג לַיהוָה, שִׁבְעַת יָמִים בַּשָּׁנָה: חֻקַּת עוֹלָם לְדֹרֹתֵיכֶם, בַּחֹדֶשׁ הַשְּׁבִיעִי תָּחֹגּוּ אֹתוֹ.	**41** And ye shall keep it a feast unto the LORD seven days in the year; it is a statute forever in your generations; ye shall keep it in the seventh month.

מב בַּסֻּכֹּת תֵּשְׁבוּ, שִׁבְעַת יָמִים; כָּל-הָאֶזְרָח, בְּיִשְׂרָאֵל, יֵשְׁבוּ, בַּסֻּכֹּת.	42 Ye shall dwell in booths seven days; all that are home-born in Israel shall dwell in booths;
מג לְמַעַן, יֵדְעוּ דֹרֹתֵיכֶם, כִּי בַסֻּכּוֹת הוֹשַׁבְתִּי אֶת-בְּנֵי יִשְׂרָאֵל, בְּהוֹצִיאִי אוֹתָם מֵאֶרֶץ מִצְרָיִם: אֲנִי, יְהוָה אֱלֹהֵיכֶם.	43 that your generations may know that I made the children of Israel to dwell in booths, when I brought them out of the land of Egypt: I am the LORD your God.
מד וַיְדַבֵּר מֹשֶׁה, אֶת-מֹעֲדֵי יְהוָה, אֶל-בְּנֵי, יִשְׂרָאֵל. {פ}	44 And Moses declared unto the children of Israel the appointed seasons of the LORD. {P}

In history and in contemporary times, world Jewish communities, irrespective of religious practice and degree of observance, use the *luaḥ Ivri* ("Hebrew calendar" popularly referenced as the "Jewish religious calendar") for matters of religious observance, holidays, rituals, rites of passage, and on. In the Jewish State of Israel, the *luaḥ Ivri* is utilized alongside the Gregorian calendar for agricultural, civil purposes, and secular events. Jewish time reckoning is lunisolar determined by the natural cycles of the Moon (month) and Sun (season) and a system of religious decisions to balance mathematical and astronomical infractions in conjunction with scriptural time.

    Succinctly stated, the amount of time for the Moon to circle the Earth is 29 ½ twenty-four-hour day period; and the Earth's complete orbit around the Sun is 365 ¼ days in a twenty-four-hour day cycle. The ½ day fraction in the Jewish lunar year is eliminated by alternating six 29 and six 30-day months equating to 354 days in the year. The ¼ fraction in the solar calendar is eliminated by attaching an extra twenty-four-hour day every four years to the shortest month, February.[1] Leviticus 23 gives a succinct statement that the biblical Holy Days (determined by the monthly lunar cycle) are to be consecrated in celebrated in sacred seasons. *"And the LORD spoke unto Moses, saying: Speak unto the children of Israel, and say unto them: The appointed seasons of the LORD, which ye shall proclaim to be holy convocations, even these are My appointed seasons* (Lev 23:1).

    In general, to balance the eleven-day deficiency between the lunar year and the solar season, rabbinic tradition adds a lunar month (29/30 days)

---

[1] Personally, a regulation of mixed emotions. Sad early childhood memories when my March 1st birthday was put off a day every four years. Later in years, I celebrated 48 hours of birth-time and insisted on doubling the presents.

seven times in a nineteenth-year cycle. The additional month is added every couple of years at the end of the calendar year. However, to avoid certain Holy Days (e.g., Rosh HaShanah) to fall on certain days of the week, a day is added to (Mar)Ḥeshvan and or dropped from Kislev. In sum, the Jewish year can be 353,354,355, 383,384,385 days in length.

The Jewish Year

1. Nisan – April, 30 Days	7. Tishrei – October, 30 Days
2. Iyar – May, 29 Days	8. Mar/Ḥeshvan – November, 29/30 Days
3. Sivan – June, 30 Days	9. Kislev – December, 30/29 Days
4. Tammuz – July, 29 Days	10. Tevet – January, 29 Days
5. Av – August, 30 Days	11. Shevet – February, 30 Days
6. Elul – September, 29 Days	12. Adar I – March, 29 Days

Adar II

Significant Days and Seasons of the Jewish Year

Tishrei 1,2 – Rosh HaShana	Nisan 15 – First Day of Passover
Tishrei 3 – Tsom Gedaliah	Nisan 27 – Yom HaSho'ah (Holocaust Day)
Tishrei 10 – Yom Kippur	Iyar 5 – Yom Ha`atsma'ut
	(Israel Independence Day)
Tishrei 15 – First Day Succot	Iyar 18 – Lag B`Omer (Scholars' Day)
Tishrei 21 – Hoshana Rabba	Iyar 28 – Yom Yerushalayim
	(United Jerusalem Day)
Tishrei 22 – Shemini `Aṣeret	Sivan 6 – First Day Shavuot
Tishrei 23 – Simchat Torah	Tammuz 17 – Shiv`ah `Asar B'Tammuz
Kislev 25 – First Day Ḥanukka	`Av 9 – Tish`ah B'Av
Tevet 10 – `Asarah B'Tevet	Rosh Ḥodesh
Shevat 15 – Jewish Arbor Day	Shabbat
Adar (I/II) 13 – Fast of Esther	`Omer/Sefira
Adar (I/II) 14 – Purim	Shlosha Shavuot
Adar (I/II) 15 – Shushan Purim	`Aseret Yemei Teshuvah

Notes

1. Leviticus 23 presents a succinct description of the major holidays and seasons in the Torah/Pentateuch calendar: Shabbat (v. 1); Pesaḥ/Passover (vv. 5–8); `Omer (vv. 9–14); Shavuot/Feast of Weeks/Pentecost (vv. 15–21); Day of Memorial/Blast/Rosh HaShanah (vv. 24–25); Yom Kippur/ Day of Atonement (vv. 26–32); and Succot/Feast of Tabernacles (vv. 33–43). The other listed holidays of the Jewish year are 1) Rabbinic related to post-Pentateuchal collective trial and judgement, e.g., Purim, Ḥanukka, Fast Days (1st and 2nd Temples), and 2) history changing events affecting contemporary Jewry, e.g., Shoah, Third Jewish Commonwealth, etc.

2. Leviticus 23 represents a biblical collective memory of holy convocations associated with Pentateuchal Israelite tradition. Notably absent is reference to the New Moon possibly because its quasi secular activity suggested that it was not celebrated as a "holy convocation." Similarly, the Rosh Ḥodesh (New Month) festival is a quasi-religious one-or-two days celebration. That is to say, a 30-day month, one day Rosh Ḥodesh; 29 day month, two days, the 30th day of the prior month and day one of the new month. A list of the sacrifices brought for the Festivals is found in Numbers 28–29.

3. The Hebrew calendar year begins in spring (Nisan, Passover) not fall (Tishrei, Rosh HaShana). The name "Rosh HaShana" derives from the rabbinic period and embraces the start of intensive religious observance conditioning-guaranteeing the beginning of a successful economic season-year.

The meaning and observance of the Passover observance is detailed in Exod 12: 1–28. Biblically speaking, the Passover Season of Freedom/ *z'man ḥerutenu* features two obligatory rituals/meals: the paschal offering at dusk on Nisan 14 and the eating of the unleavened bread starting on Nisan 15. Hence the designated names of the spring holiday, *Ḥag Ha-Pesaḥ* and *Ḥag Ha-Matsot*. The names also express economic concern, animal, and agriculture.

The `Omer, the gathering of the barley harvest which ripened three weeks before the wheat harvest; both were deemed as fruitfulness of the Land (Deut 8:8) and whose first sheaf was presented at the Sanctuary (see Deut 26:2). The seven weeks of gathering was legislated to begin on *maharat ha-shabbat*/ the morrow after the *sabbath*/rest (Lev 23:11), interpreted in pharisaic-rabbinic tradition as the day after Feast of the Unleavened Bread (Nisan 15), not the day after Shabbat (Sadducees). The joy of bringing the first fruits of the spring season is converted to weeks of sadness and mourning caused by the occupation and destruction of the Land and Temple and prohibition/restriction of Torah study by Ancient Rome. The slaughter of multitudes of Rabbi Akiba's students of Torah is illustrative. LaG B'Omer/ Thirty-Third Day of 'Omer, it is said, the killing ended hence transmitting from sadness to joy on this Scholars Day. The period of the *Sefirah*/ "Counting of the 'Omer" has transcended ill-fated historical memory and time to the present. On the second night of Passover the counting of the forty-nine days of barley harvest ending with Shavuot (Lev 23: 10–14).

Shavuot/ "Festival of Weeks" is so-called because of the counting (*sefirat 'Omer*) of forty-nine days ("seven weeks") from the start of the spring barley harvest (Nisan 16, second day Passover) to the bringing of a next meal offering fifty days later (Sivan 6; Lev 23:16). Leviticus 23 speaks of Shavuot as the first agricultural festival, which is connected with the time of the Revelation at Sinai, *zeman matan torateinu*. Rabbinic teaching references Shavuot as '*atseret*, the spiritual "completion"/ complement to the physical freedom story told and reenacted at Passover time.

4. Day of Memorial/Blast/Rosh HaShana are alternate names for Tishrei 1 (and Tisrei 2 for traditional Diaspora Jewry). Lev 23:24 speaks of no servile work on this day. Num 29:1 refers to this occasion, "a day of blowing the horn/Shofar"; a wake-up call to remember personal sin and contraction and engage in contrition and repentance. This concludes the month of Elul preparation and inaugurates the '*Aseret Yemei Teshuvah*/"Ten Days of Repentance" which climaxes with Yom HaKippurim/ "Day of Atonements." From the medieval Rosh HaShana–Yom Kippur liturgy, we read that Tefilah/Prayer–Teshuvah/Return–Tsedakah/Charity/Righteous Deeds can divert the evil decree. That is to teach, individual and collective *Teshuvah*: (Re)Turn inward (self, people), upward (prayer, God) and outward (charitable good deeds) are reciprocated in God's *teshuvah* (returning response) of mercy and love. Hence the plural spelling of Yom Hakippurim.

Lev 23:33–43 speaks of the seven-day festival of Succot/ "Festival of Tabernacles," Tishrei 15–21. The first (and second day among traditional Diaspora Jews) and seventh days are holy convocations, and the intermediate days between are religious-secular *ḥol ha-moed*. The seventh day in post-Pentateuchal age is called Hoshanah Rabba since it connected people with Yom Kippur. Shemini ʿAtseret is not the eight *(shemini)* day of Succot. Rather, on the day that follows the seven days of Tabernacles, it is a holiday festival on its own, and in the spirit of Succot is called ʿAtseret. In traditional Jewish Diaspora communities, a ninth day of convocation is added called Simchat Torah/ "Rejoicing of the Teaching-Law" (Tishrei 23), the day when the annual synagogue reading of the Five Books of Moses is completed and restarted. Simchat Torah is observed on Shemini ʿAtseret in Israel and in Reform and other liberal Diaspora Jewish communities. The Torah makes clear that Pesaḥ, Shavuot, and Succot, irrespective of later religio-historical associations (Passover, Freedom from Slavery; Pentecost, Sinai Revelation, Succot, Wilderness experience) are primarily noted as pilgrimage holidays of agriculture. Three times a yearly feast before the Lord is requested: the feast of the unleavened bread (Pesaḥ), the feast of harvest, the first fruits of your labors (Shavuot), and the feast of the gathering [*ḥag ha-ḳatsir= Succot*] (Exod 23:14–16). Rabbinic liturgy designates the Week of Tabernacles as *zeman śimḥatenu/* "time of our rejoicing" as *he-ḥag/* "the holiday" due to rewards related to the end of year labor harvest, ending-starting cycle of weekly and Shabbat Torah readings, and the festive Temple rain rituals and subsequent prayers for rain. The central rain ceremony in Second Temple Judaism was the *simḥat beit ha-shoeva/* "rejoice over Temple water ritual," that is, priests drew water from nearby brooks (e.g., Siloam Tunnel, Hezekiah's Pool), carried it to the Temple courtyard, poured it on the ground thereby bidding the Almighty to *imitateo Kohanim* and bring on a bountiful rainy season. The joyous proceedings in Temple days of pilgrims with *Etrog* and *Lulav* in hand (Lev 23: 40) singing songs of praise created a messianic aura. The Hallel praise and thanksgiving Psalms 113–118 are featured in the pilgrimage holidays of Succot, Passover, and other festival calendar dates. Finally, in the *musaf/* "additional" service of Shemini ʿAtseret, *tefilat geshem/*"Prayer for the Rain" is recited.

The centrality of rain and rain rituals (and the alternate Torah way) cannot be overestimated in the Ancient Near East. Three times the Torah (Exod 23:19, 34:26 and Deut 14:21) forbids an ancient Cannanite/Ugaritic fertility rite possibly related to bringing rain, "You shall not boil a kid in its mother's milk." The sanctity of life (mother's milk), separation from death (killing of the living) in the way of Torah validates the safety of the People and the Land of Israel. Neglecting *Halakha* (Torah direction, legalism) is viewed religiously as a blemish in a season for Israel's collective rejoicing. A teaching example: Opposition to foreign rule, yes, but murder, of an appointed governor, however contested/detested, no. The assassination of Gedaliah Ben Achikam, the appointed Governor of Judea during the days of Nebuchadnetzar King of Babylonia, led to the destruction of the First Temple, massive death, and expulsion of the people from the Land. Jewish Sages commemorate the tragic killing of a righteous individual/leader, a cause of the Babylonian Exile by instituting Tsom Gedaliah/ "Fast of Gedaliah" on Tishrei 3 in the midst of `Aseret Yemei Teshuvah*, a period of sincere contemplation and repentance on sinful acts of personal and group behavior. The sunrise to sunset "Fast (Gedaliah) of the Seventh (month Tishrei)" is not commemorated on Tshrei 1, the date of Gedalianh's murder, due to Rosh HaShanah observance. Similarly, in contemporary times, a religio-nationalist law student, Yigal Amir, assassinated the sitting Prime Minister Yitzchak Rabin at a rally in support of the Oslo Accords. The murder occurred at Kings of Israel Square on November 4, 1995, 15 (Mar)Heshvan 5756. Remembering Rabin's assassination on Tsom Gedaliah was first proposed and observed. Ultimately and rightly, official State recognition of the death of Rabin was moved to the day of his murder.

In law and lore, the 29-day month of Heshvan features two unique features: 1) in certain years, it is observed as a 30 day month to balance the lunisolar cycle of the Jewish calendar; and 2) *mar/* "bitter" has been affixed to its name. In lore, Marheshvan/"Bitter Heshvan" because a) it is month with no holidays like the High Holidays of proceeding month of Tishrei and the following month Kislev, which observes Hanukka or b) the serious disappointment if the rains prayed for during Succot are not beholden in Heshvan.

5. There are two ancient sources of the origin of Hanukka, one from the books of the Maccabees and the other from Rabbinic literature. I Maccabees 4:36–59 informs us that Judah Maccabee and his men defeated Lysius (164 BCE) three years to the day when the Greek Seleucid King Antiochus Epiphones decreed idolatrous worship on the altar of the sacred Temple in Jerusalem (167 BCE). Judah and his brethren cleansed the Temple and reintroduced burnt offerings with songs and praises to Heaven, accompanied by musical

instruments as an expression of deliverance and rededication (*hanukka*). II Maccabees, an abridgement of a lost five-book narrative by Jason of Cyrene, echoes the motif of I Maccabees, and adds that the eight day feast is an analogy to Solomon's dedication of the First Temple (2 Macc 2:2; cf. 1 Kgs 8 and 2 Chr 6,7) and also "they kept eight day with gladness as in the feast of Tabernacles, remembering that not long before they had held the feast of Tabernacles, when as they wander in the mountains and dens like beasts" (2 Macc 10:6). From the reference cited it is clear that history's first "feast of dedication" (John 10:22) was an opportunity to reenact the Tabernacles (Succot) festival of the Fall High Holiday season. "Therefore, they bare branches, and bare boughs, and palms, and sang Psalms unto Him that had given them good success in cleansing His place" (2 Macc 10:7). Note well that the "fruit of the goodly trees" (Lev 23:40) was not celebrated because winter was not the season for Etrogs.

Why celebrate "the feast of Tabernacles in the month of Kislev"? Possibly because the *simhat beit ha-shoeva*, the eight-day Temple cult ritual for rain, normally practice on the eve of the rainy season, was denied the Jewish loyalists during the several years of the Temple's pollution by the Seleucids. At the first favorable juncture, then, when the Temple was no longer defiled, and with torches lighting up the sky, the consecrated priesthood conducted the "drawing of the water" ceremony. Nine months later, however, the act was relegated to its proper season, month of Tishrei. Also, fire at the altar burnt offerings connected the success of the Second Jewish Commonwealth with the glory of the Lord during the days of Moses (Wilderness Tabernacle), Solomon (First Temple), and Nehemiah (Second Temple). And the evolving name for the holiday reflects the origin of Hanukka: from "the feast of Tabernacles and of fire" to "Festival of Lights." Talmudic tradition, however, differs decisively from the Maccabean explanation of the eight-day Hanukkah festival. The Rabbis taught that the Greeks contaminated all the Temple oils, but the Maccabees searched and found one cruse of oil with the seal of the High Priest sufficient for one day's lighting only; yet a miracle occurred and they lit the lamp for eight days. The following year these days were appointed a festival with the recital of Hallel (Pss 113–118) and thanksgiving (*b. Šabb.*23b).

Clearly there are major differences between the Talmud and the books of Maccabees, regarding not "why the Festival of Lights?" but "*why* eight days?" The miracle of oil is unreported in the latter.

For example, in 2 Macc 10:3, we read: "And having cleansed the Temple they (Maccabees) made another altar, and *striking stones they took fire out of them* (italics added), and offered a sacrifice after two years (sic) and set forth incense, and lights, and showbread." How then to explain the different origins of the source of fire, one from celestial intervention and the other from facts-on-the-ground guerilla warfare? The Kislev dilemma on the origins of Ḥanukka equates in significance to the Four Questions at the Passover Seder table.

6. Fast Days. Fasting in Jewish tradition is a serious conviction to remember, atone, correct, and cleanse private and public acts of contrition, sadness, disaster. Judaism's defining creed, ethical monotheism, exhibited in deed, is the motivating factor. There are two major and five minor mandatory public fast days noted by fasting sunset to sunset (major) and sunrise to sunset (minor). The twenty-four-hour fast days of Yom Kippur (the Day of Atonement) and Tisha B'Av (the Ninth of Av, commemorating various tragedies of Jewish history, including the destruction of the Two Temples) are major. Three of the five sunrise-to-sunset minor fast days relate to the fate of the First and Second Temples; one to the destiny of the Jews in ancient Persia; and a fast of the firstborn male child on the eve of Passover. *Shiva Asar be-Tammuz*, the 17th of Tammuz is noted for breaching the walls of Jerusalem by the Romans in 70 CE and culminating three weeks later in the destruction of the Second Temple, *Tisha B'Av*, the 9th of Av. The First Temple was said to have been breached on the 9th of Tammuz, but the date has been moved to the 17th of Tammuz; the date commemorates other tragic associations, namely, Moses smashing the tablets of the Ten Commandments, and idolatrous Seleucid worship in the Second Temple before the Maccabean revolt. Related to the fate of the First Temple. *Tsom Gedaliah*, the Fast of Gedaliah, the third of Tishrei, commemorating the killing of the Babylonian-appointed Jewish governor of Judah by other Jews; an assassination viewed as the starting point of the Babylonian Exile of the Judeans/Jews in 586 BCE *Asarah be-Tevet*, the 10th of Tevet: *Asarah be-Tevet* marks the beginning of the siege of Jerusalem by Nebuchadnezzar. A fast day related to the fate of the Jews in Persia as recorded in the Book of Esther is *Ta'anit Esther*, the Fast of Esther which commemorates the saving of Jews from the evil decrees of Haman of old. This minor fast day is commemorated on 13 Adar I/II before 14 Adar, Purim day. Exception: if Purim day falls on Sunday, the Fast of Esther is moved back to Thursday due to Sabbath observance.

Lastly, *Ta'anit Bekhorim*/ "Fast of the First Born" male children obligated to fast on Passover eve (Nisan 14) to demonstrate empathic mercy to the obligatory death of the Egyptian first-born children for the freedom from the Egyptian bondage as told in the Ten Plagues narrative of the Seder reading.

Yom Kippur is the only commanded fast day recorded in the Torah. Fast Days and traditions associated with them are basically the achievement of the Talmudic Sages, derived from scriptural events related to the destruction of the Temple and Jerusalem. For example, Zechariah 8:19, responding to why the people cannot replace days of group tragedy by keeping moral virtues: "Thus saith the Lord of hosts: the fast of the fourth month, and the fast of the fifth, and the fast of the seventh, and the fast of the 10th, shall be to the house of Judah joy and gladness and cheerful seasons; therefore, love you truth and peace." Meaning, clothe communal tragic events in the words of the Lord, so to derive tranquility, security, peace. Rabbinical clarification of the fast days: the first referred to is the 17th of Tammuz, the second is Tisha B'Av, the third is the Fast of Gedaliah, and the last is the 10th of Tevet. In sum, major and minor fast days speak of the mission and destiny of Israel: destruction-restoration, exile-return of People and Land.

7. Israel national holidays. Since the establishment of the State of Israel in 1948, four national holidays have been added to the Hebrew calendar. *Yom Ha-`Atsma'ut*, Israel Independence Day, was proclaimed on May 14, 1948/5 Iyar 5708 in Tel Aviv by David Ben Gurion, Chairman of the Jewish Agency and first elected prime minister of the newly established State of Israel. Selected sentences from the proclamation of sovereignty speak of the Jewish religious-nationalistic democracy of the Third Jewish Commonwealth. *The Land of Israel was the birthplace of the Jewish People. Here their spiritual, religious, and political identity was shaped. Here they first attained to statehood, created cultural values of national and universal significance and gave the world the eternal "Book of Books. Placing our trust in the "Rock of Israel" (2 Sam 23)*[2] ... Thirty-eight members at this session of the provincial council of the State signed the proclamation of statehood. Three years *after* the proclamation of Israel Independence Day, on April 12, 1951, the Knesset of Israel decreed Nisan 27 to be the official day for observing *Yom Ha-Shoah U-Mered Ha-Getaot*, Shoah and Ghetto

---

[2] "The God of Israel has spoken; the Rock of Israel has said to me: When one rules justly over men, ruling in the fear of God..."

Revolt Remembrance Day. The date is commemorated worldwide by all who wish to recall the Great Catastrophe, honor its victims and heroes, and pledge that the devastation done by the Nazis will *never again* be repeated. Questions prevail, however; why the mention of Yom ha-`Atsmaut, and *before* Yom ha-Shoah in the Knesset declaration? Why the uniqueness of Nisan 27 over other dates of World War II infamy and the other Fast Days, and on.[3] *Yom Ha-Zikaron le-Halalei Ma'arakhot Yisrael Ule-Nifge'ei Pe'ulot Ha-Eivah,* Memorial Day for the Fallen Soldiers of Israel and Victims of Terrorism was enacted into law by an act of Knesset in 1963. Yom ha-Zikaron is celebrated on Iyar 4, the day before Iyar 5, Yom ha-`Atsma'ut, Israel Independence Day. *Yom Yerushalayim,* United Jerusalem Day was proclaimed a holiday on May 12, 1968 and ratified as a national holiday by Knesset enactment on March 23, 1998. United Jerusalem Day commemorates the binding of Old and New Jerusalem by Israel's victorious IDF during the Six Day War of 1967 and it is celebrated on the Hebrew date of the unification of the divided city, Iyar 28. A powerful prophetic-messianic-religious message is foreseen and celebrated by the national celebrations of Yom ha-`Atsma'ut and Yom Yerushalayim and greeted by the recitation of the festive Hallel Psalms 113–118, Pesukei DeZimra, and other religio-celebratory rites proclaiming *yerushalayim ha-b'nuyah*/Rebuilt Jerusalem (Ps 122:3).

---

[3] See Z. Garber, "Dating the Shoah: In Your Blood Shall You Live," in *Idem, Shoah the Paradigmatic Genocide: Essays in Exegesis and Eisegesis* (University Press of America, 1994 *first printing*) 67–78.

Bedikat Chametz

בדיקת חמץ

Zev Garber

Exodus 13:7

ז מַצּוֹת, יֵאָכֵל, אֵת, שִׁבְעַת הַיָּמִים; וְלֹא-יֵרָאֶה לְךָ חָמֵץ--וְלֹא-יֵרָאֶה לְךָ שְׂאֹר--בְּכָל-גְּבֻלֶךָ.

7 Unleavened bread shall be eaten throughout the seven days; and there shall no leavened bread be seen with thee, neither shall there be leaven seen with thee, in all thy borders.

In many observant Jewish homes and gathering places, the process of creating a chametz (leaven)-free environment begins shortly after the Purim holiday (Adar I/II, 13–14/15) and comes to its climax the night (14 Nisan) before Passover (15 Nisan).[1] If the eve of Passover falls out on Saturday night then the search for chametz is on Thursday evening. We conduct a veritable "search and destroy" mission to find any remaining chametz in our home and eradicate it. The search is traditionally conducted with a beeswax candle, using a feather, wooden spoon, and a paper bag for collecting any chametz found. It is customary to place ten

---

[1] In Judaism, following biblical tradition, a 24-hour day commences from sunset to sunset ("And there was evening and there was morning," one day,' Gen1:5, and throughout *bri'at `olam*/ Creation of the World, Gen 1–2:3). Minimally, Sunset in Rabbinic tradition commences at the sighting of three stars in heaven. *Pesach*/Passover in the Torah is a seven-day observance, 15 Nisan-21 Nisan. It commences at the sunset of 14 Nisan and ends at sunset 21 Nisan. The first and last days are days of holy convocation and religious restriction; and the intermediate days, *chol ha-moed*, are religio-secular days of observance. Talmudic Rabbinic tradition due to calendar mishap between Jerusalem and Jewish communities off the Land of Zion has tacked an eighth day to Passover observance (22 Nisan) and mandated second day of Passover as an obligatory day of holy convocation and observance. The distinction continues to this day. Jews of Eretz Israel and world-wide Liberal Jewish communities observe a Seven Day Passover with first and last days of obligation. Diaspora traditional Jews (Orthodox, Conservative, and others) observe a Eight day Passover, days 1,2, 7, 8 days of religious obligation and restriction.

pieces of bread throughout the house to be "found" during the search and to note where they are located.[2] If not found the blessing recited before the search for leaven would be *levadala*, in vain. The leaven remains should be wrapped in paper or some other flammable wrapping (but not silver foil, as it does not burn), and perhaps then in plastic bags to prevent crumbs.

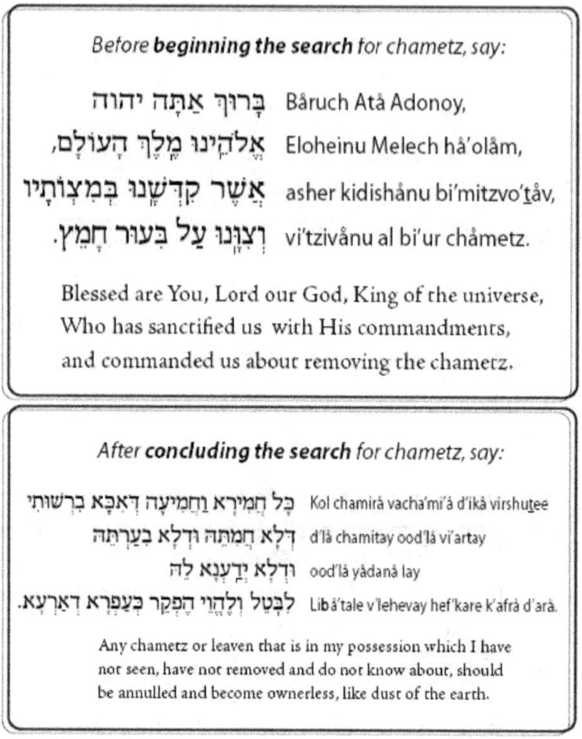

---

*Before **beginning the search** for chametz, say:*

בָּרוּךְ אַתָּה יהוה Båruch Atå Adonoy,

אֱלֹהֵינוּ מֶלֶךְ הָעוֹלָם, Eloheinu Melech hå'olåm,

אֲשֶׁר קִדְּשָׁנוּ בְּמִצְוֹתָיו asher kidishånu bi'mitzvo'tåv,

וְצִוָּנוּ עַל בִּעוּר חָמֵץ. vi'tzivånu al bi'ur chåmetz.

Blessed are You, Lord our God, King of the universe,
Who has sanctified us with His commandments,
and commanded us about removing the chametz.

---

*After **concluding the search** for chametz, say:*

כָּל חֲמִירָא וַחֲמִיעָה דְּאִכָּא בִרְשׁוּתִי Kol chamirå vacha'mi'å d'ikå virshutee

דְּלָא חֲמִתֵּהּ וּדְלָא בְעַרְתֵּהּ d'lå chamitay ood'lå vi'artay

וּדְלָא יְדַעְנָא לֵהּ ood'lå yådanå lay

לִבָּטֵל וְלֶהֱוֵי הֶפְקֵר כְּעַפְרָא דְאַרְעָא. Lib å'tale v'lehevay hef'kare k'afrå d'arå.

Any chametz or leaven that is in my possession which I have
not seen, have not removed and do not know about, should
be annulled and become ownerless, like dust of the earth.

Fig. 3 Public Domain

The next morning, between the 10–11 a.m. hour, the last meal of chamets, breakfast leftovers are added to the crumbs gathered the previous night, and are burned or thrown out. At the burning/casting of the leaven the following prayer is recited:

כָּל־חֲמִירָא חֲמִירָא וַחֲמִיעָה דְּאִכָּא בִרְשׁוּתִי, דְּלָא חֲמִתֵּהּ וּדְלָא בְעַרְתֵּהּ וּדְלָא יְדַעְנָא לֵהּ לִבָּטֵל וְלֶהֱוֵי הֶפְקֵר בְּעַפְרָא דְאַרְעָא.

---

[2] Why ten? Some say it is related to the Passover Ten Plagues narrative and others to the ten *sefirot*/emanations of the Kabbalah.

And a slightly longer recitation:

Kol hamira vahamia d'ika virshuti dahaziteih udla haziteih, dahamiteih udla hamiteih, d'viarteih udla viarteih libateil v'lehevei hefkeir k'afra d'ara. All hameitz in my possession, whether I have seen it or not, whether I have removed it or not, is hereby nullified and ownerless as the dust of the earth.

Concise discussion of *Bedika* laws and traditions are found in a number of internet sources. They range from lofty teachings to necessary changes reflecting contemporary safety. Examples, of the former, flame penetrating darkness in the quest of the last particles of leaven and of the latter, the replacement of the chamets candle by flashlight for safety reasons. Of particular interest to the contemporary traditionalist religious household, see the Orthodox Union website.

`Eruv Tavshilin: עירוב תבשילין
"Mixing of [cooked] Dishes"

Zev Garber

In Jewish law no start-up cook food preparation is permitted from e*rev Shabbat* (Friday sunset) to *motsaei Shabbat* (Saturday night). Since Second Temple Judaism, the question has risen how does one prepare properly, if at all, Shabbat cooked food if perchance an obligatory festival falls on the proceeding days? The permissive response was `*eruv tavshilin*/ "mixing of (cooked) dishes," a rabbinic *halakhic* decision that enables one to cook food on the *chag*/ "festival" to be consumed on the Shabbat. Hence, cooking food on Shabbat is *'asur* (forbidden) but to cook the Shabbat food on the festival is *mutar* (permitted). Thus, if a Passover day falls on Friday, in order to prepare Shabbat cooked food, the head of the household is obligated to perform the act of `*eruv tavshilin before Pesach* begins and not on Passover day. Also, if the last day(s) of *Pesach* fall before Shabbat then `*eruv tavshilin* is performed on the last day of *chol ha-mo`ed*/ intermediate day of the holiday. Food *koshered* by the `*eruv* prayers permit all household members and guests to partake. A sample Passover `*eruv* is taking some *matsa* and something cooked, for example, boiled egg, piece of fish, meat, placing them on a plate, raising it, and saying the following prayers:

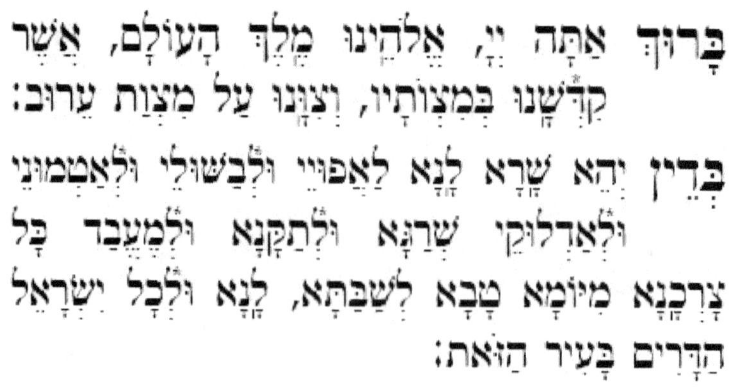

בָּרוּךְ אַתָּה יְיָ, אֱלֹהֵינוּ מֶלֶךְ הָעוֹלָם, אֲשֶׁר
קִדְּשָׁנוּ בְּמִצְוֹתָיו, וְצִוָּנוּ עַל מִצְוַת עֵרוּב:

בְּדֵין יְהֵא שָׁרֵא לָנָא לַאֲפוּיֵי וּלְבַשּׁוּלֵי וּלְאַטְמוּנֵי
וּלְאַדְלוּקֵי שְׁרָגָא וּלְתַקָּנָא וּלְמֶעְבַּד כָּל
צָרְכָנָא מִיּוֹמָא טָבָא לְשַׁבַּתָּא, לָנָא וּלְכָל יִשְׂרָאֵל
הַדָּרִים בָּעִיר הַזֹּאת:

Fig. 4 Public Domain

Blessed are you, Lord our God, king of the universe, who has sanctified us with his commandments, and commanded us concerning the mitsvah of `eruv.

Through this [eruv] it shall be permissible for us to bake, cook, put away a dish [to preserve its heat], kindle a light, prepare, and do on the holiday all that is necessary for Shabbat—for us and for all the Israelites who dwell in this city.

The Traditional Seder Table

Zev Garber

1. **Candles** are lighted by the mother/wife/daughter/female of the house to usher in the *Pesach* festival. The benediction she pronounces over the candles conveys that the act symbolizes joy and festivity, and that the soft candle glow adds an aura of spirituality at the table.
2. **A Cup of Wine** is placed at each table setting. The sanctification of the Holiday (and Shabbat if they coincide) is pronounced over the first cup. Three additional cups are drunk during the course of the seder, making a total of four, to symbolize the four expressions of the Lord's promise to redeem the Children of Israel and deliver them from the bondage of Egyptian slavery (Exodus 6:6–7).
3. **The Haggadah** meaning the "telling" contains the complete seder night ritual in their prescribed *seder* (order). The first section of the Haggadah relates the story of Israelite bondage and freedom and is read before the seder festive meal. The second section follows the evening dinner and consists of prayers of praise and thanksgiving to the Almighty for the memory and reenactment of this unique event in Jewish history.
4. **Matsa** "bread of affliction" eaten by the Israelites in Egypt and the bread that had to be baked in hasty flight when there was no time for fermenting/leavening. Three *matsot* are placed on the seder plate separated by cloth, which makes it possible to cover and uncover for ritual instruction. One *matsa* fulfills the seder obligation; the other two is necessary if seder night falls on Shabbat eve which requires two loaves of bread. *Matsa sh'murah* ("watched *matsa*"), ritually supervised from the planting of the grain through the baking of the unleavened bread, is the preferred *matsa* of the seder ritual. Half the middle *matsa* is broken, hidden, found by child/ren and ransomed for a reward. The *Afikoman* is the requisite *dessert* to end the seder meal no later than *chatsot ha-laylah* (midnight).
5. **The Z'ro`a**, a roasted shank bone is placed on the seder plate. It represents the Temple paschal lamb sacrifice (*korban pesach*). The Hebrew name *pesach* for Passover refers to the Lord's passing over

(*pose'ach*) the Israelite homes during the plague visited upon the Egyptian first born. The *z'ro'a* is commemorative but must be made edible.

6. **The Beitsah**, a roasted egg is placed left of the *z'ro'a* on the seder plate. It symbolizes the required Temple offerings brought on festivals during days of yore. On the seder plate it also serves as a mournful reminder of the loss of the Temple where the Paschal sacrifices were once brought. Commemorative but must be edible.

7. **The Maror** "bitter herbs" (most often horseradish) is placed in the middle of the seder plate and eating it fulfills the commandment of identification with the bitter suffering of the Israelites under the yoke of Egypt. In some traditions, a second bitter herb, *chazeret* (lettuce, endives), is found directly below the *maror*. It commemorates the custom of eating *maror* (*merorim*, bitter herbs) sandwiched between two pieces of *matsot* before the meal. In the Haggadah reading, bitter herbs in the plural is required for the Hillel sandwich.

8. **The Charoset**, placed beneath the *z'ro'a*, is a mixture of chopped apple, nuts, cinnamon, and wine designed to connote the mortar used by the Israelites to build the palaces and pyramids of Pharonic Egypt during centuries of forced labor. Before the *maror* is eaten, it is dipped into the *charoset*. To lessen or enhance the taste of slavery?

9. **The Karpas**, a piece of parsley or celery placed to the left of the *charoset*, symbolizes the meager diet of the Israelites in Egyptian bondage, It is dipped into salt water in remembrance of the tears they shed in their misery. Other vegetables, such as radishes and potatoes may replace parsley/celery. The *karpas* also signifies the start of Spring, the season of Passover.

10. **The Cup of Elijah**, filled with wine, is kept on the seder table throughout the seder ritual in the hope that the Prophet Elijah at the quest of the Almighty may appear to proclaim the coming of the Mashiach and the dawning of messianic times. Thus, in retelling their memories of Egyptian bondage and "in all generations" thereafter, contemporary Jews look forward to a day of universal peace, love, and brother-sisterhood.

11. **Dish of Salt Water or Vinegar** by the seder plate to dip the *karpas*.

38 *Annotated Passover Haggadah*

Fig. 5 Public Domain

Fig. 6 Passover seder plate, 20th century, modelled on a 19th century exemplar.
On display at the Jewish Museum, London

Order of the Passover Seder

Kadesh קַדֵּשׁ

The first of four cups of wine is poured; the blessing is said to sanctify the feast day.

Urechats וּרְחַץ

The hands are washed before handling the *karpas*. No blessing is recited.

Karpas כַּרְפַּס

A green vegetable is dipped in saltwater and then eaten.

Yachats יַחַץ

The middle of three *matsot* is broken. The larger half is wrapped in a napkin and hidden for *Afikoman* (dessert).

Maggid מַגִּיד

The second cup of wine is poured, and the story of the flight of the Israelite slaves from Egypt is told.

Rachatsah רָחְצָה

The hands are washed with blessing before the meal.

Motsi מוֹצִיא

The *motsi* prayer is said over bread followed by the blessing over the *matsa*.

Matsa מַצָּה

Special blessing is recited over the unleavened bread. The eating of the *matsah* follows.

Maror מָרוֹר

The bitter herbs are tasted.

Korech כּוֹרֵךְ

A "sandwich" of *matsa*, bitter herbs, and *charoset* is eaten.

Shulchan Orech שֻׁלְחָן עוֹרֵךְ

The festive meal is served.

Tsafun צָפוּן

A child discovers the *Afikoman,* which is then eaten.

Barech בָּרֵךְ

The third cup of wine is poured, and the grace after meals is recited. An extra cup of wine is also poured for the prophet Elijah, and a child opens the door of the house to invite him in.

Hallel הַלֵּל

The fourth cup of wine is poured, followed by psalms of praise and a prayer.

Nirtsah נִרְצָה

The service concludes with a hymn, a prayerful request that the seder ritual was done appropriately, and a request that next year may it be celebrated in *yerushalayim ha-b'nuyah,* redeemed-rebuilt Jerusalem.

The order of the seder is summed up in fifteen parts; others count fourteen parts by combining *motsi* and *matsa.* Interesting coincidence (or is it?) that the second century B.C.E. *Dayyenu* paragraphs which speak of God's mercies from the time of the Israelite Exodus from Egypt to entrance and settlement in the Promise Land contains fourteen strophes and mentions fifteen blissful acts. *HalleluYaH.*[1]

The complex parts of the seder night ritual are contained in this hallowed mnemonic device to remember the order and content of the seder:

Kaddesh (Sanctification), ***Urechats*** (Wasshing), ***Karpas*** (Vegetable), ***Yachats*** (Breaking), ***Maggid*** (The Story), ***Rachatsah*** (Washing), ***Motzi Matsa*** (Blessings), ***Maror*** (Bitter Herbs), ***Korech*** (Sandwich), ***Shulchan*** Orech (Dinner), ***Tsafun*** (Dessert), ***Barech*** (Grace), ***Hallel*** (Song), ***Nirtsah*** (Closing).

---

[1] YaH, the Lord's Name (one of many) equates to number 15. *Haleluyah,* "praise the Lord."

Annotated Haggadah for Passover

Zev Garber
Kenneth Hanson

KADESH קַדֵּשׁ

Make Kiddush

The first cup of wine is poured, and the leader of the Seder recites the Kiddush (Sanctification) over wine (normally) or grape juice. If Shabbat and Seder coincide, the blessing over the wine is recited before the benediction over the festive occasion. This follows the School of Hillel over the School of Shammai who teaches the reverse, the blessing of the day before the blessing over the wine (m. Pesach 10.2; see m.Ber 8.1).

—Zev Garber

The Mishnah (Pesachim 10:1) relates:

> On the eve of Passover [from] close to [the time of] the afternoon offering, no one must eat until nightfall. Even the poorest person in Israel must not eat [on the night of Passover] unless he reclines. And they must give him no fewer than four cups of wine, even [if he receives relief] from the charity plate.

The four cups of wine at the Seder correspond to the four "salvations" as expressed in the book of Exodus. The Jerusalem Talmud (*y. Pesach.* 68b:20–21) explains:

> From where [do we know the requirement to drink] four cups? Rabbi Yochanan [said] in the name of Rav, "Rabbi Banniah said, 'Corresponding to the four [expressions of] salvations: "Therefore say unto the children of Israel, I am the Lord, and I will bring you out, etc. And I will take you to Me for a people, etc."(Exod 6:6–7). "And I will

bring you out, and I will rescue you, and I will save you, And I will take you."'

An alternate interpretation found in the same passage relates:

> Rabbi Yehoshua ben Levi said, 'Corresponding to the four cups of Pharaoh: "And the cup of Pharaoh was in my hand and I squeezed them into the cup of Pharaoh and I placed the cup onto the palm of Pharaoh... and you will place the cup of Pharaoh, etc." (Gen 40:11–13).'

Yet another explanation hints at the four kingdoms which oppressed the Israelites in antiquity, to which the rabbis responded:

> Corresponding to the four punishments that the Holy One, blessed be He, will pour upon the nations of the world in the future: "For so said the Lord, the God of Israel to me, 'Take the cup of wine of anger, etc." (Jer 25:15); "A golden cup is Babylonia in the hand of the Lord" (Jer 51:7); "As it is a cup in the hand of the Lord" (Ps 75:9); "Upon the wicked He will cause to rain coals; fire and brimstone and burning wind shall be the portion of their cup" (Ps 11:6)."

The number four is echoed elsewhere in the Seder, in the four questions, the four sons, and the four kinds of food (*matsa*, lamb, *maror* and *charoset*).

In rabbinic commentary (*Maarechet Heidenheim*, by Rabbi Tevele Bondi, 1898, on *Pesach* Haggadah, Magid, Four Questions 1:1) we also read:

> "I will take you out" implies from the sea, as we see in Psalm 107. God hinted in this promise that he would not take them by way of the land of the Philistines but rather by the way of the sea. The Israelites had no reason to fear the "labors of Egyptians" because God planned to drown the Egyptians in the sea. "I will take you out of the labors of Egypt." This verse implies that I am taking you and not the Egyptians out.

The *kiddush* is appropriately recited over the first cup, which represents salvation from harsh labor, when the plagues were sent down on the Egyptians. Traditionally, the cup is filled to the brim, suggesting the fullness of this redemption. However, the participants are admonished to remain sober, fully appreciating the meaning of story yet to be told. For this reason, only half of the cup is required to be consumed.

—Kenneth Hanson

בְּשַׁבָּת מַתְחִילִין

On Shabbat, begin here:

וַיְהִי עֶרֶב וַיְהִי בֹקֶר יוֹם הַשִּׁשִּׁי. וַיְכֻלּוּ הַשָּׁמַיִם וְהָאָרֶץ וְכָל־צְבָאָם. וַיְכַל אֱלֹהִים בַּיּוֹם הַשְּׁבִיעִי מְלַאכְתּוֹ אֲשֶׁר עָשָׂה וַיִּשְׁבֹּת בַּיּוֹם הַשְּׁבִיעִי מִכָּל מְלַאכְתּוֹ אֲשֶׁר עָשָׂה. וַיְבָרֶךְ אֱלֹהִים אֶת יוֹם הַשְּׁבִיעִי וַיְקַדֵּשׁ אוֹתוֹ כִּי בוֹ שָׁבַת מִכָּל־מְלַאכְתּוֹ אֲשֶׁר בָּרָא אֱלֹהִים לַעֲשׂוֹת.

And there was evening and there was morning, the sixth day. And the heaven and the earth were finished, and all their host. And on the seventh day God finished His work which He had done; and He rested on the seventh day from all His work which He had done. And God blessed the seventh day, and sanctified it; because He rested on it from all of His work which God created in doing (Genesis 1:31–2:3).

בחול מתחילין:

On weekdays, begin here:

בָּרוּךְ אַתָּה ה', מְקַדֵּשׁ (לשבת: הַשַׁבָּת וְ) יִשְׂרָאֵל וְהַזְּמַנִּים.

Blessed are You, Lord our God, King of the universe, who creates the fruit of the vine.

בָּרוּךְ אַתָּה ה', אֱלֹהֵינוּ מֶלֶךְ הָעוֹלָם אֲשֶׁר בָּחַר בָּנוּ מִכָּל־עָם וְרוֹמְמָנוּ מִכָּל־לָשׁוֹן וְקִדְּשָׁנוּ בְּמִצְוֹתָיו. וַתִּתֶּן לָנוּ ה' אֱלֹהֵינוּ בְּאַהֲבָה (לשבת: שַׁבָּתוֹת לִמְנוּחָה וּ) מוֹעֲדִים לְשִׂמְחָה, חַגִּים וּזְמַנִּים לְשָׂשׂוֹן, (לשבת: אֶת יוֹם הַשַׁבָּת הַזֶּה וְ) אֶת יוֹם חַג הַמַּצּוֹת הַזֶּה זְמַן חֵרוּתֵנוּ, (לשבת: בְּאַהֲבָה) מִקְרָא קֹדֶשׁ זֵכֶר לִיצִיאַת מִצְרָיִם. כִּי בָנוּ בָחַרְתָּ וְאוֹתָנוּ קִדַּשְׁתָּ מִכָּל הָעַמִּים, (לשבת: וְשַׁבָּת) וּמוֹעֲדֵי קָדְשֶׁךָ (לשבת: בְּאַהֲבָה וּבְרָצוֹן) בְּשִׂמְחָה וּבְשָׂשׂוֹן הִנְחַלְתָּנוּ.

Blessed are You, Lord our God, King of the universe, who has chosen us from all peoples and has raised us above all tongues and has sanctified us with His commandments. And You have given us, Lord our God, [Sabbaths for rest], appointed times for happiness, holidays, and special times for joy, [this Sabbath day, and] this Festival of *Matsot*, our season of freedom [in love] a holy convocation in memory of the Exodus from Egypt. For You have chosen us and sanctified us above all peoples. In Your gracious love, You granted us Your [holy Sabbath, and] special times for happiness and joy.

רוּךְ אַתָּה ה', מְקַדֵּשׁ (לשבת: הַשַׁבָּת וְ) יִשְׂרָאֵל וְהַזְּמַנִּים.

Blessed are You, O Lord, who sanctifies [the Sabbath,] Israel, and the appointed times.

במוצאי שבת מוסיפים:

On Saturday night add the following two paragraphs:

בָּרוּךְ אַתָּה ה', אֱלֹהֵינוּ מֶלֶךְ הָעוֹלָם, בּוֹרֵא מְאוֹרֵי הָאֵשׁ. בָּרוּךְ אַתָּה ה', אֱלֹהֵינוּ מֶלֶךְ הָעוֹלָם הַמַּבְדִּיל בֵּין קֹדֶשׁ לְחֹל, בֵּין אוֹר לְחֹשֶׁךְ, בֵּין יִשְׂרָאֵל לָעַמִּים, בֵּין יוֹם הַשְּׁבִיעִי לְשֵׁשֶׁת יְמֵי הַמַּעֲשֶׂה. בֵּין קְדֻשַּׁת שַׁבָּת לִקְדֻשַּׁת יוֹם טוֹב הִבְדַּלְתָּ, וְאֶת־יוֹם הַשְּׁבִיעִי מִשֵּׁשֶׁת יְמֵי הַמַּעֲשֶׂה קִדַּשְׁתָּ. הִבְדַּלְתָּ וְקִדַּשְׁתָּ אֶת־עַמְּךָ יִשְׂרָאֵל בִּקְדֻשָּׁתֶךָ.

Blessed are You, Lord our God, King of the universe, who creates the light of the fire. Blessed are You, Lord our God, King of the universe, who distinguishes between the holy and the profane, between light and darkness, between Israel and the nations, between the seventh day and the six working days. You have distinguished between the holiness of the Sabbath and the holiness of the Festival, and You have sanctified the seventh day above the six working days. You have distinguished and sanctified Your people Israel with Your holiness.

בָּרוּךְ אַתָּה ה', הַמַּבְדִּיל בֵּין קֹדֶשׁ לְקֹדֶשׁ.

Blessed are You, O Lord, who distinguishes between the holy and the holy.

בָּרוּךְ אַתָּה ה', אֱלֹהֵינוּ מֶלֶךְ הָעוֹלָם, שֶׁהֶחֱיָנוּ וְקִיְּמָנוּ וְהִגִּיעָנוּ לַזְּמַן הַזֶּה.

Blessed are You, Lord our God, King of the universe, who has granted us life and sustenance and permitted us to reach this season.

שותה בהסיבת שמאל ואינו מברך ברכה אחרונה.

Drink while reclining to the left (free person's posture) and do not recite a blessing after drinking.

The Kiddush is a formal public and home (so seen by many) ritual consecrating the holiness of the Sabbath and festivals. All who sit, stand, and participate in the cosmic-religious-historical message of the Kiddush. If Seder night falls on *erev Shabbat,* remember and observe the Sabbath commandment to abstain from work, rest, reflect that the cosmos is not a product by chance, meaning as the Creator rests so too Created Man (generic), *imitateo Dei.* The universe is not an unpredictable event by chance or accident but the creativity of an Intelligent Power. In historic terms, God the Creator is portrayed as Israel's Redeemer, a weekly-festive reminder of Israel's natal origins, deliverance from Egypt (explicit) and revelation at Sinai (implicit). Twinning origins of the World and Israel's natal birth teaches a distinct teaching of Judaism. Slavery in Egypt is timeless work and oppression; *Shabbat menucha*, peaceful 24-hour Sabbath day of rest from work, toil, and anxiety distinguishes a free-person work ethic from the dreadfulness of a slave mentality. In the weekly *erev Shabbat Kiddush*, the holy Sabbath is referenced "as an inheritance, a memorial of the creation—that day being also the first of the holy convocations (Shabbat is listed as the first of the Holy Convocations commanded by God to Moses to instruct Israel to observe; see Lev 23), in remembrance of the departure from Egypt."

Sanctifying the Sabbath-Seder/Festivals table meal is over wine. Jewish Shabbat and festive meals are traditionally accompanied by a cup of wine in honor of the day and accompanied by two blessings: One over the wine and the other on the sanctity of the day ("rejoicing this day of the festival of the unleavened bread, the season of our deliverance" recited at Kiddush for *Pesach*). If there is no wine nor grape juice, then no blessing over the wine. On Shabbat and Festivals, bread is substituted and the *Motsi* blessing is recited. But on Passover night unleavened bread would be required and this would occur before the priority blessing of the *matsa*. A *Shanda* at the table that no *Zeyda* would tolerate.

Havdalah ("separation") paragraph is recited if Seder night occurs at the end of the Sabbath. Kiddush and Havdalah are religious rituals dated to ancient antiquity and ascribed to the Men of the Great Assembly (*'anshei keneset ha-gedolah*). Best identify with the end of the Sabbath, Havdalah is also recited at the end of all festival holy days separating sacred time and obligations from secular time and endeavors. *Nota Bene*, Havdalah on Seder night separates the Shabbat from *yemei ha-chol* (weekdays) but not sacred time which is ongoing with Passover eve. Hence basic symbols of the Havdalah ritual (wine, spices, twin candles) are suspended.

Ethical morality themed in *separation* connects Kiddush and Havdalah, the incoming and outgoing of sacred time, here, the Sabbath. Kiddush narrates *Creation*: God separates, makes distinctions, categorizes, and thus creates. In Genesis, creation is the imposition of order on chaotic Nature and strict definition of categories. God distinguishes light from dark, heavenly bodies from earthly ones, sea, land, and all creatures, man from God, woman from man, workdays from rest days; and freedom from slavery, Exodus. And this mirrors the teaching of Havdalah, *separation* in areas of holy and profane, sacred and secular, light from darkness, Shabbat from *yemei ha-chol*, Israel (*goy kadosh*, Exod 19:6) from the heathen nations.

—Zev Garber

Urchatz (and Wash)

וּרְחַץ

נוטלים את הידים ואין מברכים "עַל נְטִילַת יָדַיִם"

Wash your hands but do not say the blessing "on the washing of the hands." A ritual action without a formal blessing may be viewed as washing before a meal but it is viewed as a requisite act of purification to start the Seder ritual. Traditionally, pitcher, bowl, and towel are handed out the Seder table. Alternatively, participants wash their hands at the kitchen sink.

Karpas (Greens)

כַּרְפַּס

לוקח מן הכרפס פחות מכזית – כדי שלא יתחייב בברכה אחרונה – טובל במי מלח, מברך "בורא פרי האדמה", ומכוין לפטור בברכה גם את המרור. אוכל בלא הסבה.

Take from parsley or celery or any green vegetable and dip a kazayit ("smallest amount" to avoid saying the blessing after eating it) into vinegar or saltwater; say the blessing "who creates the fruit of the earth." The same procedure and blessing for eating the bitter herbs (maror). If green vegetable is wanting, potatoes and radishes are appropriate. Greens symbolize the season of spring when Passover is celebrated. The karpas is dipped into vinegar or saltwater to evoke the tears shed by the Israelites in the Egyptian slavery. Eat without reclining.

בָּרוּךְ אַתָּה ה', אֱלֹהֵינוּ מֶלֶךְ הָעוֹלָם, בּוֹרֵא פְּרִי הָאֲדָמָה.

Blessed are you, Lord our God, King of the universe, who creates the fruit of the earth.

Yachatz (Break)

יַחַץ

חותך את המצה האמצעית לשתים, ומצפין את הנתח הגדול לאפיקומן.

The leader of the Seder breaks the middle matsa in two, and leaving half of it on the Seder plate, he conceals the larger piece to use it after supper for the Afikoman.

Matsa, crisp, flat unleavened bread. *Matsa*, the dominant food symbol of Passover week, commemorates the flight of the Israelites from Egypt. They left in such haste that there was no time for their bread dough to rise (Exod 12:39). The Passover *matsa* symbolizes freedom and redemption and its simplicity teaches us to be modest and humble. Three *matsa* separated by cloth or napkin for easy accessibility during the Seder ritual. To honor the Seder ritual, *matsa shemurah* ("watched *matsa*," supervised from the planting of the grain through the baking of the unleavened bread) is the preferable *matsa* of *haste*. However, during the week of Passover, most households prefer regular Kosher for Passover *matsa* not *matsa shemurah* as the *matsa* of *taste*.

The twist and turn of Seder *she'elot u-teshuvot* (Q & A) begin here. If one *matsa shemurah* is sufficient for the Seder, then why show three unleavened breads? Two *matsot* are required if Seder night falls on *erev Shabbat* symbolizing the double portion of *manna* (*man hu'/* "what's it? food) for Sabbath observance during the Israelite wilderness experience (Exodus 16). Respectfully, they are not removed if Seder night does not fall on Sabbath eve. Kabbalists name the Three *matsot, Kohen(priest)-Levi* (levite)-*Yisrael* (Israelite) following the three divisions of Jewish peoplehood associated with Second Temple Judaism and still in vogue today. The breaking-hiding-retrieving of the Levi *matsa* for *gelt* or presents is to encourage children and others to stay wake to the climatic end of the Seder service. Of note, Messianic Jewish and Christian oriented Last Supper Seders view Christological Messianic themes in the Three *matsot*/Trinity; breaking/crucifixion the middle *matsa*; and restoration of the broken *matsa*/ Resurrection of Jesus, the messianic *dessert/Afikoman* climaxing the Exodus *desert* story.

—Zev Garber

Magid, Ha Lachma Anya

מַגִּיד

The Recitation [of the Exodus story]

מגלה את המצות, מגביה את הקערה ואומר בקול רם:

The shankbone and egg are removed from the Seder plate. The leader of the Seder uncovers the matsot, raises the Seder plate, and says with all present:

הָא לַחְמָא עַנְיָא דִּי אֲכָלוּ אַבְהָתָנָא בְּאַרְעָא דְמִצְרָיִם. כָּל דִּכְפִין יֵיתֵי וְיֵיכֹל, כָּל דִּצְרִיךְ יֵיתֵי וְיִפְסַח. הָשַׁתָּא הָכָא, לְשָׁנָה הַבָּאָה בְּאַרְעָא דְיִשְׂרָאֵל. הָשַׁתָּא עַבְדֵי, לְשָׁנָה הַבָּאָה בְּנֵי חוֹרִין.

This is the bread of destitution that our ancestors ate in the land of Egypt. Anyone who is famished should come and eat, anyone who is in need should come and partake of the *Pesach* sacrifice. Now we are here, next year we will be in the land of Israel; *this year we are slaves, next year we will be free people.*

The vernacular Aramaic language and *Pesaḥ* sacrifice meal component suggest composition in the period of the Second Temple before the destruction of *bayit sheni* in 70 C.E. This invitation to the poor to participate is inserted before the telling of the Exodus story and not before the Kaddish. The Kiddush inaugurates festival time in general and not exclusively the Passover freedom story. Also, the *bread of destitution* eaten in the land of Egypt suggests that the *matsa* is not exclusively identified as the hasty baked bread of flight. *Next year we will be free people* mirrors the final refrain of the Passover Haggadah, *Next Year in Rebuilt Jerusalem.* Exodus—Return—Zion are converging themes of Freedom chiseled in midrashic tradition in the month of Nisan, the month of redemption when Israel was freed from Egypt and when Israel will again be freed (see *Exod. Rab.* XV.12).

—Zev Garber

This year we are slaves, next year we will be free people. When the Haggadah emphasizes that "once we were slaves in Egypt," it is constructive to consider what the nature of this "slavery" and what it may have entailed. The "minimalist" camp of textual critics have long argued for a late date of composition of the biblical accounts (the seventh century B.C.E. or later), allowing none of this to be read as history. Others, such as Israeli archaeologist Amihai Mazar, have noted that details in the Bible's narrative coincide well with what archaeology tells us about the ancient days they presume to detail. For example, we know that there were major building projects during the long reign of Pharaoh Ramses II, and the presence of slaves in Egypt and their migration from Egypt is well-attested in the archaeological and historical record.

In any case, the traditional conception of vast throngs of Hebrews wearing shackles and toiling under the cruel whips of their taskmasters may well be literary hyperbole. While standard English translations tell us they are "slaves," the actual Hebrew word is `avadim*, meaning "laborers," which could even refer to "corvée laborers," or "day laborers." The Hebrews, according to this theory, were not "owned" in the way we imagine slaves in bondage to have been the property of their masters. Rather, such servitude may have involved only the dispensation of their labor.

To the editors of the Bible, looking back anachronistically, it may have seemed that entering into the pharaoh's employ, however it came about, was a grievous form of bondage. Who would not argue that it might have been better for the children of Abraham to suffer the ravages of famine in the land of Canaan than to enter the relative "safety" of servitude in Egypt? But enter they did, and in the end, they would require nothing less than a revolution. They would need an exodus.

—Kenneth Hanson

Magid, Four Questions

מסיר את הקערה מעל השולחן. מוזגין כוס שני. הבן שואל:

The Seder plate is placed back or removed from the table. Participants pour a second cup of wine. The youngest son/child/ participant then asks:

מַה נִּשְׁתַּנָּה הַלַּיְלָה הַזֶּה מִכָּל הַלֵּילוֹת? שֶׁבְּכָל הַלֵּילוֹת אָנוּ אוֹכְלִין חָמֵץ וּמַצָּה, הַלַּיְלָה הַזֶּה – כֻּלּוֹ מַצָּה. שֶׁבְּכָל הַלֵּילוֹת אָנוּ אוֹכְלִין שְׁאָר יְרָקוֹת – הַלַּיְלָה הַזֶּה (כֻּלּוֹ) מָרוֹר. שֶׁבְּכָל הַלֵּילוֹת אֵין אָנוּ מַטְבִּילִין אֲפִילוּ פַּעַם אֶחָת – הַלַּיְלָה הַזֶּה שְׁתֵּי פְעָמִים. שֶׁבְּכָל הַלֵּילוֹת אָנוּ אוֹכְלִין בֵּין יוֹשְׁבִין וּבֵין מְסֻבִּין – הַלַּיְלָה הַזֶּה כֻּלָּנוּ מְסֻבִּין.

What differentiates this night from all [other] nights? On all [other] nights we eat *chamets* and *matsa*; this night, only *matsa*? On all [other] nights we eat other vegetables; tonight (only) *maror*. On all [other] nights, we don't dip [our food], even one time; tonight [we dip it] twice. On [all] other nights, we eat either sitting or reclining; tonight we all recline.

Fig. 7 The Four Questions (Ma Nishtana) from the Sarajevo Haggadah, circa 1350 CEd7

The Seder meal of days of yore modeled after the Greco-Roman dinner of antiquity—hors d'oeuvre, multiple cups of wine (before, beginning, during, after), and the main meal – was endowed by three not four questions: 1) why dipped vegetables twice, *karpas* dipped in salt water and dipped in *haroset* during the eating of the main meal; 2) why eating unleavened bread and food products; and 3) why, in the period of Second Temple sacrifices, only roasted not stewed or boiled paschal lamb is permitted? (*m. Pesach* 10.4). Question Three became obsolete after the Fall of the Temple and abandonment of paschal sacrifice. Questions One and Two remain; and the question of the *maror* was added to fill the lacuna of bitter herbs. The Fourth Question about reclination (suggesting full freedom as an Israelite/Jew) is post-talmudic and never answered in and by the Seder reading. May it not be because there is no definitive sign/end of generational antisemitism, rhetoric and action, which increases not decreases in contemporary times? Then *inclination* (concerned and focused *she'elot u-teshuvot*) not *reclination* (illusory freedom telling).

Asking and understanding the Passover Questions is obligatory. Ideally, for children to ask; an introduction to their heritage of slavery and freedom. No children then adults. If done alone, the individual recites the questions. The importance of this procedure is underscored by scholars knowledgeable in the laws of *Pesach* are obliged to ask (*b. Pesach* 116a), Rambam (Maimonides, 12th century) requires that the leader of the Seder recites the questions (*Mishneh Torah*, *Hametsu-Matsah*, VIII.2) and the school of Rashi (11th century) requires that the leader of the Seder explains the questions in the vernacular (*Mahzor Vitry*, p. 295). In sum, the obligatory significance of asking/initiating the Passover story negates any distinction between scholarly wisdom and the innocence of an inquisitive child.

—Zev Garber

Magid, We Were Slaves in Egypt

מחזיר את הקערה אל השולחן. המצות תהיינה מגלות בשעת אמירת ההגדה.

Replace Seder plate if it has been removed from the table. The matsot should be uncovered during the saying of the Haggadah.

עֲבָדִים הָיִינוּ לְפַרְעֹה בְּמִצְרָיִם, וַיּוֹצִיאֵנוּ ה' אֱלֹהֵינוּ מִשָּׁם בְּיָד חֲזָקָה וּבִזְרֹעַ נְטוּיָה. וְאִלּוּ לֹא הוֹצִיא הַקָּדוֹשׁ בָּרוּךְ הוּא אֶת אֲבוֹתֵינוּ מִמִּצְרַיִם, הֲרֵי אָנוּ וּבָנֵינוּ וּבְנֵי בָנֵינוּ מְשֻׁעְבָּדִים הָיִינוּ לְפַרְעֹה בְּמִצְרָיִם. וַאֲפִילוּ כֻּלָּנוּ חֲכָמִים כֻּלָּנוּ נְבוֹנִים כֻּלָּנוּ זְקֵנִים כֻּלָּנוּ יוֹדְעִים אֶת הַתּוֹרָה מִצְוָה עָלֵינוּ לְסַפֵּר בִּיצִיאַת מִצְרָיִם. וְכָל הַמַּרְבֶּה לְסַפֵּר בִּיצִיאַת מִצְרַיִם הֲרֵי זֶה מְשֻׁבָּח.

We were slaves to Pharaoh in the land of Egypt. And the Lord, our God, took us out from there with a strong hand and an outstretched forearm. And if the Holy One, blessed be He, had not taken our ancestors from Egypt, behold we and our children and our children's children would [all] be enslaved to Pharaoh in Egypt. And even if we were all sages, all discerning, all elders, all knowledgeable about the Torah, it would be a commandment upon us to tell the story of the exodus from Egypt. And anyone who adds [and spends extra time] in telling the story of the Exodus from Egypt, behold he is praiseworthy.

Mishnah *Pesach* 10.4 instructs that the Seder Leader/Response begins with the disgrace and ends with the glory. A midrashic exposition of *A wandering Aramean (Jacob) was my father* (Deut 26:5–8) is the prologue of the Response which expounds in two different teachings (*b. Pesach* 116a). Here *We were slaves to Pharaoh in the land of Egypt* that of Samuel and later in the Haggadah reading that of Rav, *In the beginning our fathers were idolaters*.

—Zev Garber

Interestingly, Moses is deliberately left out of the Haggadah, so that no one would be confused about who liberated the Israelites from slavery in Egypt. Participants of the Seder were not to consider Moses as the one who performed the miracles and who "took us out from there with a strong hand and an outstretched forearm." The traditional Haggadah of Rabbi Philip Birnbaum (Hebrew Publishing Company, New York 1953 and 1976) mentions Moses only once, in a direct quotation of Exodus 14:31: וַיַּרְא יִשְׂרָאֵל אֶת־הַיָּד הַגְּדֹלָה אֲשֶׁר עָשָׂה יְהוָה בְּמִצְרַיִם וַיִּירְאוּ הָעָם אֶת־יְהוָה וַיַּאֲמִינוּ בַּיהוָה וּבְמֹשֶׁה ("And Israel saw the great work which the Lord did upon the Egyptians, and the people feared the Lord; and they believed in the Lord, and in His servant Moses").

—Kenneth Hanson

Magid, Story of the Five Rabbis and Rabbi Elazar ben Azariah Dictum

מַעֲשֶׂה בְּרַבִּי אֱלִיעֶזֶר וְרַבִּי יְהוֹשֻׁעַ וְרַבִּי אֶלְעָזָר בֶּן־עֲזַרְיָה וְרַבִּי עֲקִיבָא וְרַבִּי טַרְפוֹן שֶׁהָיוּ מְסֻבִּין בִּבְנֵי־בְרַק וְהָיוּ מְסַפְּרִים בִּיצִיאַת מִצְרַיִם כָּל־אוֹתוֹ הַלַּיְלָה, עַד שֶׁבָּאוּ תַלְמִידֵיהֶם וְאָמְרוּ לָהֶם רַבּוֹתֵינוּ הִגִּיעַ זְמַן קְרִיאַת שְׁמַע שֶׁל שַׁחֲרִית.

It happened once [on *Pesach*] that Rabbi Eliezer, Rabbi Yehoshua, Rabbi Elazar ben Azariah, Rabbi Akiva and Rabbi Tarfon were reclining in Bnei Brak and were telling the story of the exodus from Egypt that whole night, until their students came and said to them, "The time of [reciting] the morning Shema has arrived."

אָמַר רַבִּי אֶלְעָזָר בֶּן־עֲזַרְיָה הֲרֵי אֲנִי כְּבֶן שִׁבְעִים שָׁנָה וְלֹא זָכִיתִי שֶׁתֵּאָמֵר יְצִיאַת מִצְרַיִם בַּלֵּילוֹת עַד שֶׁדְּרָשָׁהּ בֶּן זוֹמָא, שֶׁנֶּאֱמַר, לְמַעַן תִּזְכֹּר אֶת יוֹם צֵאתְךָ מֵאֶרֶץ מִצְרַיִם כֹּל יְמֵי חַיֶּיךָ. יְמֵי חַיֶּיךָ הַיָּמִים. כֹּל יְמֵי חַיֶּיךָ הַלֵּילוֹת. וַחֲכָמִים אוֹמְרִים יְמֵי חַיֶּיךָ הָעוֹלָם הַזֶּה. כֹּל יְמֵי חַיֶּיךָ לְהָבִיא לִימוֹת הַמָּשִׁיחַ:

Rabbi Elazar ben Azariah said, "Behold I am like a man of seventy years (in biblical-talmudic tradition, a lifetime) and I have not merited [to understand why] the Exodus from Egypt should be said at night until Ben Zoma explicated it, as it is stated (Deut 16:3), 'In order that you remember the day of your going out from the land of Egypt all the days of your life;' 'the days of your life' [indicates that the remembrance be invoked during] the days, 'all the days of your life' [indicates that the remembrance be invoked also during] the nights." But the Sages say, "'the days of your life' [indicates that the remembrance be invoked in] this world, 'all the days of your life' [indicates that the remembrance be invoked also] in the days of the Messiah."

Three paragraphs compose the Shema's section of the *Shaḥarit* (morning) and *Ma'ariv* (evening) services: Deut 6:4–9 (the oneness of God and Israel's absolute commitment to Him); Deut 11:13–21(Land of Israel, Reward and Punishment); and Num 15: 37–41(*Tsitsit*, "see, remember all the commandments of the Lord, and do"). The story of the Five Rabbis, including, the famed Rabbi Akiba, supporter of the Bar Kokhba revolt against Roman rule in Eretz Israel, is a lesson in current intrigue and revolt against oppressive presence in one's land. The sages, who lived from ca.100–130 C.E., inspired by the Exodus story of freedom, engaged intensely in discussion of freedom in their day that they failed to complete the Seder reading by the required time of midnight. Hence, the wake-up call by their students.

The dictum of Rabbi Eleazar follows the Five Rabbis but it has nothing to do with the political intrigue against Rome. The original context (*m. Ber*.I.5; *Mek.* on Exod 13:3, "remember this day" every year) dealt with saying the third paragraph of the Shema (Num 15: 37:41) at night. Thus, the connection in the Haggadah is the Seder *night* reading in Bnei Brak. Hence a linguistic discussion whether the Exodus narrative can be recited at night or is it restricted to daytime. Conclusion, "*all* the days" not "the days" embrace day and night and the Messianic times. Message conveyed: Israel's birth story is restricted neither by daily time nor limited by time period.

—Zev Garber

Magid, The Four Sons

בָּרוּךְ הַמָּקוֹם, בָּרוּךְ הוּא, בָּרוּךְ שֶׁנָּתַן תּוֹרָה לְעַמּוֹ יִשְׂרָאֵל, בָּרוּךְ הוּא. כְּנֶגֶד אַרְבָּעָה בָנִים דִּבְּרָה תּוֹרָה: אֶחָד חָכָם, וְאֶחָד רָשָׁע, וְאֶחָד תָּם, וְאֶחָד שֶׁאֵינוֹ יוֹדֵעַ לִשְׁאוֹל.

Blessed be the Place [of all = Omnipresent], Blessed be He; Blessed be the One who Gave the Torah to His people Israel, Blessed be He. Corresponding to four sons did the Torah speak; one [who is] wise, one [who is] evil, one who is innocent and one who doesn't know to ask.

The passage of the Four Sons (Children) is a definitive midrashic interpretation of the Exodus story as to why 'the testimonies, and the statutes, and the ordinances" are given to the Children of Israel (Exod 13:14; Deut 6:20–24). *"According to the wisdom* of the son/child does the father instruct him" (*m. Pesaḥ* 10.4) is conditioned by the four Torah passages which inspire the parent-child instruction, namely, Deut 6:20–24; Exod 12:26 ff.; Exod 13:14; and Exod 13:8.

"Blessed be the Omnipresent/Place, Blessed be He" is a post-talmudic equivalent to "The Holy One, Blessed be He." However, God as *Ha-Maḳom* is noted in the Mishnah and explained as meaning, "He is the Place of the world and the world is not His place" (*Gen. Rab.* 68.9*).*

—Zev Garber

חָכָם מָה הוּא אוֹמֵר? מָה הָעֵדוֹת וְהַחֻקִּים וְהַמִּשְׁפָּטִים אֲשֶׁר צִוָּה ה' אֱלֹהֵינוּ אֶתְכֶם. וְאַף אַתָּה אֱמוֹר לוֹ כְּהִלְכוֹת הַפֶּסַח: אֵין מַפְטִירִין אַחַר הַפֶּסַח אֲפִיקוֹמָן:

What does the wise [son] say? "'What are these testimonies, statutes and judgments that *the Lord our God commanded you?*'" (Deut 6:20) And accordingly you will say to him, as per the laws of the *Pesach* sacrifice, "We may not eat an *afikoman* [a dessert or other foods eaten after the meal] till after [we are finished eating] the *Pesach* sacrifice (*m. Pesach* 10:8)."

רָשָׁע מָה הוּא אוֹמֵר? מָה הָעֲבוֹדָה הַזֹּאת לָכֶם. לָכֶם – וְלֹא לוֹ. וּלְפִי שֶׁהוֹצִיא אֶת עַצְמוֹ מִן הַכְּלָל כָּפַר בְּעִקָּר. וְאַף אַתָּה הַקְהֵה אֶת שִׁנָּיו וֶאֱמוֹר לוֹ: "בַּעֲבוּר זֶה עָשָׂה ה' לִי בְּצֵאתִי מִמִּצְרָיִם". לִי וְלֹא־לוֹ. אִלּוּ הָיָה שָׁם, לֹא הָיָה נִגְאָל:

What does the evil [son] say? "'*What is this worship to you?*'" (Exod 12:26) 'To you' and not 'to him.' And since he excluded himself from the collective, he denied a principle [of the Jewish faith]. And accordingly, you will blunt his teeth and say to him, "'For the sake of this, did the Lord do [this] for me in my going out of Egypt' (Exodus 13:8)." 'For me' and not 'for him.' If he had been there, he would not have been saved.

תָּם מָה הוּא אוֹמֵר? מַה זֹּאת? וְאָמַרְתָּ אֵלָיו "בְּחֹזֶק יָד הוֹצִיאָנוּ ה' מִמִּצְרַיִם מִבֵּית עֲבָדִים."

What does the innocent [son] say? "'What is this?'" (Exod 13:14) And you will say to him, "'With the strength of [His] hand did the Lord take us out from Egypt, from the house of slaves' (Exodus 13:14).'"

וְשֶׁאֵינוֹ יוֹדֵעַ לִשְׁאוֹל – אַתְּ פְּתַח לוֹ, שֶׁנֶּאֱמַר, וְהִגַּדְתָּ לְבִנְךָ בַּיּוֹם הַהוּא לֵאמֹר, בַּעֲבוּר זֶה עָשָׂה ה' לִי בְּצֵאתִי מִמִּצְרָיִם.

And [regarding] the one who doesn't know to ask, *you* (fem. *'at* not masc. *'atta* is written; Aramaism?) will open [the conversation] for him. As it is stated, "And you will speak to your son on that day saying, for the sake of this, did the Lord do [this] for me in my going out of Egypt."(Exod 13:8)

The wise child asks about the precepts and testimonies related to the meaning of the Exodus story and s/he is instructed in the precepts of Passover. The question from the wicked child suggests exclusion but the cited biblical source is an innocent query, "What is the meaning of the paschal sacrifice," without the intent of exclusivity. The innocent child asks, and s/he is instructed on the meaning and particulars of the law of redemption and the role of the first-born therein. The child who does not know to ask—no question is given—is not excluded from the lessons of the paschal lamb and the Passover story. The father/parent instructs him/her accordingly.

The prooftexts for both the wise child and the wicked child objectify "you." Wise: 'What are these testimonies, statutes and judgments that the Lord our God commanded you?'" (Deut 6:20); Wicked, "'What is this worship to you?'" (Exod 12:26). Older Haggadot render "has commanded us" by the wise child and reverted to the masoretic biblical reading in the Middle Ages and universal today.

Afikoman [a dessert or other foods eaten after the meal] is also explained as entertainment, revelry, or going from one gathering to another. All are forbidden till after the present gathering finished eating the *Pesach* sacrifice (*m. Pesach* 10:8; *b. Pesach* 119b; *y. Pesach* 37d).

—Zev Garber

Magid, Yechol Me'rosh Chodesh

יָכוֹל מֵרֹאשׁ חֹדֶשׁ? תַּלְמוּד לוֹמַר בַּיּוֹם הַהוּא. אִי בַּיּוֹם הַהוּא יָכוֹל מִבְּעוֹד יוֹם? תַּלְמוּד לוֹמַר בַּעֲבוּר זֶה – בַּעֲבוּר זֶה לֹא אָמַרְתִּי, אֶלָּא בְּשָׁעָה שֶׁיֵּשׁ מַצָּה וּמָרוֹר מֻנָּחִים לְפָנֶיךָ.

It could be from Rosh Chodesh [that one would have to discuss the Exodus. However] we learn [otherwise, since] it is stated, "on that day." If it is [written] "on that day" it could be from while it is still day [before the night of the fifteenth of Nissan. However] we learn [otherwise, since] it is stated, "for the sake of this" I didn't say 'for the sake of this' except [that it be observed] when [this] *matsa* and *maror* are resting in front of you [meaning, on the night of the fifteenth].

Paragraph suggests that the preparation for the Passover should begin at the start of the month Nisan and should that not include the time to instruct the children on the regulations of the Passover night? However, the rabbinic instruction of "for the *sake of this* which the Lord did for me when I came out of Egypt" (Exod 13:8) encompasses the *matsa* (unleavened bread), *maror* (bitter herbs), and paschal lamb (Second Temple period) and they are uncovered on *Pesach* eve, Nisan 15, and not at the start of the month.

—Zev Garber

Magid, In the Beginning Our Fathers Were Idol Worshipers

מִתְּחִלָּה עוֹבְדֵי עֲבוֹדָה זָרָה הָיוּ אֲבוֹתֵינוּ, וְעַכְשָׁיו קֵרְבָנוּ הַמָּקוֹם לַעֲבֹדָתוֹ, שֶׁנֶּאֱמַר: וַיֹּאמֶר יְהוֹשֻׁעַ אֶל־כָּל־הָעָם, כֹּה אָמַר ה' אֱלֹהֵי יִשְׂרָאֵל: בְּעֵבֶר הַנָּהָר יָשְׁבוּ אֲבוֹתֵיכֶם מֵעוֹלָם, תֶּרַח אֲבִי אַבְרָהָם וַאֲבִי נָחוֹר, וַיַּעַבְדוּ אֱלֹהִים אֲחֵרִים.

From the beginning, our ancestors were idol worshipers. And now, the Omnipresent/Place [of all] has brought us close to His worship, as it is stated (Joshua 24:2–4), "Yehoshua said to the whole people, so said the Lord, God of Israel, 'Over the river did your ancestors dwell from always,' Terach the father of Avraham and the father of Nachor, and they worshiped other gods."

וָאֶקַּח אֶת־אֲבִיכֶם אֶת־אַבְרָהָם מֵעֵבֶר הַנָּהָר וָאוֹלֵךְ אוֹתוֹ בְּכָל־אֶרֶץ כְּנָעַן, וָאַרְבֶּה אֶת־זַרְעוֹ וָאֶתֶּן לוֹ אֶת־יִצְחָק, וָאֶתֵּן לְיִצְחָק אֶת־יַעֲקֹב וְאֶת־עֵשָׂו. וָאֶתֵּן לְעֵשָׂו אֶת־הַר שֵׂעִיר לָרֶשֶׁת אֹתוֹ, וְיַעֲקֹב וּבָנָיו יָרְדוּ מִצְרָיִם.

And I took your father, Avraham, from over the river and I made him walk in all the land of Canaan and I increased his seed and I gave him Yitschak. And I gave to Yitschak, Ya'akov and Esav; and I gave to Esav, Mount Seir [in order that he] inherit it; and Yaakov and his sons went down to Egypt.'"

Two introductory replies are recorded to the midrashic exposition of *A wandering Aramean (Jacob) was my father* (Deut 26:5–8). Above "*We were slaves to Pharaoh in the land of Egypt*" (Samuel) and here, "*In the beginning our fathers were idolaters*" (Rav).

—Zev Garber

בָּרוּךְ שׁוֹמֵר הַבְטָחָתוֹ לְיִשְׂרָאֵל, בָּרוּךְ הוּא. שֶׁהַקָּדוֹשׁ בָּרוּךְ הוּא חִשַּׁב אֶת־הַקֵּץ, לַעֲשׂוֹת כְּמוֹ שֶׁאָמַר לְאַבְרָהָם אָבִינוּ בִּבְרִית בֵּין הַבְּתָרִים, שֶׁנֶּאֱמַר: וַיֹּאמֶר לְאַבְרָם, יָדֹעַ תֵּדַע כִּי־גֵר יִהְיֶה זַרְעֲךָ

בְּאֶרֶץ לֹא לָהֶם, וַעֲבָדוּם וְעִנּוּ אֹתָם אַרְבַּע מֵאוֹת שָׁנָה. וְגַם אֶת־הַגּוֹי אֲשֶׁר יַעֲבֹדוּ דָּן אָנֹכִי וְאַחֲרֵי־כֵן יֵצְאוּ בִּרְכֻשׁ גָּדוֹל.

Blessed be the One who keeps His promise to Israel, blessed be He; since the Holy One, blessed be He, calculated the end [of the exile,] to do as He said to Avraham, our father, in the *Covenant between the Pieces* (*berit bein hab-betarim*), as it is stated (Gen 15:13–14), "And He said to Avram, 'you should surely know that your seed will be a stranger in a land that is not theirs, and they will enslave them and afflict them *four hundred* years. Also, that nation for which they shall toil will I judge, and afterwards they will go out with much property.'"

According to *m. Pesaḥ* 10.4, the core of the Haggadah story is a midrash on Deut 26: 5–8, *A wandering Aramean (Jacob) was my father*. The midrashic exposition is preceded by assurance of divine protection. *Covenant between the Pieces* refers to the sacrificial rite that Avram/Abraham undertook to assure the promise of an heir and the longevity of his seed. The projected 400 years is recorded as 430 years in Exod 12:40. However, this is not the duration of the enslavement period. Tradition starts the 430-year count from the birth of Isaac and suggests that the additional 30 years mark when the period of the affliction was foretold to Avram/Abraham to the birth of Isaac. The Rabbis deduce that the Egyptian enslavement was 210 years based on the Exodus narrative and the genealogies mentioned in Exod 6.

In the Torah, *My father was a fugitive Aramean* (Deut 26:5–8) continues with the sentiment that the Lord brought the people into a land flowing with milk and honey; and to wit the people are instructed to annually remember by bringing their first fruits to the Temple at Shavuot, the Feast of Weeks, to the *place where the LORD your God will choose to establish His name* (Deut 26:2). The place is rabbinically associated with the *Har Ha-Bayit*, the Temple Mount; and the offering ritual is the sign that God has fulfilled His promise of redeeming the people from slavery. Alas, after the destruction of the Second Temple by the Romans and the dispersion of the people from the land this thought was excluded from the Haggadah text.

—Zev Garber

מכסה המצה ומגביה את הכוס בידו, ואומר:

The Seder leader covers the matsa and participants lift up their cups of wine and say:

וְהִיא שֶׁעָמְדָה לַאֲבוֹתֵינוּ וְלָנוּ. שֶׁלֹּא אֶחָד בִּלְבָד עָמַד עָלֵינוּ לְכַלּוֹתֵנוּ, אֶלָּא שֶׁבְּכָל דּוֹר וָדוֹר עוֹמְדִים עָלֵינוּ לְכַלּוֹתֵנוּ, וְהַקָּדוֹשׁ בָּרוּךְ הוּא מַצִּילֵנוּ מִיָּדָם.

And it is this that has stood for our ancestors and for us; since it is not [only] one [person or nation] that has stood [against] us to destroy us, but rather in each generation, they stand [against] us to destroy us, but the Holy One, blessed be He, rescues us from their hand.

Magid, First Fruits Declaration

יניח הכוס מידו ויגלה את המצות.

All put down their cups; and the Seder leader uncovers the matsa.

צֵא וּלְמַד מַה בִּקֵּשׁ לָבָן הָאֲרַמִּי לַעֲשׂוֹת לְיַעֲקֹב אָבִינוּ: שֶׁפַּרְעֹה לֹא גָזַר אֶלָּא עַל הַזְּכָרִים, וְלָבָן בִּקֵּשׁ לַעֲקֹר אֶת־הַכֹּל. שֶׁנֶּאֱמַר: אֲרַמִּי אֹבֵד אָבִי, וַיֵּרֶד מִצְרַיְמָה וַיָּגָר שָׁם בִּמְתֵי מְעָט, וַיְהִי שָׁם לְגוֹי גָּדוֹל, עָצוּם וָרָב.

Go out and learn what *Lavan the Aramean* sought to do to Ya'akov, our father; since Pharaoh only decreed [the death sentence] on the males but Lavan sought to uproot the whole [people]. As it is stated (Deut 26:5), "An Aramean was destroying my father and he went down to Egypt, and he resided there with a small number and he became there a nation, great, powerful and numerous."

Ya`akov, Jacob named Yisrael/Israel (cf. Gen 32:29, *for you have striven with God and with men have prevailed*), here called Aramean due to his many years spent in Aram and that his mother, Rivkah/Rebecca was born there.

Confronting generational antisemitism is a leitmotif in the retelling of the Passover story ("in each generation, they stand [against] us to destroy us"); meaning, what is the lesson of slavery-freedom for my generation.

Three possible suggestions to explain the insertion of Lavan the Aramean in the Passover story and the distorted citation of "Wandering/`oved (אֹבֵד) Aramean was my father (Jacob)" to "An Aramean (Lavan) was destroying/`ibbed (עִבֵּד) my father" (Deut 26:5): (1) Pre-Maccabean explanation: to placate the Egyptian Ptolemies over Syria/Aram regarding the status of Palestine similar to the reply of Rav which avoids direct referencing to Egyptian slavery in contrast to that of Samuel (*we were Pharoah's slaves in Egypt*) (2) Second Temple period: Lavan the Aramean (הָאֲרַמִּי) decoded is Rome (רומאי) current destroyer

Fig. 8 Pharaoh Ramses II

of the Jews of Judea; and (3) Historio-Theological: *Lavan sought to uproot (la`akor) the whole*, that is to say, the people and its motivating Principle (*Ikkar*).

—Zev Garber

וַיֵּרֶד מִצְרַיְמָה – אָנוּס עַל פִּי הַדִּבּוּר. וַיָּגָר שָׁם. מְלַמֵּד שֶׁלֹּא יָרַד יַעֲקֹב אָבִינוּ לְהִשְׁתַּקֵּעַ בְּמִצְרַיִם אֶלָּא לָגוּר שָׁם, שֶׁנֶּאֱמַר: וַיֹּאמְרוּ אֶל-פַּרְעֹה, לָגוּר בָּאָרֶץ בָּאנוּ, כִּי אֵין מִרְעֶה לַצֹּאן אֲשֶׁר לַעֲבָדֶיךָ, כִּי כָבֵד הָרָעָב בְּאֶרֶץ כְּנָעַן. וְעַתָּה יֵשְׁבוּ-נָא עֲבָדֶיךָ בְּאֶרֶץ גֹּשֶׁן.

"And he went down to Egypt"—helpless on *account of the word* [in which God told Avraham that his descendants would have to go into exile]. "And he resided there"—[this] teaches that Ya'akov, our father, didn't go down to settle in Egypt, but rather [only] to reside there, as it is stated (Gen 47:4), "And they said to Pharaoh, 'To reside in the land have we come, since there is not enough pasture for your servant's flocks, since the famine is heavy in the land of Canaan, and now please grant that your servants should dwell in the Land of Goshen.'"

בִּמְתֵי מְעָט. כְּמָה שֶׁנֶּאֱמַר: בְּשִׁבְעִים נֶפֶשׁ יָרְדוּ אֲבוֹתֶיךָ מִצְרָיְמָה, וְעַתָּה שָׂמְךָ ה' אֱלֹהֶיךָ כְּכוֹכְבֵי הַשָּׁמַיִם לָרֹב.

"As a *small number*"—as it is stated (Deut 10:22), "With seventy souls did your ancestors come down to Egypt, and now the Lord your God has made you as numerous as the stars of the sky."

וַיְהִי שָׁם לְגוֹי. מְלַמֵּד שֶׁהָיוּ יִשְׂרָאֵל מְצֻיָּנִים שָׁם. גָּדוֹל עָצוּם – כְּמָה שֶׁנֶּאֱמַר: וּבְנֵי יִשְׂרָאֵל פָּרוּ וַיִּשְׁרְצוּ וַיִּרְבּוּ וַיַּעַצְמוּ בִּמְאֹד מְאֹד, וַתִּמָּלֵא הָאָרֶץ אֹתָם.

"And he became there a nation"—[this] teaches that Israel [became] *distinguishable* there. "Great, powerful"—as it is stated (Exodus 1:7), "And the Children of Israel multiplied and swarmed and grew numerous and strong, most exceedingly and the land became full of them."

וָרָב. כְּמָה שֶׁנֶּאֱמַר: רְבָבָה כְּצֶמַח הַשָּׂדֶה נְתַתִּיךְ, וַתִּרְבִּי וַתִּגְדְּלִי וַתָּבֹאִי בַּעֲדִי עֲדָיִים, שָׁדַיִם נָכֹנוּ וּשְׂעָרֵךְ צִמֵּחַ, וְאַתְּ עֵרֹם וְעֶרְיָה. וָאֶעֱבֹר עָלַיִךְ וָאֶרְאֵךְ מִתְבּוֹסֶסֶת בְּדָמָיִךְ, וָאֹמַר לָךְ בְּדָמַיִךְ חֲיִי, וָאֹמַר לָךְ בְּדָמַיִךְ חֲיִי.

"And numerous"—as it is stated (Ezek 16:7), "I have given you to be numerous as the vegetation of the field, and you increased and grew and became highly ornamented, your breasts were set and your hair grew, but you were naked and barren." "When I passed by you and saw you wallowing in your blood, I said to you: "Live in spite of your blood." Yea, I said to you, *"Live in spite of your blood"* (Ezek 16:6).

Going down to Egypt on the assurance by God that Israel/Hebrews will sustain and come forth from there a great and multitudinous nation (Gen 46:3–4). *Few in number*, to avoid the association that Israel's objective is royalty and conquest. Hence absence of Joseph narrative in the Haggadah narrative. Also, conscientious disassociation of the Israelites with the Hyksos who invaded Egypt and were later expelled. *Distinguishable* by the Israelites/Hebrews not assimilating into Egypt and its culture; they kept their Hebrew names, language, customs, and clothing. *Live in spite of your blood* (Ezek 16:6). In the Haggadah reading, Ezek 16 verses 6 and 7 are reversed. The text in Ezekiel 16 speaks of the abandon infant in the field whom no one pities but God passed by and seeing the infant in the field said "live in spite of your blood" suggesting that due to the privilege of your bloodline, you will prevail. These words are circumscribed in the ritual drop of blood of the *berit milah/Covenant of the Circumcision*. They are words clearly adverse to the decree of Pharoah to wipe out all male Hebrews. And these words were pronounced on 6 Nisan 5711/ April 12, 1951 when act of the Knesset of

Israel signed into law the Shoah and Ghetto Revolt Remembrance Day/*Yom ha-Shoah u-Mered ha-Getaot.*

—Zev Garber

וַיָּרֵעוּ אֹתָנוּ הַמִּצְרִים וַיְעַנּוּנוּ, וַיִּתְּנוּ עָלֵינוּ עֲבֹדָה קָשָׁה. וַיָּרֵעוּ אֹתָנוּ הַמִּצְרִים – כְּמָה שֶׁנֶּאֱמַר: הָבָה נִתְחַכְּמָה לוֹ פֶּן יִרְבֶּה, וְהָיָה כִּי תִקְרֶאנָה מִלְחָמָה וְנוֹסַף גַּם הוּא עַל שֹׂנְאֵינוּ וְנִלְחַם־בָּנוּ, וְעָלָה מִן־הָאָרֶץ.

"And the Egyptians did bad to us" (Deut 26:6)—as it is stated (Exod 1:10), "Let us be wise towards him, lest he multiply and it will be that when war is called, he too will join with our enemies and fight against us and go up from the land."

וַיְעַנּוּנוּ. כְּמָה שֶׁנֶּאֱמַר: וַיָּשִׂימוּ עָלָיו שָׂרֵי מִסִּים לְמַעַן עַנֹּתוֹ בְּסִבְלֹתָם. וַיִּבֶן עָרֵי מִסְכְּנוֹת לְפַרְעֹה. אֶת־פִּתֹם וְאֶת־רַעַמְסֵס.

"And afflicted us"—as is is stated (Exod 1:11); "And they placed upon him leaders over the work-tax in order to afflict them with their burdens; and they built storage cities, Pithom and Ra'amses."

וַיִּתְּנוּ עָלֵינוּ עֲבֹדָה קָשָׁה. כְּמָה שֶׁנֶּאֱמַר: וַיַּעֲבִדוּ מִצְרַיִם אֶת־בְּנֵי יִשְׂרָאֵל בְּפָרֶךְ.

"And put upon us hard work —as it is stated (Exod 1:11), "And they enslaved the children of Israel with breaking work."

וַנִּצְעַק אֶל־ה' אֱלֹהֵי אֲבֹתֵינוּ, וַיִּשְׁמַע ה' אֶת־קֹלֵנוּ, וַיַּרְא אֶת־עָנְיֵנוּ וְאֶת עֲמָלֵנוּ וְאֶת לַחֲצֵנוּ.

"And we we cried out to the Lord, the God of our ancestors, and the Lord heard our voice, and He saw our affliction, and our toil and our duress" (Deut 26:7).

וַנִּצְעַק אֶל־ה' אֱלֹהֵי אֲבֹתֵינוּ – כְּמָה שֶׁנֶּאֱמַר: וַיְהִי בַיָּמִים הָרַבִּים הָהֵם וַיָּמָת מֶלֶךְ מִצְרַיִם, וַיֵּאָנְחוּ בְנֵי־יִשְׂרָאֵל מִן־הָעֲבוֹדָה וַיִּזְעָקוּ, וַתַּעַל שַׁוְעָתָם אֶל־הָאֱלֹהִים מִן הָעֲבֹדָה.

"And we cried out to the Lord, the God of our ancestors"—as it is stated (Exodus 2:23); "And it was in those great days that the king of Egypt died and the Children of Israel sighed from the work and yelled out, and their supplication went up to God from the work."

וַיִּשְׁמַע ה' אֶת קֹלֵנוּ. כְּמָה שֶׁנֶּאֱמַר: וַיִּשְׁמַע אֱלֹהִים אֶת־נַאֲקָתָם, וַיִּזְכֹּר אֱלֹהִים אֶת־בְּרִיתוֹ אֶת־אַבְרָהָם, אֶת־יִצְחָק וְאֶת־יַעֲקֹב.

"And the Lord heard our voice"—as it is stated (Exod 2:24); "And God heard their groans and God remembered His covenant with Avraham and with Yitschak and with Ya'akov."

וַיַּרְא אֶת־עָנְיֵנוּ. זוֹ פְּרִישׁוּת דֶּרֶךְ אֶרֶץ, כְּמָה שֶׁנֶּאֱמַר: וַיַּרְא אֱלֹהִים אֶת בְּנֵי־יִשְׂרָאֵל וַיֵּדַע אֱלֹהִים.

"And He saw our affliction"—this [refers to] the separation from the way of the world, as it is stated (Exod 2:25); "And God saw the Children of Israel and God knew."

וְאֶת־עֲמָלֵנוּ. אֵלוּ הַבָּנִים. כְּמָה שֶׁנֶּאֱמַר: כָּל־הַבֵּן הַיִּלּוֹד הַיְאֹרָה תַּשְׁלִיכֻהוּ וְכָל־הַבַּת תְּחַיּוּן.

"And our toil"—this [refers to the killing of the] sons, as it is stated (Exod 1:24); "Every boy that is born, throw him into the Nile and every girl you shall keep alive."

Fig. 9 Death of the Firstborn, from the "Sister Haggadah," 14th century, Catalonia

וְאֶת־לַחֲצֵנוּ. זֶה הַדְּחַק, כְּמָה שֶׁנֶּאֱמַר: וְגַם־רָאִיתִי אֶת־הַלַּחַץ אֲשֶׁר מִצְרַיִם לֹחֲצִים אֹתָם.

"And our duress"—this [refers to] the pressure, as it is stated (Exod 3:9); "And I also saw the duress that the Egyptians are applying on them."

וַיּוֹצִאֵנוּ ה' מִמִּצְרַיִם בְּיָד חֲזָקָה, וּבִזְרֹעַ נְטוּיָה, וּבְמֹרָא גָּדֹל, וּבְאֹתוֹת וּבְמֹפְתִים.

"And the Lord took us out of Egypt with a strong hand and with an outstretched forearm and with great awe and with signs and with wonders" (Deut 26:8).

וַיּוֹצִאֵנוּ ה' מִמִּצְרַיִם. לֹא עַל־יְדֵי מַלְאָךְ, וְלֹא עַל־יְדֵי שָׂרָף, וְלֹא עַל־יְדֵי שָׁלִיחַ, אֶלָּא הַקָּדוֹשׁ בָּרוּךְ הוּא בִּכְבוֹדוֹ וּבְעַצְמוֹ. שֶׁנֶּאֱמַר: וְעָבַרְתִּי בְאֶרֶץ מִצְרַיִם בַּלַּיְלָה הַזֶּה, וְהִכֵּיתִי כָל־בְּכוֹר בְּאֶרֶץ מִצְרַיִם מֵאָדָם וְעַד בְּהֵמָה, וּבְכָל אֱלֹהֵי מִצְרַיִם אֶעֱשֶׂה שְׁפָטִים. אֲנִי ה'.

"And the Lord took us out of Egypt"—not through an angel and not through a seraph and not through a messenger, but [directly by] the Holy One, blessed be He, Himself, as it is stated (Exodus 12:12); "And I will pass through the Land of Egypt on that night and I will smite every firstborn in the Land of Egypt, from men to animals; and with all the gods of Egypt, I will make judgments, I am the Lord."

וְעָבַרְתִּי בְאֶרֶץ מִצְרַיִם בַּלַּיְלָה הַזֶּה – אֲנִי וְלֹא מַלְאָךְ; וְהִכֵּיתִי כָל בְּכוֹר בְּאֶרֶץ־מִצְרַיִם. אֲנִי וְלֹא שָׂרָף; וּבְכָל־אֱלֹהֵי מִצְרַיִם אֶעֱשֶׂה שְׁפָטִים. אֲנִי וְלֹא הַשָּׁלִיחַ; אֲנִי ה'. אֲנִי הוּא וְלֹא אַחֵר.

"And I will pass through the Land of Egypt"—I and not an angel. "And I will smite every firstborn"—I and not a seraph. "And with all the gods of Egypt, I will make judgments"—I and not a messenger. "I am the Lord"—I am He and there is no other.

"And the Egyptians did bad to us" (Deut 26:6) is suggested because Egypt considered the Israelites as evil. The scriptural passages that follow support this claim. The cry of affliction, suffering, oppression was heard; *"And the Lord took us out of Egypt with a strong hand and with an outstretched forearm and with great **awe** (root carries association of divine appearance/Rome [mora';mor'ah; roma] and with signs and with wonders. Repetitive assertions that God alone will execute judgments against the gods of Egypt* and that He and not the messenger will redeem the people from slavery another suggests the superiority of Israel monolatry and a subtle rejection of messianic redemption. *I am the Lord, I am He, and no other* may also be seen as biblical and Haggadic rejection of Trinatarianism and rejection of other means of salvation including messianic deliverance.

—Zev Garber

בְּיָד חֲזָקָה. זוֹ הַדֶּבֶר, כְּמָה שֶׁנֶּאֱמַר: הִנֵּה יַד־ה' הוֹיָה בְּמִקְנְךָ אֲשֶׁר בַּשָּׂדֶה, בַּסּוּסִים, בַּחֲמֹרִים, בַּגְּמַלִּים, בַּבָּקָר וּבַצֹּאן, דֶּבֶר כָּבֵד מְאֹד.

"With a strong hand"—this [refers to] the pestilence, as it is stated (Exod 9:3); "Behold the hand of the Lord is upon your herds that are in the field, upon the horses, upon the donkeys, upon the camels, upon the cattle and upon the flocks, [there will be] a very heavy pestilence."

וּבִזְרֹעַ נְטוּיָה. זוֹ הַחֶרֶב, כְּמָה שֶׁנֶּאֱמַר: וְחַרְבּוֹ שְׁלוּפָה בְּיָדוֹ, נְטוּיָה עַל־יְרוּשָׁלָיִם.

"And with an outstretched forearm"—this [refers to] the sword, as it is stated (I Chr 21:16); "And his sword was drawn in his hand, leaning over Jerusalem."

וּבְמוֹרָא גָּדֹל. זוֹ גִּלּוּי שְׁכִינָה. כְּמָה שֶׁנֶּאֱמַר, אוֹ הֲנִסָּה אֱלֹהִים לָבוֹא לָקַחַת לוֹ גוֹי מִקֶּרֶב גּוֹי בְּמַסֹּת בְּאֹתֹת וּבְמוֹפְתִים וּבְמִלְחָמָה וּבְיָד חֲזָקָה וּבִזְרוֹעַ נְטוּיָה וּבְמוֹרָאִים גְּדֹלִים כְּכֹל אֲשֶׁר־עָשָׂה לָכֶם ה' אֱלֹהֵיכֶם בְּמִצְרַיִם לְעֵינֶיךָ.

"And with great awe"—this [refers to the revelation of] the Divine Presence, as it is stated (Deut 4:34), "Or did God try to take for Himself a nation from within a nation with enigmas, with signs and with wonders and with war and with a strong hand and with an outstretched forearm and with great and awesome acts, like all that the Lord, your God, did for you in Egypt in front of your eyes?"

וּבְאֹתוֹת. זֶה הַמַּטֶּה, כְּמָה שֶׁנֶּאֱמַר: וְאֶת הַמַּטֶּה הַזֶּה תִּקַּח בְּיָדְךָ, אֲשֶׁר תַּעֲשֶׂה־בּוֹ אֶת הָאֹתוֹת.

"And with signs"—this [refers to] the staff, as it is stated (Exodus 4:17); "And this staff you shall take in your hand, that with it you will preform signs."

וּבְמֹפְתִים. זֶה הַדָּם, כְּמָה שֶׁנֶּאֱמַר: וְנָתַתִּי מוֹפְתִים בַּשָּׁמַיִם וּבָאָרֶץ.

"And with wonders"—this [refers to] the blood, as it is stated (Joel 3:3); "And I will place my wonders in the skies and in the earth":

Fig. 10 Gustave Doré (1866), "Moses and Aaron Appear before Pharaoh"

Magid, The Ten Plagues

כשאומר דם ואש ותימרות עשן, עשר המכות ודצ"ך עד"ש באח"ב – ישפוך מן הכוס מעט יין:

And when the head of the Seder says, "blood and fire and pillars of smoke" and the ten plagues and "detsakh," "adash" and "baachab," he should pour out a little wine from his cup.

דָּם וָאֵשׁ וְתִימְרוֹת עָשָׁן.

"blood and fire and pillars of smoke."

דָּבָר אַחֵר: בְּיָד חֲזָקָה שְׁתַּיִם, וּבִזְרֹעַ נְטוּיָה שְׁתַּיִם, וּבְמֹרָא גָּדֹל – שְׁתַּיִם, וּבְאֹתוֹת – שְׁתַּיִם, וּבְמֹפְתִים – שְׁתַּיִם.

Another [explanation]: "With a strong hand" [corresponds to] two [plagues]; "and with an outstretched forearm" [corresponds to] two [plagues]; "and with great awe" [corresponds to] two [plagues]; "and with signs" [corresponds to] two [plagues]; "and with wonders" [corresponds to] two [plagues].

Fig. 11 John Martin (1828)
"The Seventh Plague of Egypt"

Deut 26:8 is discussed exegetically ("with a strong hand, with an outstretched forearm, and with great awe, and with signs, and with wonders") and ends hermeneutically; that is to say, counting the first two words of each standard equates to ten setting the stage for the Ten Plagues that follow. Anthropomorphic portrayal of God's attributes and hermeneutical counting are not unknown in midrashic literature. Though anthro-pomorphisms may be restrictive in formalize liturgy they are conducive in *Haggadah* (story telling).

—Zev Garber

אֵלּוּ עֶשֶׂר מַכּוֹת שֶׁהֵבִיא הַקָּדוֹשׁ בָּרוּךְ הוּא עַל־הַמִּצְרִים בְּמִצְרַיִם, וְאֵלּוּ הֵן:

These are [the] ten plagues that the Holy One, blessed be He, brought on the Egyptians in Egypt and they are:

Blood   דָּם

Frogs   צְפַרְדֵּעַ

Lice/Gnats   כִּנִּים

[The] Mixture [of Wild Animals]   עָרוֹב

Pestilence   דֶּבֶר

Boils   שְׁחִין

Hail   בָּרָד

Locusts   אַרְבֶּה

Darkness   חֹשֶׁךְ

Slaying of [the] Firstborn   מַכַּת בְּכוֹרוֹת

רַבִּי יְהוּדָה הָיָה נוֹתֵן בָּהֶם סִמָּנִים: דְּצַ"ךְ עֲדַ"שׁ בְּאַחַ"ב.

Rabbi Yehuda was accustomed to giving [the plagues] mnemonics: Detsakh [the Hebrew initials of the first three plagues], Adash [the Hebrew initials of the second three plagues], Beachav [the Hebrew initials of the last four plagues].

The classic exposition of the `aseret ham-makkot* ("Ten Plagues") is dispersed in Exod 7:14–12–36. Plague 1/Water into Blood (Exod 7:14–25); Plague 2/Frogs (Exod 7:26–8:11); Plague 3/Lice/Gnats (Exod 8:12–15); Plague 4/Mixture of Insects/Beetles (Exod 8:16–28); Plague 5/Pestilence

(Exod 9:1–7); Plague 6/Boils (Exod 9:8–12); Plague 7/Hail (Exod 9:17–35); Plague 8/Locusts (Exod 10:1–20); Plague 9/Darkness (Exod 10:21–23); Plague 10/Slaying of Firstborn (Exod 12: 9–36). Variants of the Ten Plagues are mentioned in Pss 78:42–51 and 105:28–36 but in different order and number. Book of Jubilees mentions the Ten Plagues but not in the same order of Exodus. Hence the mnemonic saying of Rabbi Yehuda *Detsakh, Adash, Beachav* דְּצַ"ךְ עֲדַ"שׁ בְּאַחַ"ב to secure the prominence of the Exodus reading/order.

—Zev Garber

Considerable critique has been offered regarding the God of the Exodus, who has been characterized as "passionately partisan" and thoroughly lacking compassion for anyone, while championing only his designated favorites. The issue of "theodicy," the goodness of God, was the subject of a play written in 1977 by Holocaust survivor, Elie Wiesel. It was set, not during the Shoah but during Purim in the year 1649. It was later adapted by BBC Television, depicting a supposed trial of God by Jewish prisoners at Auschwitz. In it, one of the prisoners delivers a poignant speech, particularly relevant to the story of the Exodus:

> God slew the first born of Egypt and led us out of Egypt. He struck down the firstborn, from the firstborn and heir of Pharaoh to the firstborn of the slave at the mill, He slew them all. Did He slay Pharaoh? It was Pharaoh who said no, but God let him live and slew his children instead. All the children. And then the people of Israel made their escape, taking with them all the gold and silver and jewelry and garments of the Egyptians, and then God drowned the soldiers who pursued them. He did not close the waters so that the soldiers could not follow; He waited until they were following, and then He closed the waters. Did the mothers of Egypt, did they think Adonai was just? Did God not make the Egyptians? Did God not make their rivers and make their crops grow? If not Him then who? Some other god? And what did He make them for? To punish them? To starve, to frighten, to slaughter them? The people of Amalek, the people of Egypt, what was it like for them when Adonai turned against them? They faced extinction at the hand of Adonai; they died for His purpose; they fell as we are falling; they were afraid as we are afraid. And what did they learn? They learned that Adonai, the Lord our God, our God is not good. He was not ever good; He was only on our side…

While there is no record of such a trial having taken place at Auschwitz, Wiesel insisted: "It happened at night; there were just three people. At the end of the trial, they used the word *chayav*, rather than 'guilty.' It means 'He owes us something'. Then we went to pray." In short God may be all-powerful, but God has not been all-fair, all-righteous, all-just. We are, at the very least, owed an explanation. Still, we never doubt God's providence, and we pray. The Haggadah makes no attempt to offer such an explanation, but with ingenious subtlety it makes the participants aware that in pouring even a small amount from the cup, to symbolize the plagues, it diminishes one's joy by the same amount. The Haggadah is wrestling with the ethical dilemmas posed by Israel's chosen-ness. One is *not* to rejoice in full measure over the demise of one's foes. Remarkably, it is the Israelites themselves who would one day, under the influence of the prophets, transform in their minds the "G-d of armies" (*Hashem tsĕva'ot*) into the G-d of infinite compassion (*El ha-rakhamim*).

—Kenneth Hanson

Bibliography

Jenni Frazer, "Wiesel: Yes, We Really Did Put God on Trial," *The JC*, Sep. 19, 2008.

Excursus

Zev Garber

The Moral Sense of the Ten Plagues

On the nature of the Ten Plagues, Nahum Sarna commented, "It will surely be noted at once that there is nothing inherently mythological of supernatural about the first nine plagues. They can all be explained within the context of the familiar vicissitudes of nature that imperil the Nile Valley and elsewhere from time to time (*Exploring Exodus*, Schocken Books, 1987, p. 69). He points out that scholar Greta Hort has proposed a theory of a chain of direct causal connection between flagellates, bacteria, and insects to explain Plagues 1–6; and seasonal climatic change to explain Plagues 7–9.

The First Plague, for instance, when Aaron (not Moses, see Exod 7: 19–20) turns the water of the Nile into Blood, most likely recalls the fact that the Nile turn red during the spring floods due to the various microorganisms floating around in it. Swarms of frogs, lice, and insects would follow the flooding. Pestilence, boils, and locusts are all common place features of Egyptian life. Hail and thunderstorms, though uncommon, are known to occur but in no season for all of Egypt. And the "darkness that can be touched" (Exod 10:21) is identified with the heavy sandstorms that are raised by the *hamsin* winds that blow in early spring.

In the words of Nahum Sarna: "The Ninth Plague, darkness for three days, was the first *hamsin* of the season, which happens in early March...this is the hot southerly Egyptian wind that blows in from the Sahara Desert carrying with it sand and dust. In that particular year, the cumulatively devastating effects of the previous plagues on the soil meant that the matter released into the atmosphere would have been extraordinarily dense and abundant blocking out the sun. A *hamsin* of two- or three-days' duration is not unusual. Since the Israelites were largely domiciled in Goshen, which is in Wadi Tumilat, they would have been little affected by such a *hamsin* from the south because the region is at right angles to the narrow Nile valley" (*loc. cit.*, pp. 72–73).

Scholars argue that the Plagues could happen in a year's duration by reading the notation of Exod 7:7 in conjunction with Deut 34:7. That is to

The Moral Sense of the Ten Plagues

say, Moses was 80 years old when he appeared before the Pharoah; he spent 40 years in the wilderness leading the Children of Israel to the Promise Land; and he died at 120 years. However, the scholarly defense of the Plagues does not explain how Moses arrange to have the plague phenomena operate on command. In this view, we are suggesting that the "miracle" of the Plagues was not that these phenomena are not possible but that they appeared intensified and concentrated on command at a very opportune time.

Furthermore, if the Plagues occur as they are reported, why two other versions and order of the Plague narrative? Compare the account of the Plagues in Exod 7:14–12:36 and Ps 78:42–51 and Ps 105: 28–36.

Exod 7:14–12:36	Ps 78:42–51	Ps 105:28-36
1. Blood	1. Blood	1. Darkness
2. Frogs	2. Insects	2. Blood
3. Lice	3. Frogs	3. Frogs
4. Swarms of Insects	4. Locusts	4. Insects
5. Pestilence	5. Hail (vines)/Frost (sycamores)	5. Lice
6. Boils		6. Hail
7. Hail	6. Hail/Bolts (beast, cattle)	7. Fire
8. Locusts		8. Locusts/ Grasshoppers
9. Darkness	7. Pestilence	
10. Killing of First Born	8. Killing of first Born	9. Killing of First Born

Also, Pharoah's reactions and concessions are somewhat out of place vis-à-vis the symmetrical scheme of the Exodus Plague narrative. Related is a moral issue, the hardening of Pharoah's heart.

> *And I will harden the heart of Pharoah and multiply my signs and my wonders in the land of Egypt.* (Exod 7:3)
>
> *The Lord said to Moses, "Go to Pharoah. For I have hardened his heart and the hearts of his courtiers, in order that I may display these my signs among them, and that you may recount in the hearing of your sons and of your sons' sons how I made a mockery of the Egyptians and how I displayed My signs among them—in order that you may know that I am the Lord.* (Exod 10:1–2)

Either God cannot or He will not show His power without using a human being. If God must use Pharoah to show His greatness, then God is limited in power. If God will not prevent an innocent one to suffer—why *not will*? Because of Pharoah, Egyptians suffer; and because of God, Pharoah suffers—then God is limited in benevolence. But if God is not limited in neither power nor benevolence why the Plagues, and particularly Plague10, the killing of the (innocent) First Born of Man and Beast?

Sarna suggests that the climatic Plague, outside of the symmetry and rationality of the other Nine Plagues, defies any rational explanation. Others explain the consequences of the Plagues as punishment of Pharoah's crimes (e.g., Exod 3:16) and open defiance of God's authority (Exod 5:2). True, but may not another approach be seen in the spirit of the Sages' injunction that the Torah speaks in the language of man (*b. Ber.* 32b). In our Plague narrative, a polemic theology which has for its object refutation of errors.

"Hardening the heart of the Pharoah" is a literary device expressing God's freedom and power. The signs constantly rejected were God's judgment on Egypt presented in such a way that Pharoah did not listen. Pharoah did not listen because he could not listen lest he share in the freedom of Israel. If Pharoah's heart were not hardened and he let the people go then the slaves and future generations would be grateful to him for the deliverance of Israel. Thus, all these instances of God hardening the heart of Pharoah testify to a basic and intrinsic feature of the Exodus story: God not Pharoah nor angels nor Moses (note the absence of the Great Deliverer in the retelling of the Exodus story in the Passover Seder) is the true liberator and succor of the Children of Israel. So, the Tenth Plague is explained as a cosmic polemic between celestial forces: God vs. Pharoah (a god) and God's son, Israel, vs. Pharoah's son. On this, see Exod 4:22–23: "You shall say unto the Pharoah: 'Thus says the Lord: Israel is my son, My firstborn. Let my son go that he may worship me. Yet you refuse to let him go. Now I will lay your firstborn son.'"

In conclusion, the Ten Plagues is a polemic against the gods of Egypt (cf. Exod 12:12b, "against all the gods of Egypt, I will execute judgments") suggesting that the way of God and Torah, however conservatively or liberally interpreted, is the guarantor of Israel's survival and not Egypt's gods (read diaspora assimilation, non-Jewish ways, etc.). This is not poor theology as some have claimed but an authentic Jewish understanding of Heilsgeschichte (salvation history), of the interdependence of God and Israel. And of dialogue between Israel and the Nations conducted without politics, politeness, and paternalism.

—Zev Garber

Excurses

Zev Garber

Pidyon Ha-Ben

The Passover narrative in the Torah tells how the Israelite tribes became a nation, through their collective experience of slavery and redemption. A perpetual reminder of this emergence from slavery to freedom is the sanctification of every male first-born, which is enacted in the ceremonial rite of *pidyon ha-ben* ("Redemption of the [First- Born] Son"): "And the Lord spoke to Moses, saying, 'Sanctify unto Me all the first-born, whatsoever opens the womb among the children of Israel, both of man and beast, it is Mine" (Exod 13: 1–2). The intention was that the first-born sons be dedicated to God not as human sacrifices but for service in the sanctuary; this duty was eventually transferred to the Levites (Exod 13:13–15; 22:28; 34:20; Num 3:11–13; 8:16–18). Nonetheless, the firstborn son was born into a priestly role and so morally and legally the act of the *pidyon ha-ben* was meant to release him from priestly obligation and allow him to assume an ordinary life.

However, one obligation of the first-born male is non-negotiable nor transferable; he is required to fast on the fourteenth day of Nisan, Passover eve, to commemorate the redemption of the Israelites from Egypt of yore, including the plague death of Egypt's first-born. Nonetheless, this fast of the first-born male is seen by the Sages as a *minchag Yisrael* (traditional custom) and can be suspended if the *bekhor* (first-born) attends a *seudat mitzvah*, a joyous meal celebrating a circumcision, Bar Mitzvah ,etc., or he engages in a *siyum masechet*, i.e., joining a group in meaningful learning and completing a tractate of *Gemarah* or finishing by oneself one of the Six Orders of the Mishnah.

The laws of the "Redemption of the First-Born Son" are Rabbinic. The first-born male child cannot be a descendent of Aaron, that is to say, father or grandfather is a priest or Levite or the mother is the daughter of a priest or Levite. According to some authorities, however, a child whose mother is a *bat kohen* ("daughter of a priest") and whose father is a non-Jew requires a *pidyon ha-ben* ceremony. Also, the firstborn son of a marriage between a *kohen* and a woman forbidden to him (e.g., a divorcee) does not have priestly rank but must be redeemed (*YD* 305:19), and the father may, in this case, keep the redemption money himself (R. Asher to *b.Bekh*. 47b). The first-born son cannot be preceded by a sister or a still-birth or delivered by Caesarian section (*t.Bekh* 8:2). Nor by an earlier miscarriage by the mother that occurred after the third month of pregnancy.

If the previous miscarriage occurred after forty days, but before the fetus developed distinguishing characteristics, redemption of the first-born is still required, but the blessing said by the father is omitted. He is redeemed on the thirty-first day of his life or the day after if the designated day is the Sabbath or festival. The father presents his child to a priest, declares his intention to redeem his son by citing a biblical verse of release (Num 18:16) from the sanctified service (Exod 13:2), and pays the redemption money of five shekels (five silver dollars) for the exchange to occur. The priest accepts the redemption money, returns the child to the father, who recites the permissive benediction to redeem the first-born. The priest then holds the money over the head of the child, acknowledges that it is God's will that the child be redeemed, and offers a wish that the child be raised to achieve a life of Torah, successful marriage, and good deeds. The service ends with the priestly blessing of peace (Num 6:24), followed by verses from Psalms and Proverbs invoking the Lord to be the guardian protector of the child, and the *she-he-cheyanu*, a well-known blessing thanking the Almighty for enabling the participants to re-Jew by rejoicing in this sacred ritual.

As mentioned, the obligation of redeeming the firstborn son falls upon the biological father. If he neglects to do so or if the child is an orphan, the son redeems himself when he reaches maturity (*b.Qidd*. 29a). At one time a small medallion bearing the inscription *ben bekhor* or *ben kohen* was hung around the neck of such a child (Isserles to *YD* 305:15). Later it became customary to inscribe the medallion with the letter *heh*, whose numerical number "five" symbolized the five shekels of redemption. To prevent tear and lost, the *heyalakh* medallion was kept by the synagogue or relative for safe keeping. The accepted tradition today if either the rabbinical court (*bet din*) or one of the child's male relatives redeems him at the required time. The ceremonial silver coins are payment to the *kohen* under Jewish law, who gives the money to charity, or returns the money to the child's father (*b.Bekh*. 51b) if the father is very poor (*TD*, 305:8). The choice of a poor *kohen*, which simultaneously fulfills the deed of charity, is meritorious. Finally, certain communities make no mention of the redemptive ceremony (e.g., the Bene Israel of India) possibly since there was no viable *kohen* present to conduct the ritual.

Ceremonial variations evolved to enhance the beauty of the commandment and they reflect ethnographic differences. Ashkenazi communities in eighteen and nineteen century Eastern Europe commissioned beautifully crafted silver trays decorated with related biblical or liturgical imagery, e.g., the offering of Isaac, priestly benediction, etc. On this tray, the *bekhor*, beautifully dressed and decorated in his mother's jewelry and/or the jewelry of the women in attendance (subconsciously recalling the scriptural Israelite women *not* offering their jewelry in the making of the Golden Calf; suggested in Exod 32:2) was offered to the *kohen*. It was a tradition for some Sephardic mothers to dress in their bridal gown; and in the Persian community, the mother wore the veil from her wedding. Playful drama was added with the mother wailed for her firstborn male child and in the Moroccan communities, the mother offered the jewelry she was wearing to the priest for the exchange of her child.

In contemporary times, five silver spoons (Turkey) and seven gold bracelets (Morocco) are offered. At the end of the ceremony all is exchanged for the priestly silver redemption, legally between 113 grams and 117 grams. The Israeli Mint has minted special edition 23.4-gram silver commemorative coins for the purpose, five of which would come to exactly 117 grams of silver. Finally, at the festive meal guests are served sugar and garlic, symbolic reminder that they have participated in the merit of *pidyon ha-ben*.

The norms of ancient Israelite society required that the first male offspring of man and the first issue of the herds, flocks, and fruit belong to the God of Israel, and in some manner are to be offered to Him, such as actual or proxy sacrificial offerings. Special socio-legal and cultic rights are granted to the biblical *bekhor*. The specification that the *bekhor* is "the first issue of the womb" (*peter rehem*; Exod 13:2, 12, 15, etc.; cf. Num 8:16) connotes the religious importance of the maternal line. The sole difference in the status of the first-born son as compared with that of his brother siblings is his right to a greater share in their father's inheritance (Deut 21:15–17). His status of *reshit' on* "the first fruit of vigor" (Deut. 21:17) is inalienable.

The text states that he is the principal heir and successor of his father as head of the family, irrespective of the status of his mother (beloved or hated by the father in a polygamous marriage) or if he is the first-born son of an "unloved" (i.e., not permitted) union (e.g., *kohen* and a divorcee). A son of a proselyte to Judaism qualifies for the inheritance of the first-born if his father had not previously sired a male child. A first-born of twin sons, who is born after his father's death, is not entitled to the inheritance of the *bekhor* since the deceased father cannot acknowledge his right (Deut. 21:17; *b.BB* 142b). The first-born is granted a double portion of his father's estate as inheritance, that is, twice the amount doled out to the other siblings. The prerogative of the firstborn never extends to a daughter, not even in a case where she has a right of inheritance (*Sif.Deut*.215).

—Zev Garber

Bibliography

Michele Klein, *A Time to be Born: Customs and Folklore of Jewish Birth* (Philadelphia, 1998).
Benzion Schereschewsky, *Dinei Mishpaḥah* (Jerusalem, 1967)
Zev Garber, "Firstborn," *Encylopedia of the Bible and Its Reception* 9 (Walter de Gruyter, Berlin/Boston, 2014).

Annotated Haggadah for Passover
-continued-

רַבִּי יוֹסֵי הַגְּלִילִי אוֹמֵר: מִנַּיִן אַתָּה אוֹמֵר שֶׁלָּקוּ הַמִּצְרִים בְּמִצְרַיִם עֶשֶׂר מַכּוֹת וְעַל הַיָּם לָקוּ חֲמִשִּׁים מַכּוֹת? בְּמִצְרַיִם מָה הוּא אוֹמֵר? וַיֹּאמְרוּ הַחַרְטֻמִּם אֶל פַּרְעֹה: אֶצְבַּע אֱלֹהִים הִוא, וְעַל הַיָּם מָה הוּא אוֹמֵר? וַיַּרְא יִשְׂרָאֵל אֶת־הַיָּד הַגְּדֹלָה אֲשֶׁר עָשָׂה ה' בְּמִצְרַיִם, וַיִּירְאוּ הָעָם אֶת־ה', וַיַּאֲמִינוּ בַּיָי וּבְמֹשֶׁה עַבְדּוֹ. כַּמָּה לָקוּ בָאֶצְבַּע? עֶשֶׂר מַכּוֹת. אֱמוֹר מֵעַתָּה: בְּמִצְרַיִם לָקוּ עֶשֶׂר מַכּוֹת וְעַל הַיָּם לָקוּ חֲמִשִּׁים מַכּוֹת.

Rabbi Yose Hagelili says, "From where can you [derive] that the Egyptians were struck with ten plagues in Egypt and struck with fifty plagues at the Sea? In Egypt, what does it state? 'Then the magicians said unto Pharaoh: 'This is the finger of God' (Exodus 8:15). And at the Sea, what does it state? 'And Israel saw the Lord's great hand that he used upon the Egyptians, and the people feared the Lord; and they believed in the Lord, and in Moshe, His servant' (Exodus 14:31). How many were they struck with the finger? Ten plagues. You can say from here that in Egypt, they were struck with ten plagues and at the Sea, they were struck with fifty plagues."

רַבִּי אֱלִיעֶזֶר אוֹמֵר: מִנַּיִן שֶׁכָּל־מַכָּה וּמַכָּה שֶׁהֵבִיא הַקָּדוֹשׁ בָּרוּךְ הוּא עַל הַמִּצְרִים בְּמִצְרַיִם הָיְתָה שֶׁל אַרְבַּע מַכּוֹת? שֶׁנֶּאֱמַר: יְשַׁלַּח־בָּם חֲרוֹן אַפּוֹ, עֶבְרָה וָזַעַם וְצָרָה, מִשְׁלַחַת מַלְאֲכֵי רָעִים. עֶבְרָה – אַחַת, וָזַעַם – שְׁתַּיִם, וְצָרָה – שָׁלֹשׁ, מִשְׁלַחַת מַלְאֲכֵי רָעִים – אַרְבַּע. אֱמוֹר מֵעַתָּה: בְּמִצְרַיִם לָקוּ אַרְבָּעִים מַכּוֹת וְעַל הַיָּם לָקוּ מָאתַיִם מַכּוֹת.

Rabbi Eliezer says, "From where [can you derive] that every plague that the Holy One, blessed be He, brought upon the Egyptians in Egypt was [composed] of four plagues? As it is stated (Psalms 78:49): 'He sent upon them the fierceness of His anger, wrath, and fury, and trouble, a sending of messengers of evil.' 'Wrath' [corresponds to] one; 'and fury' [brings it to] two; 'and trouble' [brings it to] three; 'a sending of messengers of evil' [brings it to] four. You can say from here that in Egypt, they were struck with forty plagues and at the Sea, they were struck with two hundred plagues."

רַבִּי עֲקִיבָא אוֹמֵר: מִנַּיִן שֶׁכָּל־מַכָּה וּמַכָּה שֶׁהֵבִיא הַקָּדוֹשׁ בָּרוּךְ הוּא עַל הַמִּצְרִים בְּמִצְרַיִם הָיְתָה שֶׁל חָמֵשׁ מַכּוֹת? שֶׁנֶּאֱמַר: יְשַׁלַּח־בָּם חֲרוֹן אַפּוֹ, עֶבְרָה וָזַעַם וְצָרָה, מִשְׁלַחַת מַלְאֲכֵי רָעִים. חֲרוֹן אַפּוֹ – אַחַת, עֶבְרָה – שְׁתַּיִם, וָזַעַם – שָׁלוֹשׁ, וְצָרָה – אַרְבַּע, מִשְׁלַחַת מַלְאֲכֵי רָעִים – חָמֵשׁ. אֱמוֹר מֵעַתָּה: בְּמִצְרַיִם לָקוּ חֲמִשִּׁים מַכּוֹת וְעַל הַיָּם לָקוּ חֲמִשִּׁים וּמָאתַיִם מַכּוֹת.

Rabbi Akiva says, says, "From where [can you derive] that every plague that the Holy One, blessed be He, brought upon the Egyptians in Egypt was [composed] of five plagues? As it is stated (Psalms 78:49): 'He sent upon them the fierceness of His anger, wrath, and fury, and trouble, a sending of messengers of evil.' 'The fierceness of His anger' [corresponds to] one; 'wrath' [brings it to] two; 'and fury' [brings it to] three; 'and trouble' [brings it to] four; 'a sending of messengers of evil' [brings it to] five. You can say from here that in Egypt, they were struck with fifty plagues and at the Sea, they were struck with two hundred and fifty plagues."

Supplementary midrashim and a thanksgiving litany (*Dayyenu*) praise the wonderment of Israel's slavery-freedom saga and divine merciful acts in leading and sustaining the Children's voyage to the Promise Land.

Tannaitic midrashim (*Mek.* on 14:10; *Exod Rab* 5.14, 23.9; *Midr. Tehilim/Psalms* on 78:49) speak in hyperboles on Exod 14:31 to magnify the divine drama of the Ten Plagues. In the teaching of Rabbi Yose Hagelili, "finger of God" in Egypt equates to "ten" and "hand (five fingers) of God" at the *yam suf*/ Sea of Reeds equates to "fifty" plagues. Rabbi Eliezer cites Ps 78:49 which mentions that God's messengers of evil, namely, anger, wrath, indignation, and trouble, accompany each plague amounting to forty in Egypt (4 x 10 = 40) and 200 at Sea (5 x 40 = 200). The intent of the exaggerated computation is not mathematical certainty but impressively enhancing God's awesome miraculous redemptive delivery.

Rabbi Akiba enhances Rabbi Eliezer's addition by adding "messengers of evil" as an additional negative accompaniment to anger, wrath, indignation, and trouble thereby equating to 50 Plagues in Egypt and 250 Plagues at Sea implying mathematical extremity is uncalled for. A less exaggerated and more compelling addition is found in '*Avot* 5.6 which speaks of Ten Plagues at the Sea derived from phrases from the Song of the Sea (Exod 15) known in Tradition and in liturgy as the *Shirah*/Song: "the horse and his rider had He thrown into the sea," "Pharoah's chariots and his host had He thrown into the sea," "You did blow with Your wind, the sea covered them," and on.

—Zev Garber

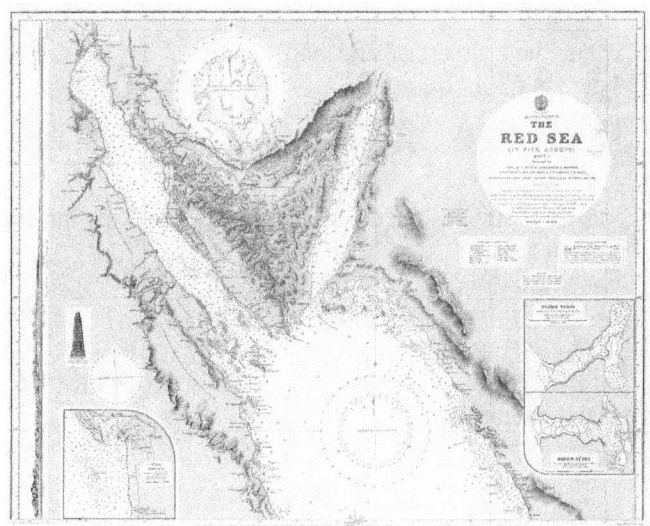

Fig. 12

Magid, Dayenu

כַּמָּה מַעֲלוֹת טוֹבוֹת לַמָּקוֹם עָלֵינוּ.

How many degrees of good did the Place [of all bestow] upon us!

אִלּוּ הוֹצִיאָנוּ מִמִּצְרַיִם וְלֹא עָשָׂה בָהֶם שְׁפָטִים, דַּיֵּנוּ.

If He had taken us out of Egypt and not made judgements on them; [it would have been] enough for us.

אִלּוּ עָשָׂה בָהֶם שְׁפָטִים, וְלֹא עָשָׂה בֵאלֹהֵיהֶם, דַּיֵּנוּ.

If He had made judgments on them and had not made [them] on their gods; [it would have been] enough for us.

אִלּוּ עָשָׂה בֵאלֹהֵיהֶם, וְלֹא הָרַג אֶת־בְּכוֹרֵיהֶם, דַּיֵּנוּ.

If He had made [them] on their gods and had not killed their firstborn; [it would have been] enough for us.

אִלּוּ הָרַג אֶת־בְּכוֹרֵיהֶם וְלֹא נָתַן לָנוּ אֶת־מָמוֹנָם, דַּיֵּנוּ.

If He had killed their firstborn and had not given us their substance; [it would have been] enough for us.

אִלּוּ נָתַן לָנוּ אֶת־מָמוֹנָם וְלֹא קָרַע לָנוּ אֶת־הַיָּם, דַּיֵּנוּ.

If He had given us their substance and had not split the Sea for us; [it would have been] enough for us.

אִלּוּ קָרַע לָנוּ אֶת־הַיָּם וְלֹא הֶעֱבִירָנוּ בְּתוֹכוֹ בֶּחָרָבָה, דַּיֵּנוּ.

If He had split the Sea for us and had not taken us through it on dry land; [it would have been] enough for us.

אִלּוּ הֶעֱבִירָנוּ בְּתוֹכוֹ בֶּחָרָבָה וְלֹא שִׁקַּע צָרֵנוּ בְּתוֹכוֹ דַּיֵּנוּ.

If He had taken us through it on dry land and had not pushed down our enemies in [the Sea]; [it would have been] enough for us.

אִלּוּ שִׁקַּע צָרֵנוּ בְּתוֹכוֹ וְלֹא סִפֵּק צָרְכֵּנוּ בַּמִּדְבָּר אַרְבָּעִים שָׁנָה דַּיֵּנוּ.

\If He had pushed down our enemies in [the Sea] and had not supplied our needs in the wilderness for forty years; [it would have been] enough for us.

אִלּוּ סִפֵּק צָרְכֵּנוּ בְּמִדְבָּר אַרְבָּעִים שָׁנָה וְלֹא הֶאֱכִילָנוּ אֶת־הַמָּן דַּיֵּנוּ.

If He had supplied our needs in the wilderness for forty years and had not fed us the manna; [it would have been] enough for us.

אִלּוּ הֶאֱכִילָנוּ אֶת־הַמָּן וְלֹא נָתַן לָנוּ אֶת־הַשַּׁבָּת, דַּיֵּנוּ.

If He had fed us the manna and had not given us the Shabbat; [it would have been] enough for us.

אִלּוּ נָתַן לָנוּ אֶת־הַשַּׁבָּת, וְלֹא קֵרְבָנוּ לִפְנֵי הַר סִינַי, דַּיֵּנוּ.

If He had given us the Shabbat and had not brought us close to Mount Sinai; [it would have been] enough for us.

אִלּוּ קֵרְבָנוּ לִפְנֵי הַר סִינַי, וְלֹא נָתַן לָנוּ אֶת־הַתּוֹרָה. דַּיֵּנוּ.

If He had brought us close to Mount Sinai and had not given us the Torah; [it would have been] enough for us.

אִלּוּ נָתַן לָנוּ אֶת־הַתּוֹרָה וְלֹא הִכְנִיסָנוּ לְאֶרֶץ יִשְׂרָאֵל, דַּיֵּנוּ.

If He had given us the Torah and had not brought us into the land of Israel; [it would have been] enough for us.

אִלּוּ הִכְנִיסָנוּ לְאֶרֶץ יִשְׂרָאֵל וְלֹא בָנָה לָנוּ אֶת־בֵּית הַבְּחִירָה דַּיֵּנוּ.

If He had brought us into the land of Israel and had not built us the 'Chosen House' [the Temple; it would have been] enough for us.

עַל אַחַת, כַּמָּה וְכַמָּה, טוֹבָה כְפוּלָה וּמְכֻפֶּלֶת לַמָּקוֹם עָלֵינוּ: שֶׁהוֹצִיאָנוּ מִמִּצְרַיִם, וְעָשָׂה בָהֶם שְׁפָטִים, וְעָשָׂה בֵאלֹהֵיהֶם, וְהָרַג אֶת־בְּכוֹרֵיהֶם, וְנָתַן לָנוּ אֶת־מָמוֹנָם, וְקָרַע לָנוּ אֶת־הַיָּם, וְהֶעֱבִירָנוּ בְתוֹכוֹ בֶּחָרָבָה, וְשִׁקַּע צָרֵנוּ בְּתוֹכוֹ, וְסִפֵּק צָרְכֵּנוּ בַּמִּדְבָּר אַרְבָּעִים שָׁנָה, וְהֶאֱכִילָנוּ אֶת־הַמָּן, וְנָתַן לָנוּ אֶת־הַשַּׁבָּת, וְקֵרְבָנוּ לִפְנֵי הַר סִינַי, וְנָתַן לָנוּ אֶת־הַתּוֹרָה, וְהִכְנִיסָנוּ לְאֶרֶץ יִשְׂרָאֵל, וּבָנָה לָנוּ אֶת־בֵּית הַבְּחִירָה לְכַפֵּר עַל־כָּל־עֲוֹנוֹתֵינוּ.

How much more so is the good that is doubled and quadrupled that the Place [of all bestowed] upon us [enough for us]; since he took us out of Egypt, and made judgments with them, and made [them] with their gods, and killed their firstborn, and gave us their money, and split the Sea for us, and brought us through it on dry land, and pushed down our enemies in [the Sea], and supplied our needs in the wilderness for forty years, and fed us the manna, and gave us the Shabbat, and brought us close to Mount Sinai, and gave us the Torah, and brought us into the land of Israel and built us the 'Chosen House' [the Temple] to atone upon all of our sins.

Dayyenu ("We Should Have Been Content") is an ancient thanksgiving hymn celebrating in fourteen stanzas fifteen instances of God's merciful acts to the Children of Israel from the time of the Exodus from Egypt until the entrance of the people into Canaan. This most ancient section of the Passover Haggadah, said to be composed in the pre-Maccabean second century B.C.E., is a litany of invocations and supplications, exalting religiosity in the slavery-freedom story seen in strophes extolling the gift of Shabbat memory and observance, revelation of Torah at Sinai, ingathering into the Land of Israel, and rebuilding the Second Temple. Highlighted themes of the *Dayyenu* are repeated in a summary fashion to emphasize that the historicity of the Passover story is enlightened by repetitive themes and transmitted by religious obligatory memory and practice. Finally, an aura of holiness emanates from the number "fifteen": it equates numerically to YaH/God and suggests the fifteen steps in the Jerusalem Temple.

—Zev Garber

Magid, Rabban Gamliel's Three Things

רַבָּן גַּמְלִיאֵל הָיָה אוֹמֵר: כָּל שֶׁלֹּא אָמַר שְׁלֹשָׁה דְּבָרִים אֵלּוּ בַּפֶּסַח, לֹא יָצָא יְדֵי חוֹבָתוֹ, וְאֵלּוּ הֵן: פֶּסַח, מַצָּה, וּמָרוֹר.

Rabban Gamliel was accustomed to say, Anyone who *has not said* these three things on *Pesach* has not fulfilled his obligation, and these are them: the *Pesach* sacrifice, *matsa* and *maror*.

פֶּסַח שֶׁהָיוּ אֲבוֹתֵינוּ אוֹכְלִים בִּזְמַן שֶׁבֵּית הַמִּקְדָּשׁ הָיָה קַיָּם, עַל שׁוּם מָה? עַל שׁוּם שֶׁפָּסַח הַקָּדוֹשׁ בָּרוּךְ הוּא עַל בָּתֵּי אֲבוֹתֵינוּ בְּמִצְרַיִם, שֶׁנֶּאֱמַר: וַאֲמַרְתֶּם זֶבַח פֶּסַח הוּא לַיי, אֲשֶׁר פָּסַח עַל בָּתֵּי בְנֵי יִשְׂרָאֵל בְּמִצְרַיִם בְּנָגְפּוֹ אֶת־מִצְרַיִם, וְאֶת־בָּתֵּינוּ הִצִּיל וַיִּקֹּד הָעָם וַיִּשְׁתַּחווּ.

The *Pesach* [passover] sacrifice that our ancestors were accustomed to eating when the Temple existed, for the sake of what [was it]? For the sake [to commemorate] that the Holy One, blessed be He, passed over the homes of our ancestors in Egypt, as it is stated (Exodus 12:27); "And you shall say: 'It is the Passover sacrifice to the Lord, for that He passed over the homes of the Children of Israel in Egypt, when He smote the Egyptians, and our homes he saved.' And the people bowed the head and bowed."

אוחז המצה בידו ומראה אותה למסובין:

The leader of the seder holds the matsa in his hand and shows it to the others there.

מַצָּה זוֹ שֶׁאָנוּ אוֹכְלִים, עַל שׁוּם מָה? עַל שׁוּם שֶׁלֹּא הִסְפִּיק בְּצֵקָם שֶׁל אֲבוֹתֵינוּ לְהַחֲמִיץ עַד שֶׁנִּגְלָה עֲלֵיהֶם מֶלֶךְ מַלְכֵי הַמְּלָכִים, הַקָּדוֹשׁ בָּרוּךְ הוּא, וּגְאָלָם, שֶׁנֶּאֱמַר: וַיֹּאפוּ אֶת־הַבָּצֵק אֲשֶׁר הוֹצִיאוּ מִמִּצְרַיִם עֻגֹת מַצּוֹת, כִּי לֹא חָמֵץ, כִּי גֹרְשׁוּ מִמִּצְרַיִם וְלֹא יָכְלוּ לְהִתְמַהְמֵהַּ, וְגַם צֵדָה לֹא עָשׂוּ לָהֶם.

This *matsa* that we are eating, for the sake of what [is it]? For the sake [to commemorate] that our ancestors' dough was not yet able to rise, before the King of the kings of kings, the Holy One, blessed be He, revealed [Himself] to them and redeemed them, as it is stated (Exodus 12:39); "And they baked the dough which they brought out of Egypt into *matsa* cakes, since it did not rise; because they were expelled from Egypt, and could not tarry, neither had they made for themselves provisions."

אוחז המרור בידו ומראה אותו למסובין.

The leader of the seder holds the maror in his hand and shows it to the others there.

מָרוֹר זֶה שֶׁאָנוּ אוֹכְלִים, עַל שׁוּם מַה? עַל שׁוּם שֶׁמֵּרְרוּ הַמִּצְרִים אֶת־חַיֵּי אֲבוֹתֵינוּ בְּמִצְרַיִם, שֶׁנֶּאֱמַר: וַיְמָרְרוּ אֶת חַיֵּיהֶם בַּעֲבֹדָה קָשָׁה, בְּחֹמֶר וּבִלְבֵנִים וּבְכָל־עֲבֹדָה בַּשָּׂדֶה אֵת כָּל עֲבֹדָתָם אֲשֶׁר עָבְדוּ בָהֶם בְּפָרֶךְ.

This *maror* [bitter greens] that we are eating, for the sake of what [is it]? For the sake [to commemorate] that the Egyptians embittered the lives of our ancestors in Egypt, as it is stated (Exodus 1:14); "And they made their lives bitter with hard service, in mortar and in brick, and in all manner of service in the field; in all their service, wherein they made them serve with rigor."

Rabban (Rabbi) Gamliel's advisory of Paschal/Passover Sacrifice, *matsa*/unleavened bread, and *maror*/bitter herbs to fulfill *halakhicly* the seder ritual is extracted from *m. Pesaḥ* 10.5. Slight emendations, changes, and instructions are noted reflecting changing historical reality. For example, Paschal Sacrifice which our forefathers ate is now "used to eat" due to the destruction of the Second Temple. Similarly, the shankbone symbolic of the Paschal offering is not lifted (venerated) but acknowledged only as a symbol of remembrance. Gamliel's injunction that anyone who *has not said* meaning has not explained the *pesach, matsa,* and *maror* has not fulfilled one's seder obligation is extraordinary since performing religious rites derived from biblical scriptures does not require an explanation in the act of doing. But the explanation subscribes to the biblical injunction of the son/child asking his father what is this? (Exod 13:14) and the meaning of the testimonies, statues, and ordinances (Deut 6:20)? Also, Gamliel's instructive counsel on the *pesach, matsa,* and *maror* is the only direct answer to the Four Questions asked at the beginning of the seder.

—Zev Garber

בְּכָל־דּוֹר וָדוֹר חַיָּב אָדָם לִרְאוֹת אֶת־עַצְמוֹ כְּאִלּוּ הוּא יָצָא מִמִּצְרַיִם, שֶׁנֶּאֱמַר: וְהִגַּדְתָּ לְבִנְךָ בַּיּוֹם הַהוּא לֵאמֹר, בַּעֲבוּר זֶה עָשָׂה ה' לִי בְּצֵאתִי מִמִּצְרָיִם. לֹא אֶת־אֲבוֹתֵינוּ בִּלְבָד גָּאַל הַקָּדוֹשׁ בָּרוּךְ הוּא, אֶלָּא אַף אוֹתָנוּ גָּאַל עִמָּהֶם, שֶׁנֶּאֱמַר: וְאוֹתָנוּ הוֹצִיא מִשָּׁם, לְמַעַן הָבִיא אוֹתָנוּ, לָתֶת לָנוּ אֶת־הָאָרֶץ אֲשֶׁר נִשְׁבַּע לַאֲבֹתֵינוּ.

In each and every generation, a person is obligated to see himself as if he left Egypt, as it is stated (Exodus 13:8); "For the sake of this, did the Lord do [this] for me in my going out of Egypt." Not only our ancestors did the Holy One, blessed be He, redeem, but rather also us [together] with them did He redeem, as it is stated (Deuteronomy 6:23); "And He took us out from there, in order to bring us in, to give us the land which He swore unto our fathers."

The text is extracted from *m. Pesach* 10.5. A central Passover message is conveyed, that is to say, the theme of slavery-freedom is not steeped in antiquity, but it is ongoing in every and all generations. Hence, constant vigil and pray for divine intervention. Similarly, we read above *And it is this that has stood for our ancestors and for us; since it is not [only] one [person or nation] that has stood [against] us to destroy us, but rather in each generation, they stand [against] us to destroy us, but the Holy One, blessed be He, rescues us from their hand.*

—Zev Garber

Magid, First Half of Hallel (Psalms 113, 114)

Psalms 113–118 were chanted by the Levites during the paschal lamb sacrifice in the Second Temple (*m. Pesach* V.7). The five Hallel Psalms are identified in Talmudic literature as *hallel d'mitsrayim*/ "the Hallel (praise) of Egypt" (see Ps 114: 1) to distinguish from the "Great Hallel," that is to say the *Songs of Ascents* (Pss 120–134) or Psalm 136, *Hymn of Praise*. Pss 113 ("Praise the Name of the Lord" and 114 (Egyptian Exodus) are recited before the Passover meal. PSS 115 ("National Trust in God"), 116 ("Personal Prayer of God's Comfort and Deliverance"), 117 ("Summon s to All Nations to Praise the Lord"), and 118 ("National Jubilation in God's Deliverance") are recited after the Passover meal. In Jewish liturgy during the morning service, the Hallel Psalms are recited on Rosh Ḥodesh, the Pilgrimage Festivals (*Pesach*/Passover, Shavuot/Pentecost, Succot/Tabernacles), and Ḥannukah/Dedication. On Rosh Ḥodesh and on the last dix days of Passover, Ps 115:1–11 and Ps 116:1–11 are omitted.

—Zev Garber

יאחז הכוס בידו ויכסה המצות ויאמר:

The leader of the seder holds the cup in his hand and he covers the matsa and says:

לְפִיכָךְ אֲנַחְנוּ חַיָּבִים לְהוֹדוֹת, לְהַלֵּל, לְשַׁבֵּחַ, לְפָאֵר, לְרוֹמֵם, לְהַדֵּר, לְבָרֵךְ, לְעַלֵּה וּלְקַלֵּס לְמִי שֶׁעָשָׂה לַאֲבוֹתֵינוּ וְלָנוּ אֶת־כָּל־הַנִּסִּים הָאֵלּוּ: הוֹצִיאָנוּ מֵעַבְדוּת לְחֵרוּת מִיָּגוֹן לְשִׂמְחָה, וּמֵאֵבֶל לְיוֹם טוֹב, וּמֵאֲפֵלָה לְאוֹר גָּדוֹל, וּמִשִּׁעְבּוּד לִגְאֻלָּה. וְנֹאמַר לְפָנָיו שִׁירָה חֲדָשָׁה: הַלְלוּיָהּ.

Therefore we are obligated to thank, praise, laud, glorify, exalt, lavish, bless, raise high, and acclaim He who made all these miracles for our ancestors and for us: He brought us out from slavery to freedom, from sorrow to joy, from mourning to [celebration of] a festival, from darkness to great light, and from servitude to redemption. And let us say a new song before Him, Halleluyah!

הַלְלוּיָהּ הַלְלוּ עַבְדֵי ה', הַלְלוּ אֶת־שֵׁם ה'. יְהִי שֵׁם ה' מְבֹרָךְ מֵעַתָּה וְעַד עוֹלָם. מִמִּזְרַח שֶׁמֶשׁ עַד מְבוֹאוֹ מְהֻלָּל שֵׁם ה'. רָם עַל־כָּל־גּוֹיִם ה', עַל הַשָּׁמַיִם כְּבוֹדוֹ. מִי כַּיי אֱלֹהֵינוּ הַמַּגְבִּיהִי לָשָׁבֶת, הַמַּשְׁפִּילִי לִרְאוֹת בַּשָּׁמַיִם וּבָאָרֶץ? מְקִימִי מֵעָפָר דָּל, מֵאַשְׁפֹּת יָרִים אֶבְיוֹן, לְהוֹשִׁיבִי עִם־נְדִיבִים, עִם נְדִיבֵי עַמּוֹ. מוֹשִׁיבִי עֲקֶרֶת הַבַּיִת, אֵם הַבָּנִים שְׂמֵחָה. הַלְלוּיָהּ.

Halleluyah! Praise, servants of the Lord, praise the name of the Lord. May the Name of the Lord be blessed from now and forever. From the rising of the sun in the East to its setting, the name of the Lord is praised. Above all nations is the Lord, His honor is above the heavens. Who is like the Lord, our God, Who sits on high; Who looks down upon the heavens and the earth? He brings up the poor out of the dirt; from the refuse piles, He raises the destitute. To seat him with the nobles, with the nobles of his people. He seats a barren woman in a home, a happy mother of children. Halleluyah! (Psalms 113)

בְּצֵאת יִשְׂרָאֵל מִמִּצְרַיִם, בֵּית יַעֲקֹב מֵעַם לֹעֵז, הָיְתָה יְהוּדָה לְקָדְשׁוֹ, יִשְׂרָאֵל מַמְשְׁלוֹתָיו. הַיָּם רָאָה וַיָּנֹס, הַיַּרְדֵּן יִסֹּב לְאָחוֹר. הֶהָרִים רָקְדוּ כְאֵילִים, גְּבָעוֹת כִּבְנֵי־צֹאן. מַה־לְּךָ הַיָּם כִּי תָנוּס, הַיַּרְדֵּן – תִּסֹּב לְאָחוֹר, הֶהָרִים – תִּרְקְדוּ כְאֵילִים, גְּבָעוֹת כִּבְנֵי־צֹאן. מִלִּפְנֵי אָדוֹן חוּלִי אָרֶץ, מִלִּפְנֵי אֱלוֹהַּ יַעֲקֹב. הַהֹפְכִי הַצּוּר אֲגַם־מָיִם, חַלָּמִישׁ לְמַעְיְנוֹ־מָיִם.

In Israel's going out from Egypt, the house of Ya'akov from a people of foreign speech. The Sea saw and fled, the Jordan turned to the rear. The mountains danced like rams, the hills like young sheep. What is happening to you, O Sea, that you are fleeing, O Jordan that you turn to the rear; O mountains that you dance like rams, O hills like young sheep? From before the Master, tremble O earth, from before the Lord of Ya'akov. He who turns the boulder into a pond of water, the flint into a spring of water. (Psalms 114)

Hallel

Biblical literature is characterized, not by flowery exposition advanced with a thesaurus of superlatives, but by leanness and brevity. Every word, every letter must be accounted for, lest it be deemed redundant. When it comes to Hebrew textuality, less is certainly more. Why, then, does the Haggadah employ nine separate verbs of *Hallel* ("praise") in order to express gratitude for deliverance from the bondage of Egypt? Perhaps this verbal torrent is designed to emphasize a concept as revolutionary as the wheel, that God, unlike the pantheon of pagan 35 deities, is separate from the physical world, beyond materiality, and fundamentally "other." Knowing before whom one stands involves no uncertain measure of obligation, and is to be expressed in a multifaceted, albeit superfluous, measure of praise. The verb *Halleluyah*, is itself obligatory, being an imperative. We see in all of this that a huge chasm has yawned between humanity and the divine realm, at once terrifying, yet strangely compelling.

The One who occupies its throne, unlike the fickle and capricious Egyptian deities, is said to "judge the world in righteousness" (Ps. 9:9). The office of judge of course involves separation (the essence of "otherness") from the objects of judgment, including the Egyptians and even the sea, which dutifully "flees" before the Israelites. Judgment, most often conceived as quintessentially negative, becomes the vehicle of deliverance. This is Israel's "new song." The "new song" is likewise an expression of a novel idea in the evolution of religious thought. In delivering Israel God has taken the side, not of mighty potentates, but of the afflicted and the oppressed. The Exodus event transcends the crossing of a Sea of Reeds; it will become an essential vehicle in the shaping of ethical religious consciousness and with it the concept of social justice—" in every generation."

—Kenneth Hanson

Magid, Second Cup of Wine

מגביהים את הכוס עד גאל ישראל.

We raise the cup until we reach "who redeemed Israel."

בָּרוּךְ אַתָּה ה' אֱלֹהֵינוּ מֶלֶךְ הָעוֹלָם, אֲשֶׁר גְּאָלָנוּ וְגָאַל אֶת־אֲבוֹתֵינוּ מִמִּצְרַיִם, וְהִגִּיעָנוּ הַלַּיְלָה הַזֶּה לֶאֱכָל־בּוֹ מַצָּה וּמָרוֹר. כֵּן ה' אֱלֹהֵינוּ וֵאלֹהֵי אֲבוֹתֵינוּ יַגִּיעֵנוּ לְמוֹעֲדִים וְלִרְגָלִים אֲחֵרִים הַבָּאִים לִקְרָאתֵנוּ לְשָׁלוֹם, שְׂמֵחִים בְּבִנְיַן עִירֶךָ וְשָׂשִׂים בַּעֲבוֹדָתֶךָ. וְנֹאכַל שָׁם מִן הַזְּבָחִים וּמִן הַפְּסָחִים אֲשֶׁר יַגִּיעַ דָּמָם עַל קִיר מִזְבַּחֲךָ לְרָצוֹן, וְנוֹדֶה לְךָ שִׁיר חָדָשׁ עַל גְּאֻלָּתֵנוּ וְעַל פְּדוּת נַפְשֵׁנוּ. בָּרוּךְ אַתָּה ה', גָּאַל יִשְׂרָאֵל.

Blessed are You, Lord our God, King of the universe, who redeemed us and redeemed our ancestors from Egypt, and brought us on this night to eat *matsa* and *maror*; so too, Lord our God, and God of our ancestors, bring us to other appointed times and holidays that will come to greet us in peace, joyful in the building of Your city and happy in Your worship; that we shall eat there from the offerings and from the *Pesach* sacrifices, the blood of which shall reach the wall of Your altar for favor, and we shall thank You with a new song upon our redemption and upon the restoration of our souls. Blessed are you, Lord, who redeemed Israel.

Rabbi Tarfon is credited with the first sentence of the Redemption benediction; and the rest is attributed to Rabbi Akiva, major supporter of the Bar Kokhba rebellion against Rome in 132 C.E. The Akiviam wish of a rebuild Jerusalem and liberated Land of Israel is a central Passover theme to this day. (cf. *m. Pesaḥ* 10.6).

—Zev Garber

The second cup signifies salvation/ deliverance from servitude and is directly linked to the meaning of the word itself. The root *gaal* (גאל), "to deliver or redeem," is distinct in connotation from another verbal root, also rendered "to redeem," *padah* (פדה), from which the noun *pidyon* (פדיון), "redemption," as in *pidyon ha-ben* (הבן פדיון), "the redemption of the firstborn," is derived. *Gaal,* unlike *padah*, specifically suggests the "redemptive" work of a near kinsman, who in antiquity would rescue a family member from trial or tribulation. In the case of the exodus, the God of Israel is fulfilling such a role. The verb *gaal* is found in Torah law, in reference to re-purchasing a field sold in dire circumstances (see Lev. 25:25ff.). Such an obligation regularly fell on the closest living relative. The term also refers to the redemption of property, including non-sacrificial animals that had been dedicated to God. The firstborn of unclean animals could likewise be "redeemed" (Lev. 27:11ff.). Additionally, a redeemer might be an "avenger of blood" for a murder victim (as in Num. 35:12ff.). In the context of the Exodus, Israel's deity may be viewed as such an avenger.

On a literary level, we find a sense, expressed in the Psalms and Prophets, in which God is Israel's kinsman-redeemer. God is said to stand up for the people in vindication, in a manner which evokes in our minds the exodus. While there is no direct mention of a redemption price, the notion of redemption as ransom is found in Isa 43:1–3. Israel is said to be delivered from a bondage more grievous than slavery. Perhaps the most poignant and powerful use of the word *ga'al* is found in the book of Job (19:25), where it appears to be employed in a peak of mystical ecstasy. Here, Job envisions a kinsman-redeemer, who will avenge his suffering. Of course, we are mindful of the Israelites being avenged for their hardships in Egypt. Job declares, "For I know that my Redeemer lives, and at last he will stand upon the earth." It has been suggested that this redeemer represents an independent, mysterious figure, who will summon God to judgment for having allowed Job's affliction. However, since there is none more omnipotent than God, Job may well be appealing, poetically, from the God of power to the God of justice and love. He is said to be appealing, as it were, from God to God.

Another way to render the verse is, "For I know that I will be redeemed while I am yet alive." For their part, the ancient Israelites constructed no great pyramids, no royal mausoleums, no gold encrusted sarcophagi in which to lay their honored dead. Perhaps the most telling contribution to human civilization was that they fixated themselves on life, not death. To this day, the Jewish prayer for the dead, the Mourners' Kaddish, does not mention death at all, but extols the greatness of God. Their leaders, including Moses, were of a different order than the great pharaonic overlords of Egypt, being defined as much by human frailty as by feigned omnipotence. In life they were authentic, in death humble. Whichever way the verse in Job is understood, the concept of redemption, and the seder cup which conveys it, is central, not only to the exodus, but to the entire contour of biblical thought.

—Kenneth Hanson

שותים את הכוס בהסבת שמאל.

We say the blessing below and drink the cup while reclining to the left.

בָּרוּךְ אַתָּה ה', אֱלֹהֵינוּ מֶלֶךְ הָעוֹלָם בּוֹרֵא פְּרִי הַגָּפֶן.

Blessed are You, Lord our God, who creates the fruit of the vine.

Rachtzah

רָחְצָה

Washing

נוטלים את הידים ומברכים:

We wash the hands and make the blessing.

בָּרוּךְ אַתָּה ה', אֱלֹהֵינוּ מֶלֶךְ הָעוֹלָם, אֲשֶׁר קִדְּשָׁנוּ בְּמִצְוֹתָיו וְצִוָּנוּ עַל נְטִילַת יָדַיִם.

Blessed are You, Lord our God, King of the Universe, who has sanctified us with His commandments and has commanded us on the washing of the hands.

מוֹצִיא מַצָּה

Motsi *matsa*

יקח המצות בסדר שהניחן, הפרוסה בין שתי השלמות, יאחז שלשתן בידו ויברך "המוציא" בכוונה על העליונה, ו"על אכילת מַצָּה" בכוונה על הפרוסה. אחר כך יבצע כזית מן העליונה השלמה וכזית שני מן הפרוסה, ויטבלם במלח, ויאכל בהסבה שני הזיתים:

The seder leader takes out the matsa in the order that he placed them, the broken one between the two whole ones; he holds the three of them in his hand and blesses ha-motsi with the intention to take from the top one and "on eating matsa" with the intention of eating from the broken one. Afterwards, he breaks off a kazayit (small piece) *from the top whole one and a second kazayit from the broken one and he dips them into salt and eats both while reclining.*

בָּרוּךְ אַתָּה ה', אֱלֹהֵינוּ מֶלֶךְ הָעוֹלָם הַמּוֹצִיא לֶחֶם מִן הָאָרֶץ.

Blessed are You, Lord our God, King of the Universe, who brings forth bread from the ground.

בָּרוּךְ אַתָּה ה', אֱלֹהֵינוּ מֶלֶךְ הָעוֹלָם, אֲשֶׁר קִדְּשָׁנוּ בְּמִצְוֹתָיו וְצִוָּנוּ עַל אֲכִילַת מַצָּה.

Blessed are You, Lord our God, King of the Universe, who has sanctified us with His commandments and has commanded us on the eating of *matsa*.

Maror

מָרוֹר

כל אחד מהמסבים לוקח כזית מרור, מטבלו בחרוסת; מנער החרוסת, מברך ואוכל בלי הסבה.

All present should take a kazayit of maror, dip into the haroset, shake off the haroset, make the blessing and eat without reclining.

בָּרוּךְ אַתָּה ה', אֱלֹהֵינוּ מֶלֶךְ הָעוֹלָם, אֲשֶׁר קִדְּשָׁנוּ בְּמִצְוֹתָיו וְצִוָּנוּ עַל אֲכִילַת מָרוֹר.

Blessed are You, Lord our God, King of the Universe, who has sanctified us with His commandments and has commanded us on the eating of *maror*.

Korech

כּוֹרֵךְ

Wrap

כל אחד מהמסבים לוקח כזית מן המצה השלישית עם כזית מרור, כורכים יחד, אוכלים בהסבה ובלי ברכה. לפני אכלו אומר.

All present should take a kazayit from the third whole matsa with a kazayit of maror, wrap them together and eat them while reclining and without saying a blessing. Before one eats it, s/he should say:

זֵכֶר לְמִקְדָּשׁ כְּהִלֵּל. כֵּן עָשָׂה הִלֵּל בִּזְמַן שֶׁבֵּית הַמִּקְדָּשׁ הָיָה קַיָּם:

In memory of the Temple according to Hillel. This is what Hillel would do when the Temple existed:

הָיָה כּוֹרֵךְ מַצָּה וּמָרוֹר וְאוֹכֵל בְּיַחַד, לְקַיֵּם מַה שֶׁנֶּאֱמַר: עַל מַצּוֹת וּמְרוֹרִים יֹאכְלֻהוּ.

He would wrap the *matsa* and *maror* and eat them together, in order to fulfill what is stated, (Exod 12:15): "You should eat it upon *matsot* and *marorim*."

Faith, it has sometimes been observed, is memory, or perhaps more accurately, sanctified memory. To be sure, every element and aspect of the seder meal recalls, with intricate detail, the events surrounding the Exodus, as the seminal episode in Israel's self-conception. The consumed *maror* evokes the bitterness of Egyptian bondage, though it is deliberately a small amount (*kazayit*), in recognition of the fact that the Israelites are now "children of freedom." Notable is the biblical command that it be eaten along with the paschal lamb and *matsa*: "They shall eat it with unleavened bread and bitter herbs" (Num. 9:11). Rabbinic sources emphasize that consuming the *maror* is in fact inseparable from eating the lamb (*b. Pesach* 120a; Minchat Chinuch 6:3; Shulchan Aruch HaRav 475:15). Whereas eating *matsa* is an independent obligation, commanded separately (Exod 12:18), the *maror* anticipates the lamb (*b. Pesach* 90a). An impossibility arises, however, since the Temple no longer stands, and animals may not be ritually slaughtered. This element of the seder might therefore be dispensed with. The Haggadah nonetheless directs that the *maror* must be consumed *as if* the Temple were standing. This is the element of memory, that has allowed for the survival of the faith of Judaism, even without a Temple, even without a sacrifice. This is why the words of Hillel appear at this point in the Haggadah, to remind each participant of the holy sanctuary that once graced the heart of Jerusalem.

—Kenneth Hanson

Shulḥan `Orech

שֻׁלְחָן עוֹרֵךְ

The Set Table

אוכלים ושותים.

We eat and drink.

Tzafun

צָפוּן

The Concealed [*matsa*]

אחר גמר הסעודה לוקח כל אחד מהמסבים כזית מהמצה שהייתה צפונה לאפיקומן ואוכל ממנה כזית בהסבה. וצריך לאוכלה קודם חצות הלילה.

After the end of the meal, all those present take a kazayit from the matsa, that was concealed for the afikoman, and eat a kazayit from it while reclining.

לפני אכילת האפיקומן יאמר: זֵכֶר לְקָרְבָּן פֶּסַח הַנֶּאֱכָל עַל הַשּׂוֹבַע.

Before eating the afikoman, he should say: "In memory of the Pesach sacrifice that was eaten upon being satiated." After the afikomen is eaten only water can be drunk; also, cups three and four of wine are permitted to complete the seder ritual.

The Bible, bolstered by Jewish tradition, conveys a powerful message, that the release from bondage in Egypt is yet incomplete. Even after crossing the Sea of Reeds, there is an expectation of something more. On one level the *afikoman* (which means "that which is to come") symbolizes the Paschal lamb, which is the last thing to be consumed during the seder. The beauty of the ritual, however, lies in its multiple levels of meaning. The *matsa* itself may be seen to represent spiritual salvation; yet it is broken, suggesting incompleteness and the failure to realize one's full potential. The shrouded *afikoman* may well embody a mystical longing for future growth and the fullness of the redemption, which must be sought and discovered. Additionally, the expectation of the *afikoman* may be paired with another kind of anticipation, beyond the seder itself, culminating at the foot of Mt. Sinai, when all Israel is to receive the Torah.

—Kenneth Hanson

Barech, Birkat Hamazon

The *birkat ha-mazon* at the seder is no different than any Grace after consuming bread at the meal except for the obligatory cup of wine poured before the grace and blessed/drunk after the meal. The three sandard blessings are attributed to Moses, Joshua, and David. The fourth blessing identified with Solomon is supplementary and credited to the sages of Yavneh following the Bar Kochba rebellion 132–135 (*b. Ber.* 48b).

Supplementary additions later composed complete the Grace. Together they speak of the universal, national and spiritual sentiments and growth of an old-new people and religion. The first benediction is *universal*; it expresses the essence of the Grace, namely, universal thanks to the One who gives food for all. The second benediction is *national*; it thanks God for the Land of Israel, freedom fom Egyptian bondage, giving of Torah and Commandments which connect major aspects of Israel's religio-national identity then and now. The third blessing is a petition for God's unlimited mercy and caring of an oppressed, dispised, outcast Nation of Israel who beckons Him not others for resettlement of a People and restoration of the Holy City. The fourth blessing appeals to God of benevolence that He "may not let us lack of all that is good." The remainder of the Grace contains later conditions that reflect personal and peoplehood concerns and petitions related to timeless issues. For example, *May the Merciful One send us multiple blessing, to this home and upon this table upon which we have eaten* (individual household) *May the Merciful One send us Eliyahu the prophet—may he be remembered for good—and he shall announce to us tidings of good, of salvation and of consolation* (repairing Jewish—Israel peoplehood from the ashes of the Shoah).

—Zev Garber

Bless

בָּרֵךְ

מוזגים כוס שלישי ומברכים בְּרכַת המזון.

We pour the third cup and recite the Grace over the Food.

שִׁיר הַמַּעֲלוֹת, בְּשׁוּב ה' אֶת שִׁיבַת צִיּוֹן הָיִינוּ כְּחֹלְמִים. אָז יִמָּלֵא שְׂחוֹק פִּינוּ וּלְשׁוֹנֵנוּ רִנָּה. אָז יֹאמְרוּ בַגּוֹיִם: הִגְדִּיל ה' לַעֲשׂוֹת עִם אֵלֶּה. הִגְדִּיל ה' לַעֲשׂוֹת עִמָּנוּ, הָיִינוּ שְׂמֵחִים. שׁוּבָה ה' אֶת שְׁבִיתֵנוּ כַּאֲפִיקִים בַּנֶּגֶב. הַזֹּרְעִים בְּדִמְעָה, בְּרִנָּה יִקְצֹרוּ. הָלוֹךְ יֵלֵךְ וּבָכֹה נֹשֵׂא מֶשֶׁךְ הַזָּרַע, בֹּא יָבֹא בְרִנָּה נֹשֵׂא אֲלֻמֹּתָיו.

A Song of Ascents; When the Lord will bring back the captivity of Zion, we will be like dreamers. Then our mouth will be full of mirth and our tongue joyful melody; then they will say among the nations; "The Lord has done greatly with these." The Lord has done great things with us; we are happy. Lord, return our captivity like streams in the desert. Those that sow with tears will reap with joyful song. He who surely goes and cries, he carries the measure of seed, he will surely come in joyful song and carry his sheaves. (Ps 126)

שלשה שֶׁאָכְלוּ כְאֶחָד חַיָּבִים לְזַמֵּן וְהַמְזַמֵּן פּוֹתֵחַ:

Three that ate together are obligated to introduce the blessing and the leader of the introduction opens as follows:

רַבּוֹתַי נְבָרֵךְ:

My masters, let us bless:

המסבים עונים:

All those present answer:

יְהִי שֵׁם ה' מְבֹרָךְ מֵעַתָּה וְעַד עוֹלָם.

May the Name of the Lord be blessed from now and forever. (Ps 113:2)

הַמְזַמֵּן אוֹמֵר:

The leader says:

בִּרְשׁוּת מָרָנָן וְרַבָּנָן וְרַבּוֹתַי, נְבָרֵךְ [אֱלֹהֵינוּ] שֶׁאָכַלְנוּ מִשֶּׁלּוֹ.

With the permission of our gentlemen and our teachers and my masters, let us bless [our God] from whom we have eaten.

המסבים עונים:

Those present answer:

בָּרוּךְ [אֱלֹהֵינוּ] שֶׁאָכַלְנוּ מִשֶּׁלּוֹ וּבְטוּבוֹ חָיִינוּ

Blessed is [our God] from whom we have eaten and from whose goodness we live.

המזמן חוזר ואומר:

The leader repeats and says:

בָּרוּךְ [אֱלֹהֵינוּ] שֶׁאָכַלְנוּ מִשֶּׁלּוֹ וּבְטוּבוֹ חָיִינוּ

Blessed is [our God] from whom we have eaten and from whose goodness we live.

כלם אומרים:

They all say:

First Benediction

בָּרוּךְ אַתָּה ה', אֱלֹהֵינוּ מֶלֶךְ הָעוֹלָם, הַזָּן אֶת הָעוֹלָם כֻּלּוֹ בְּטוּבוֹ בְּחֵן בְּחֶסֶד וּבְרַחֲמִים, הוּא נוֹתֵן לֶחֶם לְכָל בָּשָׂר כִּי לְעוֹלָם חַסְדּוֹ. וּבְטוּבוֹ הַגָּדוֹל תָּמִיד לֹא חָסַר לָנוּ, וְאַל יֶחְסַר לָנוּ מָזוֹן לְעוֹלָם וָעֶד. בַּעֲבוּר שְׁמוֹ הַגָּדוֹל, כִּי הוּא אֵל זָן וּמְפַרְנֵס לַכֹּל וּמֵטִיב לַכֹּל, וּמֵכִין מָזוֹן לְכָל בְּרִיּוֹתָיו אֲשֶׁר בָּרָא. בָּרוּךְ אַתָּה ה', הַזָּן אֶת הַכֹּל.

Blessed are You, Lord our God, King of the Universe, who nourishes the entire world in His goodness, in grace, in kindness and in mercy; He gives bread to all flesh since His kindness is forever. And in His great goodness, we always have not lacked, and may we not lack nourishment forever and always, because of His great name. Since He is a Power that feeds and provides for all and does good to all and prepares nourishment for all of his creatures that he created. Blessed are You, Lord, who sustains all.

Second Benediction

נוֹדֶה לְךָ ה' אֱלֹהֵינוּ עַל שֶׁהִנְחַלְתָּ לַאֲבוֹתֵינוּ אֶרֶץ חֶמְדָּה טוֹבָה וּרְחָבָה, וְעַל שֶׁהוֹצֵאתָנוּ ה' אֱלֹהֵינוּ מֵאֶרֶץ מִצְרַיִם, וּפְדִיתָנוּ מִבֵּית עֲבָדִים, וְעַל בְּרִיתְךָ שֶׁחָתַמְתָּ בִּבְשָׂרֵנוּ, וְעַל תּוֹרָתְךָ שֶׁלִּמַּדְתָּנוּ, וְעַל חֻקֶּיךָ שֶׁהוֹדַעְתָּנוּ, וְעַל חַיִּים חֵן וָחֶסֶד שֶׁחוֹנַנְתָּנוּ, וְעַל אֲכִילַת מָזוֹן שָׁאַתָּה זָן וּמְפַרְנֵס אוֹתָנוּ תָּמִיד, בְּכָל יוֹם וּבְכָל עֵת וּבְכָל שָׁעָה:

We thank you, Lord our God, that you have given as an inheritance to our ancestors a lovely, good and broad land, and that You took us out, Lord our God, from the land of Egypt and that You redeemed us from a house of slaves, and for Your covenant which You have sealed in our flesh, and for Your Torah that You have taught us, and for Your statutes which You have made known to us, and for life, grace and kindness that You have granted us and for the eating of nourishment that You feed and provide for us always, on all days, and at all times and in every hour.

וְעַל הַכֹּל ה' אֱלֹהֵינוּ, אֲנַחְנוּ מוֹדִים לָךְ וּמְבָרְכִים אוֹתָךְ, יִתְבָּרַךְ שִׁמְךָ בְּפִי כָּל חַי תָּמִיד לְעוֹלָם וָעֶד. כַּכָּתוּב: וְאָכַלְתָּ וְשָׂבָעְתָּ וּבֵרַכְתָּ אֶת ה' אֱלֹהֶיךָ עַל הָאָרֶץ הַטּוֹבָה אֲשֶׁר נָתַן לָךְ. בָּרוּךְ אַתָּה ה', עַל הָאָרֶץ וְעַל הַמָּזוֹן:

And for everything, Lord our God, we thank You and bless You; may Your name be blessed by the mouth of all life, constantly forever and always, as it is written (Deut 8:10); "And you shall eat and you shall be satiated and you shall bless the Lord your God for the good land that He has given you." Blessed are You, Lord, for the land and for the nourishment.

Third Benediction

רַחֵם נָא ה' אֱלֹהֵינוּ עַל יִשְׂרָאֵל עַמֶּךָ וְעַל יְרוּשָׁלַיִם עִירֶךָ וְעַל צִיּוֹן מִשְׁכַּן כְּבוֹדֶךָ וְעַל מַלְכוּת בֵּית דָּוִד מְשִׁיחֶךָ וְעַל הַבַּיִת הַגָּדוֹל וְהַקָּדוֹשׁ שֶׁנִּקְרָא שִׁמְךָ עָלָיו. אֱלֹהֵינוּ אָבִינוּ, רְעֵנוּ זוּנֵנוּ פַּרְנְסֵנוּ וְכַלְכְּלֵנוּ וְהַרְוִיחֵנוּ, וְהַרְוַח לָנוּ ה' אֱלֹהֵינוּ מְהֵרָה מִכָּל צָרוֹתֵינוּ. וְנָא אַל תַּצְרִיכֵנוּ ה' אֱלֹהֵינוּ, לֹא לִידֵי מַתְּנַת בָּשָׂר וָדָם וְלֹא לִידֵי הַלְוָאָתָם, כִּי אִם לְיָדְךָ הַמְּלֵאָה הַפְּתוּחָה הַקְּדוֹשָׁה וְהָרְחָבָה, שֶׁלֹּא נֵבוֹשׁ וְלֹא נִכָּלֵם לְעוֹלָם וָעֶד.

Please have mercy, Lord our God, upon Israel, Your people; and upon Jerusalem, Your city; and upon Zion, the dwelling place of Your Glory; and upon the monarchy of the House of David, Your appointed one; and upon the great and holy house that Your name is called upon. Our God, our Father, tend us, sustain us, provide for us, relieve us and give us quick relief, Lord our God, from all of our troubles. And please do not make us needy, Lord our God, not for the gifts of flesh and blood, and not for their loans, but rather from Your full, open, holy and broad hand, so that we not be embarrassed and we not be ashamed forever and always.

בשבת מוסיפין:
On Shabbat, we add the following paragraph:

רְצֵה וְהַחֲלִיצֵנוּ ה' אֱלֹהֵינוּ בְּמִצְוֹתֶיךָ וּבְמִצְוַת יוֹם הַשְּׁבִיעִי הַשַּׁבָּת הַגָּדוֹל וְהַקָּדוֹשׁ הַזֶּה. כִּי יוֹם זֶה גָּדוֹל וְקָדוֹשׁ הוּא לְפָנֶיךָ לִשְׁבָּת בּוֹ וְלָנוּחַ בּוֹ בְּאַהֲבָה כְּמִצְוַת רְצוֹנֶךָ. וּבִרְצוֹנְךָ הָנִיחַ לָנוּ ה' אֱלֹהֵינוּ שֶׁלֹּא תְהֵא צָרָה וְיָגוֹן וַאֲנָחָה. בְּיוֹם מְנוּחָתֵנוּ. וְהַרְאֵנוּ ה' אֱלֹהֵינוּ בְּנֶחָמַת צִיּוֹן עִירֶךָ וּבְבִנְיַן יְרוּשָׁלַיִם עִיר קָדְשֶׁךָ כִּי אַתָּה הוּא בַּעַל הַיְשׁוּעוֹת וּבַעַל הַנֶּחָמוֹת.

May You be pleased to embolden us, Lord our God, in your commandments and in the command of the seventh day, of this great and holy Shabbat, since this day is great and holy before You, to cease work upon it and to rest upon it, with love, according to the commandment of Your will. And with Your will, allow us, Lord our God, that we should not have trouble, and grief and sighing on the day of our rest. And may You show us, Lord our God, the consolation of Zion, Your city; and the building of Jerusalem, Your holy city; since You are the Master of salvations and the Master of consolations.

אֱלֹהֵינוּ וֵאלֹהֵי אֲבוֹתֵינוּ, יַעֲלֶה וְיָבֹא וְיַגִּיעַ וְיֵרָאֶה וְיֵרָצֶה וְיִשָּׁמַע וְיִפָּקֵד וְיִזָּכֵר זִכְרוֹנֵנוּ וּפִקְדוֹנֵנוּ, וְזִכְרוֹן אֲבוֹתֵינוּ, וְזִכְרוֹן מָשִׁיחַ בֶּן דָּוִד עַבְדֶּךָ, וְזִכְרוֹן יְרוּשָׁלַיִם עִיר קָדְשֶׁךָ, וְזִכְרוֹן כָּל עַמְּךָ בֵּית יִשְׂרָאֵל לְפָנֶיךָ, לִפְלֵיטָה לְטוֹבָה לְחֵן וּלְחֶסֶד וּלְרַחֲמִים, לְחַיִּים וּלְשָׁלוֹם בְּיוֹם חַג הַמַּצּוֹת הַזֶּה זָכְרֵנוּ ה' אֱלֹהֵינוּ בּוֹ לְטוֹבָה וּפָקְדֵנוּ בוֹ לִבְרָכָה וְהוֹשִׁיעֵנוּ בוֹ לְחַיִּים. וּבִדְבַר יְשׁוּעָה וְרַחֲמִים חוּס וְחָנֵּנוּ וְרַחֵם עָלֵינוּ וְהוֹשִׁיעֵנוּ, כִּי אֵלֶיךָ עֵינֵינוּ, כִּי אֵל מֶלֶךְ חַנּוּן וְרַחוּם אָתָּה. וּבְנֵה יְרוּשָׁלַיִם עִיר הַקֹּדֶשׁ בִּמְהֵרָה בְיָמֵינוּ. בָּרוּךְ אַתָּה ה', בּוֹנֵה בְרַחֲמָיו יְרוּשָׁלָיִם. אָמֵן.

God and God of our ancestors, may there ascend and come and reach and be seen and be acceptable and be heard and be recalled and be remembered— our remembrance and our recollection; and the remembrance of our ancestors; and the remembrance of the messiah, the son of David, Your servant; and the remembrance of Jerusalem, Your holy city; and the remembrance of all Your people, the house of Israel—in front of You, for survival, for good, for grace, and for kindness, and for mercy, for life and for peace on this day of the Festival of *Matsot*. Remember us, Lord our God, on it for good and recall us on it for survival and save us on it for life, and by the word of salvation and mercy, pity and grace us and have mercy on us and save us, since our eyes are upon You, since You are a graceful and merciful Power. And may You build Jerusalem, the holy city, quickly and in our days. Blessed are You, Lord, who builds Jerusalem in His mercy. Amen.

Fourth Benediction

בָּרוּךְ אַתָּה ה', אֱלֹהֵינוּ מֶלֶךְ הָעוֹלָם, הָאֵל אָבִינוּ מַלְכֵּנוּ אַדִּירֵנוּ בּוֹרְאֵנוּ גּוֹאֲלֵנוּ יוֹצְרֵנוּ קְדוֹשֵׁנוּ קְדוֹשׁ יַעֲקֹב רוֹעֵנוּ רוֹעֵה יִשְׂרָאֵל הַמֶּלֶךְ הַטּוֹב וְהַמֵּטִיב לַכֹּל שֶׁבְּכָל יוֹם וָיוֹם הוּא הֵטִיב, הוּא מֵטִיב, הוּא יֵיטִיב לָנוּ. הוּא גְמָלָנוּ הוּא גוֹמְלֵנוּ הוּא יִגְמְלֵנוּ לָעַד, לְחֵן וּלְחֶסֶד וּלְרַחֲמִים וּלְרֶוַח הַצָּלָה וְהַצְלָחָה, בְּרָכָה וִישׁוּעָה נֶחָמָה פַּרְנָסָה וְכַלְכָּלָה וְרַחֲמִים וְחַיִּים וְשָׁלוֹם וְכָל טוֹב, וּמִכָּל טוּב לְעוֹלָם עַל יְחַסְּרֵנוּ.

Blessed are You, Lord our God, King of the Universe, the Power, our Father, our King, our Mighty One, our Creator, our Redeemer, our Shaper, our Holy One, the Holy One of Ya'akov, our Shepard, the Shepard of Israel, the good King, who does good to all, since on every single day He has done good, He does good, He will do good, to us; He has granted us, He grants us, He will grant us forever—in grace and in kindness, and in mercy, and in relief—rescue and success, blessing and salvation, consolation, provision and relief and mercy and life and peace and all good; and may we not lack any good ever.

Additional Supplications

הָרַחֲמָן הוּא יִמְלוֹךְ עָלֵינוּ לְעוֹלָם וָעֶד. הָרַחֲמָן הוּא יִתְבָּרַךְ בַּשָּׁמַיִם וּבָאָרֶץ. הָרַחֲמָן הוּא יִשְׁתַּבַּח לְדוֹר דּוֹרִים, וְיִתְפָּאַר בָּנוּ לָעַד וּלְנֵצַח נְצָחִים, וְיִתְהַדַּר בָּנוּ לָעַד וּלְעוֹלְמֵי עוֹלָמִים. הָרַחֲמָן הוּא יְפַרְנְסֵנוּ בְּכָבוֹד. הָרַחֲמָן הוּא יִשְׁבּוֹר עֻלֵּנוּ מֵעַל צַוָּארֵנוּ, וְהוּא יוֹלִיכֵנוּ קוֹמְמִיּוּת לְאַרְצֵנוּ. הָרַחֲמָן הוּא יִשְׁלַח לָנוּ בְּרָכָה מְרֻבָּה בַּבַּיִת הַזֶּה, וְעַל שֻׁלְחָן זֶה שֶׁאָכַלְנוּ עָלָיו. הָרַחֲמָן הוּא יִשְׁלַח לָנוּ אֶת אֵלִיָּהוּ הַנָּבִיא זָכוּר לַטּוֹב, וִיבַשֶּׂר לָנוּ בְּשׂוֹרוֹת טוֹבוֹת יְשׁוּעוֹת וְנֶחָמוֹת. הָרַחֲמָן הוּא יְבָרֵךְ אֶת בַּעְלִי / אִשְׁתִּי. הָרַחֲמָן הוּא יְבָרֵךְ אֶת [אָבִי מוֹרִי] בַּעַל הַבַּיִת הַזֶּה. וְאֶת [אִמִּי מוֹרָתִי] בַּעֲלַת הַבַּיִת הַזֶּה, אוֹתָם וְאֶת בֵּיתָם וְאֶת זַרְעָם וְאֶת כָּל אֲשֶׁר לָהֶם. אוֹתָנוּ וְאֶת כָּל אֲשֶׁר לָנוּ, כְּמוֹ שֶׁנִּתְבָּרְכוּ אֲבוֹתֵינוּ אַבְרָהָם יִצְחָק וְיַעֲקֹב בַּכֹּל מִכֹּל כֹּל, כֵּן יְבָרֵךְ אוֹתָנוּ כֻּלָּנוּ יַחַד בִּבְרָכָה שְׁלֵמָה, וְנֹאמַר, אָמֵן. בַּמָּרוֹם יְלַמְּדוּ עֲלֵיהֶם וְעָלֵינוּ זְכוּת שֶׁתְּהֵא לְמִשְׁמֶרֶת שָׁלוֹם. וְנִשָּׂא בְרָכָה מֵאֵת ה', וּצְדָקָה מֵאֱלֹהֵי יִשְׁעֵנוּ, וְנִמְצָא חֵן וְשֵׂכֶל טוֹב בְּעֵינֵי אֱלֹהִים וְאָדָם. בשבת: הָרַחֲמָן הוּא יַנְחִילֵנוּ יוֹם שֶׁכֻּלּוֹ שַׁבָּת וּמְנוּחָה לְחַיֵּי הָעוֹלָמִים. הָרַחֲמָן הוּא יַנְחִילֵנוּ יוֹם שֶׁכֻּלּוֹ טוֹב.[יוֹם שֶׁכֻּלּוֹ אָרוּךְ. יוֹם שֶׁצַּדִּיקִים יוֹשְׁבִים וְעַטְרוֹתֵיהֶם בְּרָאשֵׁיהֶם וְנֶהֱנִים מִזִּיו הַשְּׁכִינָה וִיהִי חֶלְקֵנוּ עִמָּהֶם]. הָרַחֲמָן הוּא יְזַכֵּנוּ לִימוֹת הַמָּשִׁיחַ וּלְחַיֵּי הָעוֹלָם הַבָּא. מִגְדּוֹל יְשׁוּעוֹת מַלְכּוֹ וְעֹשֶׂה חֶסֶד לִמְשִׁיחוֹ לְדָוִד וּלְזַרְעוֹ עַד עוֹלָם. עֹשֶׂה שָׁלוֹם בִּמְרוֹמָיו, הוּא יַעֲשֶׂה שָׁלוֹם עָלֵינוּ וְעַל כָּל יִשְׂרָאֵל וְאִמְרוּ, אָמֵן. יְראוּ אֶת ה' קְדֹשָׁיו, כִּי אֵין מַחְסוֹר לִירֵאָיו. כְּפִירִים רָשׁוּ וְרָעֵבוּ, וְדֹרְשֵׁי ה' לֹא יַחְסְרוּ כָל טוֹב. הוֹדוּ לַיי כִּי טוֹב כִּי לְעוֹלָם חַסְדּוֹ. פּוֹתֵחַ אֶת יָדֶךָ, וּמַשְׂבִּיעַ לְכָל חַי רָצוֹן. בָּרוּךְ הַגֶּבֶר אֲשֶׁר יִבְטַח בַּיי, וְהָיָה ה' מִבְטַחוֹ. נַעַר הָיִיתִי גַם זָקַנְתִּי, וְלֹא רָאִיתִי צַדִּיק נֶעֱזָב, וְזַרְעוֹ מְבַקֶּשׁ לָחֶם. יי עֹז לְעַמּוֹ יִתֵּן, ה' יְבָרֵךְ אֶת עַמּוֹ בַשָּׁלוֹם.

May the Merciful One reign over us forever and always. May the Merciful One be blessed in the heavens and in the earth. May the Merciful One be praised for all generations, and exalted among us forever and ever, and glorified among us always and infinitely for all infinities. May the Merciful One sustain us honorably. May the Merciful One break our yolk from upon our necks and bring us upright to our land. May the Merciful One send us multiple blessing, to this home and upon this table upon which we have eaten. May the Merciful One send us Eliyahu the prophet—may he be remembered for good—and he shall announce to us tidings of good, of salvation and of consolation. May the Merciful One bless my husband/my wife. May the Merciful One bless [my father, my teacher,] the master of this home and [my mother, my teacher,] the mistress of this home, they and their home and their offspring and everything that is theirs. Us and all that is ours; as were blessed Avraham, Yitschak and Ya'akov, in everything, from everything, with everything, so too should He bless us, all of us together, with a complete blessing and we shall say, Amen. From above, may they advocate upon them and upon us merit, that should protect us in peace; and may we carry a blessing from the Lord and charity from the God of our salvation; and find grace and good understanding in the eyes of God and man. [On Shabbat, we say: May the Merciful One give us to inherit the day that will be completely Shabbat and rest in everlasting life.] May the Merciful One give us to inherit the day that will be all good. [The day that is all long, the day that the righteous will sit and their crowns will be on their heads and they will enjoy the radiance of the Divine presence and my our share be with them.] May the Merciful One give us merit for the times of the messiah and for life in the world to come. A tower of salvations is our King; may He do kindness with his messiah, with David and his offspring, forever (II Sam 22:51). The One who makes peace above, may He make peace upon us and upon all of Israel; and say, Amen. Fear the Lord, His holy ones, since there is no lacking for those that fear Him. Young lions may go without and hunger, but those that seek the Lord will not lack any good thing (Ps 34:10–11). Thank the Lord, since He is good, since His kindness is forever (Ps 118:1). You open Your hand and satisfy the will of all living things (Ps 146:16). Blessed is the man that trusts in the Lord and the Lord is his security (Jer 17:7). I was a youth and I have also aged and I have not seen a righteous man forsaken and his offspring seeking bread (Ps 37:25). The Lord will give courage to His people. The Lord will bless His people with peace (Ps 29:11).

Barech, Third Cup of Wine

בָּרוּךְ אַתָּה ה', אֱלֹהֵינוּ מֶלֶךְ הָעוֹלָם בּוֹרֵא פְּרִי הַגָּפֶן.

Blessed are You, Lord our God, King of the universe, who creates the fruit of the vine.

ושותים בהסיבה ואינו מברך ברכה אחרונה.

We drink while reclining and do not say a blessing afterwards.

At the conclusion of the grace after meals, the third cup is drunk. It is often said to signify the splitting of the sea, after which the Israelites no longer had need to fear the Egyptians. Following the order of the four verbs in Exod 2:6–7, we find, *after* "I will bring you out" (וְהוֹצֵאתִי): "I will save you" (וְהִצַּלְתִּי), "I will redeem you" (וְגָאַלְתִּי), and "I will take you" (וְלָקַחְתִּי). It would appear that the second cup would correspond to "I will save you" (וְהִצַּלְתִּי); yet the Haggadah, with the blessing "... who redeemed Israel (גָּאַל יִשְׂרָאֵל)," links it with "I will redeem you" (וְגָאַלְתִּי), which we would otherwise expect to be identified with the third cup. Either we have two cups expressing "redemption" (גְאֻלָה), or we should reverse the order of the biblical verse and consider the third cup in the context of "I will save you" (וְהִצַּלְתִּי). In rabbinic commentary (Maarechet Heidenheim on *Pesach* Haggadah, Magid, Four Questions 1:1), we find the following:

- I will save you—from the wilderness. The Israelites might also be fearful that God would bring the people into the dangerous wilderness where they would face many difficult tasks. Since the wilderness is not a place where things grow, they would have to work very hard to find food. God reassured them by saying, "I will save you" implies from the wilderness, as in Psalm 107. Even if sin made it necessary to remain in the wilderness for an extended period, God reassured them by saying it will not be necessary for you to do hard labor. God rained down bread from heaven, quail to eat each day during the desert sojourn as well as ample water from a well.

- I will redeem you—Having reassured the people that he would protect them both at the sea and in the wilderness, the people might become anxious that Pharaoh would not let them leave at all; that he would give them freedom but keep them in Egypt. Therefore, God made a third promise: "I will redeem you with an outstretched arm and with extraordinary judgments." This was a reassurance that God would pass judgment on the Egyptians and their gods while they were in Egypt.
—Kenneth Hanson

Fig. 13 Gustave Doré (1866), "The Egyptians Ask Moses to Depart"

Barech, Pour Out Thy Wrath

מוזגים כוס של אליהו ופותחים את הדלת:

We pour the cup of Eliyahu and open the door.

שְׁפֹךְ חֲמָתְךָ אֶל־הַגּוֹיִם אֲשֶׁר לֹא יְדָעוּךָ וְעַל־מַמְלָכוֹת אֲשֶׁר בְּשִׁמְךָ לֹא קָרָאוּ. כִּי אָכַל אֶת־יַעֲקֹב וְאֶת־נָוֵהוּ הֵשַׁמּוּ. שְׁפָךְ־עֲלֵיהֶם זַעְמֶךָ וַחֲרוֹן אַפְּךָ יַשִּׂיגֵם. תִּרְדֹּף בְּאַף וְתַשְׁמִידֵם מִתַּחַת שְׁמֵי ה'.

Pour your wrath upon the nations that did not know You and upon the kingdoms that did not call upon Your Name! Since they have consumed Ya'akov and laid waste his habitation (Ps 79:6–7). Pour out Your fury upon them and the fierceness of Your anger shall reach them (Ps 69:25)! You shall pursue them with anger and eradicate them from under the skies of the Lord (Lam 3:66).

Certain rabbinic sources suggested the presence of a fifth cup, poured prior to the obligatory fourth and now understood as Elijah's cup. This may be based on an additional verb in Exod 6:7: "...*who brought you out* (הַמּוֹצִיא) from under the burdens of the Egyptians." According to this reading of the passage, this potential fifth cup may be seen as memorializing the Exodus itself (in contrast to the first cup, which celebrates the release from suffering under the Egyptians). We read (Rif Pesaḥim, by Isaac ben Jacob Alfasi ha-Cohen, c. 1085 C.E. – c. 1105 C.E., 26b:1): "On the fifth cup [of wine] one recites the great Hallel. This is the opinion of Rabbi Tarfon." We also read (Rosh on Pesaḥim, by Rabbi Asher ben Yechiel, c. 1275 C.E. – c. 1325 C.E., 10:33:1): "Our rabbis learned, 'We say the Great Hallel over a fifth cup—these are the words of Rabbi Tarfon, and there are those that say, "The Lord is my shepherd, I shall not lack" (Psalms 23).'" Rambam characteristically adopt a moderate approach, suggesting that a fifth cup should be poured but not consumed (Mishneh Torah, "Leavened and Unleavened Bread," 8:10):

> And he should mix (pour) a fifth cup and say upon it the Great Hallel (Psalms 136), from "Give thanks to the Lord, for He is good" (Ps 136:1) to "Upon the waters of Babylon" (Ps 137:1). And this cup is not obligatory like the [other] four cups. And he can finish the Hallel any place that he desires, even though he is not in the place of the meal.

In light of the justification for its presence, a fifth cup is occasionally, though rarely consumed. This is perhaps because it may also be seen to signify the arrival and dwelling of Israel in the Land of Promise, a hope which has been only partially fulfilled. An effort was actually undertaken, after the creation of the modern Jewish state in 1948, to convince the Israeli rabbinate to add a fifth cup, but it was never adopted. To this day its presence at the seder table remains, like the return of all Jews from the diaspora, an unfulfilled option.

—Kenneth Hanson

Excursus

Kenneth Hanson

The Image of Elijah

The most illustrious of the early brand of Israelite prophets is doubtless Elijah, around whom an entire folklore was destined to arise. Together with Samuel and Nathan, Elijah forms a trifecta of early prophets who firmly establish that God is, in the words of Abraham Joshua Heschel, "no patron of kings." It is Elijah who confronts the despotic King Ahab over his monarchal tyranny, for having effectively pilfered the property of a simple vinedresser named Naboth. It is Elijah who, while the land is in the grip of a terrible drought, wanders through the hills, bedecked in a hairy mantle and loincloth, to bemoan the mounting disloyalty to Israel's deity. In a direct challenge to the Baal worship imported into the land by Queen Jezebel, the prophet summons Ahab and all the people to the summit of Mt. Carmel, where a great contest demonstrates, once and for all, who is God and who is not. The prophet must ultimately flee for his life to a cave on "Horeb the mount of God" (1 Kgs 19:8, clearly recalling Mt. Sinai and the Exodus), to hide himself from Ahab's wrath. There on the holy mountain, several "special effects" manifest themselves—a mighty wind, an earthquake, a fire—but God is in none of them.

Finally, a gentle breeze blows. This is how the prophet meets his God, in the paradoxical expression of a "still small voice" (1 Kgs 19:12), as it were, a voiced silence. Elijah is subsequently taken up into heaven on a chariot of fire but will return one day to usher in the "anointed one"—the Messiah. This tradition is developed by the last of Israel's prophets, Malachi, who declares: "Behold, I will send you Elijah the prophet before the coming of the great and dreadful day of the Lord. And he will turn the hearts of the fathers to the children, And the hearts of the children to their fathers, lest I come and strike the earth with a curse" (Mal 3:23–24). In summoning the image of Elijah, Malachi simultaneously looks backward to the pre-classical prophetic era and forward to a glorious messianic future age. Therefore, an empty chair is set for the prophet, and why the door is opened, to see whether he may have come to this home on this night.

Bibliography

Abraham Joshua Heschel, *The Prophets* (New York: Harper & Row, 1962), 524.
Karen Armstrong, *A History of God: The 4,000 Year Quest of Judaism, Christianity and Islam* (New York: Ballantine, 1993), 26–7.

Annotated Haggadah for Passover
-continued-

Hallel, Second Half of Hallel (Pss 115–118) הַלֵּל

מוזגין כוס רביעי וגומרין עליו את ההלל

We pour the fourth cup and complete the Hallel

לֹא לָנוּ, ה', לֹא לָנוּ, כִּי לְשִׁמְךָ תֵּן כָּבוֹד, עַל חַסְדְּךָ עַל אֲמִתֶּךָ. לָמָּה יֹאמְרוּ הַגּוֹיִם אַיֵּה נָא אֱלֹהֵיהֶם. וֵאלֹהֵינוּ בַשָּׁמַיִם, כֹּל אֲשֶׁר חָפֵץ עָשָׂה. עֲצַבֵּיהֶם כֶּסֶף וְזָהָב מַעֲשֵׂה יְדֵי אָדָם. פֶּה לָהֶם וְלֹא יְדַבֵּרוּ, עֵינַיִם לָהֶם וְלֹא יִרְאוּ. אָזְנַיִם לָהֶם וְלֹא יִשְׁמָעוּ, אַף לָהֶם וְלֹא יְרִיחוּן. יְדֵיהֶם וְלֹא יְמִישׁוּן, רַגְלֵיהֶם וְלֹא יְהַלֵּכוּ, לֹא יֶהְגּוּ בִּגְרוֹנָם. כְּמוֹהֶם יִהְיוּ עֹשֵׂיהֶם, כֹּל אֲשֶׁר בֹּטֵחַ בָּהֶם. יִשְׂרָאֵל בְּטַח בַּיְיָ, עֶזְרָם וּמָגִנָּם הוּא. בֵּית אַהֲרֹן בִּטְחוּ בַיְיָ, עֶזְרָם וּמָגִנָּם הוּא. יִרְאֵי ה' בִּטְחוּ בַיְיָ, עֶזְרָם וּמָגִנָּם הוּא. יְיָ זְכָרָנוּ יְבָרֵךְ. יְבָרֵךְ אֶת בֵּית יִשְׂרָאֵל, יְבָרֵךְ אֶת בֵּית אַהֲרֹן, יְבָרֵךְ יִרְאֵי ה', הַקְּטַנִּים עִם הַגְּדוֹלִים. יֹסֵף ה' עֲלֵיכֶם, עֲלֵיכֶם וְעַל בְּנֵיכֶם. בְּרוּכִים אַתֶּם לַיְיָ, עֹשֵׂה שָׁמַיִם וָאָרֶץ. הַשָּׁמַיִם שָׁמַיִם לַיְיָ וְהָאָרֶץ נָתַן לִבְנֵי אָדָם. לֹא הַמֵּתִים יְהַלְלוּ יָהּ וְלֹא כָּל יֹרְדֵי דוּמָה. וַאֲנַחְנוּ נְבָרֵךְ יָהּ מֵעַתָּה וְעַד עוֹלָם. הַלְלוּיָהּ.

Not to us, not to us, but rather to Your name, give glory for your kindness and for your truth. Why should the nations say, "Say, where is their God?" But our God is in the heavens, all that He wanted, He has done. Their idols are silver and gold, the work of men's hands. They have a mouth but do not speak; they have eyes but do not see. They have ears but do not hear; they have a nose but do not smell. Hands, but they do not feel; feet, but do not walk; they do not make a peep from their throat. Like them will be their makers, all those that trust in them. Israel, trust in the Lord; their help and shield is He. House of Aharon, trust in the Lord; their help and shield is He. Those that fear the Lord, trust in the Lord; their help and shield is He. The Lord who remembers us, will bless; He will bless the House of Israel; He will bless the House of Aharon. He will bless those that fear the Lord, the small ones with the great ones. May the Lord bring increase to you, to you and to your children. Blessed are you to the Lord, the maker of the heavens and the earth. The heavens, are the Lord's heavens, but the earth He has given to the children of man. It is not the dead that will praise the Lord, and not those that go down to silence. But we will bless the Lord from now and forever. Halleluyah! (Psalms 115)

אָהַבְתִּי כִּי יִשְׁמַע ה' אֶת קוֹלִי תַּחֲנוּנָי. כִּי הִטָּה אָזְנוֹ לִי וּבְיָמַי אֶקְרָא. אֲפָפוּנִי חֶבְלֵי מָוֶת וּמְצָרֵי שְׁאוֹל מְצָאוּנִי, צָרָה וְיָגוֹן אֶמְצָא. וּבְשֵׁם ה' אֶקְרָא: אָנָּא ה' מַלְּטָה נַפְשִׁי. חַנּוּן ה' וְצַדִּיק, וֵאלֹהֵינוּ מְרַחֵם. שֹׁמֵר פְּתָאיִם ה', דַּלּוֹתִי וְלִי יְהוֹשִׁיעַ. שׁוּבִי נַפְשִׁי לִמְנוּחָיְכִי, כִּי ה' גָּמַל עָלָיְכִי. כִּי חִלַּצְתָּ נַפְשִׁי מִמָּוֶת, אֶת עֵינִי מִן דִּמְעָה, אֶת רַגְלִי מִדֶּחִי. אֶתְהַלֵּךְ לִפְנֵי ה' בְּאַרְצוֹת הַחַיִּים. הֶאֱמַנְתִּי כִּי אֲדַבֵּר, אֲנִי עָנִיתִי מְאֹד. אֲנִי אָמַרְתִּי בְחָפְזִי כָּל הָאָדָם כֹּזֵב.

I have loved the Lord—since He hears my voice, my supplications. Since He inclined His ear to me—and in my days, I will call out. The pangs of death have encircled me and the straits of the Pit have found me and I found grief. And in the name of the Lord I called, "Please Lord, Spare my soul." Gracious is the Lord and righteous, and our God acts mercifully. The Lord watches over the silly; I was poor and He has saved me. Return, my soul to your tranquility, since the Lord has favored you. Since You have rescued my soul from death, my eyes from tears, my feet from stumbling. I will walk before the Lord in the lands of the living. I have trusted, when I speak—I am very afflicted. I said in my haste, all men are hypocritical. (Psalms 116:1–11)

מָה אָשִׁיב לַיי כֹּל תַּגְמוּלוֹהִי עָלָי. כּוֹס יְשׁוּעוֹת אֶשָּׂא וּבְשֵׁם ה' אֶקְרָא. נְדָרַי לַיי אֲשַׁלֵּם נֶגְדָה נָּא לְכָל עַמּוֹ. יָקָר בְּעֵינֵי ה' הַמָּוְתָה לַחֲסִידָיו. אָנָּה ה' כִּי אֲנִי עַבְדֶּךָ, אֲנִי עַבְדְּךָ בֶּן אֲמָתֶךָ, פִּתַּחְתָּ לְמוֹסֵרָי. לְךָ אֶזְבַּח זֶבַח תּוֹדָה וּבְשֵׁם ה' אֶקְרָא. נְדָרַי לַיי אֲשַׁלֵּם נֶגְדָה נָּא לְכָל עַמּוֹ. בְּחַצְרוֹת בֵּית ה', בְּתוֹכֵכִי יְרוּשָׁלָיִם. הַלְלוּיָהּ.

What can I give back to the Lord for all that He has favored me? A cup of salvations I will raise up and I will call out in the name of the Lord. My vows to the Lord I will pay, now in front of His entire people. Precious in the eyes of the Lord is the death of His pious ones. Please Lord, since I am Your servant, the son of Your maidservant; You have opened my chains. To You will I offer a thanksgiving offering and I will call out in the name of the Lord. My vows to the Lord I will pay, now in front of His entire people. In the courtyards of the house of the Lord, in your midst, Jerusalem. Halleluyah! (Psalms 116:12–19)

הַלְלוּ אֶת ה' כָּל גּוֹיִם, שַׁבְּחוּהוּ כָּל הָאֻמִּים. כִּי גָבַר עָלֵינוּ חַסְדּוֹ, וֶאֱמֶת ה' לְעוֹלָם. הַלְלוּיָהּ. הוֹדוּ לַיי כִּי טוֹב כִּי לְעוֹלָם חַסְדּוֹ. יֹאמַר נָא יִשְׂרָאֵל כִּי לְעוֹלָם חַסְדּוֹ. יֹאמְרוּ נָא בֵית אַהֲרֹן כִּי לְעוֹלָם חַסְדּוֹ. יֹאמְרוּ נָא יִרְאֵי ה' כִּי לְעוֹלָם חַסְדּוֹ.

Praise the name of the Lord, all nations; extol Him all peoples. Since His kindness has overwhelmed us and the truth of the Lord is forever. Halleluyah! Thank the Lord, since He is good, since His kindness is forever. Let Israel now say, "Thank the Lord, since He is good, since His kindness is forever." Let the House of Aharon now say, "Thank the Lord, since He is good, since His kindness is forever." Let those that fear the Lord now say,

"Thank the Lord, since He is good, since His kindness is forever." (Psalms 117–118:4)

מִן הַמֵּצַר קָרָאתִי יָּהּ, עָנָנִי בַמֶּרְחַב יָהּ. ה' לִי, לֹא אִירָא – מַה יַּעֲשֶׂה לִי אָדָם, ה' לִי בְּעֹזְרָי וַאֲנִי אֶרְאֶה בְשֹׂנְאָי. טוֹב לַחֲסוֹת בַּיי מִבְּטֹחַ בָּאָדָם. טוֹב לַחֲסוֹת בַּיי מִבְּטֹחַ בִּנְדִיבִים. כָּל גּוֹיִם סְבָבוּנִי, בְּשֵׁם ה' כִּי אֲמִילַם. סַבּוּנִי גַם סְבָבוּנִי, בְּשֵׁם ה' כִּי אֲמִילַם. סַבּוּנִי כִדְבֹרִים, דֹּעֲכוּ כְּאֵשׁ קוֹצִים, בְּשֵׁם ה' כִּי אֲמִילַם. דָּחֹה דְחִיתַנִי לִנְפֹּל, וַיי עֲזָרָנִי. עָזִּי וְזִמְרָת יָהּ וַיְהִי לִי לִישׁוּעָה. קוֹל רִנָּה וִישׁוּעָה בְּאָהֳלֵי צַדִּיקִים: יְמִין ה' עֹשָׂה חָיִל, יְמִין ה' רוֹמֵמָה, יְמִין ה' עֹשָׂה חָיִל. לֹא אָמוּת כִּי אֶחְיֶה, וַאֲסַפֵּר מַעֲשֵׂי יָהּ. יַסֹּר יִסְּרַנִּי יָּהּ, וְלַמָּוֶת לֹא נְתָנָנִי. פִּתְחוּ לִי שַׁעֲרֵי צֶדֶק, אָבֹא בָם, אוֹדֶה יָהּ. זֶה הַשַּׁעַר לַיי, צַדִּיקִים יָבֹאוּ בוֹ.

From the strait I have called, Lord; He answered me from the wide space, the Lord. The Lord is for me, I will not fear, what will man do to me? The Lord is for me with my helpers, and I shall glare at those that hate me. It is better to take refuge with the Lord than to trust in man. It is better to take refuge with the Lord than to trust in nobles. All the nations surrounded me—in the name of the Lord, as I will chop them off. They surrounded me, they also encircled me—in the name of the Lord, as I will chop them off. They surrounded me like bees, they were extinguished like a fire of thorns—in the name of the Lord, as I will chop them off. You have surely pushed me to fall, but the Lord helped me. My boldness and song is the Lord, and He has become my salvation. The sound of happy song and salvation is in the tents of the righteous, the right hand of the Lord acts powerfully. I will not die but rather I will live and tell over the acts of the Lord. The Lord has surely chastised me, but He has not given me over to death. Open up for me the gates of righteousness; I will enter them, thank the Lord. This is the gate of the Lord, the righteous will enter it. (Psalms 118:5–20)

The following four verses are repeated:

אוֹדְךָ כִּי עֲנִיתָנִי וַתְּהִי לִי לִישׁוּעָה. אוֹדְךָ כִּי עֲנִיתָנִי וַתְּהִי לִי לִישׁוּעָה. אֶבֶן מָאֲסוּ הַבּוֹנִים הָיְתָה לְרֹאשׁ פִּנָּה. אֶבֶן מָאֲסוּ הַבּוֹנִים הָיְתָה לְרֹאשׁ פִּנָּה. מֵאֵת ה' הָיְתָה זֹּאת הִיא נִפְלָאת בְּעֵינֵינוּ. מֵאֵת ה' הָיְתָה זֹּאת הִיא נִפְלָאת בְּעֵינֵינוּ. זֶה הַיּוֹם עָשָׂה ה'. נָגִילָה וְנִשְׂמְחָה בוֹ. זֶה הַיּוֹם עָשָׂה ה'. נָגִילָה וְנִשְׂמְחָה בוֹ.

I will thank You, since You answered me and You have become my salvation. The stone that was left by the builders has become the main cornerstone. From the Lord was this, it is wondrous in our eyes. This is the day of the Lord, let us exult and rejoice upon it. (Psalms 118:21–24)

The following verses are repeated:

אָנָּא ה', הוֹשִׁיעָה נָּא. אָנָּא ה', הוֹשִׁיעָה נָּא. אָנָּא ה', הַצְלִיחָה נָא. אָנָּא ה', הַצְלִיחָה נָא.

Please, Lord, save us now; please, Lord, give us success now! (Psalms 118:25)

בָּרוּךְ הַבָּא בְּשֵׁם ה', בֵּרַכְנוּכֶם מִבֵּית ה'. בָּרוּךְ הַבָּא בְּשֵׁם ה', בֵּרַכְנוּכֶם מִבֵּית ה'. אֵל ה' וַיָּאֶר לָנוּ. אִסְרוּ חַג בַּעֲבֹתִים עַד קַרְנוֹת הַמִּזְבֵּחַ. אֵל ה' וַיָּאֶר לָנוּ. אִסְרוּ חַג בַּעֲבֹתִים עַד קַרְנוֹת הַמִּזְבֵּחַ. אֵלִי אַתָּה וְאוֹדֶךָּ, אֱלֹהַי – אֲרוֹמְמֶךָּ. אֵלִי אַתָּה וְאוֹדֶךָּ, אֱלֹהַי – אֲרוֹמְמֶךָּ. הוֹדוּ לַיי כִּי טוֹב, כִּי לְעוֹלָם חַסְדּוֹ. הוֹדוּ לַיי כִּי טוֹב, כִּי לְעוֹלָם חַסְדּוֹ.

Blessed be the one who comes in the name of the Lord, we have blessed you from the house of the Lord. God is the Lord, and He has illuminated us; tie up the festival offering with ropes until it reaches the corners of the altar. You are my Power and I will Thank You; my God and I will exalt You. Thank the Lord, since He is good, since His kindness is forever. (Psalms 118:26–29)

יְהַלְלוּךָ ה' אֱלֹהֵינוּ כָּל מַעֲשֶׂיךָ, וַחֲסִידֶיךָ צַדִּיקִים עוֹשֵׂי רְצוֹנֶךָ, וְכָל עַמְּךָ בֵּית יִשְׂרָאֵל בְּרִנָּה יוֹדוּ וִיבָרְכוּ, וִישַׁבְּחוּ וִיפָאֲרוּ, וִירוֹמְמוּ וְיַעֲרִיצוּ, וְיַקְדִּישׁוּ וְיַמְלִיכוּ אֶת שִׁמְךָ, מַלְכֵּנוּ. כִּי לְךָ טוֹב לְהוֹדוֹת וּלְשִׁמְךָ נָאֶה לְזַמֵּר, כִּי מֵעוֹלָם וְעַד עוֹלָם אַתָּה אֵל.

All of your works shall praise You, Lord our God, and your pious ones, the righteous ones who do Your will; and all of Your people, the House of Israel will thank and bless in joyful song: and extol and glorify, and exalt and acclaim, and sanctify and coronate Your name, our King. Since, You it is good to thank, and to Your name it is pleasant to sing, since from always and forever are you the Power.

---

m. Pesaḥ 10.7 reports that over the fourth cup of wine one completes the Hallel and says after it the Benediction over song. "All of your works" and "The breath of every living thing," chanted later, are examples.

—Zev Garber

Hallel, Songs of Praise and Thanks

הוֹדוּ לַיי כִּי טוֹב כִּי לְעוֹלָם חַסְדּוֹ. הוֹדוּ לֵאלֹהֵי הָאֱלֹהִים כִּי לְעוֹלָם חַסְדּוֹ. הוֹדוּ לַאֲדֹנֵי הָאֲדֹנִים כִּי לְעוֹלָם חַסְדּוֹ. לְעֹשֵׂה נִפְלָאוֹת גְּדֹלוֹת לְבַדּוֹ כִּי לְעוֹלָם חַסְדּוֹ. לְעֹשֵׂה הַשָּׁמַיִם בִּתְבוּנָה כִּי לְעוֹלָם חַסְדּוֹ. לְרוֹקַע הָאָרֶץ עַל הַמָּיִם כִּי לְעוֹלָם חַסְדּוֹ. לְעֹשֵׂה אוֹרִים גְּדֹלִים כִּי לְעוֹלָם חַסְדּוֹ. אֶת הַשֶּׁמֶשׁ לְמֶמְשֶׁלֶת בַּיּוֹם כִּי לְעוֹלָם חַסְדּוֹ. אֶת הַיָּרֵחַ וְכוֹכָבִים לְמֶמְשְׁלוֹת בַּלַּיְלָה כִּי לְעוֹלָם חַסְדּוֹ. לְמַכֵּה מִצְרַיִם בִּבְכוֹרֵיהֶם כִּי לְעוֹלָם חַסְדּוֹ. וַיּוֹצֵא יִשְׂרָאֵל מִתּוֹכָם כִּי לְעוֹלָם חַסְדּוֹ. בְּיָד חֲזָקָה וּבִזְרוֹעַ

נְטוּיָה כִּי לְעוֹלָם חַסְדּוֹ. לְגֹזֵר יַם סוּף לִגְזָרִים כִּי לְעוֹלָם חַסְדּוֹ. וְהֶעֱבִיר יִשְׂרָאֵל בְּתוֹכוֹ כִּי לְעוֹלָם חַסְדּוֹ. וְנִעֵר פַּרְעֹה וְחֵילוֹ בְיַם סוּף כִּי לְעוֹלָם חַסְדּוֹ. לְמוֹלִיךְ עַמּוֹ בַּמִּדְבָּר כִּי לְעוֹלָם חַסְדּוֹ. לְמַכֵּה מְלָכִים גְּדֹלִים כִּי לְעוֹלָם חַסְדּוֹ. וַיַּהֲרֹג מְלָכִים אַדִּירִים כִּי לְעוֹלָם חַסְדּוֹ. לְסִיחוֹן מֶלֶךְ הָאֱמֹרִי כִּי לְעוֹלָם חַסְדּוֹ. וּלְעוֹג מֶלֶךְ הַבָּשָׁן כִּי לְעוֹלָם חַסְדּוֹ. וְנָתַן אַרְצָם לְנַחֲלָה כִּי לְעוֹלָם חַסְדּוֹ. נַחֲלָה לְיִשְׂרָאֵל עַבְדּוֹ כִּי לְעוֹלָם חַסְדּוֹ. שֶׁבְּשִׁפְלֵנוּ זָכַר לָנוּ כִּי לְעוֹלָם חַסְדּוֹ. וַיִּפְרְקֵנוּ מִצָּרֵינוּ כִּי לְעוֹלָם חַסְדּוֹ. נֹתֵן לֶחֶם לְכָל בָּשָׂר כִּי לְעוֹלָם חַסְדּוֹ. הוֹדוּ לְאֵל הַשָּׁמָיִם כִּי לְעוֹלָם חַסְדּוֹ.

Thank the Lord, since He is good, since His kindness is forever. Thank the Power of powers since His kindness is forever. To the Master of masters, since His kindness is forever. To the One who alone does wondrously great deeds, since His kindness is forever. To the one who made the Heavens with discernment, since His kindness is forever. To the One who spread the earth over the waters, since His kindness is forever. To the One who made great lights, since His kindness is forever. The sun to rule in the day, since His kindness is forever. The moon and the stars to rule in the night, since His kindness is forever. To the One that smote Egypt through their firstborn, since His kindness is forever. And He took Israel out from among them, since His kindness is forever. With a strong hand and an outstretched forearm, since His kindness is forever. To the One who cut up the Reed Sea into strips, since His kindness is forever. And He made Israel to pass through it, since His kindness is forever. And He jolted Pharaoh and his troop in the Reed Sea, since His kindness is forever. To the One who led his people in the wilderness, since His kindness is forever. To the One who smote great kings, since His kindness is forever. And he killed mighty kings, since His kindness is forever. Sichon, king of the Amorite, since His kindness is forever. And Og, king of the Bashan, since His kindness is forever. And he gave their land as an inheritance, since His kindness is forever. An inheritance for Israel, His servant, since His kindness is forever. That in our lowliness, He remembered us, since His kindness is forever. And he delivered us from our adversaries, since His kindness is forever. He gives bread to all flesh, since His kindness is forever. Thank the Power of the heavens, since His kindness is forever. (Psalm 136)

Ps. 136 referenced as the *Hallel HaGadol*/ "The Great Hallel" (*m. Ta'an.* 3.9; *b. Ber.* 4b; *b. Pesaḥ* 118a) praises God as the controlling power of nature and history of Israel. A liturgical compilation sung by the choir of Levites or the congregation made popular by the refrain, "His kindness endures forever."

—Zev Garber

First Section: God the King, Redeemer, and Helper

נִשְׁמַת כָּל חַי תְּבָרֵךְ אֶת שִׁמְךָ, ה' אֱלֹהֵינוּ, וְרוּחַ כָּל בָּשָׂר תְּפָאֵר וּתְרוֹמֵם זִכְרְךָ, מַלְכֵּנוּ, תָּמִיד. מִן הָעוֹלָם וְעַד הָעוֹלָם אַתָּה אֵל, וּמִבַּלְעָדֶיךָ אֵין לָנוּ מֶלֶךְ גּוֹאֵל וּמוֹשִׁיעַ, פּוֹדֶה וּמַצִּיל וּמְפַרְנֵס וּמְרַחֵם בְּכָל עֵת צָרָה וְצוּקָה. אֵין לָנוּ מֶלֶךְ אֶלָּא אַתָּה. אֱלֹהֵי הָרִאשׁוֹנִים וְהָאַחֲרוֹנִים, אֱלוֹהַּ כָּל בְּרִיּוֹת, אֲדוֹן כָּל תּוֹלָדוֹת, הַמְהֻלָּל בְּרֹב הַתִּשְׁבָּחוֹת, הַמְנַהֵג עוֹלָמוֹ בְּחֶסֶד וּבְרִיּוֹתָיו בְּרַחֲמִים. וַיי לֹא יָנוּם וְלֹא יִישָׁן – הַמְעוֹרֵר יְשֵׁנִים וְהַמֵּקִיץ נִרְדָּמִים, וְהַמֵּשִׂיחַ אִלְּמִים וְהַמַּתִּיר אֲסוּרִים וְהַסּוֹמֵךְ נוֹפְלִים וְהַזּוֹקֵף כְּפוּפִים. לְךָ לְבַדְּךָ אֲנַחְנוּ מוֹדִים.

The soul of every living being shall bless Your Name, Lord our God; the spirit of all flesh shall glorify and exalt Your remembrance always, our King. From the world and until the world, You are the Power, and other than You we have no king, redeemer, or savior, restorer, rescuer, provider, and merciful one in every time of distress and anguish; we have no king, besides You! God of the first ones and the last ones, God of all creatures, Master of all Generations, Who is praised through a multitude of praises, Who guides His world with kindness and His creatures with mercy. The Lord neither slumbers nor sleeps. He who rouses the sleepers and awakens the dozers; He who makes the mute speak, and frees the captives, and supports the falling, and straightens the bent. We thank You alone.

This and the succeeding paragraphs comprise the *Nishmat Kol Ḥai* ("the soul of every living being") prayer, which extols divine mercy for sustaining humanity. It forms part of the Shabbat end festival morning services and is uttered at the end of the *Pesukei de-Zimra* hymns. It was included in the Haggadah on the basis of R. Jonathan's opinion. The first of its four sections represent a proclamation of unpolluted monotheism: "You are the Power, and other than You we have no king, redeemer, or savior, restorer, rescuer, provider... We have no king, besides You!" It has been proposed that this paragraph may have been the work of the apostle Peter, in an attempt to counter threats to the divine unity. See A. Jellinek, *Beit ha-Midrash*, 6 (1938, 1967), 12; *Maḥzor Vitry*, ed. by S. Hurwitz (1923), 282.

—Kenneth Hanson

Second Section: No human phrase can encompass God's praises

אִלּוּ פִינוּ מָלֵא שִׁירָה כַיָּם, וּלְשׁוֹנֵנוּ רִנָּה כַּהֲמוֹן גַּלָּיו, וְשִׂפְתוֹתֵינוּ שֶׁבַח כְּמֶרְחֲבֵי רָקִיעַ, וְעֵינֵינוּ מְאִירוֹת כַּשֶּׁמֶשׁ וְכַיָּרֵחַ, וְיָדֵינוּ פְרוּשׂוֹת כְּנִשְׁרֵי שָׁמָיִם, וְרַגְלֵינוּ קַלּוֹת כָּאַיָּלוֹת – אֵין אֲנַחְנוּ מַסְפִּיקִים לְהוֹדוֹת לְךָ, ה' אֱלֹהֵינוּ וֵאלֹהֵי אֲבוֹתֵינוּ, וּלְבָרֵךְ אֶת שְׁמֶךָ עַל אַחַת מֵאֶלֶף, אַלְפֵי אֲלָפִים וְרִבֵּי רְבָבוֹת פְּעָמִים הַטּוֹבוֹת שֶׁעָשִׂיתָ עִם אֲבוֹתֵינוּ וְעִמָּנוּ.

Were our mouth as full of song as the sea, and our tongue as full of joyous song as its multitude of waves, and our lips as full of praise as the breadth of the heavens, and our eyes as sparkling as the sun and the moon, and our hands as outspread as the eagles of the sky and our feet as swift as deers—we still could not thank You sufficiently, Lord our God and God of our ancestors, and to bless Your Name for one thousandth of the thousand of thousands of thousands, and myriad myriads, of goodnesses that You performed for our ancestors and for us.

This paragraph most likely dates to the tannaitic period and echoes the thanksgiving benediction for abundant rainfall, recited during the rainy season. The notion that "lips full of praise" would still be insufficient to thank God reflects the position of Judah bar Ezekiel, that each drop of rain carries with it the obligation to praise God for the multitude of "goodnesses" bestowed upon Israel. See *b. Ber.* 59b; *b. Ta'an.* 6b; Maim. *Yad, Berakhot*, 10:5.

—Kenneth Hanson

Third Section: Praise the Lord with all our existence

מִמִּצְרַיִם גְּאַלְתָּנוּ, ה' אֱלֹהֵינוּ, וּמִבֵּית עֲבָדִים פְּדִיתָנוּ, בְּרָעָב זַנְתָּנוּ וּבְשָׂבָע כִּלְכַּלְתָּנוּ, מֵחֶרֶב הִצַּלְתָּנוּ וּמִדֶּבֶר מִלַּטְתָּנוּ, וּמֵחֳלָיִם רָעִים וְנֶאֱמָנִים דִּלִּיתָנוּ.

From Egypt, Lord our God, did you redeem us and from the house of slaves you restored us. In famine You nourished us, and in plenty you sustained us. From the sword you saved us, and from plague you spared us; and from severe and enduring diseases you delivered us.

The third section of *Nishmat Kol Ḥai*, beginning with praise to God for redeeming Israel from "the house of slaves," was likely composed in the tenth century, C.E., during the geonic period.

—Kenneth Hanson

עַד הֵנָּה עֲזָרוּנוּ רַחֲמֶיךָ וְלֹא עֲזָבוּנוּ חֲסָדֶיךָ, וְאַל תִּטְּשֵׁנוּ, ה' אֱלֹהֵינוּ, לָנֶצַח. עַל כֵּן אֵבָרִים שֶׁפִּלַּגְתָּ בָּנוּ וְרוּחַ וּנְשָׁמָה שֶׁנָּפַחְתָּ בְּאַפֵּינוּ וְלָשׁוֹן אֲשֶׁר שַׂמְתָּ בְּפִינוּ – הֵן הֵם יוֹדוּ וִיבָרְכוּ וִישַׁבְּחוּ וִיפָאֲרוּ וִירוֹמְמוּ וְיַעֲרִיצוּ וְיַקְדִּישׁוּ וְיַמְלִיכוּ אֶת שִׁמְךָ מַלְכֵּנוּ. כִּי כָל פֶּה לְךָ יוֹדֶה, וְכָל לָשׁוֹן לְךָ תִּשָּׁבַע, וְכָל בֶּרֶךְ לְךָ תִכְרַע, וְכָל קוֹמָה לְפָנֶיךָ תִשְׁתַּחֲוֶה, וְכָל לְבָבוֹת יִירָאוּךָ, וְכָל קֶרֶב וּכְלָיוֹת יְזַמְּרוּ לִשְׁמֶךָ. כַּדָּבָר שֶׁכָּתוּב, כָּל עַצְמֹתַי תֹּאמַרְנָה, ה' מִי כָמוֹךָ מַצִּיל עָנִי מֵחָזָק מִמֶּנּוּ וְעָנִי וְאֶבְיוֹן מִגֹּזְלוֹ. מִי יִדְמֶה לָּךְ וּמִי יִשְׁוֶה לָּךְ וּמִי יַעֲרָךְ לָךְ הָאֵל הַגָּדוֹל, הַגִּבּוֹר וְהַנּוֹרָא, אֵל עֶלְיוֹן, קֹנֵה שָׁמַיִם וָאָרֶץ. נְהַלֶּלְךָ וּנְשַׁבֵּחֲךָ וּנְפָאֶרְךָ וּנְבָרֵךְ אֶת שֵׁם קָדְשֶׁךָ, כָּאָמוּר: לְדָוִד, בָּרְכִי נַפְשִׁי אֶת ה' וְכָל קְרָבַי אֶת שֵׁם קָדְשׁוֹ. הָאֵל בְּתַעֲצֻמוֹת עֻזֶּךָ, הַגָּדוֹל בִּכְבוֹד שְׁמֶךָ, הַגִּבּוֹר לָנֶצַח וְהַנּוֹרָא בְּנוֹרְאוֹתֶיךָ, הַמֶּלֶךְ הַיּוֹשֵׁב עַל כִּסֵּא רָם וְנִשָּׂא. שׁוֹכֵן עַד מָרוֹם וְקָדוֹשׁ שְׁמוֹ. וְכָתוּב: רַנְּנוּ צַדִּיקִים בַּייָ, לַיְשָׁרִים נָאוָה תְהִלָּה. בְּפִי יְשָׁרִים תִּתְהַלָּל, וּבְדִבְרֵי צַדִּיקִים תִּתְבָּרַךְ, וּבִלְשׁוֹן חֲסִידִים תִּתְרוֹמָם, וּבְקֶרֶב קְדוֹשִׁים תִּתְקַדָּשׁ.

Until now Your mercy has helped us, and Your kindness has not forsaken us; and do not abandon us, Lord our God, forever. Therefore, the limbs that You set within us and the spirit and soul that You breathed into our nostrils, and the tongue that You placed in our mouth—verily, they shall thank and bless and praise and glorify, and exalt and revere, and sanctify and coronate Your name, our King. For every mouth shall offer thanks to You; and every tongue shall swear allegiance to You; and every knee shall bend to You; and every upright one shall prostrate himself before You; all hearts shall fear You; and all innermost feelings and thoughts shall sing praises to Your name, as the matter is written (Ps 35:10), "All my bones shall say, 'Lord, who is like You? You save the poor man from one who is stronger than he, the poor and destitute from the one who would rob him.'" Who is similar to You and who is equal to You and who can be compared to You, O great, strong and awesome Power, O highest Power, Creator of the heavens and the earth. We shall praise and extol and glorify and bless Your holy name, as it is stated (Ps 103:1), "[A Psalm] of David. Bless the Lord, O my soul; and all that is within me, His holy name." **The Power**, in Your powerful boldness; the Great, in the glory of Your name; the Strong One forever; **the King** who sits on His high and elevated throne. **He who dwells alway**s; lofty and holy is His name. And as it is written (Ps 33:10), "Sing joyfully to the Lord, righteous ones, praise is beautiful from the upright." By the mouth of the upright You shall be praised; By the lips of the righteous shall You be blessed; By the tongue of the devout shall You be exalted; And among the holy shall You be sanctified.

Most prayer books enlarge the words *ha-El* (הָאֵל), *ha-Melekh* (הַמֶּלֶךְ), and *Shokhen ad* (שׁוֹכֵן עַד), found in this paragraph. This is to cue the *hazzan* (on High Holy Days, Sabbath and festivals, respectively) to begin the central section of the morning service at these places.

—Kenneth Hanson

Section Four: May God be worshipped in the assemblies of the tens of thousands

וּבְמַקְהֲלוֹת רִבְבוֹת עַמְּךָ בֵּית יִשְׂרָאֵל בְּרִנָּה יִתְפָּאַר שִׁמְךָ, מַלְכֵּנוּ, בְּכָל דּוֹר וָדוֹר, שֶׁכֵּן חוֹבַת כָּל הַיְצוּרִים לְפָנֶיךָ, ה' אֱלֹהֵינוּ וֵאלֹהֵי אֲבוֹתֵינוּ, לְהוֹדוֹת לְהַלֵּל לְשַׁבֵּחַ, לְפָאֵר לְרוֹמֵם לְהַדֵּר לְבָרֵךְ, לְעַלֵּה וּלְקַלֵּס עַל כָּל דִּבְרֵי שִׁירוֹת וְתִשְׁבָּחוֹת דָּוִד בֶּן יִשַׁי עַבְדְּךָ מְשִׁיחֶךָ.

And in the assemblies of the myriads of Your people, the House of Israel, in joyous song will Your name be glorified, our King, in each and every generation; as it is the duty of all creatures, before You, Lord our God, and God of our ancestors, to thank, to praise, to extol, to glorify, to exalt, to lavish, to bless, to raise high and to acclaim—beyond the words of the songs and praises of David, the son of Yishai, Your servant, Your anointed one.

The Yishtabaḥ is the Daily, Shabbat and Festivals benediction after the reading of "Psalms and Passages of Song." Fifteen distinct terms of adoration and praise of the Lord are enumerated.

—Zev Garber

יִשְׁתַּבַּח שִׁמְךָ לָעַד מַלְכֵּנוּ, הָאֵל הַמֶּלֶךְ הַגָּדוֹל וְהַקָּדוֹשׁ בַּשָּׁמַיִם וּבָאָרֶץ, כִּי לְךָ נָאֶה, ה' אֱלֹהֵינוּ וֵאלֹהֵי אֲבוֹתֵינוּ, שִׁיר וּשְׁבָחָה, הַלֵּל וְזִמְרָה, עֹז וּמֶמְשָׁלָה, נֶצַח, גְּדֻלָּה וּגְבוּרָה, תְּהִלָּה וְתִפְאֶרֶת, קְדֻשָּׁה וּמַלְכוּת, בְּרָכוֹת וְהוֹדָאוֹת מֵעַתָּה וְעַד עוֹלָם. בָּרוּךְ אַתָּה ה', אֵל מֶלֶךְ גָּדוֹל בַּתִּשְׁבָּחוֹת, אֵל הַהוֹדָאוֹת, אֲדוֹן הַנִּפְלָאוֹת, הַבּוֹחֵר בְּשִׁירֵי זִמְרָה, מֶלֶךְ אֵל חֵי הָעוֹלָמִים.

May Your name be praised forever, our King, the Power, the Great and holy King—in the heavens and in the earth. Since for You it is pleasant—O Lord our God and God of our ancestors—song and lauding, praise and hymn, boldness and dominion, triumph, greatness and strength, psalm and splendor, holiness and kingship, blessings and thanksgivings, from now and forever. Blessed are You Lord, Power, King exalted through laudings, Power of thanksgivings, Master of Wonders, who chooses the songs of hymn—King, Power of the life of the worlds.

Nishmat Kol Ḥai, as a whole, is believed to rely on an earlier, truncated version, which originated in ancient times. It is referenced talmudically (*m. Pesaḥ* 10:7, and *b. Pesaḥ* 117b–118a) as *Birkat ha-Shir* ("Benediction of the Song"). Both Ashkenazi and Sephardic renderings of *Nishmat* are remarkably congruent, diverging in only two or three lines and supporting the notion of an underlying source. See *Seder R. Amram Ga'on*, 27b and *Maḥzor Vitry* (1923), 148–54.

—Kenneth Hanson

Hallel, Fourth Cup of Wine

בָּרוּךְ אַתָּה ה', אֱלֹהֵינוּ מֶלֶךְ הָעוֹלָם בּוֹרֵא פְּרִי הַגָּפֶן.

Blessed are You, Lord our God, King of the universe, who creates the fruit of the vine.

וְשׁוֹתֶה בַּהֲסִיבַת שְׂמֹאל.

We drink while reclining to the left

The fourth cup is said to represent becoming a nation at Sinai, and is drunk at the end of the *Nishmat* hymn (*Birkat ha-Shir*), as indicated in the Talmud (*b. Pesaḥ* 118a): "The Sages taught in a *baraita*: With regard to the fourth cup, one completes Hallel over it and recites "The Great Hallel" (Ps 136); this is the statement of Rabbi Tarfon."

—Kenneth Hanson

בָּרוּךְ אַתָּה ה' אֱלֹהֵינוּ מֶלֶךְ הָעוֹלָם, עַל הַגֶּפֶן וְעַל פְּרִי הַגֶּפֶן, עַל תְּנוּבַת הַשָּׂדֶה וְעַל אֶרֶץ חֶמְדָּה טוֹבָה וּרְחָבָה שֶׁרָצִיתָ וְהִנְחַלְתָּ לַאֲבוֹתֵינוּ לֶאֱכוֹל מִפִּרְיָהּ וְלִשְׂבּוֹעַ מִטּוּבָהּ. רַחֵם נָא ה' אֱלֹהֵינוּ עַל יִשְׂרָאֵל עַמֶּךָ וְעַל יְרוּשָׁלַיִם עִירֶךָ וְעַל צִיּוֹן מִשְׁכַּן כְּבוֹדֶךָ וְעַל מִזְבְּחֶךָ וְעַל הֵיכָלֶךָ וּבְנֵה יְרוּשָׁלַיִם עִיר הַקֹּדֶשׁ בִּמְהֵרָה בְיָמֵינוּ וְהַעֲלֵנוּ לְתוֹכָהּ וְשַׂמְּחֵנוּ בְּבִנְיָנָהּ וְנֹאכַל מִפִּרְיָהּ וְנִשְׂבַּע מִטּוּבָהּ וּנְבָרֶכְךָ עָלֶיהָ בִּקְדֻשָּׁה וּבְטָהֳרָה [בשבת: וּרְצֵה וְהַחֲלִיצֵנוּ בְּיוֹם הַשַּׁבָּת הַזֶּה] וְשַׂמְּחֵנוּ בְּיוֹם חַג הַמַּצּוֹת הַזֶּה, כִּי אַתָּה ה' טוֹב וּמֵטִיב לַכֹּל, וְנוֹדֶה לְךָ עַל הָאָרֶץ וְעַל פְּרִי הַגָּפֶן.

Blessed are You, Lord our God, King of the universe, for the vine and for the fruit of the vine; and for the bounty of the field; and for a desirable, good and broad land, which You wanted to give to our fathers, to eat from its fruit and to be satiated from its goodness. Please have mercy, Lord our God upon Israel Your people; and upon Jerusalem, Your city: and upon Zion, the dwelling place of Your glory; and upon Your altar; and upon Your sanctuary; and build Jerusalem Your holy city quickly in our days, and bring us up into it and gladden us in its building; and we shall eat from its fruit, and be satiated from its goodness, and bless You in holiness and purity. [On Shabbat: And may you be pleased to embolden us on this Shabbat day] and gladden us on this day of the Festival of *Matsot*. Since You, Lord, are good and do good to all, we thank You for the land and for the fruit of the vine.

Nirtzah, Chasal Siddur Pesach

נִרְצָה

Accepted

חֲסַל סִדּוּר פֶּסַח כְּהִלְכָתוֹ, כְּכָל מִשְׁפָּטוֹ וְחֻקָּתוֹ. כַּאֲשֶׁר זָכִינוּ לְסַדֵּר אוֹתוֹ כֵּן נִזְכֶּה לַעֲשׂוֹתוֹ. זָךְ שׁוֹכֵן מְעוֹנָה, קוֹמֵם קְהַל עֲדַת מִי מָנָה. בְּקָרוֹב נַהֵל נִטְעֵי כַנָּה פְּדוּיִם לְצִיּוֹן בְּרִנָּה.

Completed is the Seder of Pesach according to its law, according to all its judgement and statute. Just as we have merited to arrange it, so too, may we merit to do [its sacrifice]. Pure One who dwells in the habitation, raise up the congregation of the community, which whom can count. Bring close, lead the plantings of the sapling, redeemed, to Zion in joy.

The Nirtzah is the last of the fifteen sections of the Seder. It consists almost entirely of singing.

—Kenneth Hanson

Nirtzah, L'Shana HaBaa

לְשָׁנָה הַבָּאָה בִּירוּשָׁלָיִם הַבְּנוּיָה.

Next year, let us be in the built Jerusalem!

In the Diaspora this line (recited also at the end of Yom Kippur, concluding the Ne'ilah service) is: *"L'Shana HaBa'a bi'Yerushalayim"* ("Next year in Jerusalem!"). It serves as a reminder of the shared experience of living in exile, which must be reconciled in order to reside in a city whose name combines "peace" (*shalom*) and "wholeness" (*shaleim*). Those already living in Jerusalem obviously have no need for such an aspiration. Therefore, in Israel the word *habenuyah* ("rebuilt") is appended, expressing the hope that a third temple will arise in the holy city. This will in turn serve to usher in the Messiah/ messianic age and bring about the ingathering of the Jewish people to the land of Israel. As both a song and a prayer, it envisions final redemption, imagining peace and completeness in all the earth.

—Kenneth Hanson

Nirtzah, And It Happened at Midnight

בליל ראשון אומרים:

On the first night we say:

וּבְכֵן וַיְהִי בַּחֲצִי הַלַּיְלָה.

And so, it was in the middle of the night [Exod 12:29]

אָז רוֹב נִסִּים הִפְלֵאתָ בַּלַּיְלָה, בְּרֹאשׁ אַשְׁמוֹרֶת זֶה הַלַּיְלָה.

Then, most of the miracles did You wondrously do at night, at the first of the watches this night. [The night is divided into three watches; the first is called *rosh ashmurot* (Lam 2:19).]

גֵּר צֶדֶק נִצַּחְתּוֹ כְּנֶחֱלַק לוֹ לַיְלָה, וַיְהִי בַּחֲצִי הַלַּיְלָה.

A righteous convert did you make victorious when it was divided for him at night [referring to Avraham in his war against the four kings—Gen 14:15], and it was in the middle of the night.

דַּנְתָּ מֶלֶךְ גְּרָר בַּחֲלוֹם הַלַּיְלָה, הִפְחַדְתָּ אֲרַמִּי בְּאֶמֶשׁ לַיְלָה.

You judged the king of Gerrar [Avimelekh] in a dream of the night; you frightened an Aramean [Lavan] in the dark of the night;

וַיָּשַׂר יִשְׂרָאֵל לְמַלְאָךְ וַיּוּכַל לוֹ לַיְלָה, וַיְהִי בַּחֲצִי הַלַּיְלָה.

and Yisrael dominated an angel and was able to withstand Him at night [Gen 32:25–30], and it was in the middle of the night.

זֶרַע בְּכוֹרֵי פַתְרוֹס מָחַצְתָּ בַּחֲצִי הַלַּיְלָה, חֵילָם לֹא מָצְאוּ בְּקוּמָם בַּלַּיְלָה, טִיסַת נְגִיד חֲרֹשֶׁת סִלִּיתָ בְּכוֹכְבֵי לַיְלָה, וַיְהִי בַּחֲצִי הַלַּיְלָה.

You crushed the firstborn of Patros [Pharaoh, as per Ezek 30:14; Egypt, as per Gen 10:14, Jer 44:1] in the middle of the night, their wealth they did not find when they got up at night; the attack of the leader Charoshet [Sisera] did you sweep away by the stars of the night [Judg 5:20], and it was in the middle of the night.

יָעַץ מְחָרֵף לְנוֹפֵף אִוּוּי, הוֹבַשְׁתָּ פְגָרָיו בַּלַּיְלָה, כָּרַע בֵּל וּמַצָּבוֹ בְּאִישׁוֹן לַיְלָה, לְאִישׁ חֲמוּדוֹת נִגְלָה רָז חֲזוֹת לַיְלָה, וַיְהִי בַּחֲצִי הַלַּיְלָה.

The blasphemer [Sennacherib whose servants blasphemed when trying to discourage the inhabitants of Jerusalem] counseled to wave off the desired ones, You made him wear his corpses on his head at night [II Kgs 19:35]; Bel and his pedestal were bent in the pitch of night [in Nebuchadnezzar's dream in Daniel 2:9]; to the man of delight [Daniel (Dan 10:11)] was revealed the secret visions at night, and it was in the middle of the night.

מִשְׁתַּכֵּר בִּכְלֵי קֹדֶשׁ נֶהֱרַג בּוֹ בַּלַּיְלָה, נוֹשַׁע מִבּוֹר אֲרָיוֹת פּוֹתֵר בִּעֲתוּתֵי לַיְלָה, שִׂנְאָה נָטַר אֲגָגִי וְכָתַב סְפָרִים בַּלַּיְלָה, וַיְהִי בַּחֲצִי הַלַּיְלָה.

The one who got drunk [Balshatsar] from the holy vessels was killed on that night [Dan 5:30], the one saved from the pit of lions [Daniel] interpreted the scary visions of the night; hatred was preserved by the Agagite [Haman] and he wrote books at night (letters to have the Jews murdered, Esth 3:13), and it was in the middle of the night.

עוֹרַרְתָּ נִצְחֲךָ עָלָיו בְּנֶדֶד שְׁנַת לַיְלָה. פּוּרָה תִדְרוֹךְ לְשׁוֹמֵר מַה מִלַּיְלָה, צָרַח כַּשּׁוֹמֵר וְשָׂח אָתָא בֹקֶר וְגַם לַיְלָה, וַיְהִי בַּחֲצִי הַלַּיְלָה.

You aroused your victory upon him by disturbing the sleep of night [of Ahasuerus, Esth 6:1], You will stomp the wine press for the one who guards from anything at night [Esav/Seir as per Isa 21:11]; He yelled like a guard and spoke, "the morning has come and also the night," and it was in the middle of the night.

קָרֵב יוֹם אֲשֶׁר הוּא לֹא יוֹם וְלֹא לַיְלָה, רָם הוֹדַע כִּי לְךָ הַיּוֹם אַף לְךָ הַלַּיְלָה, שׁוֹמְרִים הַפְקֵד לְעִירְךָ כָּל הַיּוֹם וְכָל הַלַּיְלָה, תָּאִיר כְּאוֹר יוֹם חֶשְׁכַּת לַיְלָה, וַיְהִי בַּחֲצִי הַלַּיְלָה.

Bring close the day which is not day and not night [referring to the end of days—Zech 14:7], High One, make known that Yours is the day and also Yours is the night (Ps 74:16), guards appoint (Isa 62:6) for Your city all the day and all the night, illuminate like the light of the day, the darkness of the night, and it was in the middle of the night.

And It Happened at Midnight, composed by the great liturgical poet of late antiquity, Yannai, dates to the fourth or fifth century, C.E. It is an alphabetic acrostic, anticipating future redemption and recounting the many miracles which rescued the Jewish people, as it were, in the middle of the night. Its refrain echoes Exod 12:29 ("And it came to pass at midnight, that the Lord smote all the firstborn in the land of Egypt...") and serves to reiterate poetically the theme of *Num. Rab.* 20. The midrash asserts that the anniversary of this night was one of deliverance for the Jewish people on many occasions, including Abraham's triumph over the kings, Jacob's wrestling match with an angel, Deborah's defeat of Sisera, and the demise of Haman. In addition to reminding the participants to finish the meal prior to midnight, the poem teaches that for the Jews, night, generally conceived as the time when people are most vulnerable, is transformed to a moment of rescue. Its conclusion looks ahead to a glorious future day, referenced by the prophet Zechariah (14:7): "And there shall be one day which shall be known as the Lord's, not day, and not night; but it shall come to pass, that at evening time there shall be light." We are also reminded of the Talmudic passage (*b. Roš Haš.*11b), which describes the fifteenth of *Nissan* as: "...a night that from the six days of creation has been anticipated." Therefore, this night is not unique on account of the departure from Egypt, but the date of the Exodus was divinely calculated according to the redemptive qualities of the fifteenth of *Nissan*.

—Kenneth Hanson

Nirtzah, Zevach Pesach

בְּלֵיל שֵׁנִי בחו"ל: וּבְכֵן וַאֲמַרְתֶּם זֶבַח פֶּסַח.

On the second night, outside of Israel: And so "And you shall say, 'it is the Pesach sacrifice'"(Exod 12:42; see too Exod 12:27).

אֹמֶץ גְּבוּרוֹתֶיךָ הִפְלֵאתָ בַּפֶּסַח, בְּרֹאשׁ כָּל מוֹעֲדוֹת נִשֵּׂאתָ פֶּסַח. גִּלִּיתָ לְאֶזְרָחִי חֲצוֹת לֵיל פֶּסַח, וַאֲמַרְתֶּם זֶבַח פֶּסַח.

The boldness of Your strong deeds did you wondrously show at Pesach; at the head of all the holidays [*m. Roš Haš.*1.1, Nisan 1 is the New Year's Day of festivals, making Passover which falls on Nisan 15, the frst in the cycle of prayers] did You raise Pesach; You revealed to the Ezrachite [Avraham, "Easterner," due to his eastern origin], midnight of the night of Pesach. "And you shall say, 'it is the Pesach sacrifice.'"

דְּלָתָיו דָּפַקְתָּ כְּחֹם הַיּוֹם בַּפֶּסַח, הִסְעִיד נוֹצְצִים עֻגוֹת מַצּוֹת בַּפֶּסַח, וְאֶל הַבָּקָר רָץ זֵכֶר לְשׁוֹר עֵרֶךְ פֶּסַח, וַאֲמַרְתֶּם זֶבַח פֶּסַח.

Upon his doors did You knock at the heat of the day on Pesach [Genesis 18:1]; he sustained shining ones [angels] with cakes of *matsa* on Pesach [Gen 18:6]; and to the cattle he ran, in commemoration of the bull that was set up for Pesach. "And you shall say, 'it is the Pesach sacrifice.'"

זֹעֲמוּ סְדוֹמִים וְלֹהֲטוּ בָּאֵשׁ בַּפֶּסַח, חֻלַּץ לוֹט מֵהֶם וּמַצּוֹת אָפָה בְּקֵץ פֶּסַח, טִאטֵאתָ אַדְמַת מוֹף וְנוֹף בְּעָבְרְךָ בַּפֶּסַח. וַאֲמַרְתֶּם זֶבַח פֶּסַח.

The Sodomites caused Him indignation and He set them on fire on Pesach; Lot was rescued from them and *matsot* did he bake at the end of Pesach [Gen 19:3; angels here connected with the angelic hosts greeted by Abraham, Gen 18:1] He swept the land of Mof and Nof [cities in Egypt; Josh 9:6; Isa 19:13] on Pesach. "And you shall say, 'it is the Pesach sacrifice.'"

יָהּ רֹאשׁ כָּל הוֹן מָחַצְתָּ בְּלֵיל שִׁמּוּר פֶּסַח, כַּבִּיר, עַל בֵּן בְּכוֹר פָּסַחְתָּ בְּדַם פֶּסַח, לְבִלְתִּי תֵּת מַשְׁחִית לָבֹא בִּפְתָחַי בַּפֶּסַח, וַאֲמַרְתֶּם זֶבַח פֶּסַח.

The head of every firstborn did You crush on the guarded night of Pesach [Exod 12:42]; Powerful One, over the firstborn son [Israel, Exod 12:22] did You pass over with the blood on Pesach; so as to not let the destroyer come into my gates on Pesach. "And you shall say, 'it is the Pesach sacrifice.'"

מְסֻגֶּרֶת סֻגְּרָה בְּעִתּוֹתֵי פֶּסַח, נִשְׁמְדָה מִדְיָן בִּצְלִיל שְׂעוֹרֵי עֹמֶר פֶּסַח, שֹׂרְפוּ מִשְׁמַנֵּי פּוּל וְלוּד בִּיקַד יְקוֹד פֶּסַח, וַאֲמַרְתֶּם זֶבַח פֶּסַח.

The enclosed one [Jericho, Josh 6:1] was enclosed in the season of Pesach; Midian was destroyed with a portion of the omer-barley on Pesach [via Gideon as per Judges 7:13]; from the fat of Pul and Lud [Assyrian soldiers of Sennacherib; but Assyrian tribes in Isa 66:19] was burnt in pyres on Pesach. "And you shall say, 'it is the Pesach sacrifice'"

עוֹד הַיּוֹם בְּנֹב לַעֲמוֹד עַד גָּעָה עוֹנַת פֶּסַח, פַּס יַד כָּתְבָה לְקַעֲקֵעַ צוּל בַּפֶּסַח, צָפֹה הַצָּפִית עָרוֹךְ הַשֻּׁלְחָן בַּפֶּסַח, וַאֲמַרְתֶּם זֶבַח פֶּסַח.

Still today [Sennacherib will go no further than] to stand in Nov [Isa 10:32], until he cried at the time of Pesach; a palm of the hand wrote [Dan 5:5] to rip up the deep one [the Bayblonian one—Belshassar] on Pesach; set up the watch, set the table [referring to Belshassar, based on Ps 21:5] on Pesach. "And you shall say, 'it is the Pesach sacrifice.'"

קָהָל כִּנְּסָה הֲדַסָּה לְשַׁלֵּשׁ צוֹם בַּפֶּסַח, רֹאשׁ מִבֵּית רָשָׁע מָחַצְתָּ בְּעֵץ חֲמִשִּׁים בַּפֶּסַח, שְׁתֵּי אֵלֶּה רֶגַע תָּבִיא לְעוּצִית בַּפֶּסַח, תָּעֹז יָדְךָ תָּרוּם יְמִינְךָ כְּלֵיל הִתְקַדֵּשׁ חַג פֶּסַח, וַאֲמַרְתֶּם זֶבַח פֶּסַח.

The congregation did Hadassah [Esther] bring in to triple a fast on Pesach; the head of the house of evil [Haman] did you crush on a tree of fifty [amot] on Pesach; these two [plagues as per Isaiah 47:9] will you bring in an instant to the Utsi [Esav descendants Edomites lived in Uts, Lam 4:21] on Pesach; embolden Your hand, raise Your right hand, as on the night You were sanctified on the festival of Pesach. "And you shall say, 'it is the Pesach sacrifice.'"

Nirtzah, Ki Lo Na'e

כִּי לוֹ נָאֶה, כִּי לוֹ יָאֶה.

Since for Him it is pleasant, for Him it is suited.

אַדִּיר בִּמְלוּכָה, בָּחוּר כַּהֲלָכָה, גְּדוּדָיו יֹאמְרוּ לוֹ: לְךָ וּלְךָ, לְךָ כִּי לְךָ, לְךָ אַף לְךָ, לְךָ ה' הַמַּמְלָכָה, כִּי לוֹ נָאֶה, כִּי לוֹ יָאֶה.

Mighty in rulership, properly chosen, his troops shall say to Him, "Yours and Yours, Yours since it is Yours, Yours and even Yours, Yours, Lord is the kingdom; since for Him it is pleasant, for Him it is suited."

דָּגוּל בִּמְלוּכָה, הָדוּר כַּהֲלָכָה, וָתִיקָיו יֹאמְרוּ לוֹ: לְךָ וּלְךָ, לְךָ כִּי לְךָ, לְךָ אַף לְךָ, לְךָ ה' הַמַּמְלָכָה, כִּי לוֹ נָאֶה, כִּי לוֹ יָאֶה.

Noted in rulership, properly splendid, His distinguished ones will say to him, "Yours and Yours, Yours since it is Yours, Yours and even Yours, Yours, Lord is the kingdom; since for Him it is pleasant, for Him it is suited."

זַכַּאי בִּמְלוּכָה, חָסִין כַּהֲלָכָה טַפְסְרָיו יֹאמְרוּ לוֹ: לְךָ וּלְךָ, לְךָ כִּי לְךָ, לְךָ אַף לְךָ, לְךָ ה' הַמַּמְלָכָה, כִּי לוֹ נָאֶה, כִּי לוֹ יָאֶה.

Meritorious in rulership, properly robust, His scribes shall say to him, "Yours and Yours, Yours since it is Yours, Yours and even Yours, Yours, Lord is the kingdom; since for Him it is pleasant, for Him it is suited."

יָחִיד בִּמְלוּכָה, כַּבִּיר כַּהֲלָכָה לִמּוּדָיו יֹאמְרוּ לוֹ: לְךָ וּלְךָ, לְךָ כִּי לְךָ, לְךָ אַף לְךָ, לְךָ ה' הַמַּמְלָכָה, כִּי לוֹ נָאֶה, כִּי לוֹ יָאֶה.

Unique in rulership, properly powerful, His wise ones say to Him, "Yours and Yours, Yours since it is Yours, Yours and even Yours, Yours, Lord is the kingdom; since for Him it is pleasant, for Him it is suited."

מוֹשֵׁל בִּמְלוּכָה, נוֹרָא כַּהֲלָכָה סְבִיבָיו יֹאמְרוּ לוֹ: לְךָ וּלְךָ, לְךָ כִּי לְךָ, לְךָ אַף לְךָ, לְךָ ה' הַמַּמְלָכָה, כִּי לוֹ נָאֶה, כִּי לוֹ יָאֶה.

Reigning in rulership, properly awesome, those around Him say to Him, "Yours and Yours, Yours since it is Yours, Yours and even Yours, Yours, Lord is the kingdom; since for Him it is pleasant, for Him it is suited."

עָנָיו בִּמְלוּכָה, פּוֹדֶה כַּהֲלָכָה, צַדִּיקָיו יֹאמְרוּ לוֹ: לְךָ וּלְךָ, לְךָ כִּי לְךָ, לְךָ אַף לְךָ, לְךָ ה' הַמַּמְלָכָה, כִּי לוֹ נָאֶה, כִּי לוֹ יָאֶה.

Humble in rulership, properly restoring, His righteous ones say to Him, "Yours and Yours, Yours since it is Yours, Yours and even Yours, Yours, Lord is the kingdom; since for Him it is pleasant, for Him it is suited."

קָדוֹשׁ בִּמְלוּכָה, רַחוּם כַּהֲלָכָה שִׁנְאַנָּיו יֹאמְרוּ לוֹ: לְךָ וּלְךָ, לְךָ כִּי לְךָ, לְךָ אַף לְךָ, לְךָ ה' הַמַּמְלָכָה, כִּי לוֹ נָאֶה, כִּי לוֹ יָאֶה.

Holy in rulership, properly merciful, His angels say to Him, "Yours and Yours, Yours since it is Yours, Yours and even Yours, Yours, Lord is the kingdom; since for Him it is pleasant, for Him it is suited."

תַּקִּיף בִּמְלוּכָה, תּוֹמֵךְ כַּהֲלָכָה תְּמִימָיו יֹאמְרוּ לוֹ: לְךָ וּלְךָ, לְךָ כִּי לְךָ, לְךָ אַף לְךָ, לְךָ ה' הַמַּמְלָכָה, כִּי לוֹ נָאֶה, כִּי לוֹ יָאֶה.

Dynamic in rulership, properly supportive, His innocent ones say to Him, "Yours and Yours, Yours since it is Yours, Yours and even Yours, Yours, Lord is the kingdom; since for Him it is pleasant, for Him it is suited."

Known also as *Adir Bimlukha* ("Mighty in Rulership"), Ki Lo Na'e is an anonymous composition of unknown date. It was originally intended for all meals but was adopted into the Seder by the thirteenth century, at the time of Rabbi Meir of Rothenburg. It contains no specific reference to Passover or the Exodus, but twice in each stanza it depicts God's majesty, to the accompaniment of innumerable angels, scholars, and the righteous. Three poetic lines comprise an ongoing acrostic, followed by the refrain: "Yours and Yours, Yours since it is Yours, Yours and even Yours, Yours, Lord is the kingdom; since for Him it is pleasant, for Him it is suited." It appears to take inspiration from Ps 74:16 ("Yours is the day, Yours also the night"), as well as *Gen. Rab.* 6:2, which expounds on this verse.

—Kenneth Hanson

Nirtzah, Adir Hu

אַדִּיר הוּא יִבְנֶה בֵּיתוֹ בְּקָרוֹב. בִּמְהֵרָה, בִּמְהֵרָה, בְּיָמֵינוּ בְּקָרוֹב. אֵל בְּנֵה, אֵל בְּנֵה, בְּנֵה בֵּיתְךָ בְּקָרוֹב.

Mighty is He, may He build His house soon. Quickly, quickly, in our days, soon. God build, God build, build Your house soon.

בָּחוּר הוּא, גָּדוֹל הוּא, דָּגוּל הוּא יִבְנֶה בֵּיתוֹ בְּקָרוֹב. בִּמְהֵרָה, בִּמְהֵרָה, בְּיָמֵינוּ בְּקָרוֹב. אֵל בְּנֵה, אֵל בְּנֵה, בְּנֵה בֵיתְךָ בְּקָרוֹב.

Chosen is He, great is He, noted is He. Quickly, quickly, in our days, soon. God build, God build, build Your house soon.

הָדוּר הוּא, וָתִיק הוּא, זַכַּאי הוּא יִבְנֶה בֵּיתוֹ בְּקָרוֹב. בִּמְהֵרָה, בִּמְהֵרָה, בְּיָמֵינוּ בְּקָרוֹב. אֵל בְּנֵה, אֵל בְּנֵה, בְּנֵה בֵיתְךָ בְּקָרוֹב.

Splendid is He, distinguished is He, meritorious is He. Quickly, quickly, in our days, soon. God build, God build, build Your house soon.

חָסִיד הוּא, טָהוֹר הוּא, יָחִיד הוּא יִבְנֶה בֵּיתוֹ בְּקָרוֹב. בִּמְהֵרָה, בִּמְהֵרָה, בְּיָמֵינוּ בְּקָרוֹב. אֵל בְּנֵה, אֵל בְּנֵה, בְּנֵה בֵיתְךָ בְּקָרוֹב.

Pious is He, pure is He, unique is He. Quickly, quickly, in our days, soon. God build, God build, build Your house soon.

כַּבִּיר הוּא, לָמוּד הוּא, מֶלֶךְ הוּא יִבְנֶה בֵּיתוֹ בְּקָרוֹב. בִּמְהֵרָה, בִּמְהֵרָה, בְּיָמֵינוּ בְּקָרוֹב. אֵל בְּנֵה, אֵל בְּנֵה, בְּנֵה בֵיתְךָ בְּקָרוֹב.

Powerful is He, wise is He, A king is He. Quickly, quickly, in our days, soon. God build, God build, build Your house soon.

נוֹרָא הוּא, סַגִּיב הוּא, עִזּוּז הוּא יִבְנֶה בֵּיתוֹ בְּקָרוֹב. בִּמְהֵרָה, בִּמְהֵרָה, בְּיָמֵינוּ בְּקָרוֹב. אֵל בְּנֵה, אֵל בְּנֵה, בְּנֵה בֵיתְךָ בְּקָרוֹב.

Awesome is He, exalted is He, heroic is He. Quickly, quickly, in our days, soon. God build, God build, build Your house soon.

פּוֹדֶה הוּא, צַדִּיק הוּא, קָדוֹשׁ הוּא יִבְנֶה בֵּיתוֹ בְּקָרוֹב. בִּמְהֵרָה, בִּמְהֵרָה, בְּיָמֵינוּ בְּקָרוֹב. אֵל בְּנֵה, אֵל בְּנֵה, בְּנֵה בֵיתְךָ בְּקָרוֹב.

A restorer is He, righteous is He, holy is He. Quickly, quickly, in our days, soon. God build, God build, build Your house soon.

רַחוּם הוּא, שַׁדַּי הוּא, תַּקִּיף הוּא יִבְנֶה בֵּיתוֹ בְּקָרוֹב. בִּמְהֵרָה, בִּמְהֵרָה, בְּיָמֵינוּ בְּקָרוֹב. אֵל בְּנֵה, אֵל בְּנֵה, בְּנֵה בֵיתְךָ בְּקָרוֹב.

Merciful is He, the Omnipotent is He, dynamic is He. Quickly, quickly, in our days, soon. God build, God build, build Your house soon.

Adir Hu ("Mighty is He") is an alphabetical acrostic hymn, recited at Ashkenazi Seders, expressing, on the one hand, awe of the uprightness of God ("chosen," "great," "noted," "splendid," "distinguished," etc.), and on the other, a fervent desire to see the restoration of the temple. The traditional lively melody is rooted in the Middle High German period, dating between the twelfth and fourteenth centuries. The Rittangel Haggadah of 1644 contains its earliest extant music, followed by the Haggadah Zevach Pesach of 1677 and the Selig Haggadah of 1769. Following synagogue services on the eve of Passover, and in reference to Adir Hu, a German greeting, *Bau Gut* ("build well") was traditionally uttered. Recently, a feminist version of the song was composed, referencing God as "She" and emphasizing the renewal of life.

—Kenneth Hanson

Nirtzah, Sefirat HaOmer

ספירת העמר בחוץ לארץ, בליל שני של פסח:

The counting of the omer outside of Israel on the second night of Pesach:

בָּרוּךְ אַתָּה ה', אֱלֹהֵינוּ מֶלֶךְ הָעוֹלָם, אֲשֶׁר קִדְּשָׁנוּ בְּמִצְוֹתָיו וְצִוָּנוּ עַל סְפִירַת הָעֹמֶר. הַיּוֹם יוֹם אֶחָד בָּעֹמֶר.

Blessed are You, Lord our God, King of the Universe, who has sanctified us with His commandments and has commanded us on the counting of the Omer. Today is the first day of the Omer.

As the Exodus narrative continues, the final redemption will only be revealed as the people make their way through the desert. The destination that lay ahead is of course Mt. Sinai, where the Torah will be delivered to Moses and to all Israel, amid peals of thunder. This will be the "constitution" which will provide structure and form for all the journey to come. It is not a map for the Promised Land, but a guidebook for the wilderness, which is, after all, where people must live their lives—in an imperfect world. In tradition the giving of the Torah at Sinai occurs exactly fifty days after Passover, being commemorated by the feast of Shavuot. These two festivals are linked by the tradition which commences on the second day of Passover, the counting of the *omer* (Lev 23:10–14). For seven full weeks, forty-nine days, the Jew is made mindful that the physical release from slavery does not comprise complete freedom unless it is consummated in the constraints, duties and disciplines embodied in the Ten Commandments and the Torah. Only then will those who have been freed be free indeed.

—Kenneth Hanson

Nirtzah, Echad Mi Yodea

אֶחָד מִי יוֹדֵעַ? אֶחָד אֲנִי יוֹדֵעַ: אֶחָד אֱלֹהֵינוּ שֶׁבַּשָּׁמַיִם וּבָאָרֶץ.

שְׁנַיִם מִי יוֹדֵעַ? שְׁנַיִם אֲנִי יוֹדֵעַ: שְׁנֵי לֻחוֹת הַבְּרִית. אֶחָד אֱלֹהֵינוּ שֶׁבַּשָּׁמַיִם וּבָאָרֶץ.

שְׁלֹשָׁה מִי יוֹדֵעַ? שְׁלֹשָׁה אֲנִי יוֹדֵעַ: שְׁלֹשָׁה אָבוֹת, שְׁנֵי לֻחוֹת הַבְּרִית, אֶחָד אֱלֹהֵינוּ שֶׁבַּשָּׁמַיִם וּבָאָרֶץ.

אַרְבַּע מִי יוֹדֵעַ? אַרְבַּע אֲנִי יוֹדֵעַ: אַרְבַּע אִמָּהוֹת, שְׁלֹשָׁה אָבוֹת, שְׁנֵי לֻחוֹת הַבְּרִית, אֶחָד אֱלֹהֵינוּ שֶׁבַּשָּׁמַיִם וּבָאָרֶץ.

חֲמִשָּׁה מִי יוֹדֵעַ? חֲמִשָּׁה אֲנִי יוֹדֵעַ: חֲמִשָּׁה חוּמְשֵׁי תוֹרָה, אַרְבַּע אִמָּהוֹת, שְׁלֹשָׁה אָבוֹת, שְׁנֵי לֻחוֹת הַבְּרִית, אֶחָד אֱלֹהֵינוּ שֶׁבַּשָּׁמַיִם וּבָאָרֶץ.

שִׁשָּׁה מִי יוֹדֵעַ? שִׁשָּׁה אֲנִי יוֹדֵעַ: שִׁשָּׁה סִדְרֵי מִשְׁנָה, חֲמִשָּׁה חוּמְשֵׁי תוֹרָה, אַרְבַּע אִמָּהוֹת, שְׁלֹשָׁה אָבוֹת, שְׁנֵי לֻחוֹת הַבְּרִית, אֶחָד אֱלֹהֵינוּ שֶׁבַּשָּׁמַיִם וּבָאָרֶץ.

שִׁבְעָה מִי יוֹדֵעַ? שִׁבְעָה אֲנִי יוֹדֵעַ: שִׁבְעָה יְמֵי שַׁבַּתָּא, שִׁשָּׁה סִדְרֵי מִשְׁנָה, חֲמִשָּׁה חוּמְשֵׁי תוֹרָה, אַרְבַּע אִמָּהוֹת, שְׁלֹשָׁה אָבוֹת, שְׁנֵי לֻחוֹת הַבְּרִית, אֶחָד אֱלֹהֵינוּ שֶׁבַּשָּׁמַיִם וּבָאָרֶץ.

שְׁמוֹנָה מִי יוֹדֵעַ? שְׁמוֹנָה אֲנִי יוֹדֵעַ: שְׁמוֹנָה יְמֵי מִילָה, שִׁבְעָה יְמֵי שַׁבַּתָּא, שִׁשָּׁה סִדְרֵי מִשְׁנָה, חֲמִשָּׁה חוּמְשֵׁי תוֹרָה, אַרְבַּע אִמָּהוֹת, שְׁלֹשָׁה אָבוֹת, שְׁנֵי לֻחוֹת הַבְּרִית, אֶחָד אֱלֹהֵינוּ שֶׁבַּשָּׁמַיִם וּבָאָרֶץ.

תִּשְׁעָה מִי יוֹדֵעַ? תִּשְׁעָה אֲנִי יוֹדֵעַ: תִּשְׁעָה יַרְחֵי לֵדָה, שְׁמוֹנָה יְמֵי מִילָה, שִׁבְעָה יְמֵי שַׁבַּתָּא, שִׁשָּׁה סִדְרֵי מִשְׁנָה, חֲמִשָּׁה חוּמְשֵׁי תוֹרָה, אַרְבַּע אִמָּהוֹת, שְׁלֹשָׁה אָבוֹת, שְׁנֵי לֻחוֹת הַבְּרִית, אֶחָד אֱלֹהֵינוּ שֶׁבַּשָּׁמַיִם וּבָאָרֶץ.

עֲשָׂרָה מִי יוֹדֵעַ? עֲשָׂרָה אֲנִי יוֹדֵעַ: עֲשָׂרָה דִּבְּרַיָּא, תִּשְׁעָה יַרְחֵי לֵדָה, שְׁמוֹנָה יְמֵי מִילָה, שִׁבְעָה יְמֵי שַׁבַּתָּא, שִׁשָּׁה סִדְרֵי מִשְׁנָה, חֲמִשָּׁה חוּמְשֵׁי תוֹרָה, אַרְבַּע אִמָּהוֹת, שְׁלֹשָׁה אָבוֹת, שְׁנֵי לֻחוֹת הַבְּרִית, אֶחָד אֱלֹהֵינוּ שֶׁבַּשָּׁמַיִם וּבָאָרֶץ.

אַחַד עָשָׂר מִי יוֹדֵעַ? אַחַד עָשָׂר אֲנִי יוֹדֵעַ: אַחַד עָשָׂר כּוֹכְבַיָּא, עֲשָׂרָה דִּבְּרַיָּא, תִּשְׁעָה יַרְחֵי לֵדָה, שְׁמוֹנָה יְמֵי מִילָה, שִׁבְעָה יְמֵי שַׁבַּתָּא, שִׁשָּׁה סִדְרֵי מִשְׁנָה, חֲמִשָּׁה חוּמְשֵׁי תוֹרָה, אַרְבַּע אִמָּהוֹת, שְׁלֹשָׁה אָבוֹת, שְׁנֵי לֻחוֹת הַבְּרִית, אֶחָד אֱלֹהֵינוּ שֶׁבַּשָּׁמַיִם וּבָאָרֶץ.

שְׁנֵים עָשָׂר מִי יוֹדֵעַ? שְׁנֵים עָשָׂר אֲנִי יוֹדֵעַ: שְׁנֵים עָשָׂר שִׁבְטַיָּא, אַחַד עָשָׂר כּוֹכְבַיָּא, עֲשָׂרָה דִּבְּרַיָּא, תִּשְׁעָה יַרְחֵי לֵדָה, שְׁמוֹנָה יְמֵי מִילָה, שִׁבְעָה יְמֵי שַׁבַּתָּא, שִׁשָּׁה סִדְרֵי מִשְׁנָה, חֲמִשָּׁה חוּמְשֵׁי תוֹרָה, אַרְבַּע אִמָּהוֹת, שְׁלֹשָׁה אָבוֹת, שְׁנֵי לֻחוֹת הַבְּרִית, אֶחָד אֱלֹהֵינוּ שֶׁבַּשָּׁמַיִם וּבָאָרֶץ.

שְׁלֹשָׁה עָשָׂר מִי יוֹדֵעַ? שְׁלֹשָׁה עָשָׂר אֲנִי יוֹדֵעַ: שְׁלֹשָׁה עָשָׂר מִדַּיָּא, שְׁנֵים עָשָׂר שִׁבְטַיָּא, אַחַד עָשָׂר כּוֹכְבַיָּא, עֲשָׂרָה דִּבְּרַיָּא, תִּשְׁעָה יַרְחֵי לֵדָה, שְׁמוֹנָה יְמֵי מִילָה, שִׁבְעָה יְמֵי שַׁבַּתָּא, שִׁשָּׁה סִדְרֵי מִשְׁנָה, חֲמִשָּׁה חוּמְשֵׁי תוֹרָה, אַרְבַּע אִמָּהוֹת, שְׁלֹשָׁה אָבוֹת, שְׁנֵי לֻחוֹת הַבְּרִית, אֶחָד אֱלֹהֵינוּ שֶׁבַּשָּׁמַיִם וּבָאָרֶץ.

Who knows one? I know one: One is our God in the heavens and the earth. Who knows two? I know two: two are the tablets of the covenant, One is our God in the heavens and the earth. Who knows three? I know three: three are the fathers, two are the tablets of the covenant, One is our God in the heavens and the earth. Who knows four? I know four: four are the mothers, three are the fathers, two are the tablets of the covenant, One is our God in the heavens and the earth. Who knows five? I know five: five are the books of the Torah, four are the mothers, three are the fathers, two are the tablets of the covenant, One is our God in the heavens and the earth. Who knows six? I know six: six are the orders of the Mishnah, five are the books of the Torah, four are the mothers, three are the fathers, two are the tablets of the covenant, One is our God in the heavens and the earth. Who knows seven? I know seven: seven are the days of the week, six are the orders of the Mishnah, five are the books of the Torah, four are the mothers, three are the fathers, two are the tablets of the covenant, One is our God in the heavens and the earth. Who knows eight? I know eight: eight are the days of circumcision, seven are the days of the week, six are the orders of the Mishnah, five are the books of the Torah, four are the mothers, three are the fathers, two are the tablets of the covenant, One is our God in the heavens and the earth. Who knows nine? I know nine: nine are the months of birth, eight are the days of circumcision, seven are the days of the week, six are the orders of the Mishnah, five are the books of the Torah, four are the mothers, three are the fathers, two are the tablets of the covenant, One is our God in the heavens and the earth. Who knows ten? I know ten: ten are the statements, nine are the months of birth, eight are the days of circumcision, seven are the days of the week, six are the orders of the Mishnah, five are the books of the Torah, four are the mothers, three are the fathers, two are the tablets of the covenant, One is our God in the heavens and the earth. Who knows eleven? I know eleven: eleven are the stars, ten are the statements, nine are the months of birth, eight are the days of circumcision, seven are the days of the week, six are the orders of the Mishnah, five are the books of the Torah, four are the mothers, three are the fathers, two are the tablets of the covenant, One is our God in the heavens and the earth. Who knows twelve? I know twelve: twelve are the tribes, eleven are the stars, ten are the statements, nine are the months of birth, eight are the days of circumcision, seven are the days of the week, six are the orders of the Mishnah, five are the books of the Torah, four are the mothers, three are the fathers, two are the tablets of the covenant, One is our God in the heavens and the earth. Who knows thirteen? I know thirteen: thirteen are the characteristics, twelve are the tribes, eleven are the stars, ten are the statements, nine are the months of birth, eight are the days of circumcision, seven are the days of the week, six are the orders of the Mishnah, five are the books of the Torah, four are the mothers, three are the fathers, two are the tablets of the covenant, One is our God in the heavens and the earth.

Echad Mi Yodea ("Who Knows One?") is a song with a simple verse structure, each progressively longer, as it enumerates traditional Jewish concepts and motifs. It is thought to have been composed in Germany in the fifteenth century and may have been patterned after the folk song *"Guter freund ich frage dich"* ("Good friend, I ask you"). Being entertaining and humorous, it is especially relevant as a teaching vehicle for the children at the Seder. Its message lies beyond the story of the Exodus, since it underscores the elements of Jewish life that make Israel not just a national entity, but a people, with a uniquely spiritual and religious heritage. As each verse adds a layered, numerical texture to what preceded, everything comes back to "One, our God." The unity of God is therefore the sum and substance of all.

—Kenneth Hanson

Nirtzah, Chad Gadya

חַד גַּדְיָא, חַד גַּדְיָא דְּזַבִּין אַבָּא בִּתְרֵי זוּזֵי, חַד גַּדְיָא, חַד גַּדְיָא.

One kid, one kid that my father bought for two zuz, one kid, one kid.

וְאָתָא שׁוּנְרָא וְאָכְלָה לְגַדְיָא, דְּזַבִּין אַבָּא בִּתְרֵי זוּזֵי. חַד גַּדְיָא, חַד גַּדְיָא.

Then came a cat and ate the kid that my father bought for two zuz, one kid, one kid.

וְאָתָא כַלְבָּא וְנָשַׁךְ לְשׁוּנְרָא, דְּאָכְלָה לְגַדְיָא, דְּזַבִּין אַבָּא בִּתְרֵי זוּזֵי. חַד גַּדְיָא, חַד גַּדְיָא.

Then came a dog and bit the cat, that ate the kid that my father bought for two zuz, one kid, one kid.

וְאָתָא חוּטְרָא וְהִכָּה לְכַלְבָּא, דְּנָשַׁךְ לְשׁוּנְרָא, דְּאָכְלָה לְגַדְיָא, דְּזַבִּין אַבָּא בִּתְרֵי זוּזֵי. חַד גַּדְיָא, חַד גַּדְיָא.

Then came a stick and hit the dog, that bit the cat, that ate the kid that my father bought for two zuz, one kid, one kid.

וְאָתָא נוּרָא וְשָׂרַף לְחוּטְרָא, דְּהִכָּה לְכַלְבָּא, דְּנָשַׁךְ לְשׁוּנְרָא, דְּאָכְלָה לְגַדְיָא, דְּזַבִּין אַבָּא בִּתְרֵי זוּזֵי. חַד גַּדְיָא, חַד גַּדְיָא.

Then came fire and burnt the stick, that hit the dog, that bit the cat, that ate the kid that my father bought for two zuz, one kid, one kid.

וְאָתָא מַיָּא וְכָבָה לְנוּרָא, דְּשָׂרַף לְחוּטְרָא, דְּהִכָּה לְכַלְבָּא, דְּנָשַׁךְ לְשׁוּנְרָא, דְּאָכְלָה לְגַדְיָא, דְּזַבִּין אַבָּא בִּתְרֵי זוּזֵי. חַד גַּדְיָא, חַד גַּדְיָא.

Then came water and extinguished the fire, that burnt the stick, that hit the dog, that bit the cat, that ate the kid that my father bought for two zuz, one kid, one kid.

וְאָתָא תוֹרָא וְשָׁתָה לְמַיָּא, דְּכָבָה לְנוּרָא, דְּשָׂרַף לְחוּטְרָא, דְּהִכָּה לְכַלְבָּא, דְּנָשַׁךְ לְשׁוּנְרָא, דְּאָכְלָה לְגַדְיָא, דְּזַבִּין אַבָּא בִּתְרֵי זוּזֵי. חַד גַּדְיָא, חַד גַּדְיָא.

Then came a bull and drank the water, that extinguished the fire, that burnt the stick, that hit the dog, that bit the cat, that ate the kid that my father bought for two zuz, one kid, one kid.

וְאָתָא הַשּׁוֹחֵט וְשָׁחַט לְתוֹרָא, דְּשָׁתָה לְמַיָּא, דְּכָבָה לְנוּרָא, דְּשָׂרַף לְחוּטְרָא, דְּהִכָּה לְכַלְבָּא, דְּנָשַׁךְ לְשׁוּנְרָא, דְּאָכְלָה לְגַדְיָא, דְּזַבִּין אַבָּא בִּתְרֵי זוּזֵי. חַד גַּדְיָא, חַד גַּדְיָא.

Then came the schochet and slaughtered the bull, that drank the water, that extinguished the fire, that burnt the stick, that hit the dog, that bit the cat, that ate the kid that my father bought for two zuz, one kid, one kid.

וְאָתָא מַלְאָךְ הַמָּוֶת וְשָׁחַט לְשׁוֹחֵט, דְּשָׁחַט לְתוֹרָא, דְּשָׁתָה לְמַיָּא, דְּכָבָה לְנוּרָא, דְּשָׂרַף לְחוּטְרָא, דְּהִכָּה לְכַלְבָּא, דְּנָשַׁךְ לְשׁוּנְרָא, דְּאָכְלָה לְגַדְיָא, דְּזַבִּין אַבָּא בִּתְרֵי זוּזֵי. חַד גַּדְיָא, חַד גַּדְיָא.

Then came the angel of death and slaughtered the schochet, who slaughtered the bull, that drank the water, that extinguished the fire, that burnt the stick, that hit the dog, that bit the cat, that ate the kid that my father bought for two zuz, one kid, one kid.

וְאָתָא הַקָּדוֹשׁ בָּרוּךְ הוּא וְשָׁחַט לְמַלְאַךְ הַמָּוֶת, דְּשָׁחַט לְשׁוֹחֵט, דְּשָׁחַט לְתוֹרָא, דְּשָׁתָה לְמַיָּא, דְּכָבָה לְנוּרָא, דְּשָׂרַף לְחוּטְרָא, דְּהִכָּה לְכַלְבָּא, דְּנָשַׁךְ לְשׁוּנְרָא, דְּאָכְלָה לְגַדְיָא, דְּזַבִּין אַבָּא בִּתְרֵי זוּזֵי. חַד גַּדְיָא, חַד גַּדְיָא.

Then came the Holy One, blessed be He and slaughtered the angel of death, who slaughtered the schochet, who slaughtered the bull, that drank the water, that extinguished the fire, that burnt the stick, that hit the dog, that bit the cat, that ate the kid that my father bought for two zuz, one kid, one kid.

Chad Gadya ("one little goat" or "one little kid") made its first appearance in a Haggadah printed in Prague, dating to 1590. It is a cumulative song (originally written in a mix of Aramaic and Hebrew) in the same vein as Echad Mi Yodea and was likewise possibly inspired by German folk music.

While it appeals to children, it may involve deep symbolism, concerning the many times the Jewish people (represented by the kid) have been conquered. Some see the cat as Assyria, the dog as Babylon, the stick as Persia, the fire as Macedonia, the water as Rome, the ox as the Saracens, the *schochet* ("slaughterer") as the Crusaders, and the angel of death as the Turks. Ultimately, God arrives, to bring the Jewish people back to their homeland. The two *zuzim* represent either Moses and Aaron, or the two tablets of the Law, delivered by God to Moses. Another interpretation sees the water as Greece, the ox as Rome, the *schochet* as the Muslim empire, and the angel of death as the European Christian nations. See Cecil Roth, *The Haggadah, a New Edition* (London: Soncino Press, 1959), 87–88.

The Vilna Gaon considered the *schochet* to be the Messiah ben Joseph, who, at some future time, will battle Israel's enemies, only to be slain by the Angel of Death, who in turn will be killed by God. At that time the messianic age will dawn. See Yisrael Isser Herczeg, *Vilna Gaon Haggadah: The Passover Haggadah with Commentaries by the Vilna Gaon and his Son, R' Avraham* (Brooklyn: Mesorah, 1993), 130–136. Alternately, the song may amount to an allegorical representation of the growth and development of the Jewish soul. Two *zuzim*, according to Targum Jonathan on 1 Sam 9:8, comprise the half-shekel tax levied upon each adult male Israelite. The song then relates the many snares and dangers encountered through the course of one's life. Yet another interpretation relates the song to the Passover sacrifice in the Jerusalem temple.

—Kenneth Hanson

Rabbinic Sages Index

Akiba/ Akiva ben Yosef: Known also as Rabbi Akiva, he was one of the foremost scholars and sages of the tannaitic period. Born around 50 C.E., in Lod, in the Roman province of Judea, he contributed greatly to the Mishnah and Midrash halakha. Martyred by the Romans in 135 C.E., he died chanting the Shema, and with the word "One!" he expired.

Alfasi ha-Cohen, Isaac ben Jacob (1013–1103): Known also as the Alfasi as well as by the Hebrew acronym Rif. He was an Algerian Talmudist and posek (decider in matters of Halakha). He is noted for his "digest" of the Talmud, Sefer Ha-halachot, which is regarded as the foundational work of halakhic literature.

Asher: Asher ben Jehiel (c. 1250–1327): Known also as Rabbenu Asher ("our Rabbi Asher"), Asheri and Rosh (the Hebrew acronym), he was one of the major codifiers of the Talmud. When his teacher, Meir ben Baruch of Rothenberg, was imprisoned, he became the foremost rabbi in Germany, writing multiple commentaries on Talmudic tractates and more than one thousand responsa.

Elazar ben Azariah: A first-century C.E. tannaitic/Mishnaic sage, his maxims are among the most well-known sayings of the Talmud. He was a junior contemporary of Eliezer b. Hyrcanus and Joshua ben Hananiah and was also a friend and colleague of Rabbi Akiva. He served as "Nasi" (head of the Sanhedrin) when Gamaliel II was, for a time, demoted.

Eliezer, Eliezer ben Hurcanus or Hyrcanus ("the Great"): One of the most prominent Sages of the first and second centuries, C.E., he is the sixth most frequently mentioned sage in the Mishnah. A disciple of Yohanan ben Zakkai and colleague of Gamaliel II and Joshua ben Hananiah, his teaching was characterized by strict devotion to tradition. He was known for his severe and domineering approach.

Gamliel: Gamaliel the Elder, or Rabban Gamaliel I: One of the earliest of the tannaim, and president of the Sanhedrin in Jerusalem in the first half of the first century. His father was Simeon ben Hillel, and his grandfather Hillel the Elder. Believed to have died in 52 C.E., he was known as "Nasi" ("prince"). He was the first to use the title Rabban ("Rabbi" or "Master").

Isserles, Moshe (Moses) Isserles (1530–1572): Known also as Rema, he became Rabbi of Krakow at the age of 20, and was respected as one of the foremost authorities of his day. His writings covered many areas of Jewish thought, including biblical commentary, philosophy, Kabbalah and aggadah. His glosses to the *Shulchan Aruch,* adding notes on Ashkenazi customs, made it an authoritative guide for Jewish practice to this day.

Jon—athan/Rabbi Jonathan: One of the *tannaim* of the second century, C.E., he is generally quoted in conjunction with his study partner, Rabbi Josiah. The two expertly propounded madrash halakha, interpreting Scriptural laws without propounding new ones. Their emendations are mainly found in Mekhilta and Sifre to Numbers.

Judah bar Ezekiel: (220–299 C.E.): Known also as Rav Yehudah, he was known for his strong personality and sharp, analytical mind. A disciple of Rav, he founded an academy in Pumbedita in 259. After the destruction of Nehardea, it became the focal point of Babylonian scholarship.

Maimonides (1138–1204): Known also by the acronym Rambam (for "Rabbi Moshe ben Maimon"), he was a medieval Sephardic Jewish philosopher. He was both a Torah scholar and physician, who composed some of the most influential commentaries on the Talmud. The first to produce a systematized compendium of Jewish law, he authored Mishneh Torah and the influential treatise of religious philosophy, *Guide for the Perplexed.*

Meir of Rothenburg (c. 1220–1293): Known also as Meir ben Baruch, and Maharam of Rothenburg, he was a German Rabbi, Talmudic scholar and religious poet. Among his unofficial titles, he was called "Father of Rabbis" and "Light of the Exile." He authored many notes, responsa and expositions, including tosafot on Rashi's Talmudic commentary.

Rashi/Rabbi Solomon ben Isaac (1040–1105): One of the most prominent of all Jewish commentators on the Hebrew Bible and the Talmud. Born in in Troyes, France, he is regarded as the greatest medieval Jewish scholar in Ashkenaz (Germany, France and England). All printed editions of the Babylonian Talmud since the sixteenth century include his commentary, featured in the margins.

Rav: Born in Kafri, Sassanid Babylonia, he was considered the greatest student of Rabbi Yehuda Ha-Nasi. He formed a "bridge" between the period of the Tannaim (the scholars of the Mishnah) and the Amoraim (the expositors of the Talmud). Both he and another of Rabbi's students, Shmuel, are frequently referenced throughout the Talmud.

Tarfon: A third generation Mishnaic Sage of priestly lineage, he occupied a prominent place between the destruction of the Second Temple in 70 C.E. and the fall of Betar in 135 C.E. He became one of the leading scholars of Jabneh, and was renowned as a halakhist and an advocate for the House of Shammai. He is frequently cited in the Mishnah, arguing with Rabbi Akiva.

Vilna Gaon (1720–1797): Properly known as Elijah ben Solomon Zalman, and sometimes referred to as Elijah of Vilna, Elijah Ben Solomon, or HaGra (a Hebrew acronym), he is considered the greatest Jewish sage of the eighteenth century. He never officially served in a rabbinic position, but as a Talmudic scholar, halakhist and Kabbalist, he wrote voluminous commentaries on almost all Jewish texts. He was also one of the leaders of the "Mitnagdim," those who opposed the rise of the Hasidic movement.

Yannai: A prominent Galilean poet (payyetan) of the late fifth to early sixth century, he is occasionally called the "father of piyyut." His poems represent the onset of the Classical Period of piyyut (Jewish liturgical poetry), extending from the fifth to eighth centuries. He was perhaps the first to introduce rhyme and acrostic into this tradition.

Yehuda/Judah ben Ilai: A second century Galilean, and one of the most prominent of the fifth generation tannaim. A pupil of Rabbi Akiva and a contemporary of Rabbi Shimon ben Gamliel, he was known simply as "Rabbi Judah." He is the sage mentioned most often in the Mishnah, his most famous maxim being: "Be meticulous in learning, for a careless misrepresentation is considered tantamount to an intentional sin" (Avot 4:16).

Yehoshua ben Levi: An early third century Palestinian amora (Talmudic scholar), he resided at Lydda (Lod), where he studied under Bar Kappara. He was a contemporary of Rav Johanan and Resh-Lakish, and was considered a renowned halakhist. His *bet midrash* was particularly devoted to *aggadah.* An aggadic account relates how he personally received the revelation of Elijah.

Yochanan/Rabbi Yochanan/Johanan bar Nafcha (180–279 C.E.): Head of the most prominent rabbinic academy in third century Palestine, he was one of the second generation of amoraim. He frequently sparred with his compatriot, Resh Lakish, and his opinion generally prevailed. He is the most quoted sage in the entire Talmud, appearing on almost every page.

Yose Hagelili/Eliezer ben Jose/Eliezer ben Yose HaGelili: A Palestinian (Galilean) tanna of the second century, he was one of the last disciples of Rabbi Akiva. Known as an expert in field of aggadah, he devised a set of thirty-two metrics for evaluating the Torah, as an expansion of the thirteen traditional principles of hermeneutics.

Source Index

Hebrew Bible
Gen
    1:31–2:3
    10:14
    14:15
    15:13–14
    18:1, 6
    19:3
    32:25–30
    40:11–13
    46:3–4
    47:4

Exod
    1:7, 10–11, 14, 24
    2: 6–7, 23–25
    3:9, 16
    4:17, 22–23
    5:2
    6:6–7
    7:3, 7
    7:14–12:36
    8:12–28
    9:1–12, 17–35
    10:1–23
    12:9–36, 39–40, 42
    13:1–2, 8, 12–15
    14:31
    15
    16:6–7
    22:28
    30:14
    32:2
    34:20

Lev
    23:10–14
    25:25ff.
    27:11ff.

Num
    3:11–13
    6:24
    8:16–18
    9:11
    15: 37–41
    18:16
    35:12ff.

Deut
    4:17, 34
    6:20–24
    8:10
    10:22
    11:11, 13–21
    16:3
    21:12, 15–17
    26:2, 5–8
    34:7

Josh
    6:1
    9:6
    24:2–4

Judg
    5:20
    7:13

I Sam
    22:51

I Kgs
    19:8, 12

II Kgs
    19:35

Isa
    10:32
    19:13
    21:11
    45:1–3
    47:9
    62:6
    66:19

Jer
    17:7
    25:15
    44:1

Ezek
    16:6
    16:7

Joel
    3:3

Zech
    14:7

Mal
    3:23–24

Ps
    9:9
    11:6
    21:5
    29:11
    33:10
    34:10–11
    35:10
    37:25
    69:25
    74:16
    75:9
    78:42–51
    79:6–7
    103:1
    105:28–36

107
113–118
120–134
136
137:1
146:16

Job
19:25

Lam
3:66
4:21

Esth
3:13

Dan
2:9
5:5
5:30
10:11

I Chron
21:16

Mishnah
*Ber.*1.5
Ber 8:1
Pesaḥ 10.1–2, 4–8
Roš Haš 1:1
Ta`an. 3.9
`Avot 5.6

Babylonian Talmud (Bavli)
Ber. 4b
Ber. 32b
Ber. 48b
Pesaḥ 116a
Pesaḥ 119b
Pesaḥ 90a
Pesaḥ 117b–118a
Pesaḥ 120a

Roš Haš. 11b
BB 142b
Qidd. 29a
Bekh. 47b
Bekh. 51b

Jerusalem Talmud (Yerushalmi)
Pesaḥ 37d
Pesaḥ. 68b:20–21
Bekh 8:2

Rabbinic Writings
Gen. Rab. 6:2
Gen. Rab. 68.9
Exod. Rab. 15.12
Exod. Rab. 5.14
Num. Rab. 20
Mek. on Exod 13:3
Mek. on Exod 14:10
Midr. Tehilim/Psalms on 78:49
Sif. Deut. 215

Rabbinical Commentaries
Bondi, Rabbi Tevele, *Maarechet Heidenheim*, 1898
Isserles to *YD* 305:15
Maimonides, *Mishneh Torah, Ḥametsu-Matsah*, VIII.2; "Leavened and Unleavened Bread," 8:10
Minchat Chinuch 6:3
Rashi, *Maḥzor Vitry*, p. 295
Rif Pesaḥim
Rosh on Pesaḥim
Seder R. Amram Ga'on
Shulchan Aruch HaRav 475:15

Supplementary Readings

Kenneth Hanson

Textual Issues: An Analysis

The "Lost" Supper, Paul and Qumran: The Tail that Wagged the Dog

The Last Supper, while undoubtedly the central element of liturgical Christianity, is equally laden with theoretical and theological issues, as well as questions of textual redaction, that directly bear on is interpretation and intrinsic meaning. With the significant help of Jewish scholarship and Qumranic studies, much new light has been shed on the Gospels' depiction of the meal as a kind of Passover meal. But was it? Looking behind the Textus Receptus, we find clear parallels with the so-called "Messianic Rule" of the Dead Sea Scrolls, which describes an eschatological "banquet," involving bread and wine (in that order), blessed by a priestly/ messianic figure (1QSa 2:17–21). This is the order depicted by Paul (1 Cor. 11:23–25), as well as well as by the Gospels of Mark (14:22–25) and Matthew (26:26–29), in which Jesus refers to the "blood of the covenant" or, according to other ancient texts, "new covenant" (as in Qumranic parlance). Luke, by contrast (22:13–20), has Jesus take the cup first, as common in Jewish ritual, followed by a second cup, which becomes, theologically, "the new covenant in my blood." Might the problematic reference to the drinking of blood represent a later redaction of the Lucan account, which depicts Jesus behaving in an otherwise "kosher" manner? Might Jesus' final repast with his disciples have been transformed from a traditional Jewish meal into, not just a Passover "Seder," but a Qumran-inspired "Messianic Banquet," influenced by a secondary Pauline wave of Judeo-Christianity?

The fabled "Last Supper" of Jesus, as recorded in all four Christian Gospels (Matthew 26:17–30; Mark 14:12–26; Luke 22:7–39; John 13:1–17, 26) has long been viewed as a traditional Jewish Passover meal (which came to be called a "Seder"), intriguing as well as inspiring believing Christians the world over. The very idea that the elements of the Christian Eucharist, bread and wine, were essential components of the

Passover meal, has captivated both theologians and popular Christian culture. On a scholarly level Joachim Jeremias' exhaustive study, *The Eucharistic Words of Jesus*, details not less than fourteen parallels between the Last Supper and the Passover Seder.[1] Mark Kinzer (from a messianic Jewish perspective) devotes considerable attention to the Eucharist within the milieu of first-century Judaism, but sadly, relatively little Jewish scholarship deals seriously with the New Testament. Kinzer stresses "the sacrificial dimension of the Eucharist, and its connection to the religious character of the Jewish way of life."[2] We would do well, in any case, to go beyond reflections on the theological significance of Last Supper, employing Jewish scholarship and Qumranic studies to gain a fresh appreciation of the event itself, framing the narrative as best we can in what might be called a "historical" context.

The Lost Seder?

To be sure, there are a number of chronological and textual inconsistencies ("passed over" in Jeremias' work and in Kinzer's commentary as in popular religious culture) that make identifying Jesus' Last Supper as a "Seder" a virtual impossibility. If the Last Supper had in fact been a "Seder," then the Jewish high priest would have convened the trial of a fellow Jew after the onset of the great festival. That of course is unthinkable, and not even a Roman prefect would have ordered a crucifixion on the first day of Passover in the "powder keg" of ancient Judea. Furthermore, the Gospels indicate that the body of the crucified Jesus had to be taken down from the cross and interred prior to the Sabbath; yet if Jesus had been crucified on Friday (the first day of Passover), it would already have been a high holy day, and the rush to burial would have been moot.

Such issues have led to speculation that perhaps there was no Last Supper at all, and that the Gospels themselves are comprised of mere theological reflections on the meaning of Jesus' death. Bruce Chilton argues that the identification of the Last Supper with a Passover "Seder" originated after the fact, among Jewish Christians who were attempting to maintain the

---

[1] Joachim Jeremias, *The Eucharistic Words of Jesus*, 3rd ed. (London: SCM Press, 1966), 42–61.
[2] Mark Kinzer, Jean-Miguel Garrigues, and Christoph Schönborn, *Searching Her Own Mystery: Nostra Aetate, the Jewish People, and the Identity of the Church* (Eugene, OR: Cascade Books, 2015), 107, 113. Kinzer sees the Last Supper as embodying an "organic connection to the Israel of old." He does not, however, address the multiple challenges to the reliability of the Gospel accounts of the Last Supper.

Jewish character of early Easter celebrations.[3] There is of course the larger issue of whether anything at all may be recovered of the "historical Jesus."

We need of course to examine the specific language of the synoptic Gospels, the Gospel of John and other relevant accounts. Mark (14:16) tells us that the disciples "prepared the Passover meal" on Jesus' behalf. Matthew (26:19) agrees with Mark, declaring, "So the disciples did as Jesus had directed them, and they prepared the Passover meal." As Luke (22:8) relates, "Jesus sent Peter and John, saying, 'Go and prepare the Passover meal for us that we may eat it.'" However, we are never told that they actually prepare it or that it is ever consumed. On this point it is reasonable to conclude that the Lucan language should be preferred over the other synoptics.

John's Gospel (13:1) simply relates that the Last Supper occurred "before the festival of the Passover." The meal is never identified as a Passover "Seder," and the Passover itself is said to have commenced a few hours after Jesus' death.[4] This it seems is a much more credible chronology. Moreover, the liturgical element of what became the Christian Eucharist is completely absent in John.

Seder on a Leash

Notably, there have been multiple attempts to recover the "lost dog" of Jesus' "Seder," dragging it as if by leash to the proper time. Perhaps Passover coincided with the Sabbath that year, since, according to John, Jesus was crucified on the "day of preparation," presumably Friday. In that case, however, Jesus' "Seder" (presumably Thursday night) would have been conducted a day too early. Perhaps there was flexibility regarding when the Passover meal might be celebrated. After all, multiple Seders have come to be observed in the long legacy of Jewish tradition. Never, of course, has a Seder been conducted before the onset of Passover. Is it reasonable to assume, in an age in which so much emphasis was placed on precise calendrical calculations, that Jesus would have conducted the Passover meal on the wrong day? It more than strains credulity to imagine any Second Temple observant Jew, Jesus included, simply dispensing with halakhic provisions as to when the Passover was to be commemorated.

---

[3] Bruce Chilton, *A Feast of Meanings: Eucharistic Theologies from Jesus Through Johannine Circles* (Leiden: E. J. Brill, 1994), 93–108. See also Jonathan Klawans, "Was Jesus' Last Supper a Seder?," *Bible Review*, October 2001.

[4] James Tabor, *The Jesus Dynasty: The Hidden History of Jesus, His Royal Family, and the Birth of Christianity* (New York: Simon & Schuster, 2006), 204. Tabor stresses the complete absence in John of any reference to the Eucharist. "If Jesus in fact had inaugurated the practice of eating bread because his body, and drinking wine as his blood at this 'Last Supper' how could John possibly have left it out? What John writes is that Jesus set down to the supper, by all indications an ordinary Jewish meal."

One possible solution, offered by Annie Jaubert, assumes that Jesus may have been operating according to a completely separate calendar, namely, the solar calendar that features prominently in both Jewish pseudepigrapha and the literature of Qumran.[5] Notable references to this alternate calendar appear in the books of Enoch and Jubilees, which were wildly popular during the Second Jewish Commonwealth.[6] In that case, what may have been observed as Passover by Jesus and his disciples was not Passover for the rest of the population of Jerusalem. The calendar began on the first of Nisan, a Wednesday, which was appropriate, since the creation account of Genesis lists the fourth day as that on which the heavenly bodies were created, affording the possibility of counting time. Subsequently, all holidays fell on Wednesdays.[7] This proposed "solution" nonetheless presents us with more problems, since it would place the Last Supper/"Seder" on a Tuesday night, in conflict with the rest of the Gospel chronology and effectively turning Jesus into a quasi-Essene. It has also been argued that Passover in the Qumran calendar (if it were intercalated) would have fallen after Passover according to the lunar Jewish calendar.[8]

James Tabor has attempted to reconcile the disparate Gospel accounts of the Last Supper and blend them into a cogent chronological sequence by proceeding on the assumption that Passover fell on a Friday that particular year, thus creating (in essence) two back-to-back Sabbaths. Matthew 28:1 seems to hint at this when it relates that the women who rushed to Jesus' tomb arrived early Sunday morning "after the *Sabbaths*," the Greek being plural. Mark 14:12 (in agreement with Luke 22:7), relates that Jesus was crucified on the day "when the Passover lamb is sacrificed," according to this reconstruction on a Thursday. This is also congruent with a

---

[5] Annie Jaubert, *The Date of the Last Supper* (trans. I. Rafferty, Staten Island: Alba House, 1965); Stephane Saulnier, *Calendrical Variations in Second Temple Judaism: New Perspectives on the 'Date of the Last Supper' Debate* (JSJSup 159; Leiden: Brill, 2012). See also Colin J. Humphreys, "Did Jesus use the solar calendar of Qumran for his last supper Passover?" in *The Mystery of the Last Supper: Reconstructing the Final Days of Jesus* (Cambridge: Cambridge University Press, 2011), 95–109. As Humphreys observes, "Only a small minority of biblical scholars support a different calendar solution of the synoptics/John last supper controversy."

[6] It is also likely that the embrace of the solar calendar was the principal reason for the initial schism which developed between the Dead Sea sectarians and the rest of Jewish society during this period. See Eshbal Ratzon, "The First Jewish Astronomers: Lunar Theory and Reconstruction of a Dead Sea Scroll," *Science in Context* 30, 2 (2017):113–139; Jonathan Ben Dov, *Head of All Years*. (Leiden-Boston: Brill, 2008).

[7] Eshbal Ratzon and Jonathan Ben-Dov, "A Newly Reconstructed Calendrical Scroll from Qumran in Cryptic Script," *JBL* 136, 4 (2017): 905–936.

[8] Humphreys, 107–9. See also Brant Pitre, *Jesus and the Last Supper* (Grand Rapids, Eerdmans, 2015), 280: "It is difficult to reconcile with the synoptic testimony that Jesus ate the Last Supper the same evening the lambs were being sacrificed by other Jews."

Talmudic passage which relates, "They hung Yeshua the Nazarene on *Erev Pesach*."[9] The Passover meal would therefore have been conducted that evening, *after* Jesus had already died and been interred in a burial cave. This of course effectively rules out identifying the Last Supper with a Passover meal, Mark and Matthew notwithstanding.

If, however, Jesus' famous repast should not be seen as a "Seder," what was it, and how do we understand the elements of bread and wine as details of the synoptic Gospel accounts? The place to begin is not with the Gospels at all, but with the apostle Paul. Chronologically, Paul's letters precede all of the Gospels, at least in their redacted forms, and it was Paul who arguably lent theological significance to Jesus' final meal, transforming it from a prophetic vehicle to showcase the immanent betrayal by Judas (we might rename it the "Judas dinner") to a liturgical formula for identifying with Jesus' sacrificial death.

It is apparent that the key element in this transformation was the evolving tradition of a communal meal, which became part of Judeo-Christian ("Nazarene") practice early on. The Acts of the Apostles pointedly alludes to the new believers in Jesus sharing such a repast: "And they, continuing daily with one accord in the temple, and breaking bread from house to house, ate their food with gladness and sincerity of heart" (Acts 2:46 NKJV). Additional details emerge in the same narrative, recounting the selling of homes and the adoption of a communal lifestyle reminiscent of the Dead Sea sect. According to David Flusser, the initial stage of the Jesus movement derived from the character of Jesus' message, which he insists was largely pre-rabbinic, while a "second stratum" was largely influenced by the Essenes/ Dead Sea Sect and later found expression in the *kerygma* of the hellenistic Christian communities.[10]

The Pauline "Tail"

In keeping with this "second stratum," the communal meal became integral in the liturgical life of the churches planted by Paul. The Pauline epistles repeatedly reference the "love feasts" of the early Christians, sometimes berating the participants for using them as an excuse for gluttony. The role of the communal meal at Qumran is likewise well attested, being central to the organization of the sect.

---

[9] *b. Sanhedrin* 67a and 43a.

[10] Jesus arguably made backhanded reference to the Dead Sea sect, castigating their exclusivity. For example, while the Dead Sea sectarians referred to themselves as "sons of light" and all outsiders as "sons of darkness," Jesus (with wry irony) is quoted as declaring (Luke 16:8) that the "the sons of this world are more shrewd in their generation than the sons of light." See David Flusser, *Judaism and the Origins of Christianity* (Jerusalem: Magnes Press, 1988), xviii.

Moreover, while gluttonous practices are never referenced, the "pure meal" of the sect is the domain, not of novices, but of full initiates into the order, who fully appreciate its solemnity. Most prominently, we find reference in the Dead Sea *Community Rule* (1QS 6:4–5) and in its addendum, the *Messianic Rule*, to a sanctified meal attended by one or both Qumranic messiahs (priestly and Davidic) and featuring the very elements of bread and wine central to the Last Supper. In latter we read:

> For he shall bless the first portion of the bread and the wine, reaching for the bread first. Afterward the Messiah of Israel shall reach for the bread. (1QSa 2:19–21)[11]

Most striking here is the liturgical order of bread first, followed by wine. Is it by any means coincidental that Paul follows the same order in recounting the meal partaken by Jesus and his disciples? Paul, writing around the year 55 of the Common Era, gave voice to what by then had become the focal point of the Christian "love feasts." It is hardly surprising that we should see the Pauline Eucharistic formula embedded in the Last Supper narratives.[12] The likely scenario is that the developing Christian sacrament required an earlier justification in Jesus' mouth. It is a literary case of the tail wagging the dog. Paul, writing to the church he planted in Corinth, records it as follows:

> For I received from the Lord that which I also delivered to you: that the Lord Jesus on the *same* night in which He was betrayed took bread; and when He had given thanks, He broke *it* and said, "Take, eat; this is My body which is broken for you; do this in remembrance of Me." In the same manner *He* also *took* the cup after supper, saying, "This cup is the new covenant in My blood. This do, as often as you drink *it*, in remembrance of Me." (1 Cor 11:23–25 NKJV)

Interestingly, Paul refrains from saying that this was the eve of Passover, only that it was the night on which Jesus was betrayed. Though Paul does not explain exactly how he "received" this, we may see him effectively

---

[11] Notably, the LXX almost always translates *tirosh* as *oinos* ("wine"). It is also notable that the Qumran meal has nothing at all to do with Passover. Neinz-Wolfgang Kuhn, "The Qumran Meal and the Lord's Supper in Paul in the Context of the Graeco-Roman World," in A. J. M. Wedderburn, and Alf Christophersen, *Paul, Luke and the Graeco-Roman World: Essays in Honour of Alexander J.M. Wedderburn* (London: T & T Clar, 2003), 221–49.

[12] James Tabor, *Paul and Jesus: How the Apostle Transformed Christianity* (New York: Simon & Schuster, 2012), 147: "We have every reason to believe that Mark got his tradition of the words of Jesus at the Last Supper from Paul. Matthew and Luke, who then use Mark as a source, also repeat what Paul had said decades earlier."

transforming Jesus' last meal into a Qumranic "messianic banquet," complete with a "new covenant" reference such as we find in the Dead Sea Damascus Rule. This is the language that we see broadly reflected in the synoptic Gospels.

As in the Messianic Rule, the bread comes first, followed by the wine. Might the historical Jesus have been enacting, not a Passover meal, but his own version of the Dead Sea sect's "messianic banquet"? There is in fact another interesting connection between the Gospel narratives of the Last Supper and the Dead Sea Scrolls in Jesus' directive: "Go into the city, and a man will meet you carrying a pitcher of water" (Mark 14:13 NKJV). A man carrying a jar of water is a detail we might expect to find in a celibate community, as the Essenes were rumored to be. It has even been argued that the location of the Last Supper was in the Essene Quarter of ancient Jerusalem.[13]

However, all attempts to find an Essene connection to the Last Supper must come to grips with a startling variation in Luke's Gospel, where we find the Pauline language prefaced by some uniquely Lucan material. Jesus says, "With fervent desire I have desired to eat this Passover with you before I suffer..." (22:15 NKJV). He next hints that he will not in fact be able to eat it: "... for I tell you, I will not eat it until it is fulfilled in the kingdom of God." Later manuscripts render the text as "eat it again," most likely to make it appear as though the Last Supper was in fact a "Seder."

The account continues: "Then He took the cup, and gave thanks, and said, 'Take this and divide it among yourselves...'" (22:17 NKJV). Thereafter we read: "And He took bread, gave thanks and broke *it*, and gave *it* to them..." (22:19 NKJV). Interestingly, the Greek word used here and in the other Gospels for "loaf" is *artos*, indicating ordinary, rather than unleavened bread. Again, we suspect that is no "Seder." Next, we find the Pauline-inspired language:

> ... saying, "This is my body, which is given for you; do this in remembrance of me." Likewise He also took the cup after supper, saying, "This cup is the new covenant in My blood..." (Luke 22:19–20 NKJV)

---

[13] Bargil Pixner, *Paths of the Messiah* (San Francisco: Ignatius Press, 2010), 192–220; idem, "Mount Zion, Jesus, and Archaeology," in *Jesus and Archaeology* (ed. James H. Charlesworth; Grand Rapids: Eerdmans, 2006), 309–22; Rainer Riesner, "Jesus, the Primitive Community, and the Essene Quarter of Jerusalem," in *Jesus and the Dead Sea Scrolls* (ed. James H. Charlesworth; New York: Doubleday, 1992), 198–234; Bargil Pixner, D. Chen, and S. Margalit, "Mount Zion: The 'Gate of the Essenes' Reexcavated," *ZDPV* 105 (1989): 85–95; Rainer Riesner, "Josephus' 'Gate of the Essenes' in Modern Discussion," *ZDPV* 105 (1989): 105–9.

Looking behind the *Textus Receptus*, we discover that these words do not appear in some of the earliest texts of Luke, leading to the conclusion that they are a later editorial gloss, picking up the Pauline eucharistic formula.[14] In that case, as Flusser noted, we are left with the traditionally Jewish order of wine first, followed by the bread. Furthermore, the problematic reference to the drinking of blood vanishes if we understand it as part of a later redaction of the Lucan account, which otherwise depicts Jesus behaving in a characteristically "kosher" manner.[15]

In the final analysis, if the "Seder" of Jesus amounts to a "lost dog," then Paul's Eucharist is the tail that wagged it. Some might be tempted to conclude that Jesus' final meal is entirely a literary invention, leaving us a tail without a dog at all. It may nonetheless be argued that the "second stratum" of Judeo-Christianity effectively "overwrote" the Gospels themselves.

Moreover, while the overwhelming majority of scholars assume that Mark, considered the earliest, is the preferred rendering, it is in fact Luke's version that arguably relates an even earlier and more reliable tradition, preserved in his telling alone. It is a tradition separately reflected in the late first or early second century document, the *Didache*, which, describing the Eucharist, also begins with the cup, followed by the bread, according to the traditional Jewish order:

> With respect to the Eucharist you shall give thanks as follows. First with respect to the cup: "We give thanks our Father for the holy vine of David, your child which you made known to us through Jesus your child. To you be the glory forever." And with respect to the bread: "We give thanks our Father for the life and knowledge that you made known to us through Jesus your child. To you be the glory forever" (*Didache* IX: 1–3).

As Aaron Milavec points out, three different traditions of a cultic meal are presumed to have arisen by the last quarter of the first century: a "regular"

---

[14] In the Uncial D and some Italian translations the last part of Luke 22:19 is missing, along with the entirety of 22:20. See Benjamin J. Burkholder, *Bloodless Atonement?: A Theological and Exegetical Study of the Last Supper Sayings* (Eugene, OR: Pickwick, 2017), 169, n. 5: "Luke 22:19 has been transposed before Luke 22:17–18, which was most likely done in order to cohere with the traditional Eucharistic practice of sharing in the bread before the wine." For a full exposition of these variations see Bruce M. Metzger, *A Textual Commentary on the Greek New Testament*, (London: United Bible Societies, 1971), 173–7.

[15] Joseph Klausner, *Jesus of Nazareth: His Life, Times and Teaching* (trans. Herbert Danby; New York: Macmillan, 1925), 329: "The drinking of blood, even if it was meant symbolically, could only have aroused horror in the minds of such simple Galilean Jews."

Eucharistic meal with the elements interpreted pneumatically (as in the *Didache*); a sacramental meal involving Jesus' flesh and blood; and a combination of Hellenistic/ Last Supper practices with synoptic elaborations of a "sacramental Last Supper."[16] Perhaps an early independent tradition in which Jesus blesses the cup, then the bread (with no mention of the wine as "blood" or the bread as "flesh") became source material for both Luke and the *Didache*, in the former case being overwritten by the Pauline Eucharistic formula and in the latter instance becoming part of an early Christian liturgical practice.[17]

We should still ask how the Last Supper should be perceived if it were not a Passover meal or a Pauline-inspired "messianic banquet." In this regard there is much merit in Tabor's assertion that the prophetic overtones of the meal are central, with Jesus seeing himself perhaps as a Davidic figure to whom the prophet Zechariah alluded.[18] This is underscored by the account of him riding into Jerusalem on the foal of an ass and going on to cleanse the temple of unclean practices. Perhaps he believed that if he and his disciples offered themselves up to the Roman authorities, the divine rule of God would be revealed on earth. We might even understand Jesus' "agenda" as politically revolutionary, inasmuch as he anticipated the supernatural overthrow of Roman rule.

Was the actual intent of Judas' betrayal to force Jesus' hand, as it were, into revealing the Kingdom of God with power and ushering in his messianic reign? Such a possibility is not as far-fetched as one might imagine, given Josephus' accounts of other would-be messiahs of that age, who sincerely believed that they might bring down the rule of Rome via supernatural agency.[19] That said, we may choose to refer to the "Judas

---

[16] Aaron Milavec, *The Didache: Faith, Hope, & Life of the Earliest Christian Communities, 50–70 C.E.* (New York: The Newman Press, 2003), 394. See also Marcello Del Verme, *Didache and Judaism: Jewish Roots of an Ancient Christian-Jewish Work* (New York: T & T Clark, 2004), 174: "The *Didache* is generally viewed as a many-layered and compound work correctly classified under the genre of progressive literature."

[17] Tabor, *Jesus Dynasty*, 205. See also Andrew B. McGowan, *Ancient Christian Worship: Early Church Practices in Social, Historical, and Theological Perspective* (Grand Rapids: Baker, 2014), 114: "Paul's interpretation of the Christian meal as a proclamation and remembrance of Jesus' death does not feature. Yet other passages in the work suggest that the *Didache* is closely connected with the Synoptic Gospels or their sources." See also See also H. van de Sandt, David Flusser, *The Didache: Its Jewish Sources and Its Place in Early Judaism and Christianity* (Minneapolis: Fortress Press, 2002), 112–31; H. van de Sandt, "Didache 3,1–6: A Transformation of an Existing Jewish Hortatory Pattern," *JSJ* 23 (1992): 21–41.

[18] Tabor, *Jesus Dynasty*, 192.

[19] Josephus recounts a certain prophet who would ascend from Egypt and lead a group of thirty thousand up the Mount of Olives, where he would, by supernatural power, command the walls of Jerusalem to fall down. Another messianic impostor named

dinner" simply as an "anticipatory" meal, in advance of Jesus' expectation of immanent betrayal, to be followed perhaps by divine intervention and deliverance. In the synoptic Gospels, however, all of this is subsumed by the Pauline addition of the Eucharistic formula, which instead becomes the central focus of a very different "Gospel of peace." That in turn would be much more palatable to the Greco-Roman sensibilities to which Paul was attempting to appeal. Only in reconstructed Luke and in John's Gospel do we find, sans Eucharist, an unfiltered picture of the event that would define the last hours in the life and purpose of Yeshua the Galilean.

Theudas would claim to be able to part the Jordan River and lead the people across, like Joshua of old: "It came to pass, while Cuspius Fadus was procurator of Judea, that a certain charlatan, whose name was Theudas, persuaded a great part of the people to take their effects with them, and follow him to the Jordan river; for he told them he was a prophet, and that he would, by his own command, divide the river, and afford them an easy passage over it" (*Antiquities* 20.97–98). See also Fernando Bermejo-Rubio, "Jesus as a Seditionist," in Zev Garber, ed., *Teaching the Historical Jesus: Issues and Exegesis* (New York: Routledge, 2015), 238–40: "Jesus should be labeled not only as a religious teacher, but also as a nationalistic two and an anti-Roman seditionist."

Eucharist and Seder:
What Should the Simple Scholar Say?

Peter Zaas

This essay aims to examine the origins of the Christian eucharist alongside those of the Pesach seder, with an aim to describing with greater precision how this comparison contributes (or detracts from) contemporary dialogue.

חָכָם מָה הוּא אוֹמֵר? *The experienced scholar (it is rare to find the wise one) knows that the connections between these two foundational liturgical moments are complex, and that getting to them bottom of them means maneuvering through a number of both exegetical and historical issues.*

רָשָׁע מָה הוּא אוֹמֵר? *The agenda-driven scholar (not really* רָשָׁע*, just motivated by a need to fit the text into a larger narrative) makes claims for the connections between eucharist and passover that match his or agenda, to make Christianity Judaism, say, or Judaism Christianity.*

תָּם מָה הוּא אוֹמֵר? *The scholar who is strictly concerned with the plain meaning of the words in the text, and the specific connections between parallel passages can draw conclusions about the formation of the text, but where does she go from there?*

שֶׁאֵינוֹ יוֹדֵעַ לִשְׁאוֹל *For the scholar who has trouble formulating a specific approach to material which is as difficult as it is vital, the solution is to sit with other scholars of good will, to find the right questions: How is this liturgical moment different from all other liturgical moments? How is it the same?*

The Passover Haggadah, the manual, the handbook, the enchiridion, the FAQ for the Passover Seder, the most elaborated of all Jewish liturgical moments, famously describes four children: The wise child, the wicked child, the simple child, and the child who knows not how to ask. Please bear with us as we try to shoehorn some thoughts about how to compare Passover and Eucharist into a model suggested by these four paschal forechildren. This will be a short presentation, but I still invite you to recline: Why should this presentation be different from any other presentation? Is there any possibility that we can figure out the *ma l'sh'ol?*

What is it that we are setting out to compare? The title of the session is "The Institution of the Lord's Supper, a Passover Seder," and we can start there, but it is only a starting-point. We can start briefly with the historical question, like the wise child: "What are the testimonies, the ordinances, and the legal decisions which the Lord our God commanded you?" leaving aside for the moment the textual question of why the Haggadah has the Lord commanding *you*, while in the Yerushalmi and the Mekhilta[1] the Lord commanded *us*. What is it that we are comparing? the wise panelist might ask: The historical event tagged "The Last Supper," the meal Jesus ate with his students after offering the Pesach sacrifice (in the Synoptic tradition) or before offering it (in the Johannine tradition) with the Jewish ritualized meal that commences the festival based in one tradition on the nostalgic memory of that same sacrifice? Event with ritual? The Christian ritualized meal that retells and reenacts Jesus' Paschal meal with the Passover Seder? Ritual with ritual?

The question is a complicated one, not least because the Christian eucharist reenacts a Passover event, whether or not the Last Supper occurred on *erev Pesach* or the night before, or whether it never occurred at all. Is the Christian eucharist a commemoration of a Passover seder in some form that later Jews would recognize? Joachim Jeremias, certainly a *ben chacham,* thought that it was, but, while he delineates fourteen connections between Jesus' Last Supper and the Jewish Pesach seder,[2] they are so general that they depend on one's prior acceptance of the connection in order to be convincing. The meal was held at night, they drank wine, the guests talked about the meaning of the meal, all descriptions of the Pesach seder and most other Jewish meals as well.

The academic consensus is presently that while Jews during the 2nd Temple period certainly ate liturgical meals connected to festival sacrifices, the Passover seder developed during the Tanaitic period, and the Christian eucharist celebrates an event that was not a Pesach seder, not yet. Jesus and his students offered the paschal sacrifice and shared it in liturgical purity, but no one before the Mishnaic period did those things in the form of what we now call a seder. The seder emerged, like a great deal of Jewish liturgical practice, as a way of commemorating a sacrifice that could no longer be offered; it is a complex exercise in sacred nostalgia. Jesus ate the Passover, but had no seder. This is what we must tell the wise child: Look carefully at the testimonies, the ordinances, and the legal decisions. Take special care in

---

[1] Jerusalem Talmud Pes. 70b; Mekhilta d'Rabbi Yishmael 13:14:1.
[2] Joachim Jeremias, *The Eucharistic Words of Jesus*, 3rd ed. (London: SCM Press, 1966), 42–61

the precision of your language: Comparing the central ritual of one community with the central ritual of another using rituals as interwoven as these is an exercise whose missteps can be more than academic.

The *tam*, the naive child, asks only "*Ma zot?*" What is this? In *tamimut*, there is *chochmah*, in naivety wisdom, it seems to me, if not so much to the sages. What is a pesach seder, and what is a Christian eucharist?

In my scholarly *minhag*, the definitional question is the functional question, "What is it?" and to me this means "What does it do?" To the naive child, we can say that both the Pesach seder and the Christian eucharist help relive moments of redemption and help look forward to new ones. We can say that while this is a characteristic of many religious rituals, it is quintessentially true of these two.

Relive Moments of Redemption

In the generations during which the Sages found ways to build a Judaism that was not dependent on a physical Temple or physical sacrifices, they discovered the force of sacred nostalgia, rebuilding the Temple and its sacrifices as an edifice whose physical existence was only in memory, and who rituals could only be performed in liturgical retrospect, nostalgically. Perhaps we should say that they re-discovered the force of sacred nostalgia, for what is the composition of the written Torah by the exiles in Babylonia an attempt to recreate an earlier Temple that they believed to be lost? This is not at all to say that our sages built a Judaism that only looked to the past, but what happened in the past was concrete, enshrined in both law and architecture, while what was to happen in the future was a matter for speculation, argument, and hope.

One of the things that makes the Pesach seder the Pesach seder is that the events it re-enacts are not the obvious ones, although they have become, through shear repetition, the expected ones. The Haggadah mentions authorities who lived while the Pesach sacrifice was still offered, but it portrays them telling a far older story. While we are enjoined to instruct the Chacham *ayn maftirin achar hapesach afikomen*, "We do not finish the afikomen after we eat the pesach sacrifice" ultimately the story we have told all four types of children, and any other children present as well, is about the *yetziat Mizraim*, the Exodus, not the sacrifice, although of course the two topics are unavoidably linked. Our sources preserve an ancient conflict about what aggadah the magid should relate: The canonical Haggadah introduces the obligation to make the story of the Exodus central to the seder with the story of the five sages who told that story all night, buttressed with the statement of one of them, Elazar ben Azariah which extends the obligation to discuss the Exodus at night to the daytime as well, and to the world to come.

But our sources yield an alternative story, oh wise children, and your wisdom will increase if you embrace this kind of conflict: The Tosefta records another seder, conducted by Sages who were absent from the one at Bnei Brak:

> Once it occurred that Rabban Gamliel and the elders were reclining at the house of Boethus ben Zonim in Lod, and they were busy with the *halakhot* of the Pesach sacrifice all night until the cock crowed. They lifted the table in front of them, prepared themselves, and went to the study house.[3]

If the account in B. Berachot 27b–28a is historical, then these two seders represent those conducted by rival *n'siim* Elazar b. Azariah and Gamliel II, presumably during the period before they reconciled their differences. But speculation aside, these two accounts demonstrate two drastically different approaches to the *aggadah* of Pesach, with the Sages surrounding Elazar recounting the *yitziat Mizraim* and the Sages surrounding Gamliel discussion the *pesach halakhot*. The approach of Elazar became the canonical approach, and it is the Exodus from Egypt, not the legal requirements for the Passover sacrifice, that we recount to our children, wise, wicked and otherwise, in our seders today.

So we should observe, my wise children, that both liturgies, the eucharist of nascent Christianity and the Passover seder are examples of sacred nostalgia, ways of preserving in liturgy something that has been lost. The eucharistic liturgy preserves not the loss of the Paschal sacrifice—that sacrifice was still being made when that liturgy was created—but the loss of the person Jesus himself, the liturgy proclaiming as it does "the Lord's death until he comes," in Paul's words,[4] written, appropriately enough, by that Jewish traveler as he prepared for his own Pesach observance, although not for a seder.

The liturgical retelling of Jesus' final meal with his students is surely the oldest liturgical artifact of nascent Christianity, if "Christianity" is the right term for this movement in such an early period. Its scriptural account can be redacted to at least two sources, the account beginning in I Cor. 11.23 and the account beginning in Mark 14.22; it is, along with Lord's Prayer, liturgy that predates the Gospel of Mark, and predates, as we have seen, the Passover Seder itself. If the historical question is did Jesus celebrate a seder, the answer must be no; he ate a liturgical meal following the *pesach* sacrifice, but no seder; no Exodus, no charoset; *matsa* yes, for *chag ha-matsot* was upon him, but no Four Questions and no Four Children to explain their answers to. It is even possible that the Sages of B'nei B'rak

---

[3] Tos., Pes. 10:12.
[4] 1 Cor 11.26.

and the Sages of Lod had the Christian eucharistic in mind when they began crafting the *pesach* seder, but it is not possible that Jesus opened the door for Elijah, at least in the sense we are talking about here.

But as we are not restricted to one type of daughter or son, so are we not restricted to one type of comparison; there are many ways to look at two sacred meals side-by-side; as the Haggadah offers us a taxonomy of four types of children, we might delineate four types of comparison.

Functional

The Christian eucharist functions as the centerpiece of nearly every instance of Christian liturgy, especially in Catholic tradition: Daily and weekly worship, sacramental observances along the rites de passage from baptism to marriage to deathbed unction. At each of these observances the worshiper reenacts events in sacred history and is reminded of the meaning of those events. The eucharist functions communally, but typically requires the presence of a priest.

Functionally, the Passover seder resembles the Christian eucharist only in part: Like the eucharist, the Passover seder transports the participant (participants in the Passover seder are unlikely to think of themselves as "worshipers" unlike participants in the Christian eucharist) into the sacred past, reenacting the Egyptian exodus in a variety of narrative and symbolic ways. But the Passover seder is an annual event conducted almost inevitably in a family setting, without the leadership of clergy. It functions in a communitarian way, but emphasizes the home-based nature of much of Jewish ritual practice.

Historical

The historical connections between Christian eucharist and Passover seder are complex, and the complexity has muddled the comparison. Jesus' students joined their teacher in celebrating the *pesach* sacrifice; their organization of the occasion in the Synoptic Gospels is recognizable to any Jewish traveler at Pesach time looking for a place to organize a seder. But Jesus' students weren't organizing a seder. They were a century too early for that. They were organizing one of the ritual meals following any major Jewish sacrifice, meals that certainly featured blessings over bread and over wine. That their teacher with whom they shared the occasion spoke to them of its importance is hardly surprising.

The Pesach seder, with its reenactment of the Egyptian exodus, is a product of Tannaitic times, and was conceived by sages who were certainly aware of Christian eucharistic practices. That the Christian eucharist is somehow modeled on the subsequent Pesach seder is a difficult claim, much more difficult historically than its opposite, that the seder is based on the eucharist, no matter how unpalatable a claim like that might be to some modern sensibilities.

Phenomenological

The phenomena of the Passover seder are similar to those of the Christian eucharist: They both involve bread and wine. There was certainly a time when the Lord's Supper consisted of more than the beverage and the starch, but churches whose sacred meals consist of more than bread and wine are almost as rare as Passover seders which limit themselves to those kinds. Both rituals involve the re-enactment, in narrative and in symbol, of events in sacred history. The participant in the eucharist joins Christ at the Lord's table; the Jewish family at its Pesach seder shares the bread of poverty with their spiritual ancestors escaping Egyptian slavery.

Anthropological

From a standpoint of cultural anthropology, at least in the Durkheim-Douglas-Smith trajectory, eucharist and seder both establish groups and grids; groups of eucharist- and seder-participants, and grids among participants. Does the eucharistic community follow the Johannine tradition and dine on leavened bread at the Lord's table? Does it follow the Synoptic tradition and celebrate the *chag ha-matsot* with Jesus over unleavened bread? Is Christ physically present in the bread and the wine or is he not? Who is invited to participate?

All of the variations in eucharistic practice and belief among the 33,000 Christian denominations (itself a traditional number, like the number of *mitzvoth*) help to locate worshipers among the many possible groups of worshipers as well as on the grids within each group. Pesach seders likewise distinguish groups; worshippers from non-worshippers, and establish grids within groups: Do the participants in the seder consume *kitnyot,* forbidden to observant Ashkenazim but permitted, in most cases, to observant Sephardim? Do they, following the lead of some feminist students from my own alma mater, add a crust of forbidden *chametz* to the seder plate, or, with Susannah Heschel, an orange? Is there a cup of Miriam? A fifth cup in memory of the Six Million? All of these variations place the seder participant on a grid with her group as definitively (or as vaguely) as do the variations in Christian eucharistic practice.

If we had more than the canonical number of Pesach children, we could surely find more ways to compare Eucharist and Passover. We could look at these two liturgical occasions against a backdrop of interfaith and ecumenical dialogue, for example: Whatever the precise historical relationship of these two sacred meals, they are ways in which Jews and their various Christian cousins each celebrate the founding moment of their mutual traditions. They celebrate through food, drink, and story, through reenactment and prayer; there is much that is common and much that is distinct, much in both columns to inform a meaty (or bread-y?) conversation with the respected other. And by the same token there is much that is different, and many of us complain when boundaries are crossed: Do we applaud or bemoan Christian seders?

"What a Difference a Difference Makes," wrote one of my late, lamented teachers[5]:

> A "theory of the other" rarely depends on the capacity "to see ourselves as others see us." By and large, "we" remain indifferent to such refractions. Rather, it would appear to imply the reverse. A "theory of the other" requires us to think, to situate, and to speak of "others" in relation to the way in which we think, situate, and speak about ourselves.[6]

As we distinguish amongst ourselves, as we distinguish amongst our various others, so we distinguish amongst our children, sorting them into the wicked and the wise, the simple and the one who doesn't know where to start, *sh'aino yodea l'sh'ol*. But perhaps our categories need some work, along with our parenting skills. Perhaps our good son is a sycophant, the wicked daughter an independent thinker, the simple child viewing the world through an artistic filter. And the one *sh'aino yodea l'shol*? perhaps that is the child who will grow to become a good scholar, always searching for the right question to ask.

---

[5] Smith, Jonathan Z. "What a Difference a Difference Makes," in Neusner, J. and Frerichs, E., eds., *To See Ourselves as Others See Us. Christians, Jews, "Others in Late Antiquity* (Chico, CA: Scholars Press, 1985. 3–48.

[6] Smith, p. 48.

Inserting Shoah at the Traditional Passover Seder: Interpreting Anew the Five Cups, and What Would Jesus Say?

Zev Garber

In the main, the pageantry of the Passover Seder (Nisan 15) focuses on two periods of Jewish history: the biblical Exodus from Egypt and the rabbinic recalling of the account. Through ritual food, drink, and animated reading and interpretation, the participant travels with the Children of Israel as if "s/he came forth out of Egypt," and sits at the table of the Sages as they observe Passover in Jerusalem and Bnei Brak. Alas, the forty year trek from wilderness into freedom succumbed in Jewish history into a long night's journey into exile. "Begin with disgrace and end with glory" (m. Pesaḥim 10.4). That is to say, talk openly and informatively about exilic degradation and destruction, so that, in contrast, the experience of Jewish freedom and triumph are cherished and appreciated. Thus, it is suggested, nay expected, that the greatest tragedy of the Jewish Night, the Shoah, be recounted on the night that accentuates Jewish birth and being. But for many Jews, it is not. How come? Also, a clarification of Last Supper-Passover Seder symmetry is in order.

In the main, the pageantry of the Passover Seder (Nisan 15) focuses on two periods of Jewish history: the biblical Exodus from Egypt and the rabbinic recalling of the account. Through ritual food, drink, and animated reading and interpretation, the participant travels with the Children of Israel as if "s/he came forth out of Egypt," and sits at the table of the Sages as they observe Passover in Jerusalem and Bnei Brak. Alas, the forty year trek from wilderness into freedom succumbed in Jewish history into a long night's journey into exile. "Begin with disgrace and end with glory" (*m. Pesaḥim* 10.4). That is to say, talk openly and informatively about exilic degradation and destruction, so that, in contrast, the experience of Jewish freedom and triumph are cherished and appreciated. Thus, it is suggested, nay expected, that the greatest tragedy of the Jewish Night, the Shoah, be recounted on the night that accentuates Jewish birth and being. But for many Jews, it is not. How come?

Four Cups

A number of questions arise for those who insert contemporary genocide in the midst of freedom. Where is the Shoah inserted, beginning, middle, or end of the Seder ceremony? Does not the message of Hell on Earth compromise the theme of redemption from Heaven? By reading the Shoah into the Haggadah, are we not turning Judeocide into a paschal sacrifice making it a biblical *holocaust* rather that a contemporary historical Shoah. Further, does not the Shoah have its own process of memorialization; why recall it at a time when *Yom HaShoah U-Mered HaGetaot* occurs less than two weeks later (Nisan 27)?

In answer to these non-traditional Passover questions, we recognize that Jewish history is reflected in the Haggadah and that affliction and suffering are transmitted in past, present, and future paradigms: Ten Plagues, "In every generation they stand up to destroy us," and "Pour out Thy Wrath," respectfully. The Shoah is not counted in the Ten Plagues because they represent a fixed Pentateuchal event, which the Torah sees as a condemnation of Pharoah and his advisors, not the Egyptian people.[1] "Thou shall not abhor the Egyptians,"[2] is the cause of the tempered joy on Passover evening, that is, sprinkling from the Second Cup when the Ten Plagues are computed and by omitting Pss 115 and 116 from the "Egyptian Hallel (Pss 113–118) during the last six days of Passover. In contrast, the Shoah was designed by the Nazi state but its program of Judeocide was carried out willingly by ordinary men and women. Further, to paint the victimization of the Shoah like that of Egyptian slavery in compassionate hues is absurd and obscene.

The idea of the Shoah as continuance may well explained why it is addressed in the second part ("future") of the service. The Four Cups at the Passover table represent the verbs of God's freedom in the biblical Exodus story (Exod 6: 6–8). The Four Cups are the matrix around which the redemptive memories are spun. Cup One, the *Kiddush*, festival benediction of blessing and joy; Cup Two, in honor of God, the Redeemer of Jewish history; Cup Three, an abbreviated *Kiddush* for the benefit of latecomers at the transition between the first and second part of the Seder service; Cup Four, the acknowledgement of the Passover of the Future. The Third Cup follows the Grace after the Meal without narrative accompaniment. Then a special cup, the Cup of Elijah, is poured to overflowing and the door is

---

[1] Exod 3:22a, 12:36b: "You shall save the Egyptians," meaning, individual acts of Egyptian kindness and reparations clear the Egyptian name and vindicate its humanity.
[2] Deut 23:8

opened and the "Pour Out Your Wrath" paragraph bellowed to the outside world. After the door is closed, the Fourth Cup is filled, and the "Egyptian Hallel"[3], "The Great Hallel"[4] (Ps 136), and "Benediction of Song"[5] are recited. Finally, the Fourth Cup is drunk at the close of the Passover Seder.

Open Door and the Cup of Elijah

At many *sedarim*, at the point of the Open Door and the Cup of Elijah, when the malediction against idolatry and antisemitism is pronounced, a requiem for the Six Million and others who perished in the Shoah is added. Its designation here is noteworthy. The Shoah is grounded in the antisemitic history of the State and in the suppersessionist teaching of the Church. The Shoah is *sui generis* and must be taken as emblematic. If the Shoah is seen as the unbearable past that bears inexplicably in the living than it must be made explicable how the enslavement of the powerless came about, how this functioned into the murder of the innocents, so that all can learn the universal message of the Shoah, that is, what all people are capable of doing and what all people are capable of suffering. Then we can speak of the end of malevolent history and the dawning of the messianic epoch.

This message cannot be overstated. The world must not forget the murdered Jewish People and that active participants and bystanders alike contributed to the Final Solution. Though killing fields may never cease in the land, we must never gain tolerate genocidal activity towards any group in any place at any time. The Third Cup is history and the Fourth Cup illuminates a revolutionary age of crumbling differences and indifference and of identifying the interdependence of mankind based on the belief in the oneness of G-d and acting morally as one humanity.

---

[3] Hymns of praise consisting of Pss 113–118, which sing of the greatness of G-d, His deliverance, and the ultimate hope that all nations will be united in the pure worship of G-d. The name "Egyptian Hallel" is associate with Ps 114, which speaks of the marvels of the Exodus. Pss 113 and 114 are recited before the meal and Pss 115–118 are chanted after the Fourth Cup is poured.

[4] The talmudic term for Ps 136 (*Ber* 4b; *Pesaḥ* 118a; *Ta'anit* 3:9). This Psalm is called "The Great Hallel" because its opening line, "O' give thanks to the Lord," is implied before most of the stanzas and "For his mercy endureth forever," concludes all the strophes.

[5] *m. Pesaḥ* 10:7 states: "the Fourth Cup is poured—(he) finishes the Hallel and says over it the *Birkat ha-Shir* ("The Blessing of the Song"). The Passover Haggadah preserves several version of the Birkat Ha-Shir :R. Yehuda's choice, "Praise Thee, O' Lord our G-d, Shall All Thy Works," which is recited at the conclusion of the "Egyptian Hallel"; and the selection of R. Yohanan (*Pesaḥ* 118a), "The Breath of Every Living Thing Shall Bless Thy Name, O' Lord Our G-d," which immediately follows the chanting of "The Great Hallel." This prayer also concludes the Sabbath and festival, *Pesukei de-Zimra* (Psalms and adorations before the "*Shema*' and its Blessings" section of the *Shaḥarit* [morning] service).

The addendum of the Shoah produces no formidable content change neither in the Seder nor in the traditional Haggadah. No additional food, drink, or *halakhic* reading. Maybe a short reading or song in association with the medieval "Pour Out Thy Wrath," but the Open Door[6] refers to the "Night of Watching"[7] and the Cup of Elijah signifies the ingathering of the exiles. We suggest that the reasons for the lacuna are paradoxical and pragmatic.

- The message of Passover is Liberation and the medium for conveying that message is the Written and Oral Torah from Sinai; the message of Shoah is Annihilation carried away in the fumes of cyanide.
- Passover represents providential design in history but Shoah evolved from history. In Jewish Halakha, the latter, however meaningful, may not trample on the former. To challenge, yes; but to obliterate, no.
- G-d as deliverer of the Passover is overpowering and messengers, such as, Moses and Elijah, are implied and anticipated but never made full-blown. In contrast, G-d's presence during the Shoah is disturbingly silent but may this not suggest that surviving *di milhomeh yohrn* requires more that G-d and Tradition; the Jews themselves have to want it. If they do not permit the memory of the Judeocide to destroy their morals or their own sense of identity then they like Elijah the Prophet, can traverse past and future, temporal and eternal, and bring Heaven down to Earth.

Behold I am sending My messenger (*malakhi*) to clear the way before Me, and the Lord whom you seek shall come to His Temple suddenly. As for the angel of the covenant[8] that you desire, he is already coming

---

[6] A number of suggestions are offered to explain the "Open Door" following the Grace after Meals and before the recitation of the Hallel: invitation to hospitality (however, extended at the start of the Seder); discredit blood libel disinformation (if so then investigate before not after the meal); connecting Jewish households by the worldwide travels of Elijah (however, Elijah's name, cup, and voyage is referenced at the Seder table), and so forth. "Open Door" policy? Probably not for mundane reasons of generosity, antisemitism, nor unity but rather for the mystical exercise of experiencing G-d's presence and salvific role on this "Night of Watching."

[7] "It was the Night of Watching unto the Lord for bringing them out from the land of Egypt; this same Night of Watching for all the Children of Israel throughout their generations" (Exod 12:42). This verse sums up the basic leitmotif of Passover: G-d alone redeemed Israel. Moreover, this night of vigil unto the Lord for all generations is understood in rabbinic lore to mean that the final redemption of the future will take place on this anniversary night. The old-new tradition of leaving the door unlocked on Passover night—a courageous action during the long night of exile in the lands of Cross and Crescent—underscores surely that divine protection is strongly felt on this "Night of Watching."

[8] Or, "Messenger of the Covenant." A response to the previous sentence, "You have wearied the Lord with your words ... 'Where is the G-d of Justice?'" (Mal 2:17).

... Be mindful of the Teaching of my servant Moses, whom I charged at Horeb (Sinai) with laws and rules for all Israel. Lo I will send the Prophet Elijah to you before the coming of the awesome, fearful day of the Lord. He shall reconcile fathers with sons and sons with fathers. (Mal 3:1, 22–24a)

The failure not to act and take responsibility for their own actions and ultimate redemption—i.e., "lest I come and smite the land with utter destruction" (Mal 3:24b)—is unthinkable.

- According to tradition of Rabbi Judah ben Bezalel, the Maharal of Prague (c. 1525–1609), one reads the "Great Hallel" with the Fifth Cup in hand, and in testimony to the passage, "Who remembered us in our low estate and has delivered us from our adversaries" (Ps 136: 23–24). So in our day, drinking from the Cup of Elijah testifies "to the land (He gave) for a heritage unto Israel" (Ps 136: 21–22). By filling the Cup of Elijah and then opening the door for the curse against the destroyers of Jews, are Jews not linking Auschwitz and Jerusalem? Not in terms of cause and effect but in the proposition that rebuilding Zion sustains Jews in their anguished lost of a vanished Jewry. It also sends forth a clear message of "Never Again" to a recurrence of the European *Churban*.

As a religious institution, Passover crosses generation, gender, cultural lines and invites all to participate in its narrative of freedom and its act of liberation. Its table drama, the Seder, has evolved into a forum on right and wrong, enslavement and empowerment, equality and inequality. Passover is thus both a feast of redemption and a memorial; its intrinsic value system provides an excellent pedagogical tool in teaching basic values and recording the sacrifice made and the vigilance necessary in the triumph of moral victory.

Shoah on Passover? Because the legacy of Remembrance is the underbelly of Freedom.

The Jesus Declaration

I question the accuracy of equating the institution of the Last Supper to be a Passover Seder meal. Luke 22:15 reads that "I (Jesus) have earnestly desire to eat this Passover (offering, meal) with you (disciples) before I suffer" and follows with the benediction of the wine (*Kiddush*) and blessing of the bread (*Motsi*) (vs., 17–19). However, Mark 14:22–23 and Matthew 26:26–27 reverse the order of bread and wine before the meal. Further, I Corinthians

---

The generation of the Shoah can identify with the Malakhian query when they see Evil seemingly prosper and aided by divine non-intervention.

11:23–25 speak of breaking bread at the start of the meal and drinking the cup of wine *after* the meal. In sum, Luke follows the order of a Seder ritual; Mark and Matthew do not; and the older Pauline version in 1 Corinthians speaks of a *Chavura* fellowship and not the ritualistic Passover meal.

Nonetheless, Christian ecclesiastical tradition maintains that the Synoptic Last Supper was a Passover Seder.[9] Festival sleep not dreadful wakefulness overcame the disciples. On this "Night of Watching," Jesus' question to Peter, "Could you not watch with me one hour?" (Matt 26:40; Mark 14:37), a poignant concern which is also suggested in verses 43 and 45 (Mark, vss. 40–41) graphically describes his state of abandonment. However, it is the seemingly silence of G-d (Matt 26:39,42,44; Mark 14: 36,40,41) that affects Jesus so deeply that he feels emotional pain: "And being in agony, he prayed more earnestly; and his sweat became like great drops of blood falling down upon the ground" (Luke 22:44). The strong language of sorrow is explained in Christian tradition as the recognition that physical death awaited Jesus and his bearing of human sins as well. Substitute "Six Million" for "Jesus" and you have a core Christian and Jewish apology for the Shoah: "theology of suffering" on the one hand and "birth pains of the Messiah" on the other explain why the crucifixion of the Jews for the saving of humanity.

On the night of the Last Supper, we read that Jesus in Gethsemane (Matt 26:36–46; Mark 14:32–42; Luke 22:40–46), abandoned by his disciples, experienced Godforsakeness, and this is echoed in the words at the cross: *"Eli, Eli lamah sabachtani,"* meaning, "My G-d, my G-d why hast Thou forsaken me?" (Matt 27:46; Mark 15:34). The parallel to his suffering and forsakenness is the hopeful refrain recited by the Jew in expectation of the promise of deliverance throughout their generations (Exod 12:42).

In like manner Psalm 115, recited immediately after the Grace and part of the "Egyptian Hallel" (Pss 113–118 which mirror future deliverance), is a call for national trust in G-d against the heathen who did not believe in the wonders which G-d performed in Egypt and Sinai. The medieval counterpart to the heathen who knew not G-d and discredited His holy site and people are the civilizations which believe in Creation and in the Exodus and in the moral teachings of Sinai, and still "devour Jacob and lay waste his habitation." Under the stress of persecution by Christians and Muslims during the period of the Crusades, the powerless wandering Jew denied the rival monotheistic claims that he is cursed by G-d and man, and invoked the Deliverer to:

---

[9] Council of Nicaea (325 C.E.) established the date of Easter to fall on the first Sunday following the first full moon of the Spring season; that is, Nisan 15, the first night of Passover (the traditional Last Supper). "We should (not) follow the practice of the Jews, who have impiously defiled the hands with enormous sins (the killing of Christ), and are, therefore, deservedly afflicted with blindness of soul."

Pour out Thy wrath upon the nations (Christianity and Islam) that know Thee not. And upon the kingdoms that call not upon Thy Name. For they have devoured Jacob (people), And laid waste his habitation (Jerusalem). Ps 79:6–7

Pour out Thine indignation upon them, And let the fierceness of Thine anger overtake them. Ps 69:25

Thou will pursue them in anger and destroy them from under the heavens of the Lord. (Lam 3:66)

These readings are not to be understood as an expression of vindictiveness toward the non-Jew—the Halakha instructs the Jew to pray continually for the welfare and success of the kingdoms and ministers, and for all states and places in which he resides[10]—but should be interpreted as invoking the Judge-of-all-the-Earth to deal justly with the Nations of the World as He continuously does with Israel (classical Jewish apologia for why Jewish suffering). Therefore, the complete messianic fulfillment of the future, a universal siblinghood inspired by the Torah way, can be realized swiftly in our day. This is not poor theology, as some have argued, but an authentic Jewish understanding of *Heilsgeschichte*, as seen, for example, in Gen 17, Deut 32, Isa 2 and Micah 4.

The significance of the "Pour out Your wrath" Seder message, retributive not vindictive justice ushers in the Great Redemption, should not be misconstrued by the post-Shoah Christian. It is a necessary wake-up call to the slumbering (related to "sleeping" above) Christian to rediscover the Jewish roots of his/her faith, which are deep and far-reaching, and to live with the *imitatio Christi* without antisemitism. It is an invitation to Christian preaching and catechism to understand Jewish belief and practice without polemics, politics and paternalism. It is a calling to see the Jew not as a fossil or ashes but as G-d's first love in His salvific plan.[11] And by encouraging lessons learned from Darkness to Rebirth, Shoah and the State

---

[10] Jewish loyalty to ruler and country has its roots in Jeremiah's letter to the exiles: "Seek he welfare of the city to which I have exiled you and pray to the Lord in its behalf; for in its prosperity you shall prosper" (Jer 29:70). Fear of Lord and king is expressed in Prov 24:21 and Ezra 6:10. Mishna Abot 3:2 reports in the name of R. Hanina, the Vice-High Priest, "Pray for the peace of the ruling power (Rome), since but for fear of it men would have swallowed each other alive." The fourth century amora, Mar Samuel of Nehardea, laid down the biding principle, *Dina deMalkuta Dina;* in civil matters, the law of the land is as binding on Jews as commandments of the Torah. "Prayers for the Government" are featured in the *Musaf* ("additional") liturgy for Sabbath and festivals.

[11] "As far as election is concerned, they (Jews) are loved on account of the patriarchs. For G-d's gift and His call are irreversible." Rom 11:28b, 29

of Israel, it is hoped that the Church can correct an ambivalent triumphalist teaching about the Jews:

> For he (Christ) himself is our peace, who has made the two (Jew and Gentile) one and has destroyed the barrier, the dividing wall of hostility, by *abolishing in his flesh the law with its commandments and regulations* (italics added). His purpose was to create in himself one new man out of the two, thus making peace, and in this one body to reconcile both of them to G-d through the cross, by which he put to death their hostility.[12] Eph 2:14–16

Then, and only then, can the Church ascend Jesus' conditional query (add, about the state of Christian belief) and proclaim: My Father, it is possible that the *cup* passeth, as I will and as you will."[13] This is Christian redemption after Shoah, any alternative is Christian suicide.

---

[12] Other noteworthy examples of supersessionist eschatology are John 4:21–26 and Gal 3:26–29.

[13] A post-Shoah re-reading of Matt 26:43b.

Sample Haggadot and Sedarim

Nathan Harpaz

Artists' Perception of the Last Supper and the Passover Seder

The Last Supper is a significant episode in Christian theology as it presents major religious concepts and evokes emotions and drama. Considered as a Passover meal by the Synoptic Gospels, the Last Supper arouses intense topics such as the departure of Jesus, the betrayal of Judas, or the establishment of the Eucharist. The full presentation of the Last Supper emerged only in the 6th century and the innovation of the Renaissance artists transformed it into a contemporary dining and increased the dramatic effects and psychological gestures associated with the Apostles as it featured by Leonardo da Vinci's mural. The Last Supper continued to attract artists in the Modern era with new visual and iconographic interpretations including a monumental Last Supper project (1986) by Andy Warhol. When Jewish artists started to illustrate the Passover Haggadah in the late Middle-Ages, their images of the Passover meal inspired visually from the Christian depiction of the Last Supper. Israeli artist Reuven Rubin, invited a diversity of Jewish immigrants and Jesus to his painting "First Seder in Jerusalem" (1949). Israeli contemporary artist Adi Nes staged Israeli soldiers in a composition based on da Vinci's Last Supper and he titled it: "The Last Supper before Going Out to Battle."

The Last Supper is a significant episode in Christian theology as it presents major religious concepts and also evokes emotions and drama. Considered as a Passover meal by the Synoptic Gospels, the Last Supper arouses intense topics such as the departure of Jesus, the betrayal of Judas, or the establishment of the Eucharist. The Gospels stated that on the first day of Passover, a day before the crucifixion, Jesus and his disciples gathered for a meal. There are no details in the Gospels in regard to specific Passover rituals that were applied during that meal and according to the Gospel of Mark it was "the first day of Unleavened Bread, when the Passover lamb is sacrificed."[1] According to Matthew, "While they were eating, Jesus took a loaf of bread, and after blessing it he broke it, gave it to the disciples, and said, 'Take, eat; this is my body.' Then he [Jesus] took a cup, and after giving thanks, he gave it to them, saying, Drink from it, all of you; for this is my blood of the covenant, which is poured out for many for the forgiveness of sins. I tell you, I will never again drink from this fruit of the vine from now on until that day when I drink it new with you in my Father's kingdom."[2]

Like other major episodes from the New Testament, the Last Supper's visual presentation emerged only at the post-Constantine era. Sceneries of group of people dining around a table dating to Early Christian period are not considered as the Last Supper but as Agape or Love Feast. Several of such dining scenes, inspired from the traditional Roman banquets, were painted inside the Christian Catacombs in Rome and had served later as models for early presentations of the Last Supper. The Catacombs' dining scenes introduce the Roman arrangement of a semicircular couch around a table with an open side in front to enable the servants to deliver the food. This opening in the front of the table enabled future artists to clearly expose all the figures around the table, including in the earliest presentations of the Last Supper.

The dining fresco inside the Catacomb of Domitilla in Rome (2nd – 4th centuries AD), which occasionally identified by mistake as a Last Supper, presents a center figure accompanied with ten younger men. There are no clear attributes on the table that support any specific event. In the Catacomb of Marcellinus and Peter in Rome (4th century AD), a Love Feast or Agape introduces a group of people dining in the typical Roman setting. A larger male figure sits at the center of the table and a woman sits on the left end. There are two elements in this scene that visually resemble the shaping of significant figures in the Last Supper: A small kid sitting next to the center male figure in the Agape will transform into Jesus and the young John next to him in the future Last Supper; and the figure of the male outstretching his hand toward the food in the Agape will transform into Judas holding his hand toward the plate during the Last Supper.

Another dining episode in the Priscilla Catacomb in Rome (2nd – 3rd centuries AD) depicts seven men sitting in a semi-circular setting and on the table are two fish and three loaves of bread. The symbol of the fish was a dominant motif in the Early Christian area. Two fish facing in opposite

---

[1] Mark 14:12 in Michael David Coogan, Marc Zvi Brettler, Carol A. Newsom, and Pheme Perkins, *The New Oxford Annotated Bible: New Revised Standard Version with the Apocrypha: An Ecumenical Study Bible* (New York, NY: Oxford University Press, 2018), 1857.

[2] Matthew 26:26–29 in *The New Oxford Annotated Bible*, 1822.

directions incorporated in the center of the mosaic floor of one of the oldest churches in the Holy Land in Megiddo, dated to the 3rd – 4th centuries AD. The fish attribute is associated with Jesus' miracle of the five loaves and two fish,[3] and later on with the initial letters of the Greek word for Fish which was interpreted as "Jesus Christ, son of God, Savior."

Early Christian artistic style and content are also linked to the third-century synagogue of Dura Europos. The synagogue was established in eastern Syria on the bank of the Euphrates River. Dura Europos was a dynamic center for a diverse population consisted of Pagans, Christians and Jews. The most significant artifacts in the synagogue are the murals that depict 28 panels portraying 58 Biblical scenes.

Ever since the discovery of the site in the 1930s scholars has been debated in regard to the religious identity of the worshipers of this synagogue. The appearance of so many figurative images was antagonistic to the Jewish tradition of Iconoclasm. Furthermore, the selected episodes from the Old Testament can be effortlessly interpreted as analogous scenes from The New Testament.[4] The majority of the scenes also promote Christian concept of transformation from suffering to salvation. The figure of the Orant and the scenery of the prophet Ezekiel in the synagogue, for example, contributed to the first presentation of the Crucifixion.[5]

Even though none of the murals of the synagogue of Dura Europos depict a Passover seder, major themes associated with the holiday were incorporated in the center of the main wall around the niche of the ark, including the rescue of the infant Moses, the crossing of the Red Sea, the miracle of the water and symbolic standing figures of Moses. Some studies suggest that one of these standing figures with the moon and the sun above him is Moses after his death. It might rationalize why the head of this man is surrounded with a dark squared halo and the hands are covered under the himation like a shroud of the dead.

Following such an interpretation, the moon and the sun represent heaven, the final destination of Moses.[6] In the early appearances of the Crucifixion the moon and the sun are emerging on top of the cross following the testimony of Mark that "When it was noon, darkness came over the

---

[3] Luke 9:16 in *The New Oxford Annotated Bible,* 1886.

[4] Joseph Gutmann in *The Dura-Europos Synagogue: A Re-evaluation (1933–1992)* raises 10 research questions about the nature of this unique synagogue including the type of Judaism that was practiced there and the violation of the Second Commandment.

[5] Nathan Harpaz, "Jewish Artists and the Perception of the Crucifixion," in *Teaching the Historical Jesus: Issues and Exegesis* (editor: Zev Garber, New York: Routledge, 2015), 168–181.

[6] Erwin Goodnough in his book *Jewish Symbols in the Greco-Roman Period* (NJ: Princeton University Press, 1988) interprets this scene as the Ascension of Moses.

whole land until three in the afternoon."[7] The darkness during the Crucifixion was analyzed later as a miracle or eclipse where the moon and the sun overlapped in the middle of the day. The fact that there is no verse from the Old Testament that is associated with Moses and the moon and the sun increasing the assumption that Moses of Dura might be the pre-figuration of Jesus.

One of the most enigmatic scenes in the cycle of the Dura Europos murals is the complex presentation of Moses striking water from the rock: Moses stands in the center dressed in a Roman toga in front of the Tabernacle, shaped like a Greek temple behind a monumental Menorah, and the water from the rock is distributed between the twelve tribes of Israel. Outside of each of the twelve tents stands a figure shaped like the Orant with its typical outstretched arms. Following the assumption that Moses is pre-figuration of Jesus, this episode might carry dual interpretation leading to the future presentation of the Last Supper where Moses represent Jesus and the twelve men who represent the tribes are the twelve disciples of Jesus shaped like the early Christian motif of the Orant. In the same manner, the motif of the water streaming from Moses to the twelve tribes resembles Jesus washing the feet of his disciples during the Last Supper.

One of the earliest visual presentation of the Last Supper is in the Rossano Gospels written and illustrated in the Byzantine style in the 6th century AD. Jesus, is reclining on a couch on the left side of the Roman style semi-circular table and one of his disciples is reclining on the right side. Besides Jesus who is depicted according to the Byzantine tradition, black hair and beard and elaborated golden halo, only two disciples can be identified: The bald-head Peter sitting next to Jesus, and Judas, the traitor, outstretching his hand to the bowl of food. John, the youngest disciple and Jesus' beloved one, which in later Last Supper presentations will sit next to Jesus, is unidentified in this illustration. On the same page of the Last Supper in the Rossano manuscript a second scene depicting Jesus washing the feet of St. Peter.

Another 6th century AD presentation of the Last Supper is the mosaic mural inside the church of Sant'Apollinare Nuovo in Ravenna, Italy. Like the Rossano's Last Supper the mosaic's composition is similar: around a Roman style semi-circular table Jesus in a Byzantine style is reclining on the left side, another disciple is reclining on the right side and St. Peter sits next to Jesus. The rest of the disciples are not identified by any gesture or attribute. The Mosaic is inspired from the dining scene of the Priscilla Catacomb in Rome by introducing 2 fish and loaves of bread on the table instead of the Passover Lamb which mentioned in the Gospels.

---

[7] Mark 15:33 in *The New Oxford Annotated Bible,* 1861.

A late example of the Byzantine version of the Last Supper is located in Sant'Angelo in Formis at Capua, Italy. The 12th century AD fresco maintains the semi-circular table and Jesus with an elaborated halo is still reclining on the left side. Like in the Rossano's Last Supper, Judas is outstretching his hand toward the food. But a new arrangement of sitting is emerging in the fresco where Peter is not sitting anymore next to Jesus but on the right end of the table and the young John is sitting next to Jesus. The food on the table consists of the Passover Lamb, loaves of bread and cups of wine. In a unique way, the artist opened the room into the outdoor depicting two buildings on each side which the one on the right, shaped like a Greek temple, is probably a presentation of the Herodian temple in Jerusalem.

The mosaic featuring the Last Supper in the Saint Mark's Basilica in Venice (13th century AD) is a transformation from the Byzantine tradition into the new Western approach. The domination of the golden shimmering color, the position of Jesus on the left end of the table and Peter on the right end, and the presentation of Judas outstretching his hand to the food—all follow the Byzantine tradition, but the new shape of the oblong table and the appearance of John leaning on Jesus are completely new iconography. The leaning of John on Jesus in the Last Supper is based on the Gospel's verse "One of his disciples – the one whom Jesus loved – was reclining next to him."[8] The significant change in the sitting arrangement around an oblong table has no theological reference but it was motivated by artistic preference. A presentation of Jesus and his disciples behind an oblong table enabled the artist to expose in better clarity all the participants of the event and to designate a panoramic format as a better fitting to the architectural space. At the same time, it was also a contemporary dining arrangement which was later attracted the artists of the Renaissance who obsessively innovated traditional sceneries and updated them to current environments.

Indeed, the Last Supper turned into one of the most desired themes in Renaissance art inside churches and refectories of monasteries. The themes evoked by the Last Supper challenged the artists to promote the significant theological messages together with the dramatic and psychological human excitement aroused by this event and they executed the image with new design innovations such as perspective and realism. In the early Renaissance, Giotto di Bondone (c. 1266–1337) already demonstrates this spirit of innovations in his fresco of the Last supper inside the Cappella degli Scrovegni (Arena Chapel) in Padua, Italy (1304–6). Giotto increases realism into the scene with more sense of perspective of the space and more individuality in shaping the faces and gestures of the participants. He applied an oblong table under a decorative canopy but to increase realism he positioned the disciples, equipped with black halos, on both sides of the tables so five of them are sowing their backs. Jesus with golden halo sitting

---

[8] John 13:23 in *The New Oxford Annotated Bible,* 1942.

on the left end of the table, young John is leaning on him next to Peter. Judas with a yellow gown is sitting on the left front and outstretching his hand toward the table.

Major frescos of the Last Supper were produced in the second half of the 15th century in the city of Florence, the most influential art center of the Renaissance at that time: Andrea del Castagno (1423–1457) in the refectory of the convent of Sant'Apollonia (1445–50); Domenico Ghirlandaio (1448–1494) in the refectory of the Convent of the Ognissanti (1480); and Pietro Perugino (1446–1523) in the refectory of the Convent of Fuligno (1493–1496). All these three frescoes depict a rich classical interior where Jesus and the disciples are sitting on one side of an oblong table. All of them present new sitting arrangement: Jesus and John leaning on him are in the center of the table and Judas is sitting by himself on a chair on the other side of the table.

Around the same time that Perugino worked on the Last Supper in the Convent of Fuligno, Leonardo da Vinci (1452–1519) was producing the most remarkable mural of the Last Supper in the refectory of the Convent of Santa Maria delle Grazie in Milan, Italy (1495–1498). Leonardo followed his contemporaries positioning Jesus and John in a center of an oblong table with the rest of the disciples on both sides. Even though early studies reveal that Leonardo was considering to position Judas on the other side of the table but he chose to distance him from the rest by depicting him leaning into the other side of the table and prevented him of interaction with any of the disciples. While other artists positioned the table in the far end of the interior, Leonardo was zooming into the table in purpose of exposing in more details the gestures and faces of the group.

To increase the realistic effect of the scene Leonardo removed the halos from the disciples' heads and he framed Jesus' head exactly in the center of the open window behind him to create a natural halo. He captured the moment immediate after Jesus revealed to his disciples that one of them will betray him.[9] A stormy drama evoked in a contrast to the very clam background of the architecture. The disciples formed groups, and each of them demonstrated different psychological expression. The four groups create the typical Leonardo's composition of pyramids that intensifies the illusion. The connection between the figures was done by gestures and the expression of the faces. Leonardo explored the psychological responses of human behavior and he brilliantly applied it to the drama of the Last Supper.

The theory that John in Leonardo's Last Supper is actually a woman, probably Jesus's wife, is baseless as John was traditionally depicted with young face and long hair and Leonardo's faces of men in his other

---

[9] "And while they were eating, he said, 'Truly I tell you, one of you will betray me,'" (Matthew 26:21 in *The New Oxford Annotated Bible,* 1822).

paintings typically seem feminine.[10] The Last Supper of Leonardo da Vinci survived bombing attack during World War II but the conservation of the painting has remained a restorer's nightmare as Leonardo did not follow the practice of fresh fresco but he painted on a dry wall in secco technique.

Albrecht Dürer (1471–1528), who implemented the principles of the Italian Renaissance in Germany, employed images of the Last Supper to promote political-religious agendas. In an early woodcut of the Last Supper (1510) he followed the more conventional version: Jesus is sitting in the center embracing young John and all twelve disciples are around a rectangular table which carries the paschal lamb. Like in the mural of Leonardo the disciples are without halos and around Jesus head a more natural halo of sizzling light is visible. Dürer also selected the same moment of the event like Leonardo and the exaggerated gestures of the disciples indicating that they had just responded to Jesus' revelation about the betrayal. Dürer's inserted the scene into a vaulted structure with a round window just on top of Jesus' head which darkness is visible through it.

In 1523, Dürer produced another woodcut of the Last Supper with a completely new approach. The new version follows the ideas of Luther and the beginning of spread of the Reformation. Dürer induced the ideology of Luther by selecting the moment where Jesus asked the disciples to love each other. Judas was omitted from the scene as it was already after Jesus' announcement about the betrayal. The love of John by Luther is also echoed by intensifying the physical attachment between Jesus and John who is sitting on Jesus' lap and falling asleep on the table. Luther's theology is also reflected by removing the pascal lamb from the table and by selecting a very simple interior where the round window in the center above Jesus changed from darkness (in the previous version) to light.

While Dürer revised the Last Supper to promote Lutheran agenda, Venetian artist Tintoretto (Jacopo Robusti, 1518–1594) re-evaluated this episode to support the Counter-Reformation by the Catholic establishment. After producing relatively more conventional paintings of the Last Supper early in his career, between 1591 and 1594 (the year of his passing) Tintoretto painted a large canvas (12 x 19 ft.) inside the Basilica di San Giorgio Maggiore in Venice, Italy. It is one of the most striking and daring presentation of the Last Supper by utilizing the Mannerist technique of special effects and extreme drama. A long table is penetrating the space in a diagonal angle where Jesus is standing with a bright shimmering halo and feeding one of his disciples with bread. Only two disciples are identified: John dressed in red and blue like Jesus is supporting his head by his hand behind Jesus and Judas dressed in red sitting at the far end of the other side

---

[10] On Leonardo's gender conflict see Sigmund Freud, *Leonardo Da Vinci; A Psychosexual Study of an Infantile Reminiscence* (London: Kegan Paul, Trench, Trubner & Co, 1922).

of the table. The darkness of the room is broken by the fiery lamp above the table and the fiery halo of Jesus.

In a radical interpretation, Jesus and the disciples are surrounded with servants, service stations and even with angels flying above. Without the halos and the flying angels, it would almost look like a secular Venetian banquet. Some of the dramatic devices including the effect of light versus dark that Tintoretto applied to his last "Last Supper" will continue into Baroque art in an attempt to deliver new spiritual experience to the Catholic believers as a Counter-Reformation.

In contrary to the fantastic or almost surrealistic atmosphere of Tintoretto's Last Supper, French artist James Tissot (1836–1902), approached to this episode almost as a scientist, archeologist or journalist in purpose of re-constructing the event in full realism. After a spiritual experience in 1885, Tissot travelled a year later to the Holy Land to research the landscape, people and customs leading to the time of Jesus. He returned to the original sites again in 1889 and 1896 and he produced 350 gouache illustrations on the life of Jesus (since 1900 in the collections of the Brooklyn Museum, NY). Tissot Last Supper images were included in his set of illustrations of the Passion. Beyond the historical documentation "Tissot allows the drama to unfold frame by frame, minute by minute, a strategy, he suggests, that not only emphasizes the importance of each successive event but also allows the viewer to focus on each passing moment with great concentration."[11] Tissot perceived the Last Supper as a chain of events and he divided the event into four episodes.

The first episode titled "The Last Supper" is based on the testimony of Mathew that "When it was evening, He took his place with the twelve."[12] Jesus and his disciples are standing around a table and outstretching their hands as they are praying. They dressed in traveling customs and holding walking staffs following the Old Testament verse "This is how you shall eat it: your loins girded, your sandals on your feet, and your staff in your hand."[13]

The second episode titled "The Last Supper: Judas Dipping His Hand in the Dish" follows Mark and John observations on the betrayal of Judas.[14] Tissot preserved in this episode some elements of the traditional iconography: Jesus is handing the dipped bread to Judas identifying him as

---

[11] Judith F. Dolkart, James Tissot, David Morgan, and Amy Sitar, *James Tissot: The Life of Christ: The Complete Set of 350 Watercolors* (London: Merrell Publishers, 2009), 200.

[12] Matthew 26:20 in *The New Oxford Annotated Bible*, 1822.

[13] Exodus 12:11 in *The New Oxford Annotated Bible*, 98.

[14] Mark 14:17–20 and John, 13:21–27 in *The New Oxford Annotated Bible*, 1857 and 1942.

the traitor, John is leaning on Jesus and Judas siting on the other side of the table with a darker outfit than the rest.

The third episode titled "The Washing of the Feet" is referred to John verse: "[Jesus] got up of the table, took off his outer robe, and tied a towel around himself. Then he poured water into a basin and began to wash his disciples' feet and to wipe them with the towel that was tied around him."[15]

The fourth image titled "The Communion of the Apostles" was recorded from the Gospel of Luke: "Then he took a loaf of bread, and when he had given thanks, he broke it, and gave it to them, saying, 'This is my body, which is given for you, Do this in remembrance of me.' And he did the same with the cup after supper, saying, 'This cup that is poured out for you is the new covenant in my blood.'"[16] Tissot perceived this episode as the highest point of the Last Supper: "For the artist, this sacramental event marked not only the apostles' liturgical initiation but also the beginning of Christ's church on earth."[17]

In spite of the enormous reduction in religious art during the modern era, the Last Supper continued to inspire artists. French Post-impressionist artist Paul Gaugin (1848–1903) moved to Tahiti in the early 1890s where he synthesized in his paintings the Catholic faith with the Polynesian myth. After a suicide attempt, he produced two paintings in 1899 where he incorporated the Last Supper into the general composition. In the painting titled "The Great Buddha" Gauguin introduced two women, one of them wears a white flower and sitting in front a dark idol which a man and a woman in a sexual embrace are carved on it. Next to the women—a female dog nursing her pups. And then in the far distance a Last Supper depicting Jesus with a bright halo and Judas the traitor.[18]

In the second painting titled "The Last Supper" Gauguin implemented similar motifs: A couple is sitting near a column decorated with a carving of Hina the goddess of the Moon and Fatu the spirit of the Earth (ancient Polynesian deities) evoking the themes of death and re-birth, and in the distance—the Last Supper with Jesus in the center of the table emerging again.[19] Gaugin blended the Last Supper with the natives' traditions to reflect the universality of themes such as betrayal, death, and re-birth. In similar manner, psychoanalyst Carl Jung (1875–1961) transformed the essence of the Last Supper in regard to the Eucharist to a collective

---

[15] John 13:4–11 in *The New Oxford Annotated Bible,* 1942.

[16] Luke 22:19–20 in *The New Oxford Annotated Bible,* 1910.

[17] Judith F. Dolkart, *James Tissot: The Life of Christ,* 200

[18] Naomi E. Maurer, Vincent van Gogh, and Paul Gauguin, *The Pursuit of Spiritual Wisdom: The Thought and Art of Vincent Van Gogh and Paul Gauguin* (Madison: Fairleigh Dickinson University Press, 1999), 172.

[19] Wayne Andersen, with the Assistance of Barbara Klein, *Gauguin's Paradise Lost* (London: Secker & Warburg, 1972), 252–253.

archetype by suggesting that "they [the disciples] recognize their oneness in agonizing pleasure,"[20] and everyone should accept the other in himself as it creates "a union with all humanity."[21]

Another early modernist, German-expressionist Emil Nolde (1867–1956), was fascinated from the power of the Last Supper and he produced a radical version of the episode. In the summer of 1909 Nolde fell severely ill and he felt an irresistible urge to paint a spiritual image. He painted the Last supper with such a subjective fashion that there are no traces of references to any previous versions of this theme. Nolde applied northern peasantry myth together with his own childhood fantasies. He zoomed into the table and showed only several figures in half torsos: Jesus in the center with a glowing yellow face, red hair and robe with a white shirt, holding a cup of wine, and the disciples' satiric faces resemble the caricatures of French artist Henri de Toulouse-Lautrec (1864–1901). According to art historian and curator Peter Selz," Nolde shows Christ offering the eucharistic wine, conveying the impression of unity and self-sacrifice."[22]

Jewish American artist David Aronson (1923–2015) also applied expressionistic method in producing a controversial version of the Last Supper. The painting was completed in 1944 and acquired by the Art Institute of Chicago two years later. Aronson concentrated only on the faces and hands of Jesus and the disciples in an oblong format (20 x 85 in.) as reference to the traditional composition of the group along a rectangular table. The faces are exaggerated in forms and colors and the hands are twisted in extreme gestures. A 1944 review of an exhibition, in which Aronson's Last Supper won first prize, commented that "the young artist [Aronson] has put himself into the linage of Grünewald, Bosch, Breughel, and Barlach."[23] Indeed, Aronson combined European old masters who utilized expressive or grotesque images and modern expressionists who distorted forms and colors. An art critic from the Boston Herald called Aronson's Last Supper "an abomination of cartoon portraiture [that] might make a footboard for the devil's bed."[24] In 1946 Aronson's Last Supper was included in the Museum of Modern Art (NY) as part of the exhibition *Fourteen Americans*. In a statement in the exhibition's catalog Aronson noted that "religion and art are two means of seeking ultimate truth. Religion has affinity for a great cross-section of humanity. Art is sympathetic to fewer

---

[20] C. G. Jung, and Sonu Shamdasani, *The Red Book = Liber novus* (New York: W.W. Norton, 2012), 317.

[21] Ibid.

[22] Peter Selz, and Emil Nolde, *Emil Nolde* (New York: Arno Press for the Museum of Modern Art NY, 1980, first print 1963).

[23] Judith Arlene Bookbinder, *Boston Modern: Figurative Expressionism as Alternative Modernism* (Durham, N.H.: University of New Hampshire Press, 2005), 201.

[24] Ibid., 202.

members."[25] Aronson, a son of a rabbi, started to feature Christian themes as a young artist as a rebellion to the restricted Jewish Orthodox practice that he experienced in his early life. In 1979 Aronson's Last Supper and 18 more of his paintings were rejected from the artist's retrospective exhibition at the Jewish Museum in New York. The rejected paintings were moved and displayed at the National Academy of Design, just few blocks away from the Jewish Museum. The Jewish Museum rationalized the rejection stating that "a display of Christological paintings at the Jewish museum would be offensive to the Jewish community and would show both lack of respect and lack of sensitivity to the perspective of our Christian friends."[26]

The Last Supper continued to attract artists in the second half of the 20th century. Surrealist artist Salvador Dali (1904–1989) painted a monumental image titled "The Sacrament of the Last Supper" in 1955 (about 6 x 9 ft. in the collection of the National Gallery, Washington DC). Dali returned to Christian subject-matters in the late 1940s as response to the atrocities of the Spanish Civil War and World War II. Following the Renaissance ideal models based on math and geometry Dali's composition is well calculated and evokes symmetry and balance. Jesus head is exactly in the center of the format and behind him a transparent partial torso of the resurrected Jesus outstretched his hands without any marks of his wounds. The modern architectural space opens to a landscape of Dali's native Catalonia.

Another iconic image which was inspired from the Last Supper is the 1979 installation work "The Dinner Party" (now in the collection of the Brooklyn Museum, NY) by Judy Chicago (b. 1939). During the production of this piece which promoted feminist agenda, the use of a dining table where women's meals were served over history drew the attention of the artist to Leonardo's Last Supper. "I become amused by the notion of doing a sort of reinterpretation of the all-male event from the point of view of those who traditionally been expected to prepare the food," recalled Chicago, "then silently disappear from the picture or, in this case, from the picture plane."[27] Chicago's Dinner Party transformed to an all-female event where historical female figures were represented symbolically around the triangle-shaped table.

In 1984, gallerist and art collector Alexandre Iolas, who gave Andy Warhol (1928–1987) his first solo exhibition in the Hugo Gallery in New York (1952), commissioned the Pop artist to produce a body of works based

---

[25] Dorothy C. Miller, *Fourteen Americans* (New York: The Museum of modern Art, 1946), 11.

[26] Grace Glueck, "Museum Drops 19 Aronson Paintings from Show over Christian Themes," *The New York Times* (May 25, 1979): section C, 7.

[27] Judy Chicago, *Beyond the Flower: The Autobiography of a Feminist Artist* (New York: Penguin, 1997), 46.

on Leonardo da Vinci's Last Supper. The intention was to display them in the Palazzo Stelline in Milan, just across Santa Maria delle Grazie, where Leonardo's mural is located. Between 1984 and 1986 Warhol obsessively produced more than 100 works related to Leonardo's Last Supper including works on paper, monumental paintings, and sculpture. Some images included screen prints of Leonardo's Last Supper, other were hand-painted and in many of them Warhol inserted commercial logos, newspaper headlines or advertisement. As in his previous works, he rationalized the process of the emergence of cultural icons by the mode of repetition and other techniques of the media in the context of pop culture. In his large painting (acrylic and silkscreen on linen) *Sixty Last Suppers* (1986) Warhol duplicated 60 black and white images of a 19th century engraving of Leonardo's Last Supper. The multiple images that resemble black and white TV screens following the artist's concepts of repetition, the media and the creation of iconic materials.

In another large-scale painting titled *The Last Super* (1986, collection of the Museum of Modern Art, NY) On top of a black and white rendering of Leonardo's Last Supper Warhol "stamped" the logos of two corporations, GE and Dove, and a price tag. According to Carolyn Lanchner, "Dove Soap's logo in rose and General Electric's in muted blue announce their presence at the holy scene. God, having separated light and darkness, found his creation to be 'good,' and, according to its slogan, GE, with beneficent intent, 'brings good things to light.' And did not the Holy Spirit descend upon Jesus at his baptism in the form of a dove? One might suspect a radically recast, reimagined transubstantiation. The much more brightly colored price tag of fifty-nine cents is more difficult to justify; might it be the cost of a Woolworth's copy of The Last Supper?"[28] Other art historians also observed that during the production of the Last Supper Warhol was struggling between his Catholic faith and his sexuality amid the AIDS crisis.[29] The show in Milan opened in January 1987 featuring 22 works from this series. Tragically, Alexandre Iolas, who initiated the commission, died of AIDS 5 months later, and for Andy Warhol, the Last Supper was his last major body of work and his last exhibition as he died just one month after the Milan's opening.

While the Last Supper of Jesus and his disciples is considered as a Passover meal it was not a Seder which Jews are celebrating today. The Torah emphasizes on the sacrifice of the Paschal lamb,[30] and Jews at the time of Jesus followed this ritual which was conducted in the Temple in

---

[28] Carolyn Lanchner, *Andy Warhol* (New York: The Museum of Modern Art, 2008), 42.

[29] Jessica Beck, "Andy Warhol: Sixty Last Suppers," *Gagosian Quarterly* (Summer 2017 Issue).

[30] Exodus 12:26–27 in *The New Oxford Annotated Bible*, 99.

Jerusalem and continued by families in communal feasts which also included unleavened bread and wine. The Seder was composed by the rabbinic establishment after the destruction of the temple and offered extensive and elaborated ritual for celebrating the Passover. The Haggadah was another step in elevating this holiday as the dispersal of Jews in the Diaspora and the rise of antisemitism turned Passover with its motifs of oppression and freedom to a more relevant festivity.

The Haggadah text which consists of prayers, commentary and hymns, follows the Torah's verse "You shall tell your son on that day, 'It is because of what the Lord did for me when I came out of Egypt.'"[31] The Haggadah was originally part of the Siddur, the Jewish prayer book, but in the 13th century it was separated into an independent book and since the 14th century illustrations were added. Some of the early Haggadah manuscripts were illustrated by Jewish artists-scribes, but according to Cecil Roth, "in others, to be sure, the Christian artist can be identified with virtual certainty on stylistic grounds."[32] As Jewish art was initially restricted by the Second Commandment, lack of artistic tradition or Jewish iconography forced artists to adapt a Christian visual vocabulary in early Jewish illuminated manuscripts.

One of the earliest surviving illustrated German Haggadah is the Bird's Head Haggadah (c. 1300, in the collection of the Israel Museum, Jerusalem) where most of human heads were replaced by birds' heads and others with blank heads or heads covered by helmets. The illuminated figures are dressed with the typical custom of southern German Jews and all men are wearing a pointed hat, the "Jewish hat," which was forced on them to wear by the church. Most scholars believe that the use of Bird's heads bypassed the Second Commandment's restriction of graven images, in particular those of humans, but others speculate that these images were antisemitic grotesque illustrated by a Christian artist. One of the illustrations of this Haggadah, inspired from Last Supper's images, depicts a Seder where a couple and other figures are dining along an oblong table raising cups of wine while another person on the right end carries the paschal lamb. The stylish folds of the tablecloth in front resemble those of Last Supper presentations in late medieval works such as the fresco of "The Last Supper and the Agony in the Garden," from the Church of Santa Monica inter Angelos near Spoleto, Italy (c. 1300) or in the Last Supper illustration from a bishop's benedictional from Regensburg, Germany (c. 1030–40).

The Sister Haggadah to the Golden Haggadah was produced in Barcelona, Spain in the 14th century (in the collection of the British Museum, London). The style of the illustrations in this Haggadah reflects

---

[31] Exodus 13:8 in *The New Oxford Annotated Bible*, 100.
[32] Cecil Roth, "Foreword," in Bezalel Narkiss, *Hebrew Illuminated Manuscripts* (New York: The Macmillan Company, 1969), 7–8.

early Italian Renaissance mixed with French Gothic motifs. The design of the illustrations is somehow primitive in the tradition of medieval images or according to Bezalel Narkiss, it was executed by "a relatively unaccomplished artist."[33] One of the images in this Haggadah, titled in Hebrew "The head of the house and his family making the Seder in the evening of Passover," is directly inspired from Christian illustrations of that time. The composition is based on framing the figures into French Gothic arches which was a common arrangement for Christian religious themes.

The setting of the figures around the table inspired from the conventional presentation of the Last Supper: the head of the house is sitting on the left end of an oblong table like the early Byzantine location of Jesus, a young kid is sitting next to him like John the apostle and one of the figures in the center is outstretching his hand toward a dish like Judas the apostle. Even the scale of colors preserved that of Christian manuscripts, and the attempt of the artist to render the table by applying moderate method of perspective links to the early Italian Renaissance. Another Jewish Spanish Haggadah from Barcelona dated c. 1350 is the Sarajevo Haggadah (in the collection of National Museum of Bosnia and Herzegovina in Sarajevo). The iconography for the illustrations in this Haggadah was also borrowed from Christian images in particular from the "Latin Bible illumination of the Franco-Spanish School."[34] The Italian Gothic style of the images was inspired from the local art school of Catalonia at that time. The illustration of the Seder in the Sarajevo Haggadah also inspired from the Last Supper: The head of the house is positioned on the right side of the oblong table holding a golden cup of wine in his hand and next to him, like Jesus and John, a young kid is sitting. Without any thematic connection, one figure with darker face is sitting alone on the other side of the table formally resembles Judas as he appeared in the late medieval Last Suppers. The ornamental folds of the tablecloth in front of the table are like those in the Seder table in the Bird's Head Haggadah.

The Darmstadt Haggadah from the Middle Rhine, Germany (early 15th century, in the collection of the Hesse State and University Library, Darmstadt, Germany) is a unique example of a Passover Haggadah featuring unusual illustrations in splendid design. Some of the odd scenes including a stag hunt or the fountain of youth. But one of the most remarkable pages in the Darmstadt Haggadah dedicated to the verse "Pour out your anger on the nations that do not know you, and on the kingdoms that do not call on your name."[35] A large blue initial letter on a golden background inserted in the center of the page and the rest of the verse is under it. The majority of the space of the composition above is dedicated to multiple figures, identified as

---

[33] Roth, "Forward," 58.
[34] Ibid. 60.
[35] Psalms 79:6 in *The New Oxford Annotated Bible,* 849.

women pupils and their male teachers, all are framed inside Gothic arches according the Christian tradition of religious illustrations.

Narkiss assumed that the presentation of women pupils and their teachers might suggest that this manuscript was executed for women.[36] Beneath the inscription from Psalm, on the bottom of the page inside an arch, the illustrator incorporated a Passover Seder which is completely based on the presentation of the Last Supper at that time: men and women are sitting around an oblong table as the majority of them are positioned behind the table in half-torso and two of them in each side of the table in full torso. Other details that are visually associated to the Last Supper are the design of the four rounded unleavened bread on top of the table and the gestured of the hands of the participants interacting with each other.

The Amsterdam Haggadah of 1695 followed the printed Haggadah of Venice (1629) but used for the first-time copper engravings instead of woodcuts for its illustrations. A rare map of the Land of Israel also printed in this Haggadah featuring the route of the Israelites traveling in the desert and the geographical locations of the twelve tribes. In the page of the Amsterdam Haggadah, where the verse "In every generation each individual is bound to regard himself as if he had gone personally fort from Egypt" is printed, a unique Passover Seder is illustrated.

The general design of this Seder was inspired from Dutch Baroque with dramatic mode: like a theatre scene, a curtain is opened on the right side revealing an oblong table surrounded with standing figures, and the interior is opened to the outdoor featuring a pastoral Dutch landscape. As Tissot captured later in his late 19th century Last Supper, the standing figures in the Amsterdam Haggadah holding walking staff in their hands following the verse "and thus shall ye eat it: with your loins girded, your shoes on your feet, and your staff in your hand."[37] The illustrations of the Amsterdam Haggadah became major models to future printed Haggadah books.

The Haggadah of van Geldern (1723) features a Passover Seder of a wealthy Jewish family in the Rococo style. The Haggadah was written and illustrated by Moses Loeb and was commissioned by Lazarus Geldern, the great-grandfather of Heinrich Heine. In a Last Supper inspired setting, the head of the family and his wife are sitting in full torso at the two ends of the oblong table and on the back side of table are "two guests, according to the custom of inviting strangers on this festive occasion."[38] A monumental door is open to welcome the arrival of Elijah and through it—a beautiful blooming of spring. "This illustration gives us an enlightening insight into the house of a wealthy Jew of this time," write Franz Landsberger, "It is

---

[36] Narkiss, *Hebrew Illuminated Manuscripts,* 126.
[37] Exodus 12:11 in *The New Oxford Annotated Bible,* 98.
[38] Franz Landsberger, *A History of Jewish Art* (Cincinnati: The Union of American Hebrew, 1946), 261.

only natural that the owner of such a cultivated home should use equally beautiful Haggadah."[39]

In the modern era, the illustrations of the Haggadah departed from past traditions and captured contemporary values. The Trieste Haggadah (1864) presents a middle-class Italian Jewish family sitting around the Seder's table in full realism: "not only are the men and women dressed in the current style, but each of them exhibited an individuality rarely encountered before."[40] In a similar fashion, an Haggadah which was published in 1879 in Chicago evokes not only realism but also humor. One of the illustrations in this Haggadah depicts a couple and four of their sons around the Seder table. The four sons following the Haggadah's Four Sons: the Wise son, the only son that wearing a kippah, is sitting next to his mother and looking at the Haggadah book, while the Wicked son is sitting at the other end of the table smoking a cigarette and raising his hand in a provocative manner.[41]

A communist Haggadah, published in Moscow by "red" Jews in 1927, is a parody and mockery on the Passover holiday and the Jewish religion. One of the illustrations in the communist Haggadah depicts a Seder where grotesque Jews with beards and kippahs sitting along the table surrounded with demons.[42] Another modern Haggadah's illustration that reflect social-political agenda is that of Bet Ha-Shitah (1947) featuring a mass communal Seder in a Kibbutz dining room by a Jewish secular society. The space is overwhelmed with long tables and a huge audience where the men's heads are without any cover.

Two years later, when the state of Israel already celebrated its independence, Israeli artist Reuven Rubin (1893–1974) produced the painting "First Seder in Jerusalem" inspired from the traditional depiction of the Last Supper. Reuven was fascinated from the figure of Jesus already in his early career and he created several paintings and prints of him.[43] The "First Seder in Jerusalem" features an oblong table where the artist is sitting on the right end with a kid next to him and in the other end of the table Jesus is sitting dressed in white showing his hands with the stigmata wounds. On the back side of the table the artist positioned diverse representatives of the

---

[39] Landsberger, *A History of Jewish Art*, 262.

[40] Yosef Hayim Yerushalmi, *Haggadah and History: A Panorama in Facsimile of Five Centuries of the Printed Haggadah from the Collections of Harvard University and the Jewish Theological Seminary of America* (Philadelphia: Jewish Publication Society, 2005), Plate 105.

[41] Ibid., Plate 115.

[42] Anna Shternshis, *Soviet and Kosher: Jewish Popular Culture in the Soviet Union, 1923–1939* (Bloomington: Indiana University Press, 2006), 27–35.

[43] Nathan Harpaz, "Jewish Artists and the Perception of the Crucifixion," in *Teaching the Historical Jesus: Issues and Exegesis* (editor: Zev Garber, New York: Routledge, 2015), 175–177.

Israeli society at that time including a rabbi, young pioneers, and new immigrants. Behind the group Reuven opened the interior to a landscape of Jerusalem seen through three arches analogues to Leonardo's three open windows in his Last Supper.

In 1999 contemporary Israeli artist Adi Nes (b. 1966) produced his project "Soldiers," a series of staged photos, and one of them was titled "Untitled: The Last Supper Before Going Out to Battle." Nes staged 13 Israeli soldiers with uniforms sitting on an oblong table made of military style folded tables in exact the same positions and gestures as Jesus and his disciples in Leonardo's Last Supper. This contemporary image and Leonardo's 500 years old mural share the same universal or collective archetypes of departure, sacrifice, and hopefully redemption.

Romaniote and Judeo-Spanish (Ladino) Passover Haggadah: Excerpts and Related Customs

Yitzchak Kerem

The article notes the particularistic Passover customs of the Romaniote, Judeo-Greek and Greek-speaking Jews of the Greek Peninsula in their preparation of the water for matsa production, their use of Judeo-Greek in the Passover liturgy, and their customs in the Passover seder. The article also highlights the unique Sephardic traditions in cuisine, their different Haggadot; including the famous Sarajevo Iberian Haggadah, and the use of medieval Castillian Ladino in the Passover Haggadah, singing, and prayer.

The Jews of Greece observed different traditions in Judeo-Greek Romaniote and Judeo-Spanish Ladino Sephardic traditions. The Romaniotes were in Epirus in northwest Greece and in Attica, in Athens and Chalkis in the Evia Peninsula. The Sephardim were in the north in Macedonia and Thrace and mixed with the Romaniotes in Thessaly in the center of the country.

The Romaniote Jews followed the Jerusalem Talmud whereas the Sephardim observed the Babylonian Talmud. According to Steven Bowman, the term Romaniote stem from the self-identification of the Greek-speaking Orthodox Christian population of the Balkans as Rhomaioi (Romans) who were descendants of the Roman Empire. The Byzantine Empire was established in 333 in Constantinople. The Jews were citizens of the Roman Empire, which in its eastern end became the Byzantine Empire and were known as the Rhomaioi (Greek) or Romani (Latin), hence the Romaniot or romaniotim in Hebrew.[1] The Byzantine Empire also was considered the Second Rome. In the Ottoman Empire after 1453 the Greek-Orthodox were coined Rum. The Jews were the Romaniotes. Hollander defined Romaniote (derived in modern Greek as Romaniotes) as the Greek-speaking communities, that wrote mainly in Hebrew, of the former Byzantine Empire

---

[1] Steven Bowman, "Romaniots (Bene Romania)" *Encyclopedia of Jews in the Islamic World, IV* (Boston and Leiden: Brill, 2010) 180–182.

after Heraclius I (610–641); of the Greek mainland, Asia Minor and Constantinople.[2] Furthermore, she claims that this denomination claims the whole Byzantine-Greek heritage as Romaniote. These Jewish communities spoke Greek and wrote it in Hebrew characters, and they adhered to a specific liturgical rite Minhag Romania. She assesses Romania as the self-designation of the Byzantine Empire during the Middle ages.

Romaniote Passover Customs

In Ioannina the communal preparations involved attaining special kosher sugar from abroad needed for *matsot*, particularistic customs in preparing the *matsot* and bringing water from the lake, baking the *matsot*, and special prayers recited in Judeo-Greek, Greek, and Hebrew during the Passover holiday.[3] Dalven depicted the bringing of the water from the lake in Ioannina as follows:

> The community bought wheat which they ground into floor for *matsa* made only with lake water. The water carrier brought lake water in two heavy, narrow necked copper jugs (dzkioumaia), one on each arm. He walked into the water on a stone path set some distance into the lake to get clear water. He was not permitted to speak to anyone, coming or going. Young people brought water from the lake in small copper jugs (koukmoules).[4]

The Jews of Ioannina in the evening service in the synagogue, before the home seder, sang "Lel Shemourim" ("The Night of the Vigil") commemorating the midnight when the Jews left Egypt; offering thanks to God. This was also chanted by Italian and Ashkenazi Jews, but is absent from, the Sephardic holiday maḥzor; prayer book.[5]

The Greek-speaking Jews of Byzantium, the Romaniote Jews, call their Passover seder *hova*, meaning obligation. The seder was called *hova*, meaning obligation. When the family sat down to the Passover seder, they put their hands on the table and recited in Hebrew "Zeh hashulhan asher lifne Ado-nai" (This is the table before God).[6]

In some Romaniote communities like Chalkis, the dough of the *matsa* was slashed three times diagonally with a knife to inhibit rising and

---

[2] Elisabeth Hollander and Jannis Niehoff-Panagiotis, "Mahzor Romania and the Judeo-Greek Hymn enas o kirios. Introduction, Critical Edition, and Commentary", *Revue des Etudes Juives* 170 (1–2) (Janvier-juin 2011) 117–171.
[3] Rae Dalven, *The Jews of Ioannina* (Philadelphia: Cadmus Press, 1996) 95–96.
[4] Ibid., 95.
[5] Ibid., 96.
[6] Ibid., 96.

these *matsot* were called *Hallels* to be used as the three special *matsot* blessed in the Hallel part of the seder service.[7] A sweet spoon-full of fanaro, usually a condiment or with honey, was served to guests symbolizing a holiday or special event taste. A dish served in Ioannina was *Pita paskalini* (Passover lamb pie) in dough with the heart, liver, lungs, kidneys, and intestines of a spring lamb. For desert in Ioannina, Arta, and Preveza the Romaniote Jews ate *Maretsini,* Passover almond cookies.

At the seder the Jews of Ioannina ate *lahan*, made of *matsa* meal, chopped spinach, chopped walnuts, and pieces of lamb; as well as *pastella*, a simple meat pie sandwiched between two layers of *matsot* and beaked to a brown crisp. They also sang parts of Songs of Songs (Shir Hashirim) in Greek in a version published by Behoraki Noikokir in Salonika in 1924. During the last two days of *Pesach* in the morning service, the Song of Songs was sung in Judeo-Greek (based on a translation from the Aramaic text of the Midrash). A cantor began chanting a verse on Hebrew, to which the congregation responded in Judeo-Greek. The cantor then chanted another verse in Hebrew, to which one member of the congregation answered in Judeo-Greek. As many as ten members of the congregation did the same in turn; each reciting one verse in Judeo-Greek.[8]

At the end of the Passover seder, the Romaniote Jews of Ioannina sang "Ehad mi Yodea" ("Who knows One") and "Had Gadia" ("One Goat") in Greek and not in Hebrew and Aramaic, respectively.[9]

In Ioannina, the Jews had numerous nicknames which became surnames.[10] Several have Passover connotations. The Ḥametz family had some connection to *ḥametz*, forbidden bread or leavened bread. Dalven noted that *hametz* (leaven) was discovered eating forbidden food on Passover. He confessed that he ate *ḥametz* and the name stuck; later turning into a patronym. The Colchemiro family has some connection to the Kol Chamira prayer said from the ceremony the evening before the holiday when the house is checked for any remains of bread and flour and in the prayer the head of the house declares he has no *ḥametz* in his possession. Dalven noted that her mother was a Kalchamira and the family explanation of the name was that her father, a cloth merchant, used to examine material as closely as if her was searching for leaven (*ḥametz*). Matza was a popular Romaniote

---

[7] Nicholas Stavrolakis, *Cookbook of the Jews of Greece* (Athens: Lycabettus Press, 1986) 52.

[8] Ibid., 96–97.

[9] Ibid., 96.

[10] Yitzchak Kerem, "On Sephardic and Romaniot Names" in Aaron Demsky, ed., *These Are The Names, Studies in Jewish Onomastics*, Vol. 2, (Ramat Gan: Bar Ilan University Press, 1999) 113–136; Asher Moissis, Les noms des Juifs de Grece (Gordes, France: Eli Carasso, 1998); Matilde Tagger and Yitzchak Kerem, Guidebook for the Sephardic and Oriental Genealogical Sources in Israel Bergenfeld, NJ: Avotaynu, 2006), and Dalven, 158.

surname in Ioannina and Corfu, but the family has no known specific traits connected to unleavened bread.

The Matza family claims descent from Sicily and there was a village there called Mazza which no longer appears on maps. Italian scholars think that the Italian Jewish Mazzas of Sicily were initially Ashkenazim from Germany who in Italy had their name Moshe changed to Mazza. In Italian mazzare means to kill or destroy which further deviates the etymology of the Jewish surname. Scholars of Greek Jewry highly disagree with this theory that Matza comes from the Jewish Moshe. Romaniote Jews who took the first name Moshe for a surname became Moisis. Sephardim who turned the first name Moshe into a patronym became Moise.

Sephardic Passover Customs

The Sephardic Jews of Ottoman Salonika and their transition into modern Greece, have numerous customs in the vernacular language Judeo-Spanish. Instead of Had Gadya, they sang Dos Levanim. However also in Salonika there was an 1894 Haggadah with a Ladino translation of Had Gadya entitled Un kavreitiko or Un Kavrito. Another unique Judeo-Spanish hymn in the Haggadah was Gaal Israel (The Redemption of Israel).

Rabbi Yosef Caro, who lived in Salonika in the 16th century, in the Shulhan Aruch made some rulings differing from Ashkenazi ritual. Karo ruled that glass is non-porous and therefore glass utensils that were used even for boiling *hametz* (leaven) may be used during Pesaḥ (Passover). He also ruled that fruit juice (or eggs) mixed with flour does not render the flour *hametz*, so it could be used on Pesaḥ, but not at the seder to fulfill the mitzvah of eating *matsa*.[11] Salonika Sephardim prepared *matsa* "shruya," which was soaked in water. In Salonika, no one hid the afikomen, but instead the grandfather told about the Exodus and the children replayed the dialogue as if they were leaving Egypt as liberated slaves with sacks on their back with their belongings. In the seder celery (karpas) was often dipped in vinegar or lemon juice. The hymn Ehad MiYodeya was sung in Judeo-Spanish, Greek, and Ottoman Turkish.

Some Sephardim eat rice on Pesaḥ and others not. In Salonika rice was forbidden. For those who eat rice the rationale comes from the Talmud as recorded by the Rambam who ruled that rice is not *hametz*.[12] Some Sephardim have the custom not to eat rice on Pesaḥ as well as refraining from some legumes. Dobrinsky noted that there was no prohibition against kitniyyot (legumes) amongst the Judeo-Spanish speaking Sephardim, but

---

[11] Rabbi Ilam Acoca, *The Sephardic Book of Why, A Guide to Sephardic Jewish traditions and Customs* (Saarbrucken, Germany: Hadassa Word Press, 2016) 47–48.

[12] Babylonian Talmud, Pesahim 35A, and Mishneh Torah, Hilchot Pesah 5:1.

that they did not eat rice "because of the necessity of checking through the rice to make sure there is no grain mixed into it."[13]

Angel noted that in Rhodes the more stringent religious Sephardic Jews ate *masza shemurah*:

> A specifically prepared type of *matsa*, *matsa shemurah*, was baked on the day before Passover (Nisan 14). Some Rhodian Jews ate only *matsa shemurah* throughout the Passover festival. These *matsot* were made from wheat which had been guarded from fermentation since the time of the harvest. Others ate regular *matsot* made from wheat which had been guarded from fermentation only since the time it was ground into flour. The first group, having stricter standards, did not eat or drink in the houses of the latter group during the Passover holiday.[14]

All vegetables grown were used for *Pesaḥ*.

Most Sephardim made the ḥaroset, sweet with dates and chopped nuts, but other communities made it bitter with vinegar, like in the mixed Romaniote/Judeo-Italian community of Zakynthos, to remind that it symbolized the mortar for cement that the Jews had to make as slaves.

Stavrolakis presented unusual recipes from Greece for *Pesaḥ*. In Rhodes the Sephardim prepared Megina, a beef and *matsa* casserole, In Trikala, the mixed Romaniote/Sephardic community, served *Pastel de Pesach*, (Lamb innards pie). In Hania, Crete, due to the Venetian influence, Sfoungato (Lamb innards, spinach, and *matsa* casserole) was served. Frikasse, a baby lamb dish, popular in general in the Balkans was served on Pesaḥ with Romaine lettuce.[15]

Today, the classic Sephardic Haggadah is the Sarajevo Haggadah that survived the 1492 Spanish expulsion, the Holocaust, and the Serbian attack on Bosnia from 1992 to 1995 when the city of Sarajevo was under siege, The Haggadah originates from ca. 1350 in Barcelona. It is handwritten on bleached calfskin and illuminated in copper and gold. In the beginning of the Haggadah there are thirty-four pages of illustration of Biblical scenes from creation until the death of Moses. The Haggadah is owned by the National Museum of Bosnia and Herzegovina in Sarajevo and displayed there under glass.

---

[13] Rabbi Herbert C. Dobrinsky, *A Treasury of Sephardic Laws and Customs* (Hoboken, NJ: Ktav Publishing House and New York: Yeshiva University Press, 1986) 274.

[14] Marc D. Angel, *The Jews of Rhodes, The History of a Sephardic Community* (New York: Sepher-Hermon Press and The Union of Sephardic Congregations, 1980) 130–131.

[15] Stavrolakis, 51–83.

Top: Moses and the burning bush
Bottom: The staff of Aaron swallows the magicians' staffs.

The Haggadah appeared in Italy in the 16th century. It was purchased from Yosef Cohen in 1894 by the Museum of Bosnia. A child of the Sephardic Jewish community of Sarajevo brought the Haggadah to school to be sold after his father died leaving the family destitute. During the Holocaust it was given by museum chief librarian Dervis Korkut for safekeeping to a Muslim cleric in the village Zenica on the Bjelasnica mountain, where it was hidden in a mosque. In 1957 Jewish scholar Sandor Scheiber, director of the Rabbinical Seminary of Budapest, made a facsimile of the rare precious Haggadah.[16]

---

[16] Shalom Sabar, *The Sarajevo Haggadah History & Art* (Sarajevo: The National Musueum of Bosnia and Herzegovina, 2018) 57–87.

Maror ze, This bitter herb.

Art historian Shalom Sabar noted that Rabbi Abudarham, Spanish halakhic authority of his time, identified the *maror* as cardoon (Cynara cardunculus, the "artichoke thistle") which was popular in the medieval Spanish kitchen and never appeared after Spain in the Sephardic seder,[17] David Gitlitz identified the artichoke, known as the Jerusalem artichoke, amongst crypto-Jews as a popular food reflecting their faint Jewish identity.[18]

> Other unusual motifs portrayed in the Sarajevo Haggadah is when Joseph's coffin was thrown into the Nile by the Egyptians, the interior of a Spanish synagogue, and three coat of arms illuminating that the Haggadah originated from Aragon. The biblical figures were portrayed as Sephardi/Aragonese Jews.

---

[17] David Stern Redemption in Catalonia and Bosnia: The Sarajevo Haggadah," Jewish Review of Books, April 16, 2019. https://jewishreviewofbooks.com/uncategorized/5279/redemption-in-catalonia-and-bosnia-the-sarajevo-haggadah/.

[18] David Gitlitz and Linda Kay Davidson, *A Drizzle of Honey: The Lives and Recipes of Spain's Secret Jews* (London St. Martin's Press, 1999).

There were Sephardim in the Balkans and Jerusalem that during the seder, opened their door after announcing the Maggid section[19] and pouring the second cup of wine. The Sephardim only recite the blessing on the first and third cups of wine in the seder. The custom is based on the ruling of Rabbi Yosef Karo that determined that "when one recites the blessing on the first cup of wine, he should have the second cup in mind, and when one recites the blessing on the third cup of wine, he should have the fourth cup in mind."[20] The Balkan Sephardim have no cup for Elijah the prophet like the Ashkenazim and they do not open the door for the part of the Haggadah for the recitation of *Shefokh hamatekha al hagoyim* (Pour out your wrath at the Gentiles).

The Sephardim have a different order for the Four Questions, which follows a more correct chronological order of the actual observances of the seder. In English translation the Sephardi version is as follows:

Why is this night different from all other nights?
For on all other nights we do not dip our vegetables even once; but tonight we dip twice.
For on all other nights we eat bread or *matsa* (unleavened bread), but tonight—only *matsa*.
For on all other nights we eat any vegetables, but tonight—*maror* (bitter herbs).
For on all other nights we eat either sitting up or reclining: but tonight—we all recline.[21]

Another classic Sephardic tradition is when the male leading the seder puts a symbolic sack, with the *Afikoman*, the broken half of the middle *matsa* of three, over his shoulder symbolically having left Egypt and heading toward Jerusalem. Dobrinsky depicted this part of the seder as follows:

After the Seder is under way, at the portion in the Haggadah where we read, "*Bekhol dor vador hayav adam lirot et azmo ke'ilu hu azmo yaza mimizrayim*" the head of the householding who is conducting the Seder throws the napkin containing the Afikoman over his shoulder and he walks out of the room, returning with a belt which is tightened, a cane in his hand, and this sack containing the Afikoman over his shoulder. This charade is to demonstrate how our ancestors went out of Egypt. When he walks back into the dining room with the special outfit, he makes the

---

[19] Dobrinsky noted that in the Sephardic Judeo-Spanish speaking tradition, "the door of the house is opened at *Kol Dikhfin* to symbolically invite all the poor who may wish to join in the Seder," Dobrinsky, 275.
[20] Acoca, 49.
[21] Dobrinsky, 256.

declaration, "*Kakha asu Yisrael kesheyazu mimizrayim. Mishearotam zerurot besimlotam al shikhmam ... uvenai /yisrael asu kidvar Moshe*" (paraphrasing Exodus 12:34–35). Everyone present then asks, Where do you come from?" to which he answers, "I have come from Egypt." They then ask, "To where are you going?" and he responds, "I am going to Jerusalem." Then everyone declares in unison, "*Leshanah habaah biYerushalayim habenuya*," which means, "May we celebrate next year in the rebuilt city of Jerusalem." This dramatic reenactment of the Exodus from Egypt is to stimulate the curiosity of the children and to encourage them to ask questions about the exodus from Egypt.

Each member of the family then takes the opportunity to carry the *Afikoman* over his shoulder in the enactment of the ceremony showing that the Jews were traveling from Egypt to Jerusalem. There is no tradition of hiding or stealing the *Afikoma*n. The *Afikoman* was regarded as a *segula* and was coupled together with a piece of *mazzah yayin* (*mazzah* made from flour and wine, or eggs), and this would be kept as a protector of the house against evil from year to year. Each Erev Pesah, they would change the pieces of *mazzah* and replace them that night with the new mazzot, which would be kept for the whole year until next Erev Pesah. This resembles the procedure for maintaining the mazzot in the synagogue for eruv hazerot (which permits one to carry within the designated boundary on the Sabbath).[22]

The part of the seder of the Ten Plagues of the Balkan Sephardim had an unusual custom: The portion of the *Eser makot* (Ten Plagues) is recited in both Hebrew and Ladino. The wine is poured into a large *legen* (special basin), and the wife brings in a pitcher of water for the head of the household to wash his hands after poring the wine for the Ten Plagues and for *Dezakh, Adash,* and *Be'ahav*. The pouring out shows the sadness of the Jews at the Almighty's killing of the Egyptians in order to get Pharoah to free the Jews, and depicts how with each drop of wine our happiness (which wine symbolizes) is diminished. No one is permitted to look at these drops of wine, which have been poured into a basin.[23]

In contemporary Sephardic Haggadot like the Chavez Family Sephardic Ladino Haggadah there are Ladino versions for El Lavado de Manos (washing hands), Halachma, the Four Questions, and Los 4 Hijos (four sons).[24]

The main course of the meal was lamb and fresh peas, as well as a dish called "levalov" (לבאלוב)which was a bundle of lamb pancreas with

---

[22] Dobrinsky, *A Treasury of Sephardic Laws and Customs*, 276–277.
[23] Ibid., 277.
[24] Steven Grossman, *The Chavez Family Sephardic Ladino Haggadah* https://www.haggadot.com/contributors-details/stevejets, 25–26.

neck tracheas cooked in oil and fried onion.[25] Esther Levy noted that in Rhodes the main courses of the seder were kebab and *kuajado de karne*, a meat curdling. She also noted that other foods served included leak patties (kiftes de prasa) migina (beef and *matsa* casserole).[26] Stavroulakis noted that in Rhodes other Passover dishes were *Peshe en saltsa* (Fish in rhubarb sauce) and *Boumwelos*, a type of fritter or doughnut.[27]

Initially the whole Sephardic Haggadah was both in Ladino (Judeo-Spanish) and Hebrew. In Contemporary Sephardic Haggadot there are several Ladino hymns for *Echad Mi Yodeah*, *Chad Gadya*, and *Who Knows One* (Ehad Ani Yodea) at the end of the seder; as well as Ladino tunes unique to the Sephardim at the end of the seder: Eloheinu Shabashamaim, and Ein Keloheinu.[28]

In 1955 the small Salonikan Jewish community, comprised of a few hundred out of 56,000 that survived the Holocaust, published a multi-lingual Hebrew/Aramaic, Ladino and Greek Haggadah. The first three Ladino verses and the finale are:

Un cavretico que lo merco mi padre,
    por dos az, por dos az bari.
Y vino el gato, y se cumio el cavrito, que lo merco mi padre,
    por dos az, por dos az bari.
Y vino el perro, y madrio al gato, que se cumio el cavrito, que lo merco mi padre,
    por dos az, por dos az bari.
....
Y vino el Mallah Amavath, y degoyo al chohet, que degoyo al buey, que se bivio el agua, que analo el fuego, que quemo ala vaa, que aharvo al perro, que mudrio al gato, que se cumio el cavrito, que lo merco mi padre,
    por dos az, por dos az bari.[29]

---

[25] Asher Vaserteil, ed., *Yalkut Minhagim, Miminhageihem She Shivtei Yisrael [A Collection of Customs of the Traditions of the Tribes of Israel]* (Jerusalem: Israel Ministry of Education of Culture, Administration of Religious Education, 1996) 327–328.

[26] Rebecca Amato Levy, *I Remember Rhodes* (New Yoprk: Sepher-Hermon Press for Sephardic House at Congregation Shearith Israel, 1987) 216.

[27] Stavroulakis, 50–60, 82.

[28] https://www.haggadot.com/haggadah/chavez-family-sephardic-ladino-haggadah/.

[29] Reprinted from the 1955 Salonikan Jewish community Haggadah in Barouch I. Shibi, ed., Hagadah, Leshana Haba beYerushalayim, Seder Hagaddat Leil Pessah "Agada Sel Pessah," (Thessaloniki: Israelite Community of Thessaloniki, 1970) 115. [Greek}

The standard Ladino version of Had Gadya was"

> Un kavrito ke lo merko mi padre por dos levanim.
> I vino al gato I se komio el kavretiko ke lo merko mi padre por dos levanim…
> I vino el Santo Bendicho El, I degoyo al malah amavet, ke degoyo al shohet, ke degoyo al buey, ke se bevyo la agua, ke amata el fuego, ke kemo el palo, ke aharvo el perro, ke modryo el gato, ke se komio el kavretiko, ke lo merko mi padre, por dos levanim.[30]

Naar made some general comments on differences between the above two versions. "But in reality, each locale involved particularities in terms of vocabulary, verses, and tune. In the Ladino versions, "goat" was varyingly called *un kavretiko* or *un kavrito*; the currency which it was purchased by the father varied among *aspros, asprikos, as bari*, lavanim, l*evanim,* or *levantikos,* with some versions using a combination; the ox is referred to as *buey* or *vaka*; the stick as *vara* or *palo*; and God as *El Santo Benditcho El* or, like the Aramaic, *El Akadosh Barukh Hu.* In several places, the song was sung with the middle eastern style ottoman musical modes known as *makams*: In Salonica, *makam saba*; in Rhodes, *makam oshok*; in Bulgarian *makam bayat*; in Ioannina, *makam hijaz*. In Corfu, it took on the upbeat style of an Italian tarantella."[31]

In conclusion, as opposed to Ashkenazim who forbid eating lamb in fear of desecrating the rabbinic prohibition of making a Passover sacrifice in the absence of a Holy Temple, Sephardim eat lamb and grill and broil for the Passover seder meal. The Sephardim have numerous different customs, in particular in cuisine, preparing the *matsa*, and conducting the seder. The Sephardim conduct the seder in Hebrew and Ladino, but the Greek-speaking Romaniote Jews conduct part of the seder in Greek and Judeo-Greek. Both the Sephardim and Romaniote Jews prepare Passover cuisine based on Mediterranean products, cuisine, and fish and meat availability and selection.

Many of the Romaniote traditions were lost with the dwindling and obscurity of the historic Mahzor Romania. When the Sephardim came to the Ottoman Empire, they outnumbered, overpowered, and dominated the Romaniotes with Sephardic religious laws and traditions. The Romaniotes remaining in Greece were mostly annihilated in the Holocaust, and those that migrated to the United States or even Egypt and Israel, greatly assimilated and over more than a century lost their communal identities.

---

[30] See Hagadah shel Pessah Kfi Minhag Sefardim (Vienna: Joseph Schlesinger, 1897).

[31] "Had Gadya in Ladino: A Sephardic Passover Tradition?" https://jewishstudies.washington.edu/sephardic-studies/had-gadya-ladino-passover/.

Thus, most customs have been lost and there is no longer any Romaniote surviving lifestyle.

The Sephardim were much more numerous in the Balkans, and even though most of the Sephardim in Greece and the ex-Yugoslavia were annihilated in the Holocaust, the Bulgarian and Turkish Sephardic Jews maintained Sephardic traditions and ethnicity in varying degrees. Primarily through scholarship and many active musical folk troupes since the 1980s, Sephardic traditions have been preserved in books and music. While there are few active Sephardic Judeo-Spanish speaking communities and synagogues, the language and traditions have been preserved by many dedicated Sephardim in their families and in cultural associations. The article has given a few examples of the rich array of Sephardic Passover cuisine, music, and prayer.

A Chassidisher Pesach: Passover Traditions and Insights from Chassidic Perspectives

Diane Mizrahi

The Chassidic movement of Eastern Europe emerged in the wake of the horrific Chmielnicki massacres in Poland and the Ukraine (1648–49), despondency over the fraudulent messianic claims of Shabbatei Zvi (1626–1676), and as a countermeasure to Jewish Enlightenment and assimilation. Founded by Israel Baal Shem Tov in 18th century Poland, Chassidism integrated Torah Judaism with joy, piety, and Lurianic Kabbalistic principles, and spread quickly throughout the region. Over time, different factions developed around their charismatic leaders and courts, but all continued to share core conventions. This paper explores the roots of Chassidic Passover traditions and 'hiddurim' (stringencies) that differ from other Ashkenazi and Sephardic groups, including "gebrochts," "shmura" (watched) matsa, and "matsot yad" (handmade matsa). Selected commentaries illuminating mystical aspects of the holiday are included; particularly surrounding the matsa, the search and removal of physical chametz (leavening) from our homes as a powerful reminder to rid ourselves of inflated egoism. The central role and power of women and femininity in the festival is discussed. Concluding the Passover holiday is the Chassidic custom of Seudat Mashiach, (Feast of the Messiah). Initiated by the Baal Shem-Tov and based on Kabbalistic precepts, this meal is eaten on the afternoon of the last day of the holiday and shares parallels with the Mimouna festival practiced by Jews of North African heritage.

Introduction

The Jewish movement known as Chassidism (*Chassidut*) developed in Poland in the 18th century, and spread quickly throughout Eastern Europe, particularly Poland, Russia, Lithuania, Latvia, Ukraine, Belorussia, Moldova, Hungary, and Romania. Chassidic "Courts" and sects sprang up around charismatic leaders and mystics known as 'Rebbes.' In general, Chassidism sought to reinfuse joy and purpose into the daily rituals and life, especially for the simple folk who could not hope to learn in the great Yeshivas and Torah centers. These folks sat lower in the social hierarchy of their communities than the scholars, and many suffered from ignorance and disestablishment but felt a keen attachment to Torah Judaism.

Established Ashkenazi Jewish leaders and their followers revered the traditional emphasis on scholarship and learning, believing that the Chassidic introduction of mysticism, emotional enthusiasm, and esoterism among the less learned would turn them away from rabbinic Judaism and its attention to Halachah (Jewish law) derived from arduous study of the Talmud and its commentaries. Trauma from the messianic fervor and monumental despair after the unravelling of the Shabatai Zvi movement in the previous century was still fresh, and now rabbis watched as Jacob Frank (1726–1791) and his growing sect promoted ideas in antithesis to Jewish values. They also felt threatened by the nascent Haskalah (Enlightenment) movement with its secularized agenda. Opponents of Chassidism, known as *mitnagdim* (or *misnagdim*), used communal banishment (*charem*), complaints to non-Jewish authorities often resulting in harassment and arrests, and even physical violence in their efforts to protect what they saw as Torah Judaism. But the Chasidim did not abandon Torah and Halachah. Quite the opposite, they increased their meticulous adherence by creating *chumrot* (protective walls) around their practices, "beautified" mitzvahs through careful stringency and going beyond the letter of the law (*ḥiddurim*), and by renewing customs that had been abandoned or not widely followed. These customs and *ḥiddurim* were usually based on Kabalistic principles.

By the 1930s there were scores of Chassidic centers and sects. Chabad-Lubavitch developed a particularly sophisticated philosophical systems based on Kabbalah and Halachah.[1] Others were more fluid. Over the centuries, communities in the various regions developed local customs and traditions (*minhagim*) while still adhering to Halachah. Today, most non-Chassidic European Jews follow *minhag Ashkenaz*. Chasidim tend to follow *minhag Sepharad*, similar to Ashkenaz but influenced by Spanish and Lurianic ideas.[2] Some smaller communities still follow their own *minhagim* including the Italian/Roman rites, and the two main Yemenite traditions of *Baladi* and *Shami*. *Minhag HaAri* (based on Kabalistic principles of Itzhak Luria, the 'Ari') is the *minhag* of Chabad-Lubavitch and

---

[1] Lubavitch is the name of the town in Russia that served as the group's center from 1813–1915. Like other Chasidic sects, it was named by its main geographic location. 'ChaBaD' is the acronym of the Kabbalistic 'sefirot' of Chochmah, Bina, and Daat, that are central to the sect's philosophical structure. The two terms are sometimes combined, Chabad-Lubavitch, as well as used interchangeably.

[2] Not to be confused with *Minhag Sephardi*—used by Jews from Spain and many parts of the Spanish diaspora.

other Chassidic practitioners. Many Chassidic customs and *minhagim* that differ from Ashkenazi traditions can be found in the Pesach celebrations.

This chapter will explore some of these Chassidic Pesach traditions from an historic and Kabbalistic perspective. We will also include insights into practices found in the seder and throughout the Passover holiday as illuminated by Chassidic Masters, particularly the late Lubavitcher Rebbe, Rabbi Menachem Mendel Schneerson (1902–1994). Two Chabad sources are used heavily in this chapter: The Kol Menachem Haggadah, compiled and adapted by Rabbi Chaim Miller, and the Passover Haggadah compiled by Rabbi Yosef Marcus. Both incorporate commentary and insights from classic texts, the Midrash, Kabbalah, Chassidic leaders, and the Lubavitcher Rebbe in particular. Rabbi Schneerson addressed his prolific teachings to a late twentieth century audience comprised of both secular and religious Jewish intellectuals and sages, as well as newcomers and novices in Judaism. Many of his teachings have been translated into English from their original Yiddish or Hebrew, and can be easily found in abridgements or in their entireties in the vast number of Chabad-Lubavitch publications and electronic libraries and websites.

In order to grasp the meanings of the customs more fully and enable an entrance into the mode of Chassidic thought, we will begin by offering a brief overview of the Chassidic movement, its leaders, and basic Chassidic philosophy and the Kabalistic principles on which they are based. We will then look at some of the more obvious differences found at a Chassidic seder and Passover celebrations before delving into selected insights. Finally, we examine the custom of the *Seudat Mashiach* (Messiah Meal) on the last day of Passover.

Personalities and Basic Philosophies of the Chassidic Movement

R 'Israel ben Eliezer (1698–1760), known as the Baal Shem Tov (Master of the Good Name) is regarded as the founder of the "modern" Chassidic movement. Kabbalists however, are known to Jewish history since the time of R 'Shimon bar Yochai in the second century C.E., and there are many references to mystics, and earlier 'Baal Shems.' A German Jewish movement in the 12th and 13th centuries, who called themselves Chassidim (Pious Ones), combined austerity with overtones of mysticism, and sought favor with the common people, who had grown dissatisfied with formalistic ritualism. The authentic Chassid, as described in the movement's main book *Sefer Chassidi*m, imbues himself with asceticism, humility, serenity, altruism, and strict ethical behavior.

In 16th century Safed (Israel), a young Kabbalist named Itzhak ben Shlomo Luria Ashkenazi (1534–1572) gathered a group of followers and developed the methodology known today as Lurianic Kabbalah, upon which modern Chassidism is based. Though he studied briefly with the revered mystic R 'Moshe Cordorvero, developer of the Cordoverian Kabbalistic framework, Luria's method soon took precedence and became the most widely accepted method in Jewish mystical circles. Luria is commonly known as "Ha'Ari" ("The Lion"), "Ha'Ari Hakadosh" (the holy Ari) or "Ari'zal" the Ari, Of Blessed Memory (*Zikhrono Livrakha*). His father was of Ashkenazi heritage but passed away when the Ari was young, and he was raised by his Sephardic maternal uncle in Egypt. Perhaps it is because of his mixed heritage that both Ashkenazi and Sephardic communities were so open to his teachings. Though he himself did not write books, his spiritual fame led to his veneration and the acceptance of his authority. We know of his teachings through the compilations by his many disciples, the most prominent being R 'Chaim Vital and his classic work *Etz HaChaim* (The Tree of Life), a summary of the Ari's teachings.

Among the concepts of Lurianic Kabbalah that are prominent in Chassidic philosophy are the *Sefirot*, the ten emanations of God with anthropomorphic representations. They include the three intellectual faculties: *Chochmah*, *Bina*, and *Daat*, and seven emotional faculties *Chessed* (kindness), *Gevurah* (severity), *Tiferet* (beauty), *Netzach* (Victory), *Hod* (Splendor), *Yesod* (Foundation), and *Malchut* (Kingship). *Chochmah* is likened to the "spark" of a thought or idea and compared to the male sperm which, if it does not find a nurturing environment, will be for naught. Bina, from the Hebrew word "building," and "to build" is that nurturing environment where thought is given dimensions and an opportunity to grow. It is likened to the womb and the strongly feminine traits of intuition and understanding of unspoken cues in the environment. *Daat*, knowledge, is the total incorporation of an idea into one's knowledge system. Chabad Rebbes explained that emotions are born from the intellect. Thinking about something deeply produces an emotional response to that thing, either good or bad. "The truly joyous situation is when intellect has healthy offspring of balanced emotions."[3] A basic goal for the Chassid is to train the mind to control the emotions—מח שליט על הלב.

Another important concept in *Chassidut* from Lurianic Kabbalah is *tzimtzum* (contraction or concealment). This is the idea that pure Godliness (Ein Sof) is too overpowering to be absorbed by life in this world, and therefore must be "filtered" through the three upper worlds until it can reach ours. This does not change the nature of Godliness, but allows beings in this world to absorb and use it. An analogy to this is the light of the sun which would overwhelm life on Earth if it were not filtered by distance, the atmosphere, even sunglasses, and clothing. The essence of the light of

---

[3] Insights on Chapter 113 in *Tehillim: The Book of Psalms* (Weiss Edition) p. 327. (Brooklyn, NY: Hachai Publishing, 2017), 327.

course, remains the same. In the process of creation of the upper worlds, vessels (*kelim*) from the first universe, *Olam HaTohu* (World of Chaos) could not handle the powerful Godliness and shattered (*shevirat hakelim*). Their shards became sparks of "light" (*netzutzot*) trapped within the next universe, *Olam HaTikun* (World of Order/Rectification). Prayer, meditation on various aspects of the divinity (*hitbonenut*), together with positive, Torah-prescribed actions (*mitzvot*), release sparks of light trapped within the physical participants of the actions (e.g., a coin given to charity), and allows them to reunite with God's essence. The goal of such repair, which can be done only by humans, is to restore all things to the world as it was before the disaster within the Godhead. Many people today are familiar with the parallel concept of *Tikkun Olam*, the effect of mitzvahs and good deeds on the "fixing" of this world and making it a better, more Godly place.[4]

The Baal Shem Tov expanded upon the Ari's teachings, but, like the Ari, did not write down his teachings. After he passed, his disciples continued to study his messages under his successor R 'Dov Ber of Mezeritch (d. 1772), known as the Maggid (Preacher) of Mezeritch. The Maggid attracted a group of talented disciples who later became Chassidic Masters and founded their own courts and sects. These included his inner circle: Rabbis Avraham HaMalach (his son), Nachum of Czernobyl, Elimelech of Lizhensk, Zusha of Hanipol, Levi Yitzchok of Berditchev, Boruch of Medzhybizh, Aharon (HaGadol) of Karlin, Menachem Mendel of Vitebsk, Shmuel Shmelke of Nikolsburg and Shneur Zalman of Liadi, the founder of Chabad-Lubavitch.[5]

Chassidic courts could be grand and opulent, or modest and humble. Chassidim would make pilgrimages to their Rebbes 'courts for holy days and other auspicious times, where they listened to learned talks, joined their Rebbe in the daily prayers, and participated in *farbrengens* (informal talks led by their Rebbe punctuated with singing, dancing and occasional le'chaims). They may enjoy a private audience with their Rebbe (*yechidut*)

---

[4] Sources discussing Kabbalistic concepts for the layperson include: Laibl Wolf, *Practical Kabbalah*, (Brooklyn, NY: Three Rivers Press, 1999); Jacob Immanuel Schochet, *Mystical concepts in Chassidism: An Introduction to Kabbalistic Concepts and Doctrines*, (Brooklyn, NY: Kehot Pubishing, 1979), Robert Kremnizer, *Sparks of Tanya* (2 volumes) (Brooklyn, NY: Kehot Publishing, 2014); Nadav Cohen, *Tanya in a Nutshell*, (Brooklyn, NY: BSD Publishers, 2017); and many of Aryeh Kaplan's work such as: *Innerspace: Introduction to Kabbalah, Meditation and Prophecy* (Jerusalem, Moznaim, 1991); *The Light Beyond: Adventures in Hassidic Thought*, (New York: Moznaim, 1981), *Sefer Yetzirah: The Book of Creation*, (York Beach, Me. : Weiser, 1990).

[5] See: Elie Wiesel, *Souls on Fire: Portraits and Legends of Hasidic Masters*, (New York, Shuster and Shuster, 1972), and Aryeh Kaplan, *Chasidic Masters: History, Biography, Thought*, (New York: Moznaim, Revised edition, 1991), for stories of the lives of early Chasidic Masters.

in which they discussed both personal and spiritual issues. The Chassid would then meticulously follow their Rebbe's advice.

Most courts were destroyed or decimated during the Holocaust. The largest and best known Chassidic communities today are Satmar, centered in New York, and Chabad-Lubavitch, headquartered in Brooklyn but with centers and adherents all over the world. Among other well-known Chassidic groups are Breslev, Tzanz, Belz, Vishnitz, and Ger.

R 'Schneur Zalman (known as Baal HaTanya and the Alter Rebbe) developed the most sophisticated philosophical system in the Chassidic world as expressed in his book *Likkutei Amarim*, more commonly known as the *Tanya* after the first word in the book. Commentaries and elucidations of the Tanya and related teachings by subsequent Chabad Rebbes and teachers ever since comprise the vast sea of Chabad literature. Tanya teaches Kabbalistic principles and how to personally apply them to improve an individual's spiritual state.[6] Improvement of an individual's spiritual state creates a positive impact on the physical and spiritual worlds and hastens the coming of the Messiah. Many see a parallel between this system and the precepts of Freudian psychology, both of which pitch the struggle of the Godly soul (super-ego) over the animalist/instinctual soul (id). But in Chabad, the animal soul is not evil—it drives our instincts to eat, procreate, survive and thrive, all essential components to the maintenance of our physical life which allows us to fulfil our purpose in this world.

However, these actions must be conducted in a Godly manner as directed by the Godly soul. The author was already recognized as an intellectual prodigy early in life. At the age of 25 he was commissioned by the Maggid of Mezeritch to update the Shulchan Aruch (Code of Jewish Laws) by sorting through and amending existing editions, and integrating the Kabbalistic principles that support the rulings. The resulting *Shulchan Aruch HaRav* is consulted and used as a Halachic authority in many communities until today. Thus, the Chabad system is seen as a synthesis of Kabbalah and grounded traditional Judaism. The seven Chabad Rebbes referred to in this chapter are R 'Schneur Zalman (1745–1812); R 'Dovber Schneuri (1773–1827); R 'Menachem Mendel Schneersohn, known as the *Tzemach Tzedek*, (1789–1866); R 'Shmuel Schneersohn (1834–1882); R 'Shalom Dovber Schneersohn (1860–1920); R 'Yosef Yitzchak Schneersohn (1880–1950); and R 'Menachem Mendel Schneerson (1902–1994), son-in-law of R'Yosef Yitzchak, and a great-grandson of his namesake, the third Rebbe of Lubavitch. In this chapter, he is often referred to as simply 'the Rebbe.'

---

[6] Yehiel Harari, *Winning Every Moment: Soul Conversations with the Baal HaTanya*, (Jerusalem: Gefen Publishing House, 2020), presents the psychological concepts in the Tanya as a self-help manual for the 21st century.

The Seder Plate

One of the first differences a guest may notice upon arriving at a Chasid's home for the seder, is the order of the seder plate. In Ashkenazi and non-Chassidic communities, it is common to use a special seder plate upon which the six ceremonial foods are arranged in a circle. In fact, over the centuries we can see examples of elaborate and beautifully decorated seder plates. The three *matsot* are stacked separately with a cloth or other divider between them. Chabad and other Chassidic communities follow the Kabbalistic tradition of the Ari as specified in the *Shulchan Aruch HaRav*. Three whole *matsot* are placed on a large plate or platter. They must be handmade round *matsot* (as detailed below) and stacked one upon the other, completely covered and separated from each other by a cloth or large napkin.

Each *matsa* represents a different tribal affiliation: *Israel, Levi*, and *Kohen*. On top of the stacked *matsot* is a cloth upon which the six ceremonial foods are arranged. Many Chasidim own a special round covering used especially for the seder consisting of an embroidered top cloth with individual cloth compartments for the *matsot*. The six ceremonial foods are placed directly on the cloth, although most people today protect the cloth with a clear plastic cover. The foods are arranged as two inverted triangles, with each food in its specific place:

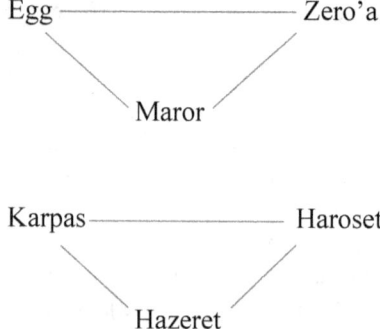

When counting the six ceremonial food items together with the tray and the three *matsot*, we reach a total of ten components. The Ari teaches that each component encompasses one of the ten Kabbalistic attributes of God, the ten Sefirot:

- Three *Matsot*=*Chochmah, Binah* and *Daat* (Wisdom, Understanding, Knowledge), the three attributes of the intellect.

- *Zero'a=Chessed* (Kindness). *Chessed* is thought to come from God's right arm (anthropomorphically speaking); the zero'a is placed in the upper right corner.
- Egg (*Beitzah*)=*Gevurah* (Strength, severity) which is thought to come from God's "left arm."
- *Maror=Tiferet* (Beauty, harmony, mercy)
- *Haroset=Netzach* (Victory, determination)
- *Karpas=Hod* (Glory, humility)
- *Chazeret=Yesod* (Foundation/Attachment)
- The tray=*Malchut* (Kingship)

Two questions arise from this arrangement: Why are the *matsot*, which represent the higher faculties of the intellect, placed under the six other items, which represent the lower, emotional faculties? And why are they not placed on a separate plate as in other traditions? R 'Shalom Dovber Schneerson, explains the Kabbalistic idea that "spiritual illumination reaches this world by intense "lights" being channeled down into "vessels" which help to restrain the "lights" so that they will not be too overwhelming for the creations. In our case, the *matsot* allude to the "vessels" and the various items allude to the "lights." The items are therefore placed upon the *matsot*, alluding to the notion of "lights" being channeled down into the "vessels."[7] Rabbi Menachem Mendel Schneerson adds that "Lights always go down into vessels."[8]

The Centrality of '*Matsa*'

In the Torah, the Pesach holiday is also known as the Holiday of Spring (חג האביב), the Holiday of Liberation (חג החרות) and the Holiday of *Matsot* (חג המצות). Liberation describes what was attained; Spring describes when this occurred and why we always commemorate the holiday when we do. Pesach refers to the Paschal lamb sacrifice, a practice that ceased when the second temple was destroyed nearly two thousand years ago. Details of worship in the Temple are found in the Torah and expanded upon in the Talmud and its commentaries. In post-Biblical times we lack the physical means to perform these rituals, therefore Rabbinic Judaism enabled us to commemorate them through prayer (e.g., the three daily prayers instead of daily sacrifices), study, and remembrance. Eating *matsa* during Passover, however, is a Biblical commandment that has been scrupulously observed by Jews all over

---

[7] From Sefer ha-Sichos 5698, p, 260, as cited in: Chaim Miller, *Haggadah: The Slager Edition*, (Brooklyn, NY: Kol Menachem, 2008), 16.

[8] Miller, 17.

the world throughout our history; it is the food most closely connected to the celebration of Passover.

Specifically, the mitzvah is to eat *matsa* on the first night of Passover in Israel, (or first two nights outside of Israel), during the Seder meal. Three Chassidic customs concerning *matsa* that are not proscribed in other traditions are the eating of *Shmura* (Guarded) *Matsa*; *Matsot Yad* (Handmade *matsot*); and the prohibition of eating "dipped" or "wet" *matsa*, known as *Shruya Matsa* or *Gebrochst*. All three developed out of the call for strict attention to the command not to eat any type of leavening (Chametz) during the Passover holiday.

What is Chametz?
Why is the Chassid so Fearful of It?

For weeks before we sit down to eat the seder meal members of the Chasid's household meticulously wash and scrub the whole house. Every item in the cupboards and closets, every piece of furniture, and the corners of every room are thoroughly cleaned. This can be particularly challenging with busy young children around—we have found Cheerios in a shoe, and half a cookie behind a toilet! After the kitchen is spotlessly clean but before the Pesach cooking preparations begin, the Chassid will cover all the countertops and other areas where food may come in contact with aluminum foil, plastic, or vinyl. Certain types of materials, such as granite countertops and steel sinks, can be koshered with boiling water, but the Chassid will probably cover them afterwards anyway. Special pots, pans, dishes, and utensils that are used only for Passover replace the daily kitchenware. Metal and glass utensils can be 'koshered' for Passover use through boiling or firing with a blow torch only after they have been thoroughly cleaned. Why all the fuss? What drives the need to be so stringent?

The Midrash tells us that chametz is a metaphor for the human being's evil inclination—our tendency towards selfish and spiritually harmful behavior. "Israel desires to fulfill God's will. Who is stopping them? The leavening that is in the dough."[9] The leavening refers to the evil inclination. Rabbi David ben Zimra (1479–1573), a leading rabbi in North Africa, discussed several logical and legal answers to the question of why Jews are so stringent in ridding their households of chametz, but dismissed them all. Finally he concluded that there can only be a mystical interpretation for the prohibition: "…I therefore rely on what our Sages stated in the Midrash, that chametz on Pesach alludes to the evil inclination…we must therefore chase it away entirely from upon us and

---

[9] Talmud, Berachot 17a as cited in: Yosef Marcus, *The Passover Haggadah*, (Brooklyn, NY: Kehot Publication Society, 2011) 16a.

search ourselves in all the pathways and hidden places in our thoughts—even a miniscule amount must be destroyed."[10]

Chassidut teaches that chametz and *matsa* are opposites. *Matsa* is simple, flat, and unpretentious; it correlates to humility and self-restraint. Chametz is inflated and tasty and correlates to the self-importance of the ego and superficial satisfaction of self-indulgence. While we are cleaning and ridding our dwelling of any trace of chametz, we must also conduct a thorough search and cleansing of our soul to rid ourselves of the negative traits of pride and selfishness. The Alter Rebbe states that during Passover:

> "the ego must be completely and unconditionally humbled. This enables us to begin the process of transforming the ego and harnessing its power for holiness…Chametz is therefore permitted after Pesach and becomes a mitzvah during the Temple service of [the holiday of] Shavuot. For our ultimate goal is not merely to subdue our inner "animal" but to gradually transform it so that it too can stand before God, face to face."[11]

The Ari'zal is quoted as saying "The person who is careful to avoid even the tiniest amount of Chametz on Pesach will be spared from [unintentional] sin throughout the entire year."[12] The Chassid is therefore meticulous throughout the holiday preparations and holiday itself.[13]

Shmura Matsa " –Guarded *Matsa*"

"You shall guard the *matsot*" (Exodus 12:17). What does this biblical command mean and how do we fulfill it?

Rabbi Moses ben Maimon, the 13th century sage known as Maimonides or the Rambam, and other sages write that the *matsa* one consumes at the seder must be supervised from the time it was harvested in order to ensure that it did not come in contact with any moisture until it is baked. A responsible Jew must ensure that the grain, usually wheat, but oat, spelt, barley, and rye are also permissible, does not come into any contact with water or moisture throughout its harvest, storage, transport, and milling processes until it is ready to be mixed and immediately baked into *matsa*. If the grain becomes moist at any point, it could cause fermentation and render it unfit for Passover use.

---

[10] Responsa of Radvaz 576 as cited in Marcus, 16a.
[11] Torah Or, Vayakhel 89c, as cited in Marcus, 16a–16b.
[12] Ba'er Heitev 447:1 as cited in Miller, 4.
[13] For more on this idea see e.g.: https://www.Chabad.org/holidays/passover/pesach_cdo/aid/273214/jewish/Chametz-What-Would-Your-Psychologist-Say.htm

Most Jewish communities did not accept the ruling of the Rambam however and considered flour that was supervised from the time of its milling, not harvest, to be 'guarded.' This became the standard practice. According to Rabbi Yaakov ben Moshe Levi Moelin (c. 1365–1427), a leading Talmudist best known for his codification of the customs of the German Jews, only the extremely pious would take care to use flour that had been guarded since the time of its harvest.[14] Writing nearly 350 years later, Rabbi Yehezkel Landau of Prague stated "It is the custom of the Jews in all the Polish lands in general, except for the very scrupulous, not to concern themselves with this [guarding the grain from the harvest]."[15]

The more stringent practice of guarding the grain from the harvest became more common as the Chassidic movement grew. The *Shulchan Aruh HaRav* states that "All of Israel are holy and ensure that all the *matsot* of the entire festival of Pesach have been supervised from the grinding on…but as far as the wheat of *matsa* mitzvah (the *matsa* used at the Seder) is concerned, it is best to be more stringent if possible and to guard it from the time of the harvest."[16] Today's Chasidim will eat only *Shmura matsa* throughout the Passover holiday, not just at the Seder night.

What are the extra precautions used in guarding the wheat from the time of the harvest? Dried sheaves of wheat do not absorb moisture from the ground, and thus they may ferment and become chametz if they come in contact with water or moisture in their environment. Therefore, the wheat must be harvested after the kernels start to harden but before the sheaves have completely dried out. The day of the harvest should be a clear, dry day. The wheat kernels are examined carefully to ensure no grains have split or begun sprouting, and the entire harvest is supervised to make sure it does not become damp while in storage. Because this may be several months, it is kept in a climate-controlled environment until transported to the mill. The mill is also inspected by supervision professionals to ensure that every piece of equipment is absolutely clean and dry.

Precautions are made for the transport of the flour to the bakery to keep it moisture free. The water used in the baking process is also 'guarded' to ensure that it contains no other grains or specks of flour. It is drawn the evening before the baking is done and kept pure until it is ready to be mixed with the flour and baked immediately. The strict supervision continues at the bakery—every piece of equipment and working area is constantly cleaned and dried after every batch to avoid any possibility of leavening. After

---

[14] Minhagei Maharil, "Hilkhos Matzos" as cited in Aaron Wertheim, *Law and Custom in Hasidism*, (Hoboken, NJ: Ktav Publishing House, 1992), 257.

[15] She'elos U-Teshuvos Noda Bi-Yehudah Tanina, 79, as cited in Wertheim, 1992, p. 258.

[16] Shulhan Arukh Ha-Rav, 553:19, as cited in Wertheim, 1992, p. 258.

baking, each *matsa* is inspected before it is boxed to check for any pockets or patches with flour.[17]

Shmura matsa can be made by machine or by hand. Either way, it must be made for the sake of the mitzvah of eating *matsa*—the bakers actually say this before beginning each new batch as a declaration of their intent. Though many people will eat handmade *shmura matsa* at the seder and automated *matsa* the rest of the holiday, most Chasidim endeavor to eat only handmade *shmura matsa* throughout Passover. What makes handmade *matsa* so special?

Matsot Yad – Handmade *Matsot*

The Talmud states that under normal conditions of climate and temperature, flour mixed with water begins to ferment in the time it takes to walk a (Roman) mile, which is estimated at 18-24 minutes (Pesachim 46a). If the temperature of the water is above normal the fermentation is accelerated, but when exposed to air during the process of kneading and manipulating the dough, the fermentation can slow down. Accepted practice today is that the entire production process; mixing the flour and water, kneading, shaping and baking the *matsa*, is completed in 18 minutes. No other ingredients besides water and flour are permitted for Passover *matsa*.

In the mid-1800s, machines were developed that automated the *matsa* baking process. This generated a major halakhic controversy: Could pieces of dough get caught in the machinery and re-attach themselves to other dough after the permitted 18 minutes? Could heat produced by the operation of the machine speed up the fermentation process? Did the milling by the machine cause the wheat to exude moisture and impact fermentation? There was also the social concern that automating the process would deprive many poor people of the income they would have normally earned through employment in the bakeries. Today, the automated process for baking *matsa* has been improved to alleviate the concerns raised above, and there are many stringent Jews who insist on using machine-made *matsa*. However, most Chassids, including Chabad, continue to use only hand-made *matsa* throughout the holiday. They contend that baking *matsa* requires the continual and conscious intent that it is being done for the purpose of the mitzvah, something beyond the capability of a machine.

Handmade *matsot* are always round. The Torah itself describes the *matsa* the Israelites ate as `*ugot* (עוגות), interpreted as round cakes from the word circle (מעגל). There are many references in both the Torah and Talmud supporting this idea that the *matsot* were round. One mystical reason for

---

[17] For a more detailed explanation of the process of *shmura matsa* preparation and baking, see: theyeshivaworld.com/news/headlines-breaking-stories/1501154/what-the-shmurah-matsa-bakeries-dont-tell-you.html

round *matsot* is that a circle has no beginning or end, symbolizing the oneness and infinite nature of God.[18]

A custom from the Middle Ages is to bake *matsa* in the afternoon before the holiday begins, the time when the Pesach offering was brought to the temple.[19] Chassidim reintroduced this practice and took upon themselves the task of baking their own *matsa* to be used for seder. In today's world this is not practical for most people, although some still follow this custom and there are several videos on YouTube demonstrating how to make *matsa* at home (though, not necessarily kosher for Passover).[20]

Matsa is the only sacred food in Judaism. Using the simple *matsa* made in the same shape and manner that our ancestors used throughout the generations lends an aura of historical authenticity to the whole holiday.

Matsa Shruya – Gebrochts

A visitor to a Chassid's home during Pesach may be disappointed to find that some well-known Passover delicacies enjoyed by most European Jews are missing: kneidlach (a form of dumpling), *matsa* balls, *matsa-brei* (*matsa* fried with eggs), and other holiday treats made from *matsa* or *matsa* flour. The standard Shuchan Aruch clearly states that once *matsa* is baked, it can no longer become chametz and is therefore permitted in any dish. However, R 'Shneur Zalman writes that in his time, one could see flour on the *matsa* even after the baking. This was around the end of the 18th century when it became the accepted custom to bake *matsot* at the 18-minute mark rather than up to 24 minutes, in order to be absolutely sure that the dough had no chance to rise before being baked.

The unfortunate consequence was that the *matsa* was not always as well kneaded as before, and it was possible that it contained pockets of flour. Some opinions state that flour which was baked without being kneaded first can still become chametz, therefore, the Alter Rebbe continues, one should not dip the *matsa* in soup. He writes that even though there is technically no concern because the Halachah follows the Rambam and Rashi who permit one to cook flour which was baked, one should still be careful to follow the words of the Arizal and "follow all stringencies on Pesach."[21]

Those who are careful to avoid *gebrochts* therefore do not cook with *matsa* at all. Additionally, when *matsa* is on the table, they are very careful to keep it covered and away from any food that may have water in it. Drinks, soups, and vegetables that have been washed and not thoroughly

---

[18] Yehuda Yaaleh, Orah Hayyim 157, as cited in Marcus, 76b.

[19] Tur and Orah Hayyim 458 as cited in Wertheim, 259.

[20] See e.g. https://www.youtube.com/watch?v=gkDlWCJqIaU; and https://www.youtube.com/watch?v=A3lkauu3f-k

[21] Responsa of Rabbi Schneur Zalman of Liadi, no. 6.

dried are all kept far away from the *matsa*. Many will keep their *matsot* in plastic bags and break off bite-sized pieces or eat the *matsa* while still in the bag in order to prevent crumbs from inadvertently landing on other foods or drink. A situation in which this stringency presents a challenge is during the Korech (sandwich) step of the Seder. This step requires that we take maror, which in Chabad is lettuce and horseradish, and put it between two pieces of *matsa*. Because the lettuce will actually be touching the *matsa*, it must be absolutely dry. Many families spend much time carefully washing the lettuce and then very meticulously drying it in preparation for the Seder.

Each Chassidic family tries to continue the traditions they learned from their parents or take on new stringencies and customs as they feel ready. Because these are traditions, not laws, one can find variations of practice from family to family. Many households make it a priority to use as few processed foods as possible, making their own condiments and delicacies from natural ingredients. Potatoes and potato starch, eggs, peeled fruits and vegetables, true nuts (not peanuts or legumes), chicken, meat, fish, sugar, salt and kosher for Passover oils (e.g., cottonseed, grapeseed, olive, walnut, safflower oil) are the basics for most holiday cooking. This commitment to a total change in the way food is prepared and eaten for the entire week serves as a constant reminder of the holiday in conscious thought and action. It exemplifies the Chassidic/Kabbalistic idea of permeating the physical, mundane world around us with holiness through thought and deed.

In the Land of Israel Jews complete the holiday of Passover after the seventh day. For diaspora Jews however, Rabbinic ordinance added an eighth day (as with the celebration of Sukkot in the autumn). Because this extra day is not directed from the Torah but of Rabbinic origin, the stringency of refraining from Gebrochts is not upheld. In fact, many Chassidim make a point to eat kneidlach and dip their *matsa* into soup and other foods. R'Menachem Mendel Schneerson, the last Lubavitcher Rebbe, presented spiritual reasons for this. Passover celebrates the Exodus, a time when we were (and are) spiritually immature. At this time, we need to be constantly on guard for the slightest bit of chametz (i.e., pride and ego), lest we be adversely affected. On the final days of Pesach, we read about and celebrate our escape from Egypt through the Red Sea into freedom.[22]

Fifty days after Passover, and after the seven weeks of character refinement we undergo with the Omer counting, we have spiritually matured and are fully immunized against the harmful side effects of chametz. We are then ready as a nation to receive the Torah. Thus, on the holiday of Shavuot,

---

[22] The last day of Passover is connected with the future redemption a time when no evil will befall us. We reflect this reality by going out of our way to eat gebrochts on this day, without fear that the *matsa* may become chametz. From a talk by Lubavitcher Rebbe, Acharon Shel Pesach 5744.

one of the communal offerings brought in the Temple was specifically made of chametz. On the last day of Passover, we have already completed the first of the seven weeks of the counting of the Omer. We are not quite ready for chametz, but we are a bit more secure. For this reason, we eat our *matsa* with liquid, without fear.[23]

Selected Chassidic Insights of *Matsa*

"*Matsa shmurah* is called by two intrinsic and inherent names: Food of Faith and Food of Healing. It strengthens the faculty of *Daat* (internalization)"—The Baal Shem Tov.[24]

"Matsa strengthens the health of the body by helping it perceive the purpose of the soul's descent into the body. Matsa is therefore also the Food of Faith, meaning that it causes the unshakable faith [of the soul] to permeate every aspect of our lives"—R 'Yosef Yitzhak of Lubavitch.[25]

R 'Schneur Zalman teaches that "The Matsa of the first night of Pesach is the "Food of Faith;" the *matsa* of the second night is the "Food of Healing." R 'Dovber adds: "When healing comes before faith, it means that you were sick, God cured you, and you thanked him. But when faith comes before healing, it means that, because of your faith, you were never sick to start with."[26]

"Faith and healing are interdependent: Simple faith is the elixir for every type of ill"—R 'Yosef Yitzhak of Lubavitch.[27]

Pesach is distinguished from all other holidays, since on Pesach we receive our physical sustenance through a Godly food. Our lives are uplifted to the loftiest heights during Pesach, and especially on the night of the Seder"—R 'Shmuel of Lubavitch.[28]

"Human beings are conditioned by their deeds. What we *do* affects how we *feel*. Hence the power of the rituals of the Seder. Eating *matsa* and doing the other rituals to remember the Exodus reinforces our belief in God as the Creator, His sovereignty over nature and His ability to suspend nature at any time, as He did in Egypt."

The above explanation describes the perspective of the "body" of Torah, its external dimension. But from the perspective of the *inner* dimension of Torah, the "soul" of Torah, *matsa* is more than a symbolic

---

[23] Talk by the Lubavitcher Rebbe, Acharon Shel Pesach 5727. For a lengthier treatment of the spiritual implications of gebrochts on the last day of Passover, see https://www.Chabad.org/holidays/passover/pesach_cdo/aid/2854/jewish/A-Speck-of-Flour.htm

[24] As retold by Marcus, 75a.
[25] Marcus, 75a.
[26] Cited by Miller, 160.
[27] Marcus, 75a.
[28] Marcus, *The Passover Haggadah*, 75a.

reminder of the Exodus—its very ingestion contains a mystical power to strengthen our faith."—The Tzemach Tzedek.[29]

Chassidic masters attached symbolic meanings to the Pesach, *matsa* and *maror* in order to help us reach deeper depths of contemplation on the concepts. *Matsa* is unleavened bread; bread represents essential nourishment without which we cannot survive "—Bread sustains a man's life," (Psalms 104:15). *Maror* is compared to toxic substances which we must avoid, and Pesach represents supplemental nutrition and the positive enjoyments of life. R 'Menachem Mendel Schneerson, asks us to think of educating a child as spiritual feeding, and sees the three types of food as representing three aspects of this task. As *matsa* (bread) is essential to sustain life, according to the Rebbe: "Our foremost obligation is providing spiritual nourishment for our children. We do so by teaching them Torah, which is compared to bread, as in the verse (Proverbs 9:5) 'Come eat bread from My bread.' The twice-mentioned bread alludes to: 1) the Written Torah and 2) the Oral Torah, as well as: 1) the legal aspects of Torah and 2) its mystical dimension. This bread should be *"matsa,"* humble bread—Torah study should be infused with humility."[30]

The Rebbe discusses the classic question of why the Haggadah states that the *matsa* was eaten due to circumstantial reasons (they were rushed to leave Egypt) when they had already been commanded to eat *matsa* before the Exodus (Shemot 12:8). The Haggadah seems to suggest that this is the only reason we eat *matsa*. Many earlier commentators asked that, if there are many reasons for why we eat *matsa*, not just one, why mention only this particular reason?[31] After discussing six different themes represented by the *matsa* we eat today, the Rebbe observes that the reason stated in the Haggadah is specifically to enhance the story. "We need to bear in mind that the current passage is part of the Haggadah's extended narration of the Exodus story. We do not mention *matsa* here because it is a mitzvah, a practice prescribed by Jewish law today, but because by relating this reason, we enhance the miraculous chronicle of the Exodus.

A second crucial point is that the mitzvah of chronicling the Exodus is to relate the story *as it happened then*, regardless of any additional layers of significance that may have been added to it subsequently. We are not here to describe the influence of the Exodus on post-Sinaitic mitzvahs, or to suggest that our celebrations today are spiritually superior to those experienced by the Jews in Egypt. Our purpose in reciting the Haggadah tonight is to get back to "grass roots" and explain how the Jewish nation was

---

[29] Marcus, *The Passover Haggadah*, 75a.
[30] Marcus, 65a–b.
[31] E.g. Abudraham (d.1300), Abarbanel (1437–1508), R' Schneur Zalman, the Tzemah Tzedek.

born; i.e., to recount and relive the events of the fifteenth of Nissan 1312 BCE.

In the final analysis, it turns out that the only explanation for why the Haggadah presents only one reason is because it is enhances the Exodus chronicle—it relates specifically to the circumstances surrounding the original Exodus: *the dough of our fathers did not have time to become leavened before the King of kings, the Holy One, blessed be He, revealed Himself to them and redeemed them.*"[32]

Women in the Passover Holiday – Chassidic Perspectives

What are Chassidic women's roles and responsibilities during the Seder and Passover holiday? Are they any different from the men's?

The distribution of Passover preparation chores in each household, including the cooking and cleaning, reflect the roles and duties already established during the rest of the year. Many Chassidic women have jobs and professions outside the home and their husbands naturally pitch in where their abilities are most suited. Everyone helps out as it is an opportunity to introduce even young children to the importance of contributing to the home.

What about the seder? According to Chana Weisberg at Chabad.org: "The role of women at the seder is the same as the role of men—to recount, discuss and delve into the miracle of the Exodus and how it relates to us today. They should definitely read from the Haggadah and they can take the leading role in the seder, in explaining the Haggadah and discussing commentary on it. Halachically, too, there is no distinction between men and women with regards to the night's obligations. The mitzvah of reclining is an exception to this rule—women of Ashkenazi heritage traditionally do not recline. (Though technically women are required to recline, as they are equally obligated in all the night's mitzvot, Ashkenazi women rely on the opinion that reclining is no longer mandatory, for today even nobility eat while sitting upright)." Women have the additional mitzvah of heralding in the holiday by lighting the Passover candles.[33]

According to our sages, women are generally exempt from time-related *active* (doing) obligations such as tefillin, but not exempt from

---

[32] Based on Likutei Sichos, vol 17, p. 79, note 20, as cited in Miller, 137–139.

[33] https://www.Chabad.org/holidays/passover/pesach_cdo/aid/494853/jewish/What-is-the-womans-role-at-a-Seder.htm . Weisberg is the author of several books on women's roles in Judaism and *Chassidut* including: *Tending the Garden: The Unique Gifts of the Jewish Woman* (2007); *Crown of Creation: The Lives of Great Biblical Women based on Rabbinic & Mystical Sources* (2010); and *The Feminine Soul* (2001).

prohibitions. Therefore, the prohibition of chametz is equally applicable to men and women. What about the active obligation of drinking the four cups of wine? The Talmud states that women are obligated to drink the four cups because "they also were a part of the miracle" of the Exodus (Pesachim 108a–b). This same expression is used by the Talmud to explain why women are obligated to observe the mitzvahs of Purim and Hanukah. The Rashbam (R. Shmuel ben Meir, 1085–1158) explains that this phrase means that women played a *primary* role in the miracle. The miracles of Purim and Hanukah came about through women (Esther and Yehudit). The miracle of Pesach is attributed to all the Jewish women "it was in the merit of the righteous women of that generation that our ancestors were redeemed from Egypt" (Sotah 11b).[34]

R 'Levi Itzhak Schneerson (1878–1944), a renown Kabbalist and father of the late Lubavitcher Rebbe, suggests that the special role of women in the Passover story refers to Miriam and Yocheved, traditionally known as Shifra and Puah, the midwives who risked their lives by refusing to kill the male Hebrew newborns in defiance of Pharaoh's decree. He states that from a Kabbalistic perspective "the four cups relate *primarily* to women." This correlates to the teaching that the four cups correspond to our four matriarchs Sarah, Rivkah, Rachel, and Leah.[35]

The Haggadah states the Jews were few in number upon their arrival in Egypt. The book of Exodus says that seventy souls of Jacob's family entered Egypt at the beginning of their sojourn, but only explicitly mentions sixty-nine. Some sages opine that the seventieth soul was God or Jacob. But the Talmud (Bava Basra 123b) states that the seventieth soul was Yocheved, the mother of Moshe, and that she was not listed because she was born just as they entered Egypt. The Lubavitcher Rebbe observes that the identity of the seventieth soul reflects a certain perception of this crucial moment when Jacob's family "went down to Egypt," where they would subsequently be enslaved, redeemed and given the Torah. Apparently, the addition of this seventieth soul was crucial to the ultimate success of the redemption process. It is easy to understand why this special soul might be Jacob or God Himself. But what was the specialness of Yocheved, a Jewish woman, beyond being the mother of Moshe?

The Rebbe answers: "Judaism is, essentially, a "feminine" religion. As a religious and ethical system, it seeks to change the world into a better place, but its approach to achieving this goal is a uniquely feminine one.

---

[34] As cited in Marcus, 9. The Rebbe also stresses that the final redemption to come is also dependent upon the women. See e.g.: https://www.Chabad.org/therebbe/livingtorah/player_cdo/aid/3212658/jewish/In-the-Merit-of-Righteous-Women.htm

[35] Likkutei Levi Itzhak, Igrot, p. 273; Maharal; Shaloh, as cited in Marcus, 10.

"A man's nature," says the Talmud, "is to conquer, but it is not a woman's nature to conquer" (Yevamot 65b). Conquering means to subdue, to overcome and to possess by force. A man wishes to acquire, to expand his empire, and he does so by utilizing whatever power he has at his disposal.

But a woman desires not to conquer, but to nurture. She takes a fertilized egg and, for nine months, patiently provides all the support required for it to develop. When the child is born, the same task continues. In the home, the woman excels in bringing beauty and serenity to her environment. Everything she touches is enhanced…and the overall mood in the home is largely to her credit.

In other words, a woman transforms her world from within, by nurturing it, bringing its latent qualities to the surface, and helping it to grow at its own pace. Judaism's mission is monotheism, to demonstrate how the diverse aspects of this world are expressions of one God. This could be done in two ways. A masculine approach would be to "impose" God on the world, to show how everything is insignificant compared to its creator, and to coerce people to be righteous.

But if God is truly One then we can do more than that: we can reveal how even the tiniest detail of this world is significant because it contains a spark of the Divine, and its inner identity is nothing other than an expression of God. We can embrace people as they are, encouraging them to come to an awareness of the truth by themselves and support their efforts to become better people.

So true monotheism is feminine. It seeks to nurture the inner sanctity of every being on this planet, not by degrading it, conquering it or replacing it with something else, but by bringing its true Godly identity to the surface.

And that is why, at this moment in history [the sojourn down to Egypt] when the monotheistic mission began to unfold, the seventy souls of Jacob's family were "completed" by Yocheved, a woman. Because the ultimate goal of monotheism—to teach all seventy nations about God (Rashi)—lies in the feminine approach."[36]

Miriam, the sister of Moshe, is attributed with many leadership roles that led to the redemption. Beyond her actions as a mid-wife with her mother described above and the well-known story of her saving her brother in the bulrushes, the Midrash describes how her words ultimately encouraged the people to rebel against Pharaoh's cruel decree against the new-born males. Her father, Amram, the leader of the Jewish people at that time, was disheartened by the decree and ceased relations with his wife so as not to bring any babies into the world, and the other Israelites followed his example. Miriam chastised him saying "You are worse than Pharaoh! For he

---

[36] Based on Likutei Sichos vol. 20, p. 218ff, as cited by Miller, 84–85.

only decreed against the males, but you have decreed against males and [the potential birth of] females. Pharaoh deprives them of this world, but you deprive them of both this world and the world to come..." Aram listened to her and the rest of Israel followed suit (Sotah 12 a).

Miriam's leadership of the Israelite women after the miraculous passing through the Red Sea is also well known. Upon safe shores, the Jewish people began to sing *Shirat Hayam*, a song expressing their ecstatic gratitude and thanksgiving to God. After Moshe and the men sang their song, Miriam and the women began theirs. "The righteous women of that generation were confident that the Holy One, Blessed be He, would perform miracles for them, so they prepared tambourines and dances." The men sang with their voices, but the women's song was composed with voice, tambourines, and dance. The women's hearts were full of a greater joy, and their song was more comprehensive, equipped with tambourines and dances of joy and faith. As bitter as their lives had become in Egypt, the women's faith in their redemption grew stronger. The women embraced Miriam's spirit of rebellion: a feminine strength borne from bitterness; a faith sewn amidst despair.[37]

Seudat Mashiach – The Messiah Meal

In the Seder at the beginning of the Passover holiday we recount the story of the Israelites' triumphant deliverance from the suffering of slavery in Egypt. The stories in the Haggadah, the Seder rituals, and the holiday Torah readings in the synagogue all focus on the events and commemorations of history; of the beginnings of the Jewish nation. The final days of Passover focus on the future, a future marked by a complete transformation of both society and nature. The Haftorah (the reading in the synagogue after the Torah reading) the on the seventh day is from the book of Samuel 2:22, King David's song of gratitude to God. It ends with an eye to the future as he expresses his assurance that God will do kindness to "David and his seed, forevermore." This is a reference to *Mashiach*, the king descending from David who will lead the Jews and the entire world into their final redemption. In the Diaspora, the Haftorah on the eighth day is from Isaiah 10:32–12:6, which describes a time when "The wolf will live with the sheep and the leopard will lie down with the kid; and a calf, a lion welp and a fatling [will walk] together, and a young child will lead them." In Chassidic tradition, this is the ultimate future of messianic times.

The Baal Shem Tov initiated a tradition for the final day known as the *Seudat Mashiach*—the Messiah Meal, which is intended to deepen our

---

[37] Chana Weisberg, https://www.Chabad.org/multimedia/video_cdo/aid/1555461/jewish/Miriam-Mother-of-Rebellion-Part-4.htm

awareness of the *Mashiach* and enable us to integrate it into our consciousness. Partaking in this special meal reinforces our belief in this principle, translating our awareness of *Mashiach* into a meal, a physical experience which leads us to associate this concept with our own flesh and blood. The meal is held after Minchah (afternoon services) of the final day, and has been adopted by all Chasidim everywhere, as well as in many non-Chassidic communities.

During the time of the Baal Shem Tov, the main ingredient of *Mashiach's Seudah* was *matsa*. The tasteless flatness of *matsa* symbolizes selfless humility, a desire to transcend oneself. In 1906 Rabbi Shalom Dov Ber incorporated four cups of wine with the *matsa* into *Mashiach's* Meal, mirroring the Seder held the week before. Wine, in contrast to the *matsa*, is flavorful and pleasurable, and thus symbolizes the assertiveness of our individual personalities. Combining *matsa* and wine in *Mashiach's Seudah* teaches us that self-transcendence does not require that we erase our personal identities. Self-transcendence may be accomplished within each individual's nature. A person can retain his or her distinctive character and identity, yet dedicate their life to spreading Godliness instead of pursuing personal fulfillment. Once they have fundamentally transformed their will, an individual can proceed to a more complete level of service of God in which their essential commitment permeates every aspect of their personality.

According to Chabad philosophy the four cups of wine also allude to the Messianic Age, for which the dissemination of *Chassidut*—especially Chabad *Chassidut*—is the preparation. The four cups symbolize:

- the four expressions of redemption.
- the four cups of retribution God will force the nations of the world to drink.
- the four cups of comfort God will bestow upon the Jews.
- the four letters of God's Name which will be revealed.
- the four general levels of repentance.[38]

It is a communal meal, meant to be a shared experience among family, friends, and congregants that can be held in the home or synagogue, and everyone participates. Wonderful stories and Torah thoughts relating to the *Mashiach* are told, punctuated with joyous songs and dancing. The actual program is flexible, and customarily extends past nightfall, ushering out Passover amid song, words of Torah and inspiration.

---

[38] R' Menachem Mendel Schneerson, *Sichah, Acharon Shel Pesach*, 5742, https://www.Chabad.org/therebbe/article_cdo/aid/2301436/jewish/Mashiachs-Seudah.htm

Parallels with Mimouna

Jews from North Africa have a similar celebration, called Mimouna, which begins as soon as the final day of Passover closes. The origins of Mimouna are uncertain. The earliest record of it is from eighteenth century Morocco, (when Chassidism was developing in Europe) but the tradition is thought to go back further. The etymological origin of the name is also unclear: some say it its roots are in the Arabic word *maymuna*, or Hebrew word *mamon*, both connected to wealth and good fortune. It may originally have marked the birth or death anniversary of R 'Maimon, the father of Maimonides; or it could come from the word *emuna*, Hebrew for faith or belief. Still there are some who contend that the holiday has Kabbalistic origins and that the word Mimouna comes from the Hebrew number *shmona* (eight) "which represents the messianic redemption, in contrast to the Passover story, which represents physical redemption."[39]

After night falls and Passover is officially over, special foods are served including *mufleta* (crepes covered in butter and honey), honey and butter wafers, and *zaben* (white almond yougat). The tables may be decorated with plates of flour decorated with seven green bean pods or with seven gold coins, milk jugs surrounded by lettuce and vegetables, sheaves of grain, or trays of fruit, apples, almonds and nuts.[40] Friends and neighbors are invited to drop-in, creating an open-house atmosphere, or families and neighbors will hold communal festivities.

Though European Chassidim may join in their neighbors' Mimouna celebrations, they have not adopted the tradition themselves. But with both Mimouna and *Seudat Mashiach* sharing mystical auras and looking forward to the ultimate redemption of the Messiah, the similarities are striking.

Conclusion

In the evening after the final day of Passover, the Chassidic household transfers their leftover foods to everyday containers. Their special dishes, silverware, and kitchenware are carefully washed, dried, and stored away in cupboards, not to be disturbed for another year. Aluminum foil or other coverings on countertops and refrigerator shelves are removed, revealing the ordinary surfaces once again. The community leader who "sold" the community's chametz to a non-Jew before the holiday began "buys" it back

---

[39] Sasha Goldstein-Sabbah "Mimouna" in *Encyclopedia of Jews in the Islamic World*, vol. 3, (Norman A. Stillman, ed). (Leiden, Brill: 2010), 428.

[40] For more information see: http://archive.jewishagency.org/mimouna/content/37171

as soon as Passover ends.[41] A mixed sense of sadness for the ending of a beautiful holiday, and relief and gratitude for the return to normalcy descends upon the household.

Acknowledgements:

The author would like to thank Rabbi Sharon and Mrs. Michal Weiss, directors of Living Chassidus, for taking the time to review and add their valuable suggestions to this manuscript.

---

[41] chabad.org/holidays/passover/pesach_cdo/aid/3640536/jewish/FAQ-About-the-Sale-of-Chametz.htm.

Why is this Haggadah different? Haggadot in the Non-orthodox Movements

Annette Boeckler

The text of the Haggadah evolved over centuries, but since the 19th century there has been a creativity in adapting Haggadot to modernity, so that today there is a variety of versions in use. They differ in that sections are missing or in their wordings and even slightly in the procedures of the ritual they describe. Even within progressive Judaism there is a large variety of versions. How and why did this come into being? And why is it important to have different versions anyway? This essay will show the roots of the development since the 19th century, demonstrate the main questions at stake and compare the Haggadot of the non-orthodox movements in regard of their attitudes and theologies.

With its request: "In each and every generation people must regard themselves as though they personally left Egypt" the Haggadah itself invites to update its message in every new age. A new sera indeed began for Jews in Europe after Napoleon had convened the so-called "Paris Sanhedrin" in 1806/1807. In its wake Judaism experienced profound changes. Jews gradually gained legal equality as citizens of their countries. With it came the free right of settlement which meant the end of the medieval ghettos, the entry into the culture of the homeland but also the end of rabbinical power over social matters. Jewish life in the 19th century got a very different character compared to previous generations. Not only daily Jewish life changed, but also philosophical views and a new approach to the meaning of Jewish prayer developed. The *Pesach* Haggadah is about all of the just mentioned: It is Jewish law and customs, but it is also prayer and most of all it is an expression of Jewish identity. So, what was the emancipation effect on the Haggadah?

Ideological Background of the Progressive Haggadah

The Progressive Haggadah is based on the principles of Progressive[1] Jewish liturgy. The oldest Progressive Siddur is the German Hamburg Temple Prayer Book, whose first edition appeared in 1818. But it was the second edition from 1841 that sparked nationwide passionate debates about Jewish prayer in these new times. The meaning of Jewish prayer shifted from mainly being the fulfilment of a Mitzvah to becoming a kind of confession and an edifying experience. Prayer now had to express the thinking and the feelings of the worshipper. Both mind and feelings had to be addressed in a manner compatible with European culture and modern views of life. Therefore, traditionally received texts were to be kept only if they would not contradict modern enlightened thinking. Customs had to be preserved only if they would not attack modern feelings. Prayers and rituals had to be honest and real, had to lift the feelings of the worshipper and needed to be meaningful in the moment of reciting the prayer.

To achieve this, the language of the service shifted from Hebrew to the vernacular as this helped to convey the meaning of texts. The service was abridged as this helped to better focus on the meaning. Repetitions were eliminated as were passages no longer relevant or contradicting modern thinking. At the same time the content was updated by adding modern texts and by adapting the traditional text to modern viewpoints. New styles of performing liturgy were tried out, like instrumental accompaniment and choral and communal singing with tunes of the time. Through the international contacts of Jewish merchants but especially through people emigrating from Germany after the failed democratization and anti-Jewish riots in 1848–1849, the new ideas quickly spread into other countries, too. The development of the progressive Haggadah mirrors this changing Jewish identity.

---

[1] I will use the term "progressive" as the general term for non-orthodox Judaism to avoid using the negative term non-orthodox, as these congregations and movements usually do not define themselves negatively according to what they are *not*. The term "progressive" came into being in 1926 when liberal, progressive, reform and German conservative congregations were looking for an umbrella term for their newly founded World Union. It refers to the common understanding of all these groups, that God's revelation was not given in one moment at Sinai but is a progressive revelation in the course of human tradition. Today also the later founded reconstructionist movement is part of progressive Judaism. When I speak, however, about a specific movement, I will use the more specific terms "Reform," "Conservative," "Liberal," and "Reconstructionist."

The Prototypes

The very first progressive Haggadah was published in 1841[2]—the same year as the 2nd edition of the above-mentioned Hamburg temple prayer book—by German poet and rabbi Dr. Leopold Stein (1810–1882). At the time of the publication Stein was the rabbi of two small Bavarian towns: Burgkunstadt and Altenkunstadt.[3] Burgkunstadt, the place mentioned in the preface of the Haggadah, was at the time a tiny town of some 1400 inhabitants,[4] a third of them being Jewish.[5] This is the place where the history of the progressive Haggadah begins. Its author had already created several poetic German adaptations of Hebrew liturgical poems.[6] In 1840 he published a collection of German prayers and songs for the High Holidays, because he thought: "It is certain that, sooner or later, the synagogue will have to open its halls to German prayer if the divine service therein is to become inspiring, attractive

---

[2] Leopold Stein, *Hagada, oder Erzählung vom Auszuge aus Aegypten.* Deutsch bearbeitet und mit neuen Liedern vermehrt (Frankfurt/Main: J.S. Adler, 1841). Later it was reprinted in: Leopold Stein, Seder Hagada. Vortrag für den Pesach-Vorabend [Familienfeier]," in: *Seder Ha'avodah. Gebetuch für Israelitische Gemeinden*, Erster Band. Mannheim: J. Schneider, 1882, p. 161–198. (2nd ed. Augsburg 1917).

[3] He officiated there from 1835–1843. In 1843 he changed to Frankfurt/Main, where he took a leading role in shaping progressive Judaism. He chaired the second modern Rabbinical Conference in 1845. At the end of his life he founded a school for girls and served as preacher in Frankfurt's Westend-Union. His poetic German singable adaptions of Jewish songs became models for American-English versions, as the Chanukkah Song "Rock of Ages" and as we will later see, his Haggadah was the model for the US Haggadot. On Leopold Stein see Friedland, Eric L.: "Leopold Stein: A Liberal Master of Prayer," in David J. Goldberg and Edward Kessler, ed., *Aspects of Liberal Judaism: Essays in Honour of John D. Rayner* (London: Vallentine Mitchell, 2004), 49–72. Carsten Wilke, ed.: *Biographisches Handbuch der Rabbiner* Vol I.2 Die Rabbiner der Emanzipationszeit in den deutschen, böhmischen und grosspolnischen Ländern 1781–1871 (Berlin: de Gruyter 2004), 834–836; *Biographisches Portal der Rabbiner*: http://www.steinheim-institut.de:50580/cgi-bin/bhr?id=1711 (accessed Aug 2020).

[4] According to the list of the population development https://de.wikipedia.org/wiki/Burgkunstadt# Einwohnerentwicklung (accessed Sep 2020). Altenkunstadt today has a Jewish Museum in the building of the former synagogue, see http://www.alemannia-judaica.de/altenkunstadt_synagoge.htm.

[5] On the Jewish history of Burgkunstadt see: *Aus der Geschichte der jüdischen Gemeinden im deutschen Sprachraum. Burgkunstadt*: https://www.xn--jdische-gemeinden-22b.de/index.php/gemeinden/a-b/515-burgkunstadt-oberfranken-bayern (accessed Sep. 2020).

[6] Leopold Stein, *Stufengesänge. Sammlung religiöser Lieder* (Würzburg: Leopold Stein, 1834); Ibid., *Königskrone von Salomo ben Gabirol, metrische deutsche Übersetzung* (Frankfurt/Main: Siegmund Schmerber, 1838); Ibid., ed., *Chissuk Habbayith. Gebete und Gesänge zum Gebrauche bei der öffentlichen Andacht der Israeliten oder Bausteine zur Auferbauung eines veredelten Synagogengottesdienstes.* Erste Lieferung: Neujahr und Versöhnungstag (Erlangen: Ferdinand Enke, 1840).

and blissful for the long term."[7] The modern, on rationality focussed services are lacking what the ancient Piyyutim added to the service: feeling and edification. Leopold Stein wanted to close this gap. He regarded his work as a first attempt, and if it succeeded, then he would also contribute a Haggadah.[8] He implemented this plan a year later. In the preface to his Haggadah he explains that he was encouraged by the series editor to go ahead with his announcement of a Haggadah.[9]

And so the first Haggadah in Progressive Judaism came into being. The 110 pages of the book are divided into two parts. If opened from right to left—like a Hebrew book—one finds 74 pages with the traditional Hebrew text of the Haggadah together with a German literal translation by Leopold Stein. But if opened from left to right—like a German (or English) book—one finds 36 pages with German text only. These are the pages of the first progressive Haggadah. They are intended as an accompaniment to the traditional Haggadah. Some traditional parts are not printed in the progressive part but are—as already the first lines shows—referred to: "After the kiddush prayer and the usual ceremonies have been performed, the host lifts the cloth that covers the Easter bread, so that they become visible, and pointing towards them, he solemnly says ..."[10] Now follows a German poetic adaptation of *Ha lachma*.

The following *maggid* section is a new German creation but based on the order of the passages of the traditional Haggadah. Footnotes refer to the specific traditional section that was redesigned in this specific German passage. Instead of *Vehi she'amda* Stein offers a song "Drum hebt die Becher feierlich"[11] (Engl.: The Festive Cup[12]). Only for the first Hallel-

---

[7] "Es ist gewiss, dass, früher oder später, die Synagoge dem deutschen Gebete ihre Hallen wird öffnen müssen, wenn der göttliche Dienst darinnen für die Dauer eindringlich, anziehend und beseligend werden soll." Stein, *Gebete und Gesänge*, 5.

[8] Stein, *Gebete und Gesänge*, VII. "Sollte mir diese Versuchsarbeit Beifall und Aufmunterung erwerben, so hoffe ich, unter dem Beistande Gottes in späteren Heften die übrigen Fest- und Feiertage auf gleiche Weise zu behandeln, damit das Werk ein Ganzes bilde. In einem Hefte für die שלש רגלים bin ich gesonnen, ein (sic!) neue Hagada-Ordnung zur häuslichen Erbauung für die Pesachabende beizulegen." [If this experimental work earns me applause and encouragement, I hope, with God's help, to treat the other festivals and holidays in the same way in later issues so that the work forms a whole. In a booklet for the *shalosh r'galim* I am inclined to enclose a new Haggadah order for domestic edification for the Pesach evenings.]

[9] Leopold Stein, *Hagada, oder Erzählung vom Auszuge aus Aegypten*. Deutsch bearbeitet und mit neuen Liedern vermehrt (Frankfurt/Main: J.S. Adler, 1841), 3.

[10] «Nachdem das Kiddusch-Gebet und die üblichen Zeremonien verrichtet sind, schlägt der Hausherr das Tuch um, welches über den Osterbroten gebreitet ist, so dass diese sichtbar werden, und darauf hindeutend, spricht er feierlich ...» Stein, *Hagada*, 5.

[11] Sein, *Hagada*, 7.

Psalms, the *B'rachot*, and the 2nd cup the text refers back to the traditional Haggadah to perform these ritual as usual.[13] The meal is concluded by a new German song[14] followed by the traditional *Birkat haMazon* and all traditional parts until *Yishtabach*.[15] Then the celebrant again turns to the progressive Haggadah for German versions of *Vay'hi b'chatzi halayla*[16] (Engl.: And it came to pass at midnight[17]), *Lekha Adonai Hamamlacha*[18] (engl.: Our Souls We Raise In Fervent Praise[19]) and *Adir hu*[20] (Engl.: God of Might[21]). The Haggadah concludes with the raising the fourth cup and a final new German poem[22] ending with the wish: «Ja, was uns drückt für Noth und Pein, mög nächstes Jahr entschwunden sein.» (So, what misery and pain depresses us, it may be gone next year.) As an encore follow German singable adaptations of *Echad mi yodea* and *Chad Gadya*.[23]

It is especially the fully reworked *maggid* part that reveals the theology and character of this first progressive Haggadah. In his preface, Leopold Stein himself explains: "We found the order of the old Haggadah generally appropriate and fitting, so we have gladly lined up our thoughts on this guide to formulate the new on this given basis. ... We imagined a pious family who had gathered to celebrate this solemn domestic celebration, and we therefore endeavoured to let its various members participate in the celebration in order to make it livelier and more varied. For this purpose, verses and songs had to be interspersed here and there to elevate and beautify the whole. We also believed that in the narrative we should not

---

[12] For the singable English adaption by Isaac S. Moses see e.g. CCAR (ed.): *The Union Haggadah: Home Service for the Passover*. Revised edition (New York: CCAR, 1923), 14f.

[13] Stein, *Hagada*, 21.

[14] "Ein Tischgesang. Componiert von Leopold Lichtenstein," Stein, *Hagada*, 22.

[15] Stein, *Hagada*, 23.

[16] "Das Lied von der Mitternacht», Stein, *Hagada*, 23–27.

[17] For the singable English adaption by Isaac S. Moses see e.g. *Union Haggadah* (1923), 115–117.

[18] "Das Lied vom Gottesreiche. Componiert von Wilhelm Speier," Stein, *Hagada*, 27–30.

[19] Singable English adaption by Isaac S. Moses see e.g. *Union Haggadah* (1923), 82–83.

[20] "Schlussgesang, Mel. Addir huh, Componiert von dem Vorsänger von Burgkundstadt," Stein, *Hagada*, 30–32. A page with the musical notation is added here, too.

[21] Singable English adaption by Isaac S. Moses see e.g. *Union Haggadah* (1923), 80.

[22] Stein, *Hagada*, 32. "Den Segen sprecht zum Weingenuss: Gott sei der Anfang und der Schluss!..."

[23] Stein, *Hagada*, 33–36.

limit ourselves to the earliest occurrences; the immediate past and present also asserted their right to be mentioned."[24]

To enable participation, Stein's *maggid* section is written like a play featuring different roles: the host, the youngest child, the housewife and the choir of the dinner party. Stage directions indicate when to stand and when to sit, when to raise the glass or uncover the *matsa*. The main roles are played by the host and the youngest child. The housewife makes two remarks.[25]

Striking from today's perspective is that *Ma Nishtanah* is revised. The child now asks about modern issues: «Why are we gathered here so solemnly today? Why is our table so festive today? Why do we eat unleavened bread today? Why the bitter herbs? What does all this mean?»[26] The four children are missing. Instead, the reader is reminded that the Torah commanded, that the inquisitive mind of the young generation should be stimulated, so that we may be given the opportunity to tell the younger generation about the greatness of God so that the attachment to Judaism is deeply impressed into the hearts of children.[27]

Present or future adversaries are eliminated from the story and instead of the traditional phrase that in every age they stand up against us to destroy us, Leopold Stein's version of *V'hi She-amdah* reads (the following is my English translation of the German):

God is with us in happiness and need;
He protects us when enemies threaten;

---

[24] "Die Anlage der alten Hagada zeigte sich uns im Allgemeinen angemessen und passend, und wir haben gerne unsere Gedanken an diesem Leitfaden angereiht, um das Neuzubietende auf einen gegeben Grund festzustellen. ... Wir stellten uns eine fromme Familie vor, welche sich zur Begehung dieses feierlichen häuslichen Aktes versammelt hat, und wir waren daher bestrebt, ihre verschiedenen Mitglieder in die Handlung zu verflechten, um diese dadurch lebendiger und abwechslungsreicher zu gestalten. Zu diesem Behufe mussten auch Verse und Lieder zur Erhebung und Verschönerung des Ganzen da und dort eingestreut werden. Auch glaubten wir, bei der Erzählung uns nicht bloss auf die frühesten Begebenheiten beschränken zu dürfen; auch die nächste Vergangenheit und die Gegenwart machten ihr Recht, in Anregung gebracht zu werden, geltend." Stein, *Hagada*, 3.

[25] On p. 12 the housewife mentions the bleak fate of women in Egypt who waited at home longing for their working husbands, not knowing, if they would survive their hardship. On p. 13 she draws attention to the feelings of the tender women when Pharaoh gave the order to kill all the boys. The housewife's two sentences correspond to the bourgeois ideal of women in the 19th century. But it is new and remarkable that the housewife gets a voice in the seder ceremony.

[26] "Warum sind wir heute so feierlich hier versammelt? warum ist unser Tisch heute so festlich bestellt? Warum geniessen wir heute das ungesäuerte Brot? Warum die bitteren Kräuter? Was bedeutet dies alles?" Stein, *Hagada*, 5.

[27] Cf. Stein, *Hagada*, 6f.

We are his—what pleasure is this!
He sets us free from all hardship and pain
as once he set free our fathers.
Thank him with all your heart![28]

Pain and Persecution belongs to the past. The presence is glorious. This becomes most striking by the addition of Deut 26:9 into the *maggid* section. The core of the traditional Haggadah is a midrash on the four verses Deut 26:5–8. Leopold Stein quotes the verses but instead of the midrash offers his own explanations and extends the narrative to the recent past of Jewish life in Western Europe. Already in his preface he announced, that when telling the story, one would also need to take into account the immediate past and present and "we therefore added to the four scriptural verses which were explained in the traditional Haggadah, the fifth final verse to complement the narrative, adhering to the prescription of the Mishnah for our subject, to begin with evil and to end with good."[29] In Steins Haggadah, the additional verse "He brought us to this place and gave us this land, a land flowing with mild and honey" does not mean Jerusalem and Israel, but Burgkunstadt and Bavaria. Quoting the first progressive Haggadah itself: "With deep appreciation of the goodness of God we declare before Him, *that He gave us this land*; that after so many, many centuries of wandering and repudiation, he finally transformed the ground on which he set us to be our home."[30]

This Haggadah is a celebration of gratefulness rather than a memory of the past and not just the fulfilment of a mitzvah. Its aim is to instill Jewish identity into the next generation and it therefore puts great emphasis to pedagogical aspects in designing the ceremony: participation of all present, especially the youngest child by creating a dialogue form, easy to understand explanations instead of difficult midrash, interspersed songs, poems and

---

[28] Gott ist mit uns in Glück und Not;
Er schirmet, wenn der Feind uns droht;
Sein sind wir—welche Lust!
Er wird von aller Not und Pein;
wie einst die Väter uns befrein
Ihm dankt aus voller Brust!—Stein, *Hagada*, 7.

[29] "Wir fügten daher an die in der alten Hagada zur Erklärung kommenden vier Schriftverse noch den fünften, die Erzählung ergänzenden Schlussvers, uns dabei an die Vorschrift der Mischna für unseren Gegenstand haltend, mit dem Bösen zu beginnen und mit dem Guten zu schliessen." Stein, *Hagada*, 3.

[30] Und mit tiefgefühlter Anerkennung der Güte Gottes sprechen auch wir es aus vor Ihm, *dass er uns eingegeben dieses Land*; dass er uns, nach so vielen, vielen Jahrhunderten des Herumirrens und der Verstossung, endlich den Boden, auf welchen er uns versetzte, zur heimathlichen Erde umgeschaffen. Stein, *Hagada*, 17. (highlighted as in the original).

responses and content relevant for the present celebrant of the Seder. And of course, all in the vernacular, so that the content can be understood, raises the feelings and shapes modern Jewish identity. All these features stayed relevant in Progressive Haggadot to this day.[31]

The first progressive Haggadah in the English language, often regarded as the very first in general, appeared only a year later. In 1942 Reverent David Woolf Mark's (1811–1909), rabbi of the recently build West London Synagogue in the UK, published *Haggadah Lepesach*: Domestic Service for the First Night of Passover. The work was created independently of Stein's work, without even knowing about the Bavarian version that appeared some months earlier. It may originally have been planned as a fundraiser for the newly founded West London Synagogue[32], but was afterwards frequently reprinted in Forms of Prayer volume II as "service for the first night of Passover,"[33] It is regarded as "something of a curiosity,"[34] "a unique document in the history of Reform Judaism"[35] and apparently it was not much used[36] and went into oblivion. In any case, it shows a very different approach than the German version published the year before. The 1842 West-London-Synagogue Haggadah presents the following surprising order of the Seder:

---

[31] Liberal Judaism in Germany only produced five Haggadot with deliberate progressive principles after Stein: Siegmund Maybaum, *Entwurf einer deutschen Haggada für den häuslichen Gottesdienst an den Vorabenden des Pessachfestes. Vorgelegt der Rabbiner-Versammlung*, (Berlin, 1891); ibid., *Haggada für den häuslichen Gottesdienst an den Vorabenden des Pessachfestes*, (Berlin, 1893); (further editions 1904 und 1910). Caesar Seligmann, *Hagada, Liturgie für die häusliche Feier der Sederabende* (Frankfurt: J. Kauffmann, 1913). [Siegfried] Guggenheim, *Offenbacher Haggadah* (Offenbach/Main: Dr. Guggenheim, 1927)—this Haggadah is based on Caesar Seligmann. Otto Geismar, *Pessach-Haggadah* (Berlin: B. Kahan, 1928). To mention is also the work of the Wissenschaft des Judentums: E.D. Goldschmidt, *Haggada* (Berlin: Schocken, 1936). The leading Haggadah in German Liberal Judaism became the one by Caesar Seligmann.

[32] Mara W. Cohen Ioannides, *Jewish Reform Movement in the U.S.: The Evolution of the Non-Liturgical Parts of the Central Conference of American Rabbis Haggadah* (Berlin/Boston: Walter de Gruyter, 2019), 11.

[33] D.W. Marks, ed., *Seder haT'fillot: Forms of Prayer used in the West London Synagogue of British Jews*, with an English Translation, Volume II. Prayers for the Festivals of Passover, Pentecost, and Tabernacles (London: J. Wertheimer, 1842), 17–28. I am very grateful to David Jacobs for many conservations about the West London Synagogue prayer books during my time in London and for making this Haggadah available to me.

[34] Michel Hilton, "When Was The Haggadah Written?" in: Paul Freedman, Yuval Keren, Colin Eimer, *Haggadateinu* (London: Reform Judaism, 2013),iii–v, v.

[35] Jakob J. Petuchowski, "Karaite Tendencies in an Early Reform Haggadah: A Study in Comparative Liturgy," *Hebrew Union College Annual* 31 (1960), 223–249, 249.

[36] Hilton, *Haggadah*, v.; Petuchowski, *Karaite Tendencies*, 249.

- Kiddush, the sanctification of the festival, as in the traditional Haggadah.
- Exod 12:40–42 in English and Hebrew, but without giving the source.
- A new English prayer, with a translation into Biblical Hebrew. It starts with: "O Lord, God of Israel! we appear before thee this night to celebrate the Feast of Passover, as thou hast commanded us through Moses thy servant, and to offer thanks and praises to thy holy name for all the goodness which thou hast wondrously vouchsafed to confer upon our fathers and upon us ...". As justification follow phrases formed from biblical cues, recurring to Ezekiel 20,33–34, Exod 12:8, 42, and 13:8. The introductory prayer then concludes with the plea: "We beseech thee, inspire our hearts with gratitude for all thy manifold mercies, and bring us speedily unto Zion, thy holy city, that we may there present the sacrifices incumbent upon us, even the sacrifice of this Passover, according to all its statutes and ordinances."[37] It is most unusual for a Reform Haggadah of this period to wish for a future temple.
- Exod 12:1–20 with mentioning of the biblical source under the headline "This is the ordinance of the Passover" / *zot chuqqat hapesach*, which is surprising, too, as this text actually deals with the generation of Egypt, not the future generations.
- Parsley dipped into vinegar with the blessing *bore pri ha'etz*, the blessing said when eating fruits from trees.
- *Mitchilah ovdei avodah,* which in fact is a quote from Joshua 24:2–4, used also in the traditional Haggadah.
- *Arami oved avi* (different from the rabbinic understanding translated as "an Assyrian had nearly caused my father to perish ..."), which is a quote from Deut 26:5–8.
- *Elu esser makkot* ... The List of the ten plagues and a passage starting with *mah rabu ma'asei adonai* "How manifold were the works of the Lord...", then listing the events as in the traditional passage *al achat kama vekama* ...even containing the phrases "he killed their firstborn" and "he build the Temple for us" but leaving out that "he gave us their money", phrases that today would not appear in a progressive Haggadah.
- The three symbols *pesach*, *matsa*, and *maror*, but without mentioning Rabban Gamliel. Instead, it starts with the phrase: "It is incumbent upon every Israelite to be mindful of three things on the

---

[37] D.W. Marks, *Forms of Prayer II*, (1842), 17–18.

Passover: the paschal lamb, the unleavened bread, and the bitter herbs."[38]
- *bechol dor va-dor* "It is incumbent upon us, throughout all generations, to consider as if we, personally, had gone forth from Egypt ..." with its quotes from Exod 13:8 and Deut 6:23.
- Psalm 113 and 114.
- The blessings Motzi *matsa*.
- The blessing "you commanded us to eat bitter herbs."
- Grace after Meals.
- Psalm 78 *Maskil le-Asaf,* a quite long psalm which is a history of Israel in poetical form. This is a completely new addition into a Haggadah without any precedent.
- *Mah rabu tuvcha...*, a short new passage praising God's goodness which he did to our ancestors, concluding: "We therefore supplicate thee, O Lord! God of the spirits of all flesh! Fountain of life and beneficence! so to inspire our hearts, that we may understand, observe and perform all the statutes of thy will, in order that it may be well with us for ever."
- Psalm 136.
- *Nishmat kol chai.*
- *Y'hal'lukha adonai kol ma-asekhah.* (The final blessing after Hallel.)

All texts are given both in English and in Hebrew. The whole British Reform Haggadah from 1842 is only 12 pages. More than the brevity of this Haggadah many readers will immediately have noticed that core passages of the traditional Haggadah are missing without any replacements: *Ma Nishtanah*, the four questions traditionally chanted by the youngest child, is missing, and so are the four children and *ha lachma anya*. This Haggadah further lacks the four cups of wine, the *charosset*, the Hillel sandwich and the *afikoman*. None of the classical Seder songs is printed, but instead this Haggadah adds in Psalm 78, a rather long Psalm reviewing Israel's sinful history.

This is the second ever published progressive Haggadah. It presents a very abridged text version, mostly based on biblical sources, and gives the passages in the chronological order of the supposedly historical events. According to J.J. Petuchowski this Haggadah shows the anti-rabbinical tendencies of the early British Reform Judaism.[39] The bible was regarded as the much older source and therefore—in the time of historicism—was given higher authority. The aim of this Haggadah was to abridge the liturgy—

---

[38] D.W. Marks, *Form of Prayer II*, (1842), 20.
[39] Petuchowski, *Karaite Tendencies*, 246–249.

which was done by leaving out rabbinic traditions. There are no ideological changes—the mentions of temple, sacrifices, joy about the killing of the Egyptians are not eliminated, as they will be in the future Progressive Jewish tradition. As already said, The West London Synagogue Haggadah from 1842 remained a unicum without reception history outside of the UK. Reform and Liberal Jews in the UK themselves did not use this Haggadah but used orthodox Haggadot and later other American-English versions and did not produce their own Reform or Liberal Haggadah until the 21st century.[40]

Development in the U.S.

The situation in the U.S. regarding the Haggadah is completely different compared to other countries with Progressive Jewish communities. In the U.S., an astonishing Haggadah creativity broke out since the end of the 19th century, repeatedly publishing new editions to this day. But also the American Haggadah-story began with a German language Haggadah, also authored by a Bavarian rabbi of about the same age as Leopold Stein. Both in fact studied at the same Yeshivah in Fürth, both studied at Würzburg University, and both later met at the second rabbinical conference in Frankfurt. We are talking about David Einhorn (1809–1879), who in 1855 arrived in Baltimore MD[41] after having served pulpits in Birkenfeld in the southwest Rhineland-Palatinate and in Mecklenburg-Schwerin in North-Eastern Germany. His Reform Prayer Book, *Olath Tamid*, published in 1858 for German Jewish immigrants to the U.S. contains on the last pages, one can't help getting the impression as if it were a very late idea, too late already to put it into the Festival section of the book—a "Hausandacht am Vorabend des Pessachfestes" (= Home Service for the Eve of *Pesach*). He does not mention his colleague Leopold Stein, but it is striking that Einhorn's Haggadah follows the same structure as Stein's starting with a paraphrase of *ha lachma* and choosing the same order and style, not presenting for example *ma nichtanah* but instead other questions closer related to the modern dinner situation—though Einhorn distributes them over the whole *maggid* section—and presenting the text in the form of a play between the host, the youngest member of the family and individual members of the family—by that creating more roles than Stein did.

However, while Leopold Stein aimed at creating a nice poetic German language and adapting the ritual to modern times by putting the focus on the gratefulness of having the right to be citizens now, David

---

[40] The first Haggadah of the British Reform movement appeared in 2013, the first Haggadah of the British Liberal Judaism appeared in 2010.

[41] His colleague Leopold Stein stayed all his life in Germany and two years after publishing his Haggadah became rabbi in Frankfurt/Main.

Einhorn vehemently changes the theology of the Haggadah. While Stein avoided talking about slavery in his *ha lachma anya* paraphrase, Einhorn deliberately does mention the many hundred years of slavery in Egypt. For Stein's congregation in 1841 slavery was something completely far away from any present experience, not so, however, for Einhorn's new congregation in Baltimore. Vice versa, slavery or abolition of slavery was a passionately debated issue in the U.S. at the time when Einhorn arrived. So Einhorn stressed that a Seder is a "night of vigilance" ("Nacht der Wache"). (He plays with the German words "Wache," "wachsam," which can mean both, "to stay awake" but also "to be attentive to something.") The unleavened bread appears in his Haggadah as "priestly bread." In this "night of vigilance" God called Israel to its special mission in the world: "Therefore it should be ... a night of vigilance for all the sons of Israel for all times, open our eyes and sharpen our view ... for the high calling that the gracious Redeemer instructs us in the midst of the nations."[42]

The bitter herbs remind us, that the battle to be God's priests among the nations never is an easy one,[43] but by this we take part in God's redemption and then one day we will celebrate "the feast of the redemption of all mankind."[44] David Einhorn's eyes were opened after arriving in the U.S. in 1855 entering right into the discussions about the abolition of slavery, a topic foreign in his previous life and as an outsider he may have taken things in with higher sensitivity. Einhorn condemned slavery deeply and vehemently.[45] His Haggadah from 1858 is a call for freedom to all human beings and a reminder of our role as Jews to fight for the freedom of others, once that freedom was granted to us, too.

Thirty-Four years later, in 1892 the Union Prayer Book appeared, which also contained a "Domestic service for the Eve of Passover."[46] It was "adapted from the German of the late Dr. Leopold Stein"[47] and it continued the dialogue form that Stein had introduced. But its editor, Isaac S. Moses,

---

[42] "Darum soll sie ... eine Nacht der Wache für alle Söhne Israels sein für alle Zeiten, unser Auge öffnen und schärfen für die Wunder, die Gott an unserem Hause gethan, wie für den hohen Beruf, den der huldreiche Erlöser inmitten der Völker uns angewiesen," *Olath Tamid* p. 478.

[43] David Einhorn, "Hausandacht am Vorabend des Pesachfestes" in: ibid, ed., *Olath Tamid: Gebetbuch für Israelitische Reform-Gemeinden* (Baltimore: C.W. Schneidereith, 1858), p. 475–486, 480.

[44] Einhorn, *Olath Tamid* 486.

[45] On Einhorn's position on slavery in the U.S. see Eric Friedland, "Olath Tamid by David Einhorn", *Hebrew Union College Annual* 45 (1974), 307–332, 309f.

[46] CCAR, "Domestic service for the Eve of Passover" in: *Union Prayer Book* (Chicago: Bloch, 1892), 227–257.

[47] Mara W. Cohen Ioannides, *Jewish Reform Movement*, 76. Mark Podwal, "CCAR Haggadot: A Feast of Haggadah Choices" in: CCAR (ed.): *RAVBLOG. Reform Rabbis speak*, Febr 21, 2014, https://ravblog.ccarnet.org/2014/02/ccar-haggadot-a-feast-of-haggadah-choices/; *Union Haggadah* (1923), 158.

not merely translated it into English but also merged it with Einhorn's theology, but the last was in a very subtle way. An impression gives the 1892 Union Prayer Book's version of the Deut 26:9, the verse Stein added to the *maggid* section, in Isaac S. Moses' American version:

> THE YOUNGEST: And He gave us this land. LEADER: With deep-felt recognition of the divine kindness do we today give expression to our thanks that God has given us this land; that He has made us co-workers in and partakers of the liberty and the free government of this glorious Republic. Here is the haven of our peace, the opportunity of our mission, to teach by our own example the faith in one God, and the love of virtue as the common bonds of humanity.[48]

In addition to the encouragement to take part in building "this glorious Republic" the stress of Israel's "mission" was completely missing in Stein's version. With this little *Pesach* eve home service at the end of the Union Prayer Book begins the creative story of American Reform Haggadot. Till 2014 the Central Conference of American Rabbis were to publish 10 revisions or new editions of official Haggadot for the Reform movement.

The first one being "The Union Haggadah" from 1907[49], an independently printed book. It therefore does not start with the *maggid* section, but of course gives the complete ritual from the beginning of the Seder including the blessings in Hebrew with English translations. The aim of the editors is to take care that the "beautiful home Service" on the eve of *Pesach* may not fall into oblivion, as "the moral and spiritual worth of such an hallowed institution, which has become a vital part of the Jewish consciousness is priceless. It would be an irretrievable loss were it to pass into neglect."[50]

The Union Haggadah reintroduces folk traditions, that Stein and Einhorn eliminated, as the four sons—but *mah nishtanah* consists only of the opening line leading to a modern question (... *umah tiwo shel seder hagadah zeh?* "and what is the meaning of this service?"[51]) and *dayenu*, but in strongly abridged and edited version.[52] In the *maggid* section some of the traditional Hebrew passages are given, while the English is not a translation but provides the progressive version, well summarized in the phrase parallel to the traditional Hebrew *lo et avoteinu bilvat ga'al hakadosh barukh hu*: "The delivered became the deliverer, when Israel was appointed the

---

[48] *Union Prayer Book* (1892), 241–42.
[49] CCAR (ed.): *The Union Haggadah* (New York: Bloch, 1907).
[50] *Union Haggadah* (1907), 5.
[51] *Union Haggadah* (1907), 19.
[52] *Union Haggadah* (1907), 20.

messenger of religion unto all mankind. Therefore, do we celebrate this night with songs and praises to the Eternal."[53]

In the 1908[54] edition of the Union Haggadah the Hebrew fonts has been replaced and as a result the Hebrew now appears more dominant on the pages. *Dayenu* has grown by two verses—*har sinai* and the building of the temple are now included.[55] But otherwise nothing is changed.

It is the third, completely revised edition of the Union Haggadah that would accompany American Reform Judaism for 51 years, and even today is still available, even in the form of an App,[56] and some years ago became the basis for the youngest CCAR Haggadah appeared first in 1923: The Union Haggadah Revised.[57] It contains quite a lot of surprising new features. First of all the Order of the Seder is now presented after the "Directions for Setting the Table," but all washing of hands are left out of course, a logical consequence that progressive Judaism does not maintain leanings on the customs of the priests in the temple.[58] As a novum the 1923 Haggadah begins with "Lighting the Festival lights. To symbolize the joy which the festival brings into the Jewish home."[59] (From now on all progressive Haggadot would begin the seder with lighting the candles, which traditionally does not belong to the seder.) New is also the feature of adding transliterations of the Hebrew of the blessings. Music is not only provided for new English songs, but also for traditional tunes as for the Kiddush in the Festival nusach and some of the Hebrew psalms. Some of the translations are closer to the Hebrew. *Ma Nishtanah* with its four strophes is reintroduced, and *Dayenu* now has 11 verses.

A need to again adapt the Haggadah to a new area arose in the 1960th.[60] Not only had the society changed between 1923 and 1960, but a modern Haggadah also needed to consider the Sho'ah and the modern State of Israel. The result was not a revision, but a completely new Haggadah, that

---

[53] *Union Haggadah* (1907), 19.

[54] CCAR (ed.): *The Union Haggadah* (Cincinnati OH: CCAR and New York: Bloch, 1908).

[55] *Union Haggadah* (1908), 22.

[56] See https://www.amazon.co.uk/Apps-Publisher-The-Union-Haggadah/dp/B0087OXYTU/.

[57] CCAR (ed.): *The Union Haggadah: Home Service for the Passover.* Revised edition (New York: CCAR, 1923).

[58] The Union Haggadah order consists of 11 steps. Besides the elimination of the washings, *motzi-matsa* and *korech-maror* are each counted as one step. The memory of 15 steps of the temple entrance was not necessary to preserve as any reminiscence to the temple was obsolete anyway.

[59] *Union Haggadah* (1923), 3.

[60] See M.W. Cohen Ioannides, *Jewish Reform Movement in the U.S.*, 120–129.

finally appeared in 1974.[61] With it began a new phase with an ongoing production of completely new works, no longer a series of revisions. The 1974 CCAR Haggadah edited by Herbert Bronstein is called "A Passover Haggadah," It offers new meditations and songs mixed with more traditional elements than in the versions before and extensive additional readings, many from Israeli poets and Holocaust literature and again makes fuller use of traditional material. But it still features the dialogue character of Leopold Stein's first progressive Haggadah, now in form of responsive readings between "Leader" and "Group." And it still offers musical notations—now they grew to 26 pages! It was reprinted in 1975 and in 1984, but it was not made for the 21st century. Now the voices of previously marginalized groups had to be heard, especially women and LGBTQ+ people. So the CCAR authorized a new Haggadah in 2002 with the title "The Open Door," [62] a 165 pages long book, among them 37 pages offering musical notations of English and Hebrew old and new songs. The choice of the title indicates that this Haggadah by its choice of texts and inclusive language welcomes all.

The new tradition of a Miriam's cup is introduced[63] at the beginning before the order of the Seder, which now contains the hand washings. A column in the inner margin of each page gives extensive advice on how to perform these sections and which alternative traditions exist, e.g., in the Sephardic tradition or in other countries or give explanations for expressions and customs. Only 10 years later it became clear, that "The Open Door" also needed to be open for people of other faiths and atheists, as nowadays many families are interreligious. Therefore in 2012 "Sharing the Journey: The Haggadah for the Contemporary Family" appeared,[64] proclaiming: "The Passover seder is a shared Jewish experience that has historical and contemporary significance to persons of all faiths," [65] The pages of this Haggadah offer questions for discussion, notes for the seder leader, and explanations, so that nobody feels excluded from the story or the ritual.

But only two years later the old 1923 Union Haggadah was rediscovered and revised by combining it with aspects from the 1974 Haggadah and the new rituals that had developed since the 70s are added, like Miriam's cup and the orange on the seder plate.[66] The aim of "The New

---

[61] Herbert Bronstein, ed., *A Passover Haggadah: The new Union Haggadah.* Prepared by the Central Conference of American Rabbis. (New York: Grossman; CCAR, 1974).

[62] Sue Levi Elwell, ed., *The Open Door: A Passover Haggadah.* (New York: CCAR, 2002).

[63] *The Open Door*, p. 12–14.

[64] Alan S. Yoffie, ed., *Sharing the Journey: The Haggadah for the Contemporary Family*, (New York, CCAR, 2012).

[65] *Sharing the journey*, half-title page.

[66] On these new rituals see in greater detail: Annette M. Boeckler, "Miriam's Cup. the Story of a New Ritual," *European Judaism* 45,2 (2012), p. 147–163. Susannah

Union Haggadah. Revised Edition"[67] is to be as inclusive as possible but at the same time show "a renewed appreciation for Reform Judaism's distinctive liturgical heritage."[68]

For a detailed analysis of the development of Reform Haggadot in the U.S. two recent articles should be noted: An overview on the history and the changing rationale of the various editions of the American Reform Haggadah was provided in the dissertation by Mara W. Cohen Ioannides.[69] Based on her research in the American Archives, studying letters and interviews, CCAR minutes, reports, speeches and documents she depicts the publication history of each of the just mentioned CCAR Haggadot and brings them also into relation with the history of the CCAR platforms and the social changes of American Jewry. The latter is the focus of the essay "Peoplehood with Purpose" by Lawrence A. Hoffman,[70] who shows how various American Haggadot mirror the changing American Jewish religious identity, how the function of the Haggadah and the Seder changed from being the performance of a Mitzvah to becoming an expression of religion or ethnicity to the need to provide spirituality and the diversity of identity in the presence.[71]

Only one of the other American Religious movements also dared very early to edit its own Haggadah. In 1941, nineteen years after founding the first Reconstructionist congregation, Mordecai Kaplan, Eugene Kohn, and Ira Eisenstein published the "New Haggadah for the Pesach Seder"[72] as the first liturgical work of the Reconstructionist movement. In a time of victories of Fascism and Communism Kaplan felt the need to stress personal and national freedom and democracy as an integral parts of Judaism.[73]

Heschel, "Orange on the Seder Plate" in: Catherine Specter, Sharon Cohen Anisfeld, Tara Mohr, *The Woman's Passover Companion* (Woodstock VT: Jewish Lights, 2003), 70–77. Sonia Zylberberg, "Oranges and Seders: Symbols of Jewish Women's Wrestlings," *Nashim* 5 (2002), 148–171.

[67] Howard A. Berman; Benjamin Yeidman (ed.): *The New Union Haggadah. Revised Edition* (New York: CCAR, 2014).

[68] *New Union Haggadah*, 1.

[69] M.W. Cohen Ioannides, *Jewish Reform Movement*, esp. 75–160.

[70] Lawrence A. Hoffman, "Peoplehood with Purpose: the American Seder and Changing Jewish Identity, in: L.A. Hoffman, David Arnow (ed.): *My People's Passover Haggadah: Traditional Texts, Modern Commentaries*, (Woodstock VT: Jewish Lights, 2008), 47–77.

[71] For a short first overview see Richard S. Sarason, "The Haggadah and Reform Judaism" in: Howard A. Berman, Benjamin Zeidman: *The New Union Haggadah*, 97–101.

[72] Mordecai M. Kaplan, Eugene Kohn, Ira Eisenstein: *The New Haggadah for the Pesah Seder*, (New York: Behrmann, 1941).

[73] A detailed history and analysis of M. Kaplan's Haggadah is given by Deborah Dash Moore: "Democracy and 'The New Haggadah'" in *American Jewish History* 95 (2009), 323–348.

The earliest Haggadah of a Religious Movement that reacted to the Sho'ah and the State of Israel was in 1982 published by the Conservative Movement: "Haggadah: The Feast of Freedom."[74] Its preface begins with the question: "Why is this Haggadah different from all other Haggadot, from the estimated 3,000 editions that have been produced during the past 500 years? This one is different primarily because it is the first that faithfully reflects Conservative ideology."[75] This means, it is committed to preserve the tradition, but is aware that the tradition is alive and evolves and adjusts—actually this is exactly the same principle that made Leopold Stein publish the first modern Haggadah. Conservative Jews no longer could use the traditional Haggadah as the facts of the *Sho'ah* and the state of Israel had to be reflected in a modern Haggadah.

Today, with the most creativity beginning in the 2nd half of the 20th century, almost each Religious Jewish movement in the different countries in the world has produced its own Haggadah-Version[76] and in addition there are Haggadot for many special interest groups, as vegetarians, social activists, feminists, special age groups, and many more.[77] But the

---

[74] Rachel Anne Rabbinowitz, ed., *Passover Haggadah: The Feast of Freedom* (New York: United Synagogue of Conservative Judaism, 1982).

[75] *The Feast of Freedom*, 6.

[76] The following editions of Progressive Haggadot were published outside of the U.S. (given in chronological order): Michael Shire, *The Illuminated Haggadah* (London: Frances Lincoln / US ed.: New York: Harry N. Abrahams, 1998) German edition transl. by Annette M. Boeckler (Berlin, 2000); French edition, (Paris 2000); Russian edition, translated into Russian by Yuriy Tkachov, (Berlin 2014). Israel Movement for Progressive Judaism ed., Пасхальная Агада [Pessach Haggadah], Russian translation by Gregory Kotlyar, (Moscow; Jerusalem: World Union for Progressive Judaism, 2007). West London Synagogue, ed., *Interfaith Haggadah* (London: West London Synagogue, 2008). Yehoram Mazor; Dalia Marx; Yehoyada Amir ed., *Haggadah laz'man hazeh. Haggadah l'pesach shel hayahadut hamitkademet b'yisrael* (Jerusalem: World Union for Progressive Judaism, 5769 [2009]). Andrew Goldstein; Pete Tobias: *Haggadah b'Chol Dor va-Dor* (London: Union of Liberal and Progressive Synagogues, 2010). Joram Rookmaaker, *Haggadah shel Pessach De brede Hagada* (Amsterdam: Stichting Sja'ar, 2011) (2nd ed. 2015) Colin Eimer; Paul Freedman; Yuval Kerem, ed., *Haggadateinu. Our Haggadah* (London: Reform Judaism, 2013). Mouvement Juif Libéral de France, ed., *Haggadah shel Pessach La Haggada de Pessah* (Paris: Mouvement juif libéral de france, s.a.). Judaisme en Mouvement, ed., *Haggadah shel Pessach La Haggada de Pessah* (Paris: Judaisme en Mouvement, s.a.).

[77] A first overview is given by Vanessa Ochs: *The Passover Haggadah. A Biography* (Princeton/Oxford: Princeton University Press, 2020), esp. 90–98 and 132f. For other Haggadot not published by a movement see also pages 139–171. See further Carole B. Balin, "Moving through the Movements. American Denominations and Their Haggadot," in: L.A. Hoffman, David Arnow (ed.): *My People's Passover Haggadah: Traditional Texts, Modern Commentaries*, (Woodstock VT: Jewish Lights, 2008), 79–84. Joel Gereboff, "One Nation, with Liberty and Haggadahs for All," in: Jack Kugelmass (ed.): *Key texts in American Jewish culture* (New Brunswick, N.J : Rutgers University Press, 2003), 275–292. Carole B. Balin, "The Modern Transformation of the Ancient

theological development of the progressive Haggadah as depicted in this article still explains the differences between orthodox Haggadot and non-orthodox Haggadot to this day.

- Leopold Stein in 1841 tried to include the dinner party by creating a dialogue form including many readers. Especially in recent years progressive Haggadot aim to be the basis for a ritual that is as inclusive as possible. Today it is far more than only participating in the reading (or singing). The wording and the ritual itself of the progressive seder must include women as equal liturgical leaders and participants. This is guaranteed by using a gender-neutral language and by putting a *"kos Miriam"* on the Seder table. A progressive Seder includes LGTBQI community, often shown by putting an orange on the Seder plate. Those aware of animal rights who will have a vegetarian meal and therefore replace the shank bone by a symbol for the shank bone. In recent years, the changes are less in the text of the Haggadah but in the rituals and symbols of the seder.
- Leopold Stein and all following editors of progressive Haggadot aimed to make the text comprehensible also for the less educated. Till today a progressive Haggadah provides a good to read translation, recently also transliterations of the Hebrew, and modern additions in the vernacular. The latest progressive Haggadot also include guests from other religions at a seder, as it is the case in interreligious families or inviting neighbors to the congregational seder and give explanatory commentaries about Judaism at the margins.
- Already the Stein Haggadah from 1841 provided musical notations for some songs and so do many progressive Haggadot since then. This serves to teach the music to those who did not grow up with the sound of the seder from childhood but also help the guests to join in. Choir—or communal singing has a become an important characteristic of any progressive liturgy.
- Progressive Haggadot abridge the text and leave out passages contradicting progressive Jewish theology, as for example multiplying the plagues in Egypt or wishing God's wrath for the nations of the world. They leave out midrashic explanations not easy to comprehend. Therefore, the *maggid* section is often abridged or paraphrased.

Passover Haggadah" in: Paul F. Bradshaw; Lawrence A. Hoffman: *Passover and Easter. Origin and History to Modern Times* (Notre Dame, IND: University of Notre Dame Press, 1999), 189–213.

- Progressive Haggadot often add activities, comments, or questions to facilitate the participation of the dinner party. Progressive Haggadot often consider the fact that many communities these days offer a communal seder, where not a family and their friends but any group of people not necessarily known to each other happen to come together for this seder.
- While the first progressive Haggadot by L. Stein, D.W. Marks, and D. Einhorn did not contain images, the Union Haggadah from 1907 and every progressive Haggadah since then pays attention to the external design of the pages. The images in today's editions either help children to follow the seder or please the artistic taste of the user.

How to make religion relevant and how to best pass on this relevancy to the next generation, this seems to be the Red Thread through the history of the Progressive Passover Haggadah.

Re-arranging Things at the Table for an Isolated and Peculiar Jewish Community at the Bottom of the World

Norman Simms

A small out-of-the-way and very peculiar Jewish community formed in Hamilton New Zealand had its own special needs in the late 20th century. To keep the group together, many of whom were in mixed-marriages and in different degrees of withdrawal or rejection of Judaism, I composed a version of the Passover Haggadah that would serve, not only as a shortened variant on the traditional text, but would include explanations of what was going on and why in the ceremonial meal. It was never meant for wider distribution nor as a substitute for the rabbinical version.

From the early 1980s through to the late 1990s, there was a Waikato Jewish Association based in Hamilton, New Zealand. Its membership varied from about ten to fifteen families most of the time to fifty or so families, at a time when there was an influx of Jewish migration from South Africa. There was also a gradual increase in the number of people coming from Israel on shorter or longer stays in the Waikato region. But most of the membership consisted of second or third generation New Zealanders, new arrivals from the UK along with a sprinkling of Americans and Russians. As there was no synagogue in Hamilton or anywhere else in the region which stretches south to Rotorua and Taupo, west to Raglan and east to Tauranga—and there never has been any formalized religious community in this central North Island area—anyone seeking to live a kosher, religious life either never comes to Hamilton to settle or, in the case of a handful of older residents, affiliates with either the Orthodox or Liberal communities in Auckland.

My experience in the organization of the Jewish Association in the last two decades of the twentieth century showed that there was either no interest in constituting a synagogue-based or rabbi-led community and, in one way or another, most members were hostile to Judaism as a religion.

Nevertheless, they felt themselves to be Jews and wanted their families to have some sort of non-intrusive, non-threatening Jewish experience. The majority, too, felt alienated from Judaism, knew very little about its modern history, and still wanted to celebrate family-based holidays, like *Hannukah, Purim* and *Pesach,* but were wary of the High Holidays (*Rosh ha-Shannah* and *Yom Kippur*) and even of Shabbat. Many families were mixed, with the female side more often non-Jewish and yet eager for their children to learn something about Judaism, much more so than their own Christian upbringings or purely secular education. In a few cases it was the gentile husband and father who kept the family coming to meetings of the Jewish Association. The members in general tended as a group to have at best ambiguous feelings about Israel, either despising it because of bad experiences growing up there or because of mis-readings of current affairs as filtered through the popular press and television news.

Something happened at the turn of the century which led to the splitting apart and recreation of something quite different than the friendly and religiously informal Jewish group[1]—a something related to scandalous political events in the University, to which many members of the Association were involved with as faculty, students or graduates—so I will restrict my remarks to the time before those unpleasant events occurred. The highpoint of the existence of the group came when virtually the only collective event of the year was a communal *seder* and for which we prepared a Hamilton Haggadah.

For the first few years we used printed *haggadot* that various families brought to the *seder*, a meal that either was set up in a rented church, if they had a big table and lots of chairs. The result was that not everyone had the same booklet in front of them. Some years, when the number of guests around the table was low enough and we could all read from the version, it was necessary for me, as the *rosh seder,* to guide the group through the text, leaving most of the Hebrew out, except form the prayers and familiar songs—which itself was a mishmash when two or more melodies were sung at the same time or alternately. It was also necessary, given who most of were, to say aloud "he or" and "him and her," as well as "sons and daughters" or "children" so as avoid complaints from the

---

[1] One of the lasting accomplishments was the running of yearly seminars to which not only overseas scholars attended but which also had room for non-academics to participate at various levels, including the giving of papers, roundtable discussions and debates on important issues of the day, dance and musical performances, food preparation and organizational arrangements. Following each of the Waikato Jewish Studies Seminars we published a collection of the Proceedings. As the local Hamilton association declined in membership and the capacity to mount such mixed scholarly and general interest weekend-long (usually Friday, Saturday and Sunday) events, other groups in Wellington and Auckland attempted to follow our lead but were stymied by jealousy between university and synagogue and different religious organizations.

feminists (male as well as female). More than that, though, I found myself giving a running commentary throughout so as to explain what was going on in the text. Given the *sitz-fleysh* (patience) of most members, and not just the young children who were there, the after-meal half of the book was omitted, except for a spirited and raucous singing of *Chad Gadya*.

At last, it seemed propitious to write out our own *Haggadah* to take in these various modernizations and deletions and make photocopies available to everyone sitting around the Passover table for the communal meal. How was this done? Sacrificing one of my own classical books, the *Maxwell House Coffee Haggadah*, I took a pair of scissors and cut out the various sections, especially the Hebrew texts we wished to retain, and laid them out in sequence. Then I typed out a new version of the given text but changed the gender to the closest neutral expression I could think of, including the references to God which were sometimes "He/She" or sometimes "He/She/They/or It" as seemed appropriate, rhythmic and euphonious. I also found myself inserting into the text an explanatory or descriptive commentary on what was meant by each passage of the narrative, homily or prayer. Then, several months for *Pesach* came around, still in a preliminary and tentative stage of preparation, I photocopied the new version and distributed it to the members and asked for their comments, questions, and objections.

Most people said they hadn't any comments, one or two asked questions about what particular words or sentences meant, and no one had any objections. That done, I went through the text again and tried to clean it up still more, here and there adding a few further explanations, and photocopied the latest version to be stapled together in sufficient number for everyone to have when we gathered for the *seder*.

This would be the real test of how well or not our emerging *Hamilton Haggadah* worked. Could everyone follow what was going on, read it aloud—including children—as we usually went round-robin for almost everything, except for (a) the passages in Hebrew assigned to the people able to read and speak aloud the language, (b) the passages sung or chanted, with each family who insisted that their own melody and pronunciation was the proper and most meaningful one allowed a turn to lead the assembled membership, and (c) certain explanations in introduction to various changes in the nature of the text being read—the indication of what various items on the *seder* plate were, why the *rosh shulchan* (the table-master or head of ceremonies) washed his hands with or without a prayer, when wine glasses should be lifted, sipped from or not, how to dip one's finger into the wine and count out the plagues, including when to lick the pinky clean with a slurping noise and so on.

The major explanatory insertion was the one near the beginning, just before the asking of the Four Questions by the children (or when there

Re-arranging Things 233

were no children present, as increasingly happened as the membership diminished and grew older) or by the newest member or youngest person present. This additional commentary explained that the Haggadah contained:

(a) a running description of what was happening as a symbolic memorial event;

(b) a special version of the story of the Exodus from Egypt, a version from which the figure of Moses was left out by the rabbis;

(c) the story of how Abraham left his father, gave up a religion of idol worship, and travelled geographically and morally to the Promised Land to found a new people and a new religion and thus a new freedom for the mind and soul;

(d) a parallel and interwoven account of how the ancient rabbis discussed the meaning and importance of performing the collective banquet as a way of remembering the Exodus story and as a substitute for enacting the holiday as it existed when the Temple was still in existence and when Israelite families came up to Jerusalem to sacrifice a kid or a lamb and celebrate this sacred act by sharing the meal together; and

(e) the various stories each of us had that brought us together in Hamilton, New Zealand, and, as Jews with various backgrounds and understandings of who we were and why we wished to identify ourselves collectively as Jews, at least on this one occasion in the year; and then

(f) the final additional ritual act: a drinking of a fifth cup of wine and the intoning together of the phrase "Never again," something that brought tears to the eyes and a lump in the throat, that confirmed that, whatever our differences in belief and intensity of belief, hesitations about allowing religious and spiritual feelings into our lives throughout the rest of the year, eventually we all knew that our fates were shared by the nature of history itself.

Aside from wanting to cut down the rabbinical Haggadah most people are familiar with, updating some locutions and ideas that seem to create negative feelings in the group, I also wanted to use the occasion to help generate positive memories in children—in terms of phrases, images and melodic patterns of speech and song. The adults with their hesitations about returning to behaviors that they spent a lifetime backing-off from indicated that they enjoyed some of the familiar modalities of speech we used from the printed *haggadot* they each brought to the *seder*, and from which I copied out a few lines here and there. The idea was not to plagiarize or pretend to be something we were not, but to have a non-threatening, understandable version of the formal Passover service useful for this one peculiar community at this time in each of our own histories and relevant to the world around us.

As we all went through the reading and performance of the *ad hoc* Hamilton Haggadah, with pencil at the ready, I noted down the places where spelling and grammatical mistakes made themselves obvious no matter how many times prior to this I had proofread the text, as well as those spots where readers, including children, stumbled over words they did not know, syntax that confused them, and passages they seemed to object to. Afterwards, as everyone packed up to go home, a few discrete—or not so discrete—suggestions on improvements needed and objections to be taken to heart were passed on to me, and duly noted. Properly humbled (and perhaps a little humiliated), I went home and in the next few weeks tried to improve the whole of the Haggadah so as to make it more acceptable to everyone next year. Needless to say, not everyone's suggestions were taken up nor all the objections acceded to. But I did, honestly, work through my changes or decisions not to make changes.

Here is how the *Hamilton Haggadah* began on its opening two pages. I cite as given with all the remaining spelling glitches, tautologies, redundancies and syntactical errors.[2]

> The festival of *Pesach*, or Passover, celebrates many things, above all the liberation of the Jewish people from slavery in Egypt. But also in this celebration from bondage, we wish for the freeing of all people in all places from oppression and slavery, from wars and privation, from ignorance and self-deceptions.
> Seder means order, and this meal; is not an ordinary meal. It is a living book, a symbolic meal through which all of us re-enter Israel—the Jewish people, its history, and its ethical values. Once more through the seder we live through the liberation from Egyptian slavery, pass through the darkness and loneliness of ignorance and superstition and return to the springtime of Israel, of joyful community living. And yet we are always mindful of our beginnings in slavery and therefore of our obligation to help other people free themselves from darkness and slavery.
> **Haggadah** is the story of departure from Egypt and our wanderings in the desert, but is not the same story of Exodus told in the Bible. For it is a Jewish story, and a special kind of rabbinical story. In this version of the narrative of our liberation from Egypt there are three main changes:

---

[2] I have never been known for my typing skills, and even my thinking runs far ahead of my formation of sentences. It would take several more years of proofing to remove all the mistakes and make the whole text read more smoothly.

First, in the narrative, this [sic] no room for a human leader, male or female, no charismatic salvation figure: it is God alone, not an angel or any other superhuman form. But the monotheistic, unnamable [sic], deeply mysterious God—a God here identified, not as the Creator of the Universe, but as the Lord who led us forth from the Land of Egypt.

And second when we join in with the Children of Israel who departed from the wickedness of Pharaoh, we are reminded of another story, a story woven into this tale of liberation and renewal.

Thus, wee *[sic]* recall how our ancestors were also idolators *[sic]*, worshippers of stone and wooden statues, and how the Jewish people emerged from that moral darkness and mental slavery to become worshipper of an unseen God.

Our God *is One who has no form, no figure, a single powerful otherness which ensures a moral, ethical, spiritual reality, and engages us, as the chosen representatives of all humanity, in a covenant to work for the harmony of the earth under the Law of justice, reason, logic, goodness and love, of loving-kindness and compassion, so that for Jews the Law and Love are not separate contending ideals but an* [sic] *and the same Power.* (The italicized passages were to be read aloud together as a group.]

In this way, the two stories, of freedom from Egypt and of emergence from superstition and self-willed blindness of idol-worship are one and the same.

But there is also a third story, a story told in the way of dialogue, of rabbinical speech. This is the conversation of the rabbis who sat in B'nei Barak all night until their students reminded them it was dawn. This is not the story of events and characters, God and the Children of Israel on their trek from Egypt or the age-old rise of civilization from the dregs of darkness and superstition.

This third dimension to the Haggadah of Passover is a dialogue of reason and love. It is a way of smashing the idols of myth and entering into the reason and love by which the universe began, the way history runs its course, and the way in which our talk, our words, our thinking, our feelings can change the world, can remedy its faults, and bring about peace and freedom for all peoples now and in the future. This is dimension of *tikkun* through the performance of *mitzvot*.

Let me give another instance of an inserted passage in the Hamilton Haggadah After the Four Questions (*"Manish tana halyla hazeh...?"* Why is this night different from all other nights...?) are asked, I included a statement to explain what is going on. These kinds of interventions seem required by the confusion members with little background in Jewish customs seemed to find in following what is going on.

> The rest of the first part of the *seder* is the answer to these Four Questions, answering which tell the three stories of Exodus from Egypt, breaking of the idols, and entering into the rabbinical discourse of reason and love....
>
> This beginning of the narrative then breaks to give a rabbinical *mashol*, a kind of riddle or parable, about four types of children. The break in the story is deliberate because it not only explains what the story of Exodus is about, it also points out that this is not a story of long ago. It is not a myth or a legend....
>
> In every generation, each and every one of us must remember that we were slaves to Pharaoh and we strangers in a strange land, and so we must never treat others as slaves nor mock them for their strangeness.

Or a little later, after the counting out of the Ten Plagues and the three abbreviated names for the plagues by Rabbi Yehuda, our Haggadah added this explanatory note:

> Yet we must not gloat over the sufferings and defeat of our enemies. When the Children of Israel crossed through the Red Sea and touched dry land, the armies and chariots of Pharaoh chased after them, and then the waters closed in on them and drowned them.
>
> At that moment the angels in heaven wanted to sing a joyous song of triumph, but the Eternal our God stopped them, and with tears in His eyes, asked: How can you be happy when my children have just been drowned in such great numbers[?]. According to this *midrash* of the rabbis, even the enemies of Israel are human beings and children of God.

Another year came and went, and it was Passover time again. I read through the text, made some further adjustments and corrections, and copied enough copies for the people who would be seated around the *seder* table. This year, with the first real rumblings and grumblings of what would split apart the community to be heard, we had smaller groups assemble. Again, with my pencil ready, we commenced the ritual meal. A few more glitches were found and no comments or objections made. But before I sat down to improve our Haggadah, with plans to start cutting out various illustrations from old *haggadot* and modern magazines,[3] the ructions broke out.[4] When it came to be *Pesach* of the next year, there very few of us left, three couples and a few odd individuals, and no children under the age of eighteen, all sufficiently agreed to what we wanted a communal celebration to be, and hence we could return to the Maxwell House traditional booklet.

We carried out the ceremonial performances with far more Hebrew than in many years, listened to each other's "classical" melodies for the songs and chants, and pushed our way through most of the second part of the seder. Along the way, there also came the usual interventions, jokes and recollections of Passovers past with family and friends, often in whatever Old Country we identified with. It was as orderly and unruly as any family gathering, given that we were old friends of many years' standing, and though none of us were "fair dinkum kiwis," we had all pretty much lived in this strange new country longer than we had anywhere else in the world.[5]

There seemed no reason thereafter to amend or reproduce the *Hamilton Haggadah* and gradually the photocopied and stapled copies fell apart and were virtually all lost or thrown away. Within the last ten years, that small somewhat cohesive group of friends disappeared too: some to other places in New Zealand, others to countries overseas, and more and more to the great study hall in the sky. Somewhere perhaps, in some box in a storage unit or at the bottom of old documents and notes there still might be more than the one copy I have kept out of nostalgia.

For a very short while, in a very peculiar part of the world, it seemed to serve a function; but today, there is no need to try to find those old bits of paper or to offer it to a world that has changed quite a bit since we started to concoct our own seder form and Haggadah style. Just as we kept the rabbis at bay, including the occasional emissary of the Lubavitcher

---

[3] The last edition of the enterprise came out as a 16-page photocopied booklet with yellow covers under the title: *Hamilton Haggadah: The Story of Passover as Recounted by the Rabbis in the Course of the Seder*, and the cover blurb added "Retold and Compiled by Norman Simms for The Waikato Jewish Association (Hamilton, New Zealand), Revised for 2002.

[4] These scandals over anti-Semitism, Holocaust Denial and denigration of Zionism as a legitimate expression of Jewish identity and nationalism occurred not only at Waikato University but also at Massey University in Palmerston North and Canterbury University in Christchurch, and came to involve the New Zealand Jewish Council. The official version of what happened is published as a formal commission of inquiry found at https://unipr.waikato.ac.nz/unipr.waikato.ac.nz › news › kupka_report › pdf › kupka-report *A Review of the Case of Hans Joachim Kupka* (PDF) by W Renwick - 2002. Further internet searches on Google should give various newspaper and magazine articles from within New Zealand and overseas, along with some of the written testimonials submitted to the Renwick Commission. What happened to the Waikato Jewish Association must remain a private matter.

[5] True blue, the real McCoy, etc.

Rebbi in Brooklyn (through his faithful followers in Australia), and thus helped protect our members from unpleasant memories and irrational fears of what their own personal demon might do if it caught them playing at being real Jews, so the *Hamilton Haggadah* helped keep a small collection of otherwise often incompatible people together. But sometimes I have a little voice inside of me in the middle of the night which asks whether or not in the long varied history of the Jewish people there might have been perhaps one or more little peculiar communities like our own. Then I whisper, "Hush, little voice: no one cares."

Select Haggadah and Exodus Topics

William Krieger

Asking for Directions on Pesach: Should Archaeological Discoveries Change Our Views of the Exodus from Egypt?

When we sit down for our seders, one question (in addition to the 4) that routinely comes up is: what does archaeology have to say about the Biblical Exodus? According to some, there is no real evidence of an Exodus from Ramses II's Egypt, and this 'fact' causes a lot of consternation around the Seder table. Putting aside questions about what 'no real evidence' means in this context, the premise, that Ramses II was the Pharaoh of the Exodus in only one hypothesis. Other Pharaohs, including Ahmose I, Amenhotep II, and Seti I, could have been that Pharaoh, and each account would have a different impact on questions surrounding 'evidence' for the Exodus. This paper will focus on two points. First, it will speak to some of these different archaeologically based proposals for an Exodus (speaking about plusses and minuses for each). Second, it will ask whether (and how) discussions of archaeological evidence should impact our understanding of Biblical Studies and Religion. The goal is to make that Exodus discussion an interesting, vibrant, living, and discordant part of the Seder, and to raise larger questions surrounding the role of Archaeology on History.

Introduction

A common discussion at the seder table (and in popular circles more generally) surrounds the historicity of the Exodus, (as well as Biblical episodes in general). Indeed, many early archaeologists in Israel focused their energies on attempts either to prove or disprove the journey of the Israelites from Egypt back to Israel. Those scholars trying to locate and confirm the Exodus have had to face two issues. First, elements in their primary information source (the Bible) seem to be in conflict with other contemporary texts, as well as with the archaeological record. Second, striving to prove a Biblical story does not sound like sound science. In fact, there are real questions as to whether Biblical (or any theological) scholarship should have a role to play in archaeological fact finding (and conversely, whether archaeological and historical data should be used to prove or disprove elements of religious belief).

While these problems might seem distinct, in fact, problem 1 lays the groundwork for problem 2, and the two together will provide a (hopefully satisfactory) starting point to a new conversation about the place, role, and impact the Exodus should have for the Jewish community, whether in scholarly circles or around the seder table.

Problem 1: What Time is the Seder?

Although there have been a range of dates proposed for the Exodus event,[1] the two serious contenders center around Egypt's 18th and 19th dynasties (1500–1400s BCE and 1200s BCE, respectively). Both accounts have evidence in their favor, and both also run into serious problems, whether textually or archaeologically.

The Traditional Chronology Thesis

According to the Traditional Chronology, the Israelites would have been expelled during the 18th dynasty. This period featured pharaohs who (in accordance with the Bible's 10th plague) lost children (Thutmose III and Amenhotep II), and contemporary texts seem to hint at events that might line up with at least parts of the Exodus story. For instance, the Tell el-Amarna letters speak of a lot of unrest in the region and of the presence of foreign agitators (including the Hyksos and the Apiru), and they report large expulsions of slaves who flee into the desert, never to be seen again.

Although this stream of foreigners sounds like an Exodus, this timeline faces significant issues with Biblical account, as well as with the archaeological record. To the former, if the Exodus had occurred during this period, there would have been a 250–300 years gap between that event and conquest of Israel and the period of Kings David and Solomon (who were supposed to have been a part of that story). In terms of the archaeology, although there was evidence of some violent overthrow of major cities in Canaan (including Jericho, a fortified city whose walls were destroyed during this period), the systematic destruction and conquest of the land mentioned in the Bible is not reflected in the archaeological record for many

---

[1] Archaeologist Aren Maeir points out that "'Egypt-originating' views have been suggested for the late EB, terminal MB, mid-LB, terminal LB, early Iron I, and late Iron II, and to a certain extent—even the Persian and Hellenistic periods" (Maeir 2015, 413).

of the major cities in existence during this era. Additionally, if Egyptian texts are to be believed, there was a strong Egyptian presence in Canaan throughout the 18th dynasty. This would have made the idea of an ascendent Israel in Canaan following an escape from Egypt unlikely.

The Late Chronology Thesis

According to the Late Chronology (following William Albright's archaeological work), the Israelites would have left Egypt at some point in the 19th dynasty. According to Egyptian records, Rameses II also lost a son (which, however personally tragic, is a good sign for a match to the Biblical account). This account is in line with early mentions of Israel, including the Merenptah (sometimes spelled Merneptah) Stele, discovered by Petrie in Thebes, where the 19th dynasty pharaoh claims victory over his enemies in Canaan, declaring in 1209 BCE that "Israel lies desolate—its seed is no more." Following this reading, Geraty suggests that, if the Exodus occurred, it must have occurred prior to this date: "Pharaoh Merneptah's 'Israel' Stele…fixes the latest date before which the Exodus must have occurred since it mentions Israel as a people among names that otherwise refer to places in Palestine" (Geraty 2015, 58). Roughly 50 years after Merenptah, Ramses III depicted his crushing defeat of the Philistines (depicted as the Biblical villains) on a Mortuary Temple at Medinat Habu, leaving the Philistines on Canaan's coastal plain (where, according to the Hebrew Bible, they would soon meet the Israelites, who were coming from the East).[2]

Other, slightly later mentions of the Israelites (referring to them as an established kingdom or people) include the Sheshonq I Victory Stele (889–887 BCE) found in Karnak, celebrating defeat of Solomon's son King Reheboam, the Shalmaneser III Monolith (853 BCE) which mentions King Ahab,[3] the Mesha Stele (850 BCE) which speaks of the sons of Omri, and the Tel Dan Inscription (9th or 8th century BCE) which lists the house of David as being conquered by the Arameans.[4]

---

[2] As a matter of fact, Ramses III lost that battle (and the Canaanite coast) to the Philistines, and simply used his inscription (the press of his era) to proclaim victory. Although this does nothing to diminish the text as a piece of evidence, it is interesting counterevidence to those who would argue that ancient texts should be read objectively, or worse, that only the Biblical account is capable of producing biased, or 'fake' news.

[3] For more work on this hypothesis, see Bietak (2015) who makes an interesting argument for a (primarily) Ramesside Exodus based on archaeology, linguistics, and historical geography.

[4] Although they fit nicely in chronological order for the 19th dynasty Exodus, these inscriptions could also be used as evidence for the earlier Exodus hypothesis. Regardless, they pretty reliably place Israel in Canaan by this time period (regardless of the time (or times) of an Exodus (or other formation processes for Judaism.) These data points are seen as problematic only to those who attempt to claim that Israelites are a

In addition to other mentions of the Israelites during this time period, this timeline is in synch with the generally accepted chronology of the united monarchy, which is based in part on a line from the book of Melachim (Kings): "In the 480th year after the Israelites left the land of Egypt, in the month of Ziv—that is, the second month—in the fourth year of his reign over Israel Solomon began to build the House of the Lord" (1 Kings 6:1).[5] As Solomon's reign was calculated to approximately 970 BCE., this would place the Exodus around 1450 BCE. The storehouse cities of Pi-Ramses (mentioned in the Bible) also existed in Egypt during this time period (and not during the 18th dynasty) and as mentioned above, this time period also saw the influx of the Philistines, a group that would be a large focus on the rest of the Biblical text.

Archaeologically, this account is problematic for reasons opposing those mentioned in the earlier Exodus account. On the positive side, the archaeological record shows a destruction layers in many major cities, and population centers shifted appreciably during this time period. However, neither Ai nor Jericho (both prominently featured in the Biblical conquest), existed as walled cities during this time, calling into question Biblical accounts of their destruction. Additional questions surround a lack of evidence of a large-scale exodus of people from Egypt during this period, leading scholars to question whether the Israelites (or how many Israelites) would have made that journey.[6]

The Trickle Exodus Thesis

While some have chosen to see the problems mentioned above as reason to dismiss the idea of an Exodus (and of an ancient Israel) out of hand, others have noted that many elements of the Exodus story (and of other portions of the Hebrew Bible) do match up with and bear out contemporary textual and archaeological findings. As such, those critics who propose to throw out the Exodus out of hand show themselves no better than their opponents. As uncritical acceptance and uncritical dismissal of an Exodus both ignore the data at hand, some scholars have turned to a third alternative, one that is more in line with the contemporary thoughts on migration, that is less ethnocentric, and that makes more sense archaeologically. This approach

---

modern phenomenon. Those who attempt to do so are forced to argue that every one of these monoliths or inscriptions are forgeries, or that they refer to another group of Israelites unrelated to those currently under study.

[5] Translation by the author.

[6] As Sweeney explains, although the Apiru (here Habiru) and Hyksos fit many of the narrative elements of the Exodus story, by the time of Ramses II these groups had already long departed from Egypt. If the Exodus occurred during the 19th dynasty, these groups could not be the subjects of the text (Sweeney 2012, 90).

views the Exodus (and ancient history more generally) as being complex, and not a single, univocal story. As Maeir explains, "I believe that a particularly compelling way to look at the complexity of the biblical text is to compare it to a multi-period archaeological site, a 'tell'—with all its layers, contexts, disturbances, and artifactual complexity" (Maeir 2015, 410).

According to this thesis, there might have been a number of small Exodus events, where people returning (or generally fleeing) from Egypt merged with people who never left, as well as with other indigenous Canaanites and members of disaffected groups. This could mean that there was some truth in both of the Exodus accounts mentioned above (along with others that might range from the Early Bronze through the Persian periods). The Biblical text could then be seen as a repository for the collective memory of its people, one that would be full of conflicts, anachronisms, and data points from each of those periods.

While this thesis has problems as well, they are not archaeological (or anthropological). This may seem surprising, as science has been branded publicly as being the source of univocal, data-driven truth. Until last quarter of the 20th century, scientific archaeologists believed that they could use the tools of 'science' to provide the researcher precise explanations for past lifeways.[7] Since that time, archaeologists have moved to a more fluid understanding of their field. This is not to say that data analysis is not central to the discipline. If anything, archaeology is more data driven than any time in its history, leading some to question whether science drives the need for data or whether scientists have so fetishized data that they would rather dispense with the complexities of theory in favor of mechanistic simplicity.[8]

However, rather than lead to unified accounts of the past, archaeological data have instead shown that human history resists reduction to a single narrative. This makes sense, as any given historical episode will mean different things to different people. For example, US History texts speak of the American Revolutionary War (1775–1783) as a fight for freedom and equality. However, at the end of the war, this freedom only applied to (and was only intended to benefit) wealthy elite white males. More recent history books have focused on the many populations that were not beneficiaries of equal rights (including women, who were not given their freedom to vote until the passage of the 19th Amendment in 1920).[9]

---

[7] For thorough treatments of the historical and philosophical rationales for this position, see Trigger1989 and Krieger 2006, respectively.

[8] Gaston Bachelard 1928 shows how technology, thought to be a scientific tool, has turned the tables and is now guiding the scientific enterprise.

[9] Although, of course, the 19th amendment only applied to white women. Voting rights for a variety of groups, including Blacks, Asians, and Native Americans, were denied or suppressed until further legislative pushes that continued through the

Applying this theoretical framework to ancient history, a multivocal, multi-part, messy and incomplete Exodus account may be in conflict with either of the unified Exodus events mentioned above, but it is entirely in line with current theories about the origins of other peoples in the region, including the aforementioned Philistines. Early archaeologically based accounts of the Philistines identified them as an invading force from Mycenae.[10] However more recent work has shown this hypothesis to have been an oversimplification. While there were Mycenean Philistines, the data show that not all Philistines were Mycenean. The Philistines were a complex people (or more appropriately, set of peoples) who were made up of a number of disaffected foreign and domestic groups.[11] This melting pot would find itself at odds (at times) with another group (the Israelites) who were also coming into their own during this period. The problem here is that accepting this thesis would require a non-literal reading of the Biblical text. However, that is a theological problem, and this tension (between an historical Exodus and a religious Exodus) moves the discussion to the final question of this paper.

Problem 2: Different Rolls at the Seder Table

If theology demands a literal reading of the Biblical text and archaeology suggests a multivocal approach to those data, it might appear that a Seder table full of questions would not be the proper place for a discussion of the Exodus. In general, there are those who do claim that as science and religion play different rolls in our lives, they need to be regulated and kept separate. Some demand a binary choice, that either science or religion reigns supreme at all times. Others expect that science and religion each have a place in our lives (but that they never inhabit the same place).

The former position is all too familiar these days, and it has resulted in a large percentage of American citizens, from elected officials to ordinary citizens, publicly denying science. A 2015 Pew research poll shows that this mistrust of science has led to significant gaps in confidence between scientists and members of the American public on a wide range of issues, from the causes of climate change, to the safety and efficacy of our food supply and vaccines. Stephen J Gould articulates the latter position, claiming that there should never be a conflict between science and religion because they are relevant in different spaces. "No such conflict should exist because

---

1970s. Recent examples of voter suppression call into question whether freedom and equality exist to date.

[10] Dothan and Dothan 1992 (and elsewhere) defended this hypothesis with a large amount of data from multiple sites.

[11] For a detailed analysis of this new reading of the Philistines, see Maeir 2017 who leads a similarly heterodox group at the ongoing excavations at Tell es-Safi/Gath.

each subject has legitimate magisterium, or domain of teaching authority—and these magisteria do not overlap" (Gould 1997, 17) One could imagine Gould at a Seder table, perhaps arguing that the Seder is no place for science. Religious events are places, for Gould, where ethics and values discussions go on. Here, theology would hold sway.

That said, Gould would also expect that the scientist at the table would leave his or her religious beliefs at home when going back to the lab or the field, as the religious views have no place when data are being gathered and analyzed. Of course, the problem with Gould's position is that religious and scientific magisteria do overlap. When Jews discuss the Exodus at a Seder, they are making factual claims about history. The Four Questions exhort parents to teach their children that they too were a part of the Exodus, they pour wine out of their glasses to lessen their joy at the actual misfortune of others. They begin to count the Omer, a record of a physical journey in the wilderness. On the other hand, despite Gould's argument that ethics are not scientific, scientific discussions routinely involves ethics, values, and in some cases, beliefs about the nature of the scientist's object of study.

Perhaps a better way to approach the Seder discussion would be to employ another analogy. Religious belief and scientific study may not rule over separable kingdoms, but they can be thought of as having different approaches, or of viewing their subject from different perspectives. This perspectival relativism can be found in, among other things, maps. "Imagine, for example, four different maps of Manhattan Island: a street map, a subway map, a neighborhood map, and a geological map. Each, I would say, represents the island of Manhattan from a different perspective, appropriate, for example, for a taxi driver, a subway rider, a social worker, and a geologist" (Giere 1999, 81). If someone were to look at a geological map of Manhattan, even if they had lived there for years, they might not be able to find their favorite pizza parlor (or even their current location). Similarly, there will be times when religious and scientific thoughts will not go well together.

When an archaeologist speaks of the Exodus, s/he is definitely using a different 'map' than the religious Jew. Guided by a scientific map of the Exodus, the archaeologist will ask (at times uncomfortable) questions. While religion asks people to bring themselves back in time, connecting themselves to the story of the Exodus, science demands that the researcher do the opposite, to remove themselves from the story, to challenge those potential sources of contact, and further, to "…critique and explore the construction of ancient social domains, those which we have overlain from contemporary culture assuming that they are 'natural' and fundamental due to our own institutionalization" (Meskell 2001, 204). Given those (hopefully explicitly stated) assumptions, Archaeologists will study natural processes and work with data driven clues to understand changes at sites and regions.

"Archaeology is best able to contribute to a general understanding of human behaviour in terms of the information that it provides about changes that occur over longer periods of time..." (Trigger 1989, 409).

Maps of Religious events, on the other hand will focus on events that demand confirmation (as opposed to skepticism. While scientific maps assume a universe governed by relatively stable processes over time, religious maps tend to focus on events and journeys that ignore the natural order. Splitting seas, plagues of frogs, mass deportations, and long winding journeys are not the sorts of things easily captured in the sorts of data that archaeologists might collect, but these map points are sources (or resources) of religious belief.

Conclusion, or Afikomen

Although science and religion look for (and to) different things, sometimes their maps do overlap. These are times when reading someone else's map might allow the reader to gain real insight into his or her own. While a subway rider may not have much interest in geology, the person constructing the subway system certainly does. A geologist, looking at a subway map, might even have some insight into the rationale for the F train's strange loop as it leaves Manhattan. In the case of the Exodus, the religious map (the Biblical account) of the Exodus can provide some data points for historical comparison to other texts (and maps).

At the same time, archaeological and historical maps can give the religious Jew insights into the range of cultures, the physical geography, and even the weather that might have existed during a personally significant time period or a religiously significant event. Rather than cause a theological crisis, this information could provide a fuller, more realistic foundation for a discussion of the Exodus (or Exoduses). This backdrop can be a source of further questions, leading to the sorts of debates that go on well after the 4th cup has been consumed, and that can be taken up again:

Next year, in Jerusalem.

Bibliography

Bachelard, Gaston 1928. Chapter IX of *Essai sur la Connaissance Approchee*. J. Vrin, Paris.

Bietak, Manfred, 2015. "On the Historicity of the Exodus: What Egyptology Today Can Contribute to Assessing the Biblical Account of the Sojourn in Egypt." p 17–37 in T.E. Levy et al. (eds.), Israel's Exodus in Transdisciplinary Perspective: Quantitative Methods in the Humanities and Social Sciences, DOI 10.1007/978-3-319-04768-3_2, Springer International Publishing Switzerland.

Geraty, Lawrence 2015. "Exodus Dates and Theories." p 55–64 in T.E. Levy et al. (eds.), Israel's Exodus in Transdisciplinary Perspective: Quantitative Methods in the Humanities and Social Sciences, DOI 10.1007/978-3-319-04768-3_2, Springer International Publishing Switzerland.

Giere, Ronald 1999. *Science Without Laws.* University of Chicago Press, Chicago.

Gould, Stephen 1997. "Nonoverlapping Magisteria" *Natural History 106: 16–22.*

Krieger, William 2006. *Can There Be a Philosophy of Archaeology?* Lexington Books, Langham.

Maeir, Aren 2015. "Exodus as a Mnemo-Narrative: An Archaeological Perspective." p 409–418 in T.E. Levy et al. (eds.), Israel's Exodus in Transdisciplinary Perspective: Quantitative Methods in the Humanities and Social Sciences, DOI 10.1007/978-3-319-04768-3_2, Springer International Publishing Switzerland.

Maeir, Aren 2017. "Philistine Gath after 20 Years: Regional perspectives on the Iron age at Tell es-Safi/Gath." p 133–154 in O Lipschits and A Maeir (eds.), *The Shephelah during the Iron Age: Recent Archaeological Studies*. Eisenbrauns, Winona Lake.

Meskell, Lynn 2001. "Archaeologies of Identity." p 187–213 in I Hodder (ed) *Archaeological Theory Today.* Polity, Cambridge

Pew Research Center poll 2015. "Public and Scientists' Views on Science and Society." Online (accessed August 1, 2020) https://www.pewresearch.org/science/2015/01/29/public-and-scientists-views-on-science-and-society/

Sweeney, Marvin 2012. *Tanak: A Theological and Critical Introduction to the Jewish Bible.* Fortress Press, Minneapolis.

Trigger, Bruce 1989. *A History of Archaeological Thought*. Cambridge University Press, Cambridge.

Exodus to Leviticus to Haggadah: The Dynamism of Torahistic Law

Jonathan Arnold, Esq.

Announcements from above or developments from below? Apodictic or casuistic law? Universals or particulars? Static statutes or case-by-case development? These are just some of the key issues which seem to vex so many legal systems—but not all. Jewish law not only embraces these myriad dualities, but dynamically adjusts them by keeping the commandments alive in present memory, of which the Haggadah stands as an exemplar.

Exodus

We begin with Exodus, which itself contains several initial progressions whereby the deposit of the law is prepared for development. First, what is provided from on high contains an invitation for Moses, as a representative of the children of Israel, to rise to meet the Almighty. "And the Lord said unto Moses: 'Come up to Me into the mount and be there; and I will give thee the tables of stone, and the law and the commandment, which I have written, that thou mayest teach them.'" (Exod 24:12)

Before we turn to the requirement of teaching, a bit of exegesis: the repeated reference to the "children of Israel" is phraseology already indicative of a nation being formed around a common concept law, and one that is given, then must be provided, then taught, next learned…and what is learned soon becomes alive. "And the Lord spoke unto Moses, saying: 'Speak thou also unto the children of Israel, saying: Verily ye shall keep My Sabbaths, for it is a sign between Me and you throughout your generations, that ye may know that I am the Lord who sanctify you." (Exod 31:12–13)

Leviticus

We next turn to Leviticus, which echoes much from Exodus—and begins to expand the law, transmuting much apodictic law (e.g., "Thou shall not murder. Though shall not commit adultery. Thou shall not steal." (Exod

20:13)) into casuistic law. "If ye walk in My statutes, and keep My commandments, and do them; then I will give your rains in their season, and the land shall yield her produce, and the trees of the field shall yield their fruit. And your threshing shall reach unto the vintage, and the vintage shall reach unto the sowing time; and ye shall eat your bread until ye have enough, and dwell in your land safely." (Lev 26:3–5)

Haggadah

Now leaving Leviticus and turning to the Haggadah we find the retelling of the giving of the law, tethered to an earlier passage from Exodus and moving from the universal to the particular. "And thou shalt tell thy son in that day, saying: It is because of that which the Lord did for me when I came forth out of Egypt. And it shall be for a sign unto thee upon thy hand, and for a memorial between thine eyes, that the law of the Lord may be in thy mouth; for with a strong hand hath the Lord brought thee out of Egypt. Thou shalt therefore keep this ordinance in its season from year to year." (Exod 13:8–10) This contemplates the law—as related to the hands, indicating writing, and memory that can be visualized, and a norm that can be spoken—becomes animated in the children of Israel yearly, and therefore always. The Passover Seder is where the story of *Exodus* is retold in a participatory manner, animating the law.

And perhaps no portion of the Haggadah resonates this more clearly than the questions posed to the "four sons" dynamically transmuting universals into particulars, as each son must give an individualized answer to a question that sounds in the Torah. In many Haggadot, the wise son asks a variation of, "What are the statutes, the testimonies, and the laws that the Lord has commanded you to do?" It is in answering this that the wise son is supposed to utilize one or more passages from Exodus to answer this question, making the history and the law personal to the son or daughter answering this at the Seder table. There are a myriad of acceptable responses, all of which recall the giving of the law and require the answering child (cf., "children of Israel") to explain it in his or her own words, referencing Exodus and its progeny. One traditional answer ends with, "And thou shalt bring his sons, and put tunics upon them. And thou shalt anoint them, as thou didst anoint their father, that they may minister unto Me in the priest's office; and their anointing shall be to them an everlasting priesthood throughout their generations." (Exod 40:14–15)

Talmud – Bava Metzia

We can see something of a parallel development of this sort of dynamism in the Talmud. Expanding on the commandments enjoining both stealing and bearing false witness, the first chapter of *Bava Metzia* delves into a discussion of both procedure and substance when it comes to promissory notes.

As discussed in Chapter One, 7A, "[i]f a borrower admits that a promissory note that has not been authenticated by the court was in fact written by him, but claims that he has already repaid it, his believed. Thus, the lender must first arrange to have the court authenticate the document, and then he can present his claim to be repaid." (*Shulhan Arukh, Hosen Mishpat* 82:1) As a practicing attorney and professor, I can't help but compare this to the modern legal concepts of the *Parol Evidence Rule* and the requirements of authenticating documents. (Cal. *Evid. Code* §1400, *et seq.*).

The Memory of God and the Blindness of Humanity: The Four Children

Leonard Greenspoon

The questions by and responses to the Four Children are among the most popular parts of the Seder. Here we will explicate this material in three separate, but interrelated sections. In the first, we will explore differences in the English translations of the Hebrew and how these affect the reader's/listener's perception of these individuals. In the second section, we will look at the rabbinic formulations from which we draw this material, their relationship to the text of the Hebrew Bible, and differences between the wording of the rabbis and the text found in today's Haggadot. The third section will focus on theological, sociological, psychological, and pedagogical approaches to this material, reflecting differing emphases and values as presented by Jewish Studies scholars, historians, rabbis, and other educators. Through this combination of diachronic and synchronic analysis, we hope to demonstrate the exegetical and pragmatic richness of this part of the Haggadah.

The number four (4) has an important role in structuring the Passover Haggadah. So, for example, there are four questions, four cups of wine, and four children.

Before we turn our attention to these four youth, I want to point out that throughout this piece I will refer to them as "children"—and not "sons," as is found in almost all English-language Haggadot, including this one. In my view, this accords with biblical usage that the Hebrew word "ben" is neither masculine nor feminine unless it is specifically marked as one or the other. And it is not here. In like manner, there is no good reason to identify the adult responder as "father." I will use the more expansive English term, "parent," since it is contextually better suited to the Haggadah.

In the introduction to this section, we are told that what follows is, at it were, the script of four distinctive and different children, each in conversation with a parent. They are characterized by a single trait. There is no doubt that the universal designation of the first child as "wise" is correct.

The biblical book of Proverbs, especially its first part, illustrates what it means to be "wise" (the Hebrew term is *ch-k-m*). Here we see that being intelligent or smart is not synonymous with being "wise," although a child or adult who is so characterized has learned a great deal from experience, observation, and obedience to God's commands. Beyond this erudition, wisdom carries with it the necessity of acting in accordance with these theological insights and imperatives. In short, wisdom can be understood as intelligence in action.

The second child, who is characterized as "evil" in English-language Haggadot, stands in opposition to the first. At first glance, this might not come across since we are likely to contrast "wise" with something like "stupid" or "ignorant" and contrast "evil" with "righteous." All well and good. But within the context of the Haggadah the "evil" (sometimes, "rebelliousness") of such children centers on their failure to act in accordance with the divine will. Thus, it is not that they don't know or can't understand what God requires. Rather, they consciously choose to move in the opposite direction.

The precise meaning of the third descriptive term, in Hebrew *t-m-m*, is difficult to capture in English. This Haggadah speaks of an "innocent" child, which does impart some of what the Hebrew term covers. However, I think "innocent" is misleading here, since for most users of the Haggadah the opposite of "innocent" is "guilty"—and that's clearly not what is on the author's mind. For the most part, we find the designation "simple" attached to this child. But to my mind that sounds too much like a disability, a negative value judgment that is not intended here.

One of the best-known usages of this term in the Hebrew Bible is at Genesis 6:9, where the New Jewish Publication Society (NJPS) translation has Noah as "blameless." The older Jewish Publication Society (OJPS) version, along with the King James Version, has "whole-hearted" at this point in its Genesis text. For me, those two renderings are very different, and further neither of them applies to this child. Possibly even better known is Job 1:1 (and elsewhere in the book), where the eponymous hero has acquired this distinction. Here again NJPS has "blameless"; OJPS repeats its gloss as "whole-hearted."

No doubt this is a difficult Hebrew root to pin down as to its meaning, since it appears to have several significations, all of which occupy related but not identical semantic fields. So maybe what we have here is a child who seeks "the big picture" without getting involved (or perhaps entangled) in the details. Perhaps the best way to capture this in English is with the adjective "uncomplicated" or perhaps "straightforward."

The fourth child "doesn't know how to ask." This English wording captures well the Hebrew expression at this point.

I ask all users of this Haggadah to look carefully at the questions posed by each of the first three children. In and of themselves, do their statements typify their categorization? In response, I offer a tentative "maybe." It is true that the first child demonstrates a linguistic and perhaps intellectual inclination when he uses three different terms to characterize God's commands: "testimonies," "statutes," and "judgments": "What are these testimonies, statutes and judgments that the Lord our God commanded you?" But, as I observed earlier, this erudition, possibly the result of much focused study, does not equate with what we understand as the defining element of "wisdom." This query could just as well come from an "evil" child who hopes to thwart spiritual considerations by introducing philological explorations.

The Haggadah clearly locates the evil of the second child in his use of "you," through which he purposefully separates himself from the Israelites of the Exodus and subsequent generations: "What is this worship to you?" But how does this child's usage distinguish him from the wise child, who in our text (as presented in the previous paragraph) likewise uses the second person pronoun, seemingly without any criticism? The only thing that seems to separate wisdom from evil here is that the "wise" child demonstrates a lexicographical prowess that the "evil" child appears to lack.

As for the third child, the most we can say, on the basis of his query, is that he seems to be seeking a comprehensive picture or understanding of all that Passover celebrates or commemorates: "What is this?" "Simple" or "simpleminded" he is not.

The responses each of these children elicit also don't seem, in a word, "responsive" to their presumed intellectual interests or spiritual levels. Of all the rituals and traditions associated with the Passover meal, how does the specific reference to the *afikomen*—"And accordingly you will say to him, as per the laws of the *Pesach* sacrifice, 'We may not eat an *afikoman* [a dessert or other foods eaten after the meal] till after [we are finished eating] the *Pesach* sacrifice'"—qualify as a clear or clever response to the "wise" child?

And why is the second child, branded as "evil" for a question that is parallel to his "wise" sibling, threatened (one might say, verbally abused) with harsh words: "'To you' and not 'to him.' And since he excluded himself from the collective, he denied a principle [of the Jewish faith]. And accordingly, you will ... say to him, 'For the sake of this, did the Lord do [this] for me in my going out of Egypt.' 'For me' and not 'for him.' If he had been there, he would not have been saved"?

And finally, what differentiates the answer to the third child's question from what the fourth child is told? That is, respectively, "And you will say to him, 'With the strength of [His] hand did the Lord take us out from Egypt, from the house of slaves,'" and "and you will open [the conversation] for him. As it is stated, And you will speak to your son on that day saying, 'for the sake of this, did the Lord do [this] for me in my going out of Egypt.'"

There is something seemingly arbitrary about this whole set up. This becomes even more apparent when we compare this text of the Haggadah with other texts that refer to four children. The oldest of this is the *Mekhilta of R. Ishmael*, a commentary on the biblical book of Exodus that dates to the third century CE. Here also we find four children and their parents within the context of discussion about the rituals and beliefs of Passover. The wise child and the child who does not know how to ask are found in the same position—first and fourth—as in the Haggadah. The wicked child appears third on this list, with the introduction of a new character, the "stupid" child, in second place.

For the wise and inarticulate children, the *Mekhilta* provides pretty much the same narrative as in our Haggadah This is also true for the third, or wicked, child. The script for the stupid child and the parent closely follows the wording the Haggadah associates with the "uncomplicated" (or "simple," if you insist) sibling, namely, "And you shall say to him, 'With a strong hand God took us out of Egypt.'" In this instance, it seems that for R. Ishmael "stupid" and "simple" serve the same function. Additionally, he sets (or transmits) an ordering in which "wise" and "stupid" are next to each other, highlighting their mutual opposition.

Is the order in which the children appear a significant factor in understanding and correctly interpreting this passage? Or is it only incidental? It is difficult to know—and this is not the only instance of such uncertainty (so, for example, there is disagreement as to whether the Ten Commandments are listed in descending or ascending order of importance). To be sure, it is tempting to hypothesize that the authors or editors of the Four Children start their account with the "best" son, in which case the other three appear as occupying successively lower rungs by comparison. But this is far from certain.

Both in the *Mekhilta* and in contemporary Haggadot the wickedness, if you will, of the wicked son is exemplified by his use of the second person plural ("you"), which distances him from the community, instead, we might suppose, of the inclusive first personal plural ("us"). But as it stands in our Haggadah, the supposedly "wiser" first child does exactly the same thing without incurring his parent's wrath. As it happens, both the *Mekhilta* and the Yerushalmi (Jerusalem Talmud) record this child's query as ending with "commanded us," not "commanded you" as in the Haggadah. Such a reading heightens the contrast between the "wise" and "wicked," but it is not in accordance with our text of Deuteronomy 6:20, which contains the second plural. So, "When thy son asketh thee in time to come, saying:

'What mean the testimonies, and the statutes, and the ordinances, which the Lord our God hath commanded you?"

Apparently the first person plural ("us") was found in the "biblical" text of Deuteronomy used by the authors/editors of the *Mekhilta* and Yerushalmi. Moreover, the third century BCE Greek or Septuagint version also read "us" here—"And it shall be, when your son asks you to-morrow, saying, 'What are the testimonies and the statutes and the judgments that the Lord our God has commanded us?'"—attesting to the appearance of the first person plural in the "biblical" Hebrew text it was translating. At some point in the medieval period, when the Masoretes completed their efforts to produce the definitive Hebrew Bible or Masoretic Text (with both consonants and vowels explicitly marked), the wording of Deuteronomy 6:20 with the second person plural pronoun was enshrined as the canonical text. Subsequent copyists of the Haggadah changed their Hebrew at this point in accordance with the "biblical" reading. The price, as it were, for their decision is the blurring of distinctions between "wise" and "wicked."

What then marks the second (or third) child as wicked? As is seemingly the case in almost all such circumstances, the rabbis were industrious in teasing out otherwise unsuspected distinctions. So it is that in the biblical passages supporting both the "wise" and "simple" (or "stupid"), Deuteronomy 6:24 ("When thy son asketh thee in time to come...") and Exodus 13:14 ("And it shall be when thy son asketh thee in time to come...) respectively, children are portrayed as "asking" their father for information, thereby showing the sincerity and seriousness of their respective questions. But the child designated as "wicked" doesn't "ask" but rather "tells" or "says," as in Exodus 12:26 ("And it shall come to pass, when your children shall say unto you..."), demonstrating to the rabbis that this child isn't truly seeking parental guidance but instead wants to make a statement independent of what he might learn from his parent. Note that this distinction can be detected in the OJPS version of 1917 (so above), but not in the newer one from 1985 ("And when your children ask you...").

The Jerusalem Talmud lists the four children in the same order as they are found in Haggadot, although retaining the designation "stupid" (rather than "simple") for one of them. But the answers the *Mekhilta* and Haggadah attribute to the parent are switched, if you will, in the Jerusalem Talmud between the "wise" son and the "stupid" ("simple" one). As a result, "the outstretched hand" of Exodus 13:14 forms the core of the response to the first or "wise" child in Yerushalmi, whereas elsewhere that's what the "stupid" (or "simple") child hears. The reference to the *afikoman* is now (that is, in the Jerusalem Talmud) offered as appropriate to the "stupid" (or "simple") child. In my view, it is not possible to determine which set of responses is original or even earlier. Each of them must have been considered meaningful within differing contexts.

We also have no way to be certain whether the authors/editors of the *Mekhilta*, the Yerushalmi, and the Haggadah were dependent on each other or perhaps they each drew independently from an earlier source. It is certain that portions of the Seder ritual date back as far as the first or second century CE. And the four children might well be part of this earliest textual stratum. But, as we noted before, over the course or many centuries and myriad translations, wording in the Haggadah changed as a result of conscious scribal intervention and probably subconscious copyist errors as well.

What are we to make of all of this? If the ordering of the children as well as the wording of responses to them was not fixed, but fluid, in the rabbinic tradition, can we say anything definitive about the meaning of this passage in terms of what constitutes "wisdom," "evilness," or "simplicity" ("stupidity") and the positive or negative evaluations assigned to each? I would guess that it's the recognition of different types or sorts of people (and not just children) that is at the heart of this narrative, with the details left to the imagination, or better pedagogical determination, of the teacher or parent.

I have been at many Seders where the leader directs our attention away from what I might term the sociological interpretation of this passage toward its psychological application. This redirection of attention is evident in those who are more comfortable in seeing the four as developmental stages within the life of a single individual (probably, most, if not all individuals) rather than as fixed descriptions of four different individuals. In my view, there is nothing inauthentic about such a re-visioning of this material. At the same time, I urge that we don't look at these differences as either/or, but both/and—with other focuses also possible.

I have read some commentators who speak of a fifth participant, namely, the parent. I am wondering if we could expand the number here beyond five to eight. What does it look like if we think of four parents in addition to the four children? In this case, attention, both positive and negative, I suppose, to the styles of parenting, or more broadly teaching, come to the fore. So, for example, the parent of the evil child exacts physical punishment—"And accordingly, you will [first] blunt his teeth and [only then] say to him"—before any attempt at instruction. For the child who does not know how to ask, the parent thoughtfully "opens" the conversation: "And [regarding] the one who doesn't know to ask, you will open [the conversation] for him." This parent does not ignore or incite but invites.

It is all well and good to think of a singular parent with multiple offspring. But it can also be salutary to imagine that each of these vignettes is characteristic of a different style of parenting or teaching. In short, there are consequences to our interactions with children or students. Although a "wise" son does not always develop out of an environment that favors or promotes "wisdom," such an environment does more easily allow for the honing of these traits.

Commentary on Cited OJPS and NJPS Verses

Here are the relevant biblical passages as rendered by the Old Jewish Publication Society version (OJPS) from 1917 and the New Jewish Publication Society version (NJPS), or *Tanakh* from 1985. The 1917 translation was consciously shaped within the literary framework of the Protestant King James Version, which consists of rather literal or formal renderings from the Hebrew. NJPS, which presents a functional equivalence version, is less literal than OJPS. It is fitting to observe that OJPS retains more distinctively Hebrew forms than NJPS, which compensates as it were for this by typically being more readable:

Deuteronomy 6:20–21 [wise]

NJPS: When, in time to come, your children ask you, "What mean the decrees, laws, and rules that the LORD our God has enjoined upon you?" you shall say to your children, "We were slaves to Pharaoh in Egypt and the LORD freed us from Egypt with a mighty hand."

OJPS: When thy son asketh thee in time to come, saying: "What mean the testimonies, and the statutes, and the ordinances, which the Lord our God hath commanded you?" Then thou shalt say unto your son, "We were Pharaoh's bondmen in Egypt; and the Lord brought us out of Egypt with a mighty hand."

Exodus 12:26–27 [wicked]

NJPS: And when your children ask you, "What do you mean by this rite?" you shall say, "It is the passover sacrifice to the LORD, because He passed over the houses of the Israelites in Egypt when He smote the Egyptians, but saved our houses." The people then bowed low in homage.

OJPS: And it shall come to pass, when your children shall say unto you, "What mean ye by this service?" That ye shall say: "It is the sacrifice of the Lord's passover, for that He passed over the houses of the children of Israel in Egypt, when He smote the Egyptians, and delivered our houses." And the people bowed the head and worshipped.

Exodus 13:14 [simple]

NJPS: And when, in time to come, your son asks you, saying, "What does this mean?" you shall say to him, "It was with a mighty hand that the LORD brought us out from Egypt, the house of bondage."

OJPS: And it shall be when thy son asketh thee in time to come, saying: "What is this?" that thou shalt say unto him: "By strength of hand the Lord brought us out from Egypt, from the house of bondage."

Exod 13:8 [doesn't know how to ask a question]
NJPS: And you shall explain to your son on that day, "It is because of what the LORD did for me when I went free from Egypt."

OJPS: And thou shalt tell thy son in that day, saying: "It is because of that which the Lord did for me when I came forth out of Egypt."

The Dawn of the Jewish Woman: Marginalization, Liberation, and the Exodus

Roberta Sabbath

Passover and the story of Exodus represent beginnings, release from slavery, and freedom. Women in the biblical story of Exodus appear in three key elements: the midwives who defy pharaohs order of genocide to the firstborn Jewish males, Miriam (four times) the prophet provides sustaining waters throughout the journey, and pharaoh's daughter who along with Miriam saves the Moses from infanticide. They serve as models for civil disobedience, social advocacy, celebration, prayer, and communal leadership. The story provides the foundation not only of the Jewish people but serves as a reflection upon the journey women have taken in Judaism from marginalization to liberation in little over the last one hundred years. Jewish women assert more power in the public realm than ever. They build on the shoulders of previous traditions. Their individual and collective action, reflecting the courageous leadership of the Exodus women, continues to nurture, celebrate, and build their communities. Talmudic rabbis instruct us to connect the story of Exodus to contemporary stories. By connecting the foundational story of Exodus to the story of contemporary women we can fulfill that reenactment. The testimony of contemporary women rabbis reports the importance of continued leadership of Jewish women.

Passover and the story of Exodus represent beginnings, release from slavery, and freedom. The parting of the Sea of Reeds suggests a birthing of the Jewish people. While Eve, whose name chava means life, is the legendary mother of all generations, Miriam, whose name means both mar bitter and yam sea, supported life through her sustaining waters and leadership. Other women of the Exodus story also save the Jewish people through their desert trials. In the Talmud, Rabbi Akiva claims "Thanks to righteous women, Israel was redeemed from Egypt" (בזכות נשים צדקניות נגאלו בני ישראל ממצרים). The salvation story provides the foundation not only of the Jewish people but serves to mirror the journey women have taken in Judaism from marginalization to liberation. Rabbis instruct us to connect the story of Exodus to our own lives. By connecting the foundational story of Exodus to the story of contemporary women we can fulfill that reenactment.

The story of the Exodus told as part of the seder includes deeds of men. Moses is at the center of the narrative as the Jewish people journey from slavery to freedom. Professor Tammi Schneider notes that those same texts are about men and through men's eyes. The portraits and treatment of women relates to their revealing the interests of men. The history of interpretation for most of these sacred texts has been in the hands of men, until fairly recently.[1] As Rachel Adler writes, "The pervasive male God images of Jewish tradition function as models of and models for…a world in which women are subordinate to men 'They both claim to tell us about the divine nature and they justify a human community that reserves power and authority for men.'"[2] The hero is male and the women characters represent the challenges and the helpers to the development of the hero self and the fulfillment of the earthly and spiritual aspirations. But what of the women?

This chapter highlights women's voices, concerns, and accomplishments in order to honor their memories and celebrate their leadership. Portraits of women in biblical and post-biblical texts are remarkable and none more so than the portraits in Exodus. Women in the biblical story of Exodus appear in three key elements: the midwives who defy pharaoh's order of genocide to the firstborn Jewish males, Miriam, who appears in four episodes as a prophet, and pharaoh's daughter, referred to as Bityah in later Talmudic literature, as righteous gentile.

The Exodus story of the courage of women, of their collective power, and of their acts of civil disobedience begins with the Hebrew midwives:

> The king of Egypt said to the Hebrew midwives, whose names were Shiphrah and Puah, "When you are helping the Hebrew women during childbirth on the delivery stool, if you see that the baby is a boy, kill him; but if it is a girl, let her live." The midwives, however, feared God and did not do what the king of Egypt had told them to do; they let the

---

[1] Tammi Schneider for the Introduction to Women & Feminism in Troubling Topics, Sacred Texts: Readings in Hebrew Bible, New Testament, Qur'an (forthcoming De Gruyter Press, 2021). For some insight into how that changed for Biblical Studies, see, *Women and the Society of Biblical Literature* (Atlanta: SBL Press, 2019).

[2] Rachel Adler, *Engendering Judaism: An Inclusive Theology and Ethics* (Jerusalem: The Jewish Publication Society, 2998) 86 with quote from Judith Plaskow, "The Right Question is Theological," in *On Being a Jewish Feminist* ed., Susannah Heschel (New York: Schocken, 1983) 227–228. And see Judith Plaskow, *Standing Again at Sinai* (San Francisco: Harper and Row, 1979) 126–7. Joshua Kul and Jason Rogoff, *Reconstructing the Talmud* (New York: Mechon Hadar, 2014) 174.

> boys live. Then the king of Egypt summoned the midwives and asked them, "Why have you done this? Why have you let the boys live?" The midwives answered Pharaoh, "Hebrew women are not like Egyptian women; they are vigorous and give birth before the midwives arrive." So God was kind to the midwives and the people increased and became even more numerous. And because the midwives feared God, he gave them families of their own. Then Pharaoh gave this order to all his people: "Every Hebrew boy that is born you must throw into the Nile, but let every girl live. (Exod 1:15–21)

Demonstrating analogous courage, the midwives Shifra and Puah work a conspiracy to save Jewish children. They defy Pharaoh's order to slay all first born Israelite male babies. An early form of civil disobedience, and notably non-violent, is memorialized in their response to oppression and attempted genocide.

As Lori Lefkovitz notes, women working together rather than alone or limited to a duo is unusual in the biblical stories.[3] Because of the success of their conspiracy, Pharaoh orders all Egyptians to slay the first born, thus ordering the first genocide recorded in the bible. Increasing their civil disobedience, the women also encourage the coupling for the specific purpose of creating children. Midrash haGadol has Miriam join this effort to encourage procreation amongst the Jews, in spite of the dire consequences, to avoid genocide.

> She girds herself with strength, this is Miriam who said to her father when he divorced her mother, "Your decrees are harder than Pharaoh's. He decreed against the boys and you have decreed against the boys and girls. He is evil, and so there is a doubt about whether his decrees will come to be or not. "You will decree, and it will be fulfilled (Job 22:28). Not only that, but I have seen that in the future there will come from you one who saves Israel." Immediately he remarried his wife, and since she gave birth to Moses and had to throw him into the Nile, her mother slapped her [Miriam] across the face and said to her, "Now where is your prophecy?" Immediately "…his sister stationed herself at a distance" (Exod 2:4). She stood by her prophecy.

Miriam is credited with encouraging her parents to couple for the sake of giving birth to another child, even a male child, to defy the Egyptian decree designed to eliminate the Jewish people, crediting her with the birth of

---

[3] Lori Lefkowitz, "Miriam's Leadership: A Reconstruction," *The Women's Passover Companion: Women's Reflections on the Festival of Freedom*, eds. Sharon Cohen Anisfeld, Tara Mohr, and Catherine Spector, Forward by Paula E. Hyman (Woodstock, VT: Jewish Lights Publishing, 2003) 113–119, 114.

Moses. Her parents would never have continued to be intimate without her urging.

Introducing the biblical entrance of Miriam on the stage is the threatened birth of her brother:

> Now a man of the tribe of Levi married a Levite woman, and she became pregnant and gave birth to a son. When she saw that he was a fine child, she hid him for three months. But when she could hide him no longer, she got a papyrus basket[a] for him and coated it with tar and pitch. Then she placed the child in it and put it among the reeds along the bank of the Nile. (Exod 2:1–3)

In Exodus, we meet her as the daughter of Yocheved (Exod 6:20), destined to save her brother.

Miriam first appears in the Bible in Exodus 2:4, as she watches her baby brother float down the Nile River in a pitch-covered basket so he would escape Pharaoh's order to kill all male Jewish infants. "His sister stood at a distance to see what would happen to him" (Exod 2:4). The authority of her prophethood status is established by her presence and deeds even before the birth of Moses. Lefkowitz notes that no other woman in the bible has a childhood.[4] Once the baby is born, the consequences continue to threaten his life.

Miriam boldly approaches Pharaoh's daughter, who found the baby, and offers her own mother—Moses' mother, unbeknownst to the Pharaoh's daughter—as a nurse for Moses. "Then his sister asked Pharaoh's daughter, 'Shall I go and get one of the Hebrew women to nurse the baby for you?'" (Exod 2:7). Miriam saves the baby Moses from certain death. Because of her courage at approaching royalty and suggesting her own mother as nurse, Miriam assures that Moses would be raised as a Jew.

We see another courageous woman in the portrait of Pharaoh's daughter. Rabbinic midrashim equally credit her with righteousness and courage. She stands for the development of allies even within alien contexts. She represents the righteous gentiles willing to risk their lives to save a Jewish child. Pharaoh's daughter is credited with rescuing the infant Moses from the basket of reeds (Exod 2). Rabbinic literature says she converts to Judaism.[5] Her importance is codified in Chronicles where the name Bitya appears in a genealogical list (4:18). From this identification, the rabbinic accounts offer precise biographical details that unite a gentile (Egyptian)

---

[4] Lefkowitz, *ibid.*

[5] Lorena Miralles Maciá, "Judaizing a Gentile Biblical Character through Fictive Biographical Reports: The Case of Bityah, Pharaoh's Daughter, Moses' Mother, according to Rabbinic Interpretations," (Open-Access Publikation im Sinne der CC-Lizenz, V&R unipress GmbH, Göttingen).

woman with the Jewish world, justifying her close relationship with a Hebrew child.

The second time we meet Miriam, named as a prophet, she leads the women in song to celebrate the successful crossing of the Sea of Reeds, dancing with timbrels. As Rabbi Pam Frydman notes, this is the first moment in the Torah when the word "prophet" (*naviim*) is used.[6] Miriam's brief words of exhortation suggest those of Moses and of women today who join together as one, "The only way to get it together is together." Most importantly, Miriam creates a collective identity for the women as a part of the Jewish future.[7] "And Miriam the prophetess, the sister of Aaron, took a timbrel in her hand; and all the women went out after her with timbrels and with dances" (Exod 15:20–21). Miriam and the women commemorate the moment of catastrophe and joy when the oppressors are destroyed, and the victims survive. The moment makes possible a future for these survivors.

The third episode presents a more complicated portrait of this prophet. We meet Miriam when Aaron and she address God, challenging Moses leadership. The two siblings use the marriage of Moses to a Cushite woman as a presumptive reason to denigrate his qualifications as leader (Num 12:2).[8] Addressing God would fit the prophetic tradition and a sign of Miriam's empowerment. When Miriam, not Aaron, is punished with a disease of the skin and isolation for seven days, Moses cries out in Hebrew, "Please God, heal her." (Num 12:13). The people do not travel again until Miriam returns among them (Num 12:15), a sign that she is a powerful, much needed, and beloved prophet.

Miriam's fourth and final appearance is at her death. The Israelites arrived in a body at the wilderness of Zin on the first new moon, and the people stayed at Kadesh. Miriam died there and was buried there. "The community was without water." (Num 20:1–2). Rashu's writes: "From here we derive that all forty years they had the well in Miriam's merit" (Rashi on Numbers 20:2).[9] As Lefkovitz writes, "It seems as if the earth itself was

---

[6] Gratitude to Rabbi Pam Frydman. Rabbi Frydman was founding Rabbi of Or Shalom Jewish Community in San Francisco, President of the Northern California Board of Rabbis and the first woman to serve as President of Ohalah, the international association of Jewish Renewal clergy. She was Director of the Holocaust Education Project at AJRCA, Coordinator of the award winning Beyond Genocide Campaign helping Yazidis and Assyrian Christians facing Genocide in Iraq and founding Co-Chair of the Rabbinic Advisory Board of Shalom Bayit, working to end domestic violence in Jewish homes. Personal Interview, 13 August 2020.

[7] Again, gratitude to Rabbi Frydman. She fondly quotes Rabbi Schachter-Shalomi who declared "The only way to get it together is together."

[8] The Cushite wife is traditionally conflated with Zipporah, an admirable persona in rabbinic literature and credited in biblical literature with saving Moses and their newborn son from God's wrath by insisting that they be circumcised (Exod 4:24).

[9] Rashi, *Rashi on Numbers* (Metsudah Publication, 2009 accessed Sefaria.org on 22 August 2020).

mourning, that Miriam's death had brought drought."[10] Indeed, Midrashic stories suggest her sustaining waters disappeared altogether. The women of Exodus use their courage, agency, and wit for the survival of the Jewish people. They build allies with those who would destroy them. They lead the community of women, forming a powerful collective that will survive in the desert. One midrash asserts that only the men contribute their wealth in the creation of the golden calf, not the women who refused to hand over their valuables and jewelry (Pirkei DeRabbi Eiezer 45). Because of their refusal, the rabbis conclude that only the men would die in the wilderness not the women (*Num. Rabbah* 21:10; *Tanhuma* [ed. Buber], *Pinhas* 7).[11]

Miriam leads the women through the Exodus, nurtures them along the way, and celebrates their victories. Like Miriam, women of the last one-hundred years have asserted more power in the public realm, leading, nurturing, celebrating. They build on the shoulders of previous traditions and the legacy of courageous women. Their individual and collective action exerts powerful impact through social advocacy, scholarship, prayer, and communal leadership, not only upon the Jewish community but on the global stage.

As leaders in the earliest stages of the suffragette movement, Jewish women served at the launch of the movement and throughout its continuing history. Gertrude Weil of North Carolina founded and served as the first president of the Goldsboro Equal Suffrage Association. Genrietta "Netta" Franklin of Britain served as president of the British National Union of Women Suffrage Societies.

As early as mid-nineteenth century, Ernestine Rose, born in a Polish shtetl and arrived in the United States in 1836, fought for an Equal Rights Amendment and women's rights. Into the twentieth century, Betty Friedan (1921–2006) founded the modern feminist movement that emphasized

---

[10] Lefkowitz, 117.

[11] Penina Adelman suggests that Rosh Hodesh, associated by the rabbis as a reward for women's refusal to provide gold for the calf, is in fact a sanitization of women's celebration of the connection between their menstrual cycle and the cycle of the moon. Penina V. Adelman, *Miriam's Well: Rituals for Jewish Women Around the Year*, 2nd ed. (New York: Biblio Press, 1990) 82. See Andrea King, "Is Israel Liberating for Ethiopian Women?" *Lilith*, Winter, 1987–88, No. 18, pp. 8–12 in which King describes the importance of the observance of the tradition of the hut and women's isolation during their menstrual cycle according the Ethiopian tradition. Also see Rabbi Elyse Goldstein, *ReVisions: Seeing Torah Through a Feminist Lens* (Key Porter Books, 1998) 127–128 for one among many expressions by Jewish women rejecting the mikveh and other practices designated to inscribe impurity upon the woman during the menstruation. In fact, Rachel Adler retracked her original judgments of the traditions to align with a rejection as marginalization of women's agency in "In Your Blood, Live: Re-visions of a Theology of Purity," in *Lifecycles 2: Jewish Women on Biblical Themes in Contemporary Life*, ed. Debra Orenstein and Jane Rachel Litman, Jewish Lights, 1997.

career oriented independence for women and Bella Abzug (1920–1998) crusaded for women's legal, economic, and human rights.[12]

Women continue to advocate for women's safety and empowerment. Organizations such as Jewish Women's International[13], Counseling Helpline and Aid Network for Abused Women (CHANA) of Baltimore[14], and Michal Sala Forum of Jerusalem[15] work to support women faced with domestic violence and to foster the ability of women to thrive. As Naomi Graetz reflects upon her seminal work about wife beating in the Talmud, Jewish families are not immune.[16] Space does not allow for the full report of how the rabbis handled wife beating, but, consistently, through the various rabbinic works the topic, wife beating is treated, referenced as a regular occurrence, and censored by payment to the wife (all of whose funds belong to the husband), granting of divorce, or even excommunication of the husband.[17] After all, as Graetz summarizes, women were property. Husbands had the right to any income from her work, to whatever she finds, to interests from her property and possessions, and to inherit her property.[18] Today, Jewish women are amongst the strongest leaders in fighting for women's equal rights and the ability to lead safe and fulfilling lives.

In scholarship and Judaic studies, giants like Judith Plaskow, the first Jewish feminist to identify herself as a theologian, wrote the groundbreaking book, *Standing Again at Sinai: Judaism from a Feminist Perspective* (1979).[19] Susannah Heschel broadened feminist academic and theological discourse with her edited collection *On Being a Jewish Feminist: A Reader* (1983).[20] Rachel Adler refined theological implications of a

---

[12] See *Jewish Women's Archive* for more detailed information on important Jewish women. Jwa.org (accessed 29 August 2020).

[13] See Jewish Women's International, jwi.org (accessed 29 August 2020).

[14] See CHANA, https://www.facebook.com/photo.php?fbid=10160300020618079&set=t.570593078&type=3 (accessed 29 August 2020).

[15] Michal Sala Safe @ Home Action fighting against domestic violence and https://www.michalsela.org.il/ (accessed 31 August 2020). Also see Facebook page Lili Ben Ami, https://www.facebook.com/lilisela.

[16] Naomi Graetz, *Silence is Deadly: Judaism Confronts Wifebeating* (Northvale, NJ: Jason Aronson Inc., 1998) traces testimonies of the reality of beating throughout the biblical, Talmudic, medieval, and modern world. See also Carol Goodman Kaufman, *Sins of Omission: The Jewish Community's Reaction to Domestic Violence; What Needs to Be Done* (Boulder, CO: Westview Press, 2003). Kaufman quotes Graetz who connects the threatening prophetic, metaphoric language to the unrepentant Israelite nation with wife beating. See 63.

[17] Graetz, *Silence*, 130.

[18] Graetz, *Silence*, 70–75.

[19] Judith Plaskow, *Standing Again at Sinai* (San Francisco: Harper and Row, 1979) 126–127. Joshua Kul and Jason Rogoff, *Reconstructing the Talmud* (New York: Mechon Hadar, 2014).

[20] Susannah Heschel, *Being a Jewish Feminist: A Reader* (Schocken Books, 1983).

theology that embraces women in an equitable fashion with *Engendering Judaism: An Inclusive Theology and Ethics* (1999).[21] All these scholars paved the way for inclusion of women at all scholarly and religious centers of Jewish learning and expression.

The creation of a new language for prayer inclusive of women but more importantly introducing new idioms of expression also developed. Originating in the early medieval period, the earliest in 1648, *Tkhines*, sometimes known as *Tehinot*, are Yiddish prayers for women. They are expressions of personal pleas that are extended to the wider community. In the Jewish tradition, redemption is communal, public, and in this world.[22] In the last twenty years, these prayers have been translated and organized for English readers.[23] Building on this earlier tradition and recognizing the power of women's prayer traditions, Marcia Falk (b. 1946) is credited with launching a contemporary tradition of prayers with fresh imagery designed to enhance spirituality.[24]

Today, for example, prayers for women's life cycle appear in many forms: online, in collections, and in prayerbooks. Here are two examples of prayers showing differing concerns and aspirations that commemorate a woman's first menstrual cycle:

> From this month on, (young woman's name), we invite you to celebrate the New Moon with us as our female ancestors have done for centuries in different ways. We hope this monthly meeting will remind you that your period is a sacred time of contemplation and rejuvenation. We

---

[21] Rachel Adler, *Engendering Judaism: An Inclusive Theology and Ethics* (Beacon Press, 1999).

[22] Especially in the late medieval and early modern period, Yiddish was thought to be the woman's language. Yiddish served as the vernacular for daily life. See Weissler, Chava. For Women and for Men Who Are like Women: The Construction of Gender in Yiddish Devotional Literature, *Journal of Feminist Studies in Religion*, vol. 5, no. 2, 1989, pp. 7–24. Also, Weissler Voices of the Matriarchs: Listening to the Prayers of Early Modern Jewish Women. (Boston: Beacon Press, 1998; paperback edition, 1999).

[23] Devra Kav (Philadelphia: The Jewish Publication Society, 2004). See also *A Book of jewish Women's Prayers: Translations from the Yiddish*, selected and with commentary by Norman Tarnor (Northvale, NJ: Jason Aronson Inc., 1995). And Chava Weissler, *Voices of the Matriarchs: Listening to the Prayers of Early Modern Jewish Women* (Boston, MA: Beacon Press, 1998). Ritualwell: Tradition & Innovation provides suggestions for contemporary women to explore their own spirituality as they share in their collective spirituality with other women and men and women. See ritualwell.org/lifecycles (website).

[24] Marcia Falk, *The Book of Blessings* (New York: CCAR Press, 1996 and reprinted 2017). Online, *Ritualwell: Tradition & Innovation* offers prayers in creative ways to bring women together in their spirituality and in celebration. https://www.ritualwell.org/ritual/new-rituals-onset-menstruation.

hope that you as you move within the rhythms of Rosh Hodesh, you will resist the negativity with which society regards your monthly blood and your womanhood.[25]

And

Prayer for a First Period

Blessed are You, Lord, for having made me a woman
For having created my body with wisdom
Such that each organ knows its time
And You gather my organs together
Bringing maturity and fertility to ripeness within me.
Now I am a complete woman
Recognizing all the wisdom of creation.
You have graciously granted me your blessed gift;
You have included me among all the women of Israel
And here I am before you
Full of Joy and thanks.[26]

In addition to prayer, a series of events can also commemorate the start of menstruation. The online website, *Ritualwell* offers suggestions of a special mother-daughter celebrations as well as events including dancing, planting a tree, a meal, singing, and sharing stories together.[27]

Women have launched not only prayers about a woman's life cycle but their relational experiences as well. Penina V. Adelman has developed rituals to commemorate the year round as well as the full life cycle experiences of women in their individual, relationship, and communal lives and aspirations including love making, birthing, and menopause.[28] And a diversity of prayers and rituals relevant to many human experiences has been developed by women.

Perhaps the most familiar is that introduced by Professor Susannah Heschel. Heschel introduced a tangerine or orange onto the seder plate to draw attention to persistent cruelty of homophobia. Each member of the seder would take a section of the orange, enjoy its flavor, and spit out the

---

[25] Adelman, *Miriam's Well*, 82.
[26] Ruth Lazare, "Prayer for a First Period," in *A Jewish Woman's Prayer Book*, ed. Aliza Lavie (New York: Spiegel & Grau, 2008) 50.
[27] "New Rituals for the Onset of Menstruation "*Ritual Well: Tradition and Innovation in Jewish Learning,* ritualwell.org (accessed 16 August 2020).
[28] Adelman, *Miriam's Well*.

seeds as ritualistic rejection of homophobia.[29] Heschel writes "the *matsa* remembers enslavement and celebrates freedom… The orange reminds us how homophobia poisons our lives and the ways homosexuality enriches our community."[30] Yet ironically Heschel herself experienced a transparent micro-aggression. She relates, "My custom was affirmed but my original intention was subverted. My idea—a woman's words—were attributed to a man, and my goal of affirming lesbians and gay men was erased." Heschel's groundbreaking work for social justice as well as her scholarly output both in the United States and around the world does not stop. Joined by many other women in their groundbreaking work, Heschel serves as a role model to all scholars.

The collective action of women continues not only in social advocacy, scholarship, creation of prayers, and gathering for celebrations, but also, like Miriam, women are taking leadership roles in Jewish congregational life. In the last one hundred years and now regularly in the last fifty years, a relatively recent phenomenon in the development of an ancient religion, Jewish denominational authorities have ordained women regularly as leaders in their congregational worship and communal life. We can see the legacy in women such as Judith Eisenstein, who was the first to become a bat mitzvah in 1922, and in the first women ordained as rabbis in various denominations: Regina Jonas (in 1935), Sally Priesand (Hebrew Union College—Jewish Institute of Religion in 1973), Sandy Sasso (Reconstructionist Rabbinical College in 1974), and Amy Eilberg (Jewish Theological Seminary in 1985).

In writing as a faculty member of the Jewish Theological Seminary in 1984, Joel Roth joined other faculty members in support of the decision of JTS to ordain women for the rabbinate "constituted a watershed in American Jewish history. Under the leadership of then-Chancellor Gerson D. Cohen, the protracted process of decision-making at the Seminary was the first time that the halakhic [laws derived from the written and oral Torah] case in favor of such an action was aired publicly." Roth himself has served as the chair of the assembly's Committee on Jewish Law and Standards. His justification for the ordination of women is testament to the changing reality of women in the Jewish public realm. Here he expounds on the appropriateness of ordination by dismissing the rabbinic judgments of prohibition as follows:

> I shall spend no time justifying my opinion that the rabbinic image of women is the sole justification for observance of the present halakhic norms regarding testimony by women, nor defending my view that the

---

[29] Susannah Heschel, "Orange on the Seder Plate," *The Women's Passover Companion: Women's Reflections on the Festival of Freedom* (Woodstock, VT: Jewish Lights Publishing, 2003) 70–78, 75.

[30] Heschel, "Orange," 77.

modern image of woman does not justify the norms, nor proving that the change in that image is desirable. The preceding analysis regarding the justification for prohibiting women from acting as witnesses, I believe, validates my opinion that it is the rabbinic image of the nature of women which is the sole justification for the prohibition. I consider the opinion that the modern image of women does not justify the prohibition, and that this change from the rabbinic image of women is desirable, to be self-evident.[31]

Today all the major Jewish movements ordain women including the orthodox movement whose women rabbis, however, cannot serve as pulpit rabbis. The living testimony of these women rabbis that follows expresses their aspirations, their concerns, their vision, and their wisdom.

Rabbi Laura Geller, ordained in 1976, writes about her experience as a rabbinical student, "One day when I sat in a class in my Rabbinical seminary...we studied the tradition of *berakhot* blessings, blessings of enjoyment, blessings relating to the performance of mizvot (commandments) and blessings of praise and thanksgiving. My teacher explained: 'There is no important moment in the lifetime of a Jew for which there is no blessing.' Suddenly I realized that it was not true. There had been important moments in my life for which there was no blessing. One such moment was when I got...first got my period."[32] Today, thanks to the creativity, dedication, and contributions of women, this blessing and many others enrich the women's lives throughout not only their own life cycles but the diversity of others.

Rabbi Cathy Felix was among the first generation of women rabbis when a substantial number of students at Hebrew Union College were women. Suggesting the collective power of women in the anecdote of Miriam celebrating with the women at the sea, Rabbi Felix, in our interview, declared that, with so many women in rabbinic school, "We asserted our importance as we believed our presence meant...one small step for women, a giant step for womankind." She opined that, while in midrash and Talmud, women were treated "Other," women today benefit from a far more inclusive experience. She retells a recent story of a conservative rabbi in Israel. One Saturday seven men and seven women appeared for minyan. Tradition says only men would qualify to fulfill the directive to have a minyan of ten. The rabbi opined aloud, "I could not look the women in the eye and say they cannot make a minyan." Women are in the process of becoming equal in Judaism, Felix reports.[33]

---

[31] Roth, "Ordination," 156.

[32] Rachel Adler, *Engendering Judaism: An Inclusive Theology and Ethics* (Philadelphia, PA: the Jewish Publication Society, 1998) 61.

[33] Rabbi Cathy Felix currently serving as rabbi at the Reform Temple Beth Am of Bayonne, New Jersey. Personal interview, 12 August 2020.

Yet, while women may receive kippot and tallit at their Bat Mitzvahs, Rabbi Felix wonders if women wear these gifts in synagogue or temple. While women pursue Jewish education and communal leadership, are they active leaders in religious spaces? She encourages women to meet their potential. She dreams of a time when there will be no gender roadblocks for women to enjoy all the privileges and responsibilities that Judaism offers. Anecdotally but perhaps also ironically, while Rabbi Yocheved Mintz sees women taking on more leadership roles in synagogue, she is concerned with a trend of men abdicating participation.[34]

Echoing the aspirations of all the women rabbis reached for this chapter, Rabbi Marcia Prager seeks a more spiritual connection with Judaism for all parishioners. Her belief in the art of prayer, or davvenology, has led her to inspire and train others. She insists, like the hundreds of others who have followed the course of davvenology, that prayer, including Jewish prayer, can be transformative. She describes "the use of music and davvenen as the carrier wave for the inner meaning of the text. Engage people with soul-expanding experiences, link generations past and generations yet-to-be in a united trajectory of self, family, community, and world healing. Engender hope and commitment." And her hopes for a seder are to follow the "flow of the classic structure—its simplicity, psycho-spiritually compelling language with the leader's guide to diverse resources and questions to share, links to traditional and contemporary music that can be learned. A Haggadah is a script for an experience."[35]

Rabbi Ariella Graetz-Bartuv in Israel sees a "big change in the role of being a rabbi." On the one hand, her identity as a woman rabbi perplexes many, but, on the other hand, others who know her have a strong affinity to a rabbi who is not a distant persona but accessible and with whom they can make a connection.[36]

---

[34] Rabbi Yocheved Mintz is Rabbi *Emerita* of Congregation P'nai Tikvah in Las Vegas, NV. She was President of OHALAH from 2008–2012, the first female rabbi to be President of the Board of Rabbis of Southern Nevada (20112013), and the first female rabbi in 18 generations of rabbis on my paternal side. Personal email, 18 August 2020.

[35] Rabbi Marcia Prager is a Reconstructionist ordained rabbi and a Jewish Renewal teacher, storyteller and artist. She is the Director and Dean of the Aleph Ordination Programs for ALEPH: Alliance for Jewish Renewal, and rabbi for the P'nai Or Jewish Renewal community of Philadelphia PA. Also, Rabbi Marcia Prager offers *the Path of Blessing: Experiencing the Energy and Abundance of the Divine* (New York: Jewish Lights, 1998). is a leading educator and practitioner in bringing a psychospiritual experience to the act of prayer for her students, audiences, and congregants. Personal email, 6 August 2020.

[36] Rabbi Ariella Graetz-Bartuv, is the rabbi of Emmet VeShalom Reform Congregation in Nahariya, West Galilee, Israel where she advocates for Movement for Progressive Judaism (IMPJ) and is the spiritual advisor for schools in northern Israel. Personal email, 10 August 2020.

Rabbi Cheryl Peretz cautions against complacent optimism.[37] She recalls the rabbinic story of Yalta, emblematic of the frustration of marginalized women through the millennia. The episode expresses the frustration of Jewish women facing sometimes opaque sometimes transparent denigration. In this talmudic anecdote, an important visitor to Rabbi Nahman does not offer the Yalta, wife of the host, the traditional cup of blessing. He justifies this refusal with byzantine, if scholarly, biblical and talmudic justifications, including a reading arguing that childbirth only comes from the fruits of a man's belly, not a woman's. In her frustration, Yalta destroys 400 jugs of wine, symbolically rebelling not only against the gesture she perceived as a personal insult to her importance and dignity but also against the male co-option of fertility and the rituals of symbolizing it.[38] Rabbis may have been empathetic to her frustration, but the institutionalization of suppressing women's agency is clear and so embedded as to have been unfixable.

Reb Mimi Feigelson, ordained as an orthodox rabbi, reports on her aspirations for the future of Judaism and Orthodox women rabbis and scholars. Yet, she expresses a frustration not unlike that expressed by Yalta in the Talmud written centuries ago in responding to an act of micro-aggression, the subtle putting down and slighting of marginalized populations.[39] "In our tradition, learning is the voice of the wisdom of revelation… When I hear an orthodox *rav* in Israel say, 'Women today are learning almost like men,' he thinks it's a compliment and to me it's an insult. Everything about that statement is an insult. Women are learning and there are multiple ways to learn Torah…[T]he orthodox world is starting baby steps…we are experimenting with a vision of what the future can and will look like."[40] The Yeshivat Maharat in New York ordains women in the orthodox tradition, calling those ordained *maharat*, a Hebrew acronym for "halachic, spiritual, and Torah leader." Currently the Rabbinical Council of American, the main Modern Orthodox rabbinic association, bars its

---

[37] Rabbi Cheryl Peretz, Associate Dean, Ziegler School of Rabbinic Studies, American Jewish University where she was ordained as a Conservative rabbi. Personal interview, 11 August 2020.

[38] Anecdote from Bavli Berakhot 51b qtd in Joshua Kul and Jason Rogoff, *Reconstructing the Talmud* (New York: Mechon Hadar, 2014) 199.

[39] Valdes, Francisco. *Crossroads, Directions and a New Critical Race Theory : And A New Critical Race Theory*, Temple University Press, 2002. 196, For a classic discussion, see Crenshaw, & Crenshaw, Kimberlé (1995). *Critical Race Theory : the key writings that formed the movement. New Press: Distributed by W. W. Norton & Co.*

[40] Reb Mimi Feigelson: Orthodox Women Owning Their Own Voices, *Women's Jewish Archive: Sharing Stories Inspiring Change.* Video interview. Accessed 16 August 2020, https://jwa.org/rabbis/narrators/feigelsonmimi.

members from ordaining or hiring female clergy, regardless of title.[41] Her hope for the future of women in the Orthodox world is clear. Women should be ordained.

Echoing the desire for inclusivity, Rabbi Iris Yaniv of Israel writes that during the Seder, we are supposed to lean to the left while enjoying our four glasses of wine. Yet, according to the Talmud Pesachim 108a, "A woman who is with her husband is not required to recline, but, if she is an important woman, she is required to recline." From a humanist perspective, we need to remember that all of us are important, regardless of our husbands or partners, and that we have the right to decide whether and when we want to recline, lean in, lean back, rest and rise up. Inspirational is the tradition of Sarah whose agency drives many of the decisions made by the patriarch Abraham. As God instructs Abraham, so should we honor these biblical words: "Whatever Sarah says, obey her" (Gen 21:12). And, like the prophetess Miriam, this new generation of women leads the Jewish people in social advocacy and scholarship, song and creativity, and prayer and communal life to a future that includes the full participation of all.

Miriam's legacy at the seder table is memorialized by Miriam's cup of water. There is no set blessing over Miriam's Cup at the seder, but here are two that might be used:

זֹאת כּוֹס מִרְיָם, כּוֹס מַיִם חַיִּים. זֵכֶר לִיצִיאַתמִצְרָיִם.

Zot Kos Miryam, kos mayim chayim. Zeicher l'tzi-at Mitztrayim.

This is the Cup of Miriam, the cup of living waters. Let us remember the Exodus from Egypt. These are the living waters, God's gift to Miriam, which gave new life to Israel as we struggled with ourselves in the wilderness.

---

[41] Josefin Dolsten, 10 years after the founding of the first Orthodox school to train female clergy, what's actually changed? *Jewish Telegraphic Agency,* 17 December 2019. Accessed 16 August 2021.

And

Blessed are You God, Who brings us from the narrows into the wilderness, sustains us with endless possibilities, and enables us to reach a new place.

מרים הנביאה עז בזמרה בידה, מרים תרקד אתנו לתקן את העולם.
במהרה בימנו היא תביאנו אל מי הישועה, אל מי הישועה.

Miriam ha-n'vi'ah oz v'zimrah b'yadah. Miriam tirkod itanu le-ta-ken et ha-olam. Bim-hayrah ve-ya-may-nu hi te-vi-ay-nu, el may ha-ye-shu-ah.

Miriam, dance with us to repair the world.
Soon she will bring us to the waters of redemption.[42]

---

[42] Rabbi Tamar Cohen, "Miriam's Cup: A Modernist Feminine Symbol." *My Jewish Learning* myjewishlearning.com quoting "Miriam's Cup Blessing," 1996 Kol Ishah, PO Box 132, Wayland, Mass. 01778 (accessed 8 November 2020). "Miriam's Cup Blessing" Copyright 1996 (Matia Rania Angelou, Janet Berkenfield, Stephanie Loo). *Kol Ishah,* PO Box 132, Wayland, MA, 01778, quoted in "Miriam's Cup, *Ritualwell: Tradition and Innovation in Jewish Learning,* ritualwell.org (accessed 16 August 2020).

Haggadah, Shoah, and the Exigency of the Holy

David Patterson

As the Passover Haggadah relates the tale of the Israelites' liberation from Egypt, we find a reference to the passage from the Torah that reads: "And the children of Israel sighed from the depths of their bondage, and they cried out, and their cry rose up to God from the depths of their bondage. And God heard their groaning and God remembered Abraham and Isaac and Jacob" (Exodus 2:23–24; my translation). This essay explores ways of reading these lines through the lens of the Shoah and reading the Shoah through the lens of these lines. The essay begins with a consideration of how we are to understand God's hearing, God's memory, and God's response. Then the essay examines a negative parallel to humanity's failure to hear, the world's silence, and the absence of response in the time of the Shoah. Here too, God is perhaps implicated, inasmuch as much of the world that fell silent during the Shoah was the Christian world, the churches that are the Body of Christ. From the faculty of hearing we proceed to the faculty of seeing and the plague of darkness, both in the time of the Passover and the time of the Shoah. The silence of the world, to use Elie Wiesel's imagery, attends the rise of the Kingdom of Night, with a plague of darkness that is the plague of Night. It is a darkness characterized by a blindness to the face: only as we behold the holiness that emanates from the face, it is argued, do we raise a cry that stirs God's memory—and God cries out to arouse our memory. For the exigency of the holy emanates from the face.

Passover is known as the *Zman Cheiruteinu*, the "Season of Our Liberation." Liberation from what? Not from a life of slavery, if slavery means forced labor for next to nothing. No, it is a liberation from Egypt, a land of darkness, in which no man could see the face of his brother, as it came to pass with the Ninth Plague (see Exodus 10:23). It is a liberation from meaninglessness, for the Season of Our Liberation finds it culmination in the Revelation at Mount Sinai. That is why we count the sacrificial offering of the omer, in a counting of the forty-nine days from Passover to the giving of the Torah, which came on the fiftieth day, on the

6th of Sivan. On that day the Israelites were gathered *betachtit hahar*, literally "beneath the mountain," and not precisely "at the foot of the mountain," as the phrase is usually translated (Exodus 19:17).

How are we to understand this gathering *beneath* the mountain? The sages of the Talmud explain that God held the mountain over the Jews and warned them that they would be buried beneath the weight of the mountain of strict materialism if they did not accept the Covenant of Torah (*Shabbat* 88a; *Avodah Zarah* 2b). The point, however, is not that God threatened the Jews, saying, "Accept the Torah, or else I'll crush you." No, it is that without the Torah, humanity is buried under the might of a merely material world, lost in a hopeless struggle that no one can win, where power is the only reality and weakness the only sin. "Materialism," Emmanuel Levinas elaborates, "does not lie in the discovery of the primordial function of the sensibility, but in the primacy of the Neuter."[1] The weight of the material mountain is the weight of indifferent Being, of the meaningless, of the crushing emptiness, that is merely "there" and that provokes only horror, what Levinas calls "the horror of the 'there is.'"[2] Telling the tale of our liberation at the Passover table, we remember and observe our liberation from the horror of meaninglessness. Indeed, we do more than just remember.

"In each generation," Rabban Gamliel teaches in the Mishnah, "a man is obligated to regard himself as if he came forth out of Egypt, as it is written: 'And you shall tell your son on that day, saying, "It is because of that which the Lord did for me when I came forth out of Egypt"' (Exodus 13:8)" (*Pesachim* 10:5). As we sit at the table and read the Haggadah, we are to view ourselves as if we have emerged *this night* from the bondage of the darkness and meaninglessness of Egypt, from the land whose king boasts, "HaShem? Who is that? I know of no HaShem" (see Exodus 5:2). The Haggadah, of course, relates this teaching from the Mishnah.[3] How can each of us be redeemed as the Israelites of the Exodus were redeemed? Through telling the tale and through the remembrance of their Exodus, says Rabbi Yeruchem Levovitz in the *Chever Maamarim*.[4]

According to Jewish tradition, the Mishnah and its teachings are part of the Oral Torah that, along with the Written Torah, was revealed at Mount Sinai. As the Haggadah incorporates the Torah into its tale, it takes on an aspect of Torah in such a way that we become contemporary with it: just as every Jewish soul was present at the giving of the Torah at Mount

---

[1] Emmanuel Levinas, *Totality and Infinity*, trans. Alphonso Lingis (Pittsburgh: Duquesne University Press, 1969), 298.

[2] Emmanuel Levinas, *Existence and Existents*, trans. Alphonso Lingis (The Hague: Martinus Nijhoff, 1978), 61

[3] *The Haggadah*, trans. Rabbi Joseph Elias (Brooklyn: Mesorah Publications, 1977), 147–49.

[4] See ibid., 147.

Sinai, as taught in the Talmud (*Shabbat* 146a; *Shavuot* 39a), so every Jew is contemporary with the tale told in the Haggadah. *This night* it is as if we emerge from the bondage, from the horror, that would consume our soul.

In his comments on the Haggadah Elie Wiesel underscores this *as if*: "Though I have not personally taken part in these events, I must live 'as if' I had. This lesson is especially relevant for those of our contemporaries who declare that all of us 'are survivors of the Holocaust.' No, all of us are not. Only those who went through the agony of Night survived that Night. Only those who knew death in Auschwitz survived Auschwitz. But all of us should think and act 'as if' we had all been there."[5] Thus, we remember some nights in some seasons when our liberation did not happen.

On the eve of Passover 5703 (1943), for example, Avraham Tory, a member of the Kovno Ghetto Jewish Council, wrote in his diary, "We believe in the Exodus taking place for each generation. The more we are being enslaved, the greater is our faith. *Am Israel Hai*"[6]—the people of Israel live! But not this time. As Tory penned these lines in Kovno, the Jews of Warsaw were about to observe Passover as they had never done before: it was the night of the Warsaw Ghetto Uprising. On the night of the first Passover the Jews were delivered from the one whom the Torah calls the *mashchit*, the "destroyer" (Exodus 12:23). On the night of Pesach 5703, however, the "destroyer" was not sent from God but was rather the Nazi angel of slaughter. And so, the Jews were not delivered.

In the case of Michael Zylberberg this reversal only heightened his need to reconnect with the Jewish community during the season of liberation, as liberation can be found only in the midst of the community. Even though he had found some safety outside the walls of the Warsaw Ghetto, Zylberberg relates, "the Passover festival was drawing closer and this, also, made me want to return to the ghetto."[7] While he managed to get inside the ghetto for a few days before Passover, he was forced to observe the holy day in isolation: "I went out into the forest and heard the reverberations of the distant gunfire. Sleep was impossible; this was to be a night of wakefulness—a *Lail Shimurim* [Exodus 12:42]. I was to hold my own vigil and service, alone, living through their experience on this night of 'blood, fire and pillars of smoke' [Joel 3:3].[8] These words, from the *Haggadah*, had acquired new meaning."[9] In his endeavor to recover a

---

[5] Elie Wiesel, *A Passover Haggadah* (New York: Simon & Schuster, 1993), 69.

[6] Avraham Tory, *Surviving the Holocaust: The Kovno Ghetto Diary*, trans. Jerzy Michalowicz, ed. Martin Gilbert (Cambridge, Mass.: Harvard University Press, 1990), 302.

[7] Michael Zylberberg, *A Warsaw Diary* (London: Valentine, Mitchell & Co., 1969), 94.

[8] *The Haggadah*, 127.

[9] Zylberberg, *A Warsaw Diary*, 95.

remnant of life and meaning Zylberberg retrieves a few words from the Haggadah that have sustained the community of Israel, words that on this night had acquired a new meaning.

Indeed, when read through the lens of the Shoah, the Haggadah acquires new meaning, as does the Shoah when read through the lens of the Haggadah. The summons to consider ourselves somehow contemporary with the events of Passovers observed by the Jewish people over the millennia acquires new meaning. The demands of the Holy One acquire new meaning. The Torah itself, both Written and Oral, acquires new meaning. Let us now consider how that might be the case.

The Memory of God

In the Haggadah's tale of the Israelites' liberation from Egypt, we find a reference to the passage from the Torah that reads: "And the children of Israel sighed from the depths of their bondage, and they cried out, and their cry rose up to God from the depths of their bondage. And God heard their groaning and God remembered His Covenant with Abraham and Isaac and Jacob" (Exodus 2:23–24).[10]

The Breslov Haggadah offers a comment from the Rebbe Nachman of Breslov: "The sigh of a Jewish heart is very dear to God, even if it be muffled and inaudible. Through it we breathe life into the world. We bring to life the things which we are lacking (*Likutei Moharan* I, 8:1)."[11] In this case, it seems, the children of Israel brought to life the memory of God. Just a few verses later God reiterates His affirmation—His confession—and drives home the point that the sighs and groans of the Israelites have stirred His memory: "I have indeed seen the affliction of My people in Egypt, and I have heard their outcry before their taskmasters, for I know their suffering....And now, behold, the outcry of the children of Israel has come unto Me, and I have seen the oppression with which Egypt has oppressed them" (Exodus 3:7, 9).[12] More than having heard the Israelites, says *The Breslov Haggadah*, "God *saw* the Jewish people. They had entered the Divine Heart. God *knew* what to do."[13] Was this the knowledge that somehow returned to God's memory?

Because the Infinite One has an infinite love for His people, His people found their way into His heart, where He, too, groans over the groaning of His beloved, as the prophet Isaiah reminds us: "In all their affliction He, too, was afflicted, and the angel of His presence saved them;

---

[10] *The Haggadah*, 115–17; translations of the Hebrew Bible are my own.

[11] *The Breslov Haggadah*, trans. Chaim Kramer, ed. Moshe Mykoff (Jerusalem: Breslov Research Institute, 1989), 69.

[12] *The Haggadah*, 119.

[13] *The Breslov Haggadah*, 70.

through His love and His compassion He redeemed them" (Isaiah 63:9). In this groaning lies His memory and His suffering. This is the meaning of "I know their suffering," for the root of "know," *daat*, means to "join together with." At first God, *Elokim*, the Creator whose act of creation was a movement into a covenant, hears and remembers the Covenant. Without this immemorial movement into a covenantal relation, there would be no hearing on the part of God: it is the covenant that imparts to God a sense of hearing. And, of course, without the Covenant there would be no revelation to consummate the liberation from Egypt.

The Midrash tells us that the ministering angels tried to talk the Creator out of bringing heaven and earth and especially humanity into being (*Bereshit Rabbah* 8:5). Why? Because they knew it would hurt Him: the Infinite One is infinite in His capacity for love and therefore infinite in His capacity for suffering. Therefore, when read that God's spirit "hovered over the waters" (Genesis 1:2), we recall that the word *merachefet*, here translated as "hovered," can also mean "hesitated." He hesitated because He knew a time would come when His children would inflict horrific suffering upon His beloved Jewish people precisely in an effort to murder Him.

"God knew their suffering…" Rabbi Kalonymos Kalmish Shapira, the Rebbe of the Warsaw Ghetto, draws this teaching into the time of the Shoah, as if he were indeed contemporary with the time of the first Pesach. Writing from the depths of the Warsaw Ghetto, he insists, "A Jew, tortured in his suffering, may think he is the only one in pain, as though his personal pain and the pain of all other Jews has no effect above, God forbid. But… we learn in the Talmud (*Chagigah* 15b; *Sanhedrin* 46a) in the name of R. Emir, … God, as it were, suffers with a Jew much more than that person himself feels it."[14] Whereas R. Yose "heard a Divine Voice like the cooing of a dove," the Rebbe goes on to say, we know from Jeremiah 25:30 that "God roars, howling over His city."[15] And His Holy City is His Shekhinah, which, in mystical terms, is the body of Israel. When does God roar? When He remembers Abraham, Isaac, and Jacob. How does God howl? Through the cry of His people, through the screams of "Mama" that reverberate throughout the camps and ghettos and shatter the souls of the Jews, through screams that threaten to undermine the very fabric of creation.

This insight into the extremity of God's suffering comes from a man whose own suffering is extreme, a man who himself roars and screams, but like a Chasid: silently.[16] Devoted to Jews and Judaism, Rabbi Shapira

---

[14] Kalonymos Kalmish Shapira, *Sacred Fire: Torah from the Years of Fury 1939–1942*, trans. J. Hershy Worch, ed. Deborah Miller (Northvale, NJ: Jason Aronson, 2000), 286–87.

[15] Ibid.

[16] Cf. Elie Wiesel, *Souls on Fire: Portraits and Legends of Hasidic Masters*, trans. Marion Wiesel (New York: Vintage Books, 1973), 235.

maintains that "possibly because God is infinite—and hence unknowable in the world—His pain at the suffering of the Jewish people is also infinite... . And so, the world continues to exist steadfast, it is not obliterated by God's pain and His voice at the suffering of His people and the destruction of His house, because God's pain never enters into the world."[17] It does not enter, Rabbi Shapira concludes, because God retreats to a place of concealment to weep.

The Talmud, in fact, speaks of a special place where He goes to weep when His suffering is too much for even Him to bear: the place is "called *Mistarim* [meaning 'concealment'], in the inner chambers" (*Chagigah* 5b).[18] For there are times when God's pain cannot enter the world without destroying it. During the days of the Shoah God did not bring His people forth "with a mighty hand and an outstretched arm" (Deuteronomy 5:15), as the Haggadah affirms He did in the days of Moses, where "a mighty hand," it says, refers to pestilence, and "an outstretched arm" refers to the sword.[19]

The Haggadah relates God's insistence that He Himself, and not an angel or a seraph, will strike the firstborn of the Land of Egypt (cf. Exodus 12:12).[20] "Why does God boast of killing innocent children," Wiesel asks, "be they Egyptian? Why does He mention it so often? Is He proud of it? One may study Midrashic and Talmudic sources in search of an explanation. In vain. And yet there must be one. Is He teaching us an essential lesson? That He alone may kill? That no one has the right to imitate Him?"[21] To imitate Him, to usurp Him, to appropriate His memory, requires killing innocent children. It is written that we are to read the Ten Utterances revealed at Mount Sinai not from top to bottom but across the tablets, from right to left (in Hebrew): the first utterance, "I am God," means "Thou shalt not murder" (see, for example, *Mekilta Bachodesh* 8; *Pesikta Rabbati* 21:19; *Zohar* I, 90a), so that "whoever sheds human blood renounces the Likeness," as it is written in the Tosefta (*Tosefta Yevamot* 8:4), the "Likeness" not only within one's own soul but also within the soul of the other. And so, it came to pass.

The Likeness of God, moreover, is manifest in our memory of God. When God, *Elokim*, the Creator of heaven and earth, hears the sighs and the groans of His children, it is as though He had awakened from some sort of sleep. And yet, we are taught, He neither sleeps nor slumbers (Psalms 121:4). Not only does He hear, but He hears and *remembers* (Exodus 2:24),

---

[17] Shapira, *Sacred Fire*, 287–88.

[18] According to the Midrash, this hiding place is the realm of darkness, from which God drew the plague of darkness, the darkness in which "a man could not see his brother" (Exodus 10:23); that is the darkness that makes God weep (see *Midrash Tehillim* 1:18:16).

[19] *The Haggadah*, 123.

[20] Ibid., 121.

[21] Wiesel, *A Passover Haggadah*, 51.

as though He might have forgotten. As the Covenant imparts the faculty of hearing, so it imparts the faculty of remembrance. Can God forget? Perhaps. He forgets when we forget. Or better: He remembers what we forget. If God can forget, the Nazis need not have undertaken their war against memory, as Elie Wiesel and Primo Levi described the Shoah,[22] which was central to their war against the God of Abraham, Isaac, and Jacob.

The Koretzer Rebbe, a disciple of the Baal Shem Tov, once said, "God and Prayer are One. God and Torah are one. God, Israel and Torah are one."[23] Just so, the Yiddish author and Holocaust diarist Yitzhak Katznelson insists, "The God of Israel and the people of Israel are one."[24] And in his diary from the Vilna Ghetto Zelig Kalmanovitch writes, "A war is being waged against the Jew. But this war is not merely directed against one link in the triad [of Israel, God, and Torah] but against the entire one: against the Torah and God, against the moral law and Creator of the universe."[25] In these diaries written from the depths of the Event, we discover that the diarists were all too aware of the profound metaphysical implications that distinguish the Event as a *novum* in the history of humanity and divinity. It was, indeed, a war against memory, against God's memory of Israel and Israel's memory of God, the very memory that is at the heart of the Haggadah.

"In our prayers on the high holy days," says a rabbi in Elie Wiesel's novel *The Forgotten*, "we beg the Lord to remember the near sacrifice of Isaac. What an idea! We beg God to remember? Can you imagine the God of Abraham an amnesiac? The truth is, we make such requests in the name of memory to prove to Him that we ourselves remember."[26] Yes: God's amnesia stems from our amnesia. Still, it takes the human outcry to awaken God from His forgetfulness—not their prayers but their outcry, their groaning, their screams, for they had run out of words and prayers. But there are times when screams are the most efficacious of prayers.

There was no shortage of screams during the Shoah. "It is a marvel," writes Rabbi Shapira, "how the world exists after so much screaming."[27] Yes, the Jews cried out, and the Jews screamed. The Jews

---

[22] Elie Wiesel, *Evil and Exile*, trans. Jon Rothschild (Notre Dame: University of Notre Dame Press, 1990), 155, and Primo Levi, *The Drowned and the Saved*, trans. Raymond Rosenthal (New York: Vintage Books, 1989), 31.

[23] Quoted in Louis I. Newman, ed., *The Hasidic Anthology* (New York: Schocken Books, 1963), 147.

[24] Yitzhak Katznelson, *Vittel Diary*, trans. Myer Cohn, 2nd Ed. (Tel-Aviv: Hakibbutz Hameuchad, 1972), 122.

[25] Zelig Kalmanovitch, "A Diary of the Nazi Ghetto in Vilna," trans. and ed. Koppel S. Pinson, *YIVO Annual of Jewish Social Studies* 8 (1953): 52.

[26] Elie Wiesel, *The Forgotten*, trans. Marion Wiesel (New York: Summit Books, 1992), 139.

[27] Shapira, *Sacred Fire*, 328.

prayed. But the others? We know the reaction of the others, as it is stated in the original title of Elie Wiesel's memoir *Night*: *Un di velt hot geshvign— And the World Remained Silent*. The silence of the world should have awakened the *Shomer Yisrael*, the "Guardian of Israel," from His slumber. Who, indeed, could sleep through such a deafening silence? And what does God remember when His memory is aroused by the screams of suffering Jews? Not only the Covenant—which He insists that *we* must remember, else the sun will lose its shining (see Joel 2:31) —but also the *names* Abraham, Isaac, and Jacob, the name of the people called Israel, called by the name that God Himself is bound to remember, the name that He bestowed upon His people. The name *Yisrael* means "one who strives with God," and striving with God entails crying out to God.

The Covenant is rooted in names: to hear and to remember is to hear and to remember *names*. How did the Nazis wage their war against the memory of God and humanity? Through the obliteration of names. "They will even take away our name," Primo Levi writes with his usual depth and insight, "and if we want to keep it"—if we want to remember it—"we will have to find ourselves the strength to do so."[28] For the Jews, the struggle to keep their names was a struggle to keep their souls.

In his commentary on the Torah, the sixteenth-century sage Ovadiah Sforno says that *naakatam*, "they groaned" (Exodus 2:24),[29] refers to the prayers of only a few of the Righteous among the Israelites. These were the *tzaddikim*, whose prayers, along with the prayers and the screams of the children whom the Pharaoh had marked for murder (Exodus 1:22), reach the ears of the Holy One. God hears and is aroused from His sleep because the righteous know His Name and cry out to Him, to HaShem, *by Name*. One must yet again wonder: in the time of the Shoah were there too few of the outcries from the Righteous, too few of the screams of "Mama!" to reach His ears? Called the Supernal Mother in the Zohar (*Zohar* I, 22b), "Mama" may well be among the Names of the Holy One. The Midrash tells us that the groaning was the sound of the Israelites strangled by the Egyptian executioners, adding that it was also the sound of the Israelite children being burned alive in the furnaces of Egypt (*Pirke de Rabbi Eliezer* 48): they too screamed, "Mama!" Other flames and furnaces, of course, immediately leap to mind—other screams that rose up from lips untainted by sin, only to meet with a terrifying silence.

God not only remembers the names of His covenantal partners Abraham, Isaac, and Jacob, but He specifically identifies Himself by attaching His Name to the names of His covenantal partners: "I am the *God of Abraham, the God of Isaac, and the God of Jacob* (Exodus 3:6), as if the

---

[28] Primo Levi, *Survival in Auschwitz*, trans. Stuart Woolf (New York: Simon & Schuster, 1996), 27.

[29] *The Haggadah*, 115.

names Abraham, Isaac, and Jacob had reminded Him of His own Name, as if their names were part of His name. Just so, He declares, "When you are My witnesses, I am God" (*Pesikta de-Rab Kahana* 12:6; see also *Sifre* on Deuteronomy 33:5), and we are God's witnesses only as long as we answer, "*Hineni!* Here I am," when we are called by name. Once again we realize that the memory of God is a memory of our names and of His Name, a memory of who we are, the memory that apart from our covenantal relation to the Name, we have neither a memory nor a name, no *yad vashem*. We are God's witnesses when we attach our name to His Name—and He is God when He attaches His Name to the name of Israel in an act of His own remembrance of Israel.

Remembering Israel, He remembers His Covenant. Remembering the Covenant, He remembers His own Name. Apart from the Covenant, God has no Name; only when He enters into the Covenant with His witnesses does He become God and take on His Name. In His *zakhor*, His "remembering," lies a *shamor*, a "watching over" His children: the two words come in a single utterance, as it is written in the Talmud (*Rosh Hashanah* 27a). For God and for humanity, to remember always means to watch over and to care for, else there is no remembrance. In God's example of remembrance and watching over lies a commandment that reverberates in the Commanding Voice of Auschwitz, where the question is not simply: Why did God not hear their groaning and remember His Covenant? No, the question at the core of the Commanding Voice is: Why do *we* not hear and remember, *zakhor veshamor*, remember and watch over—remember and watch over not only our fellow human beings but also Our Father, Our King?

In Exodus 3:9, as cited in the Haggadah,[30] it is not God Elokim the Creator who hears but God HaShem, the bearer of the Ineffable Name, who hears not only the groaning but also the outcry and, hearing the outcry, sees and knows the suffering. When the Israelites cried out to God, calling upon His Name, their cry was a groan of "Where are you?" as when God groaned to Adam, "*Ayeka!?* Where are you!?" It was also a cry of "Why?" as when the Jews of Europe cried out to God—by Name. To be sure, the cry of *Where!?* is a cry of *Why!?*, a cry of *How!?*, a cry of *How could you!?* Emmanuel Levinas points out that the face forbids murder,[31] and so it is with the name: the name and the face are of a piece, just as the Name of God and the divine prohibition against murder are of a piece. Names find their meaning in this prohibition.

"The nakedness of the face," Levinas explains further, "is destituteness. To recognize the Other is to recognize a hunger. To recognize

---

[30] *The Family Haggadah*, 35.

[31] Emmanuel Levinas, *Ethics and Infinity*, trans. Richard A. Cohen (Pittsburgh: Duquesne University Press, 1985), 86.

the Other is to give… to him whom one approaches as 'You' in a dimension of height."[32] God the Creator, who, as the Haggadah reiterates,[33] hears the groaning of the Israelites (Exodus 2:24), is the Creator of the You, who begins Creation with the creation of the heavens, of the dimension of height. Only the You is the bearer of a name; only the bearer of a name suffers the destitution of a hunger that calls out to us by name. Thus we begin the *Maggid* or storytelling in the Haggadah with an invitation to all who are hungry to come and eat.[34] "On Passover eve, the poor, the uprooted, the unhappy were the most sought-after, the most beloved guests," Elie Wiesel comments. "Without comforting our impoverished guest, our riches would shame us. And so we were grateful to him."[35] So we see what is anti- in the anti-world: "the Lager is hunger,"[36] says Primo Levi, a hunger that came with the erasure of the name and the face. And, just as the sick and hungry prisoners abandoned to Auschwitz cried out Levi's name, so did the Israelites call out the Name of God. "I felt like crying," says Levi. "I could have cursed them."[37] Could God have felt the same way?

Recalling that the movement out of Egypt was initiated by God's remembrance of the names and of the Covenant, we realize that presence—the presence of God and the presence of humanity—is tied to remembrance: the One who is *presence* is the One who is *remembrance*. With His remembrance comes the summons—even the outcry—of God Himself, as if He were crying out: "Please come to Me! For if you do not come to Me—if you do not *come back* to Me—Pharaoh will be the god he thinks he is. And the darkness that is *choshekh* will rule." So it came to pass in the time of the Shoah.

The Blindness of Humanity

From the depths of the Warsaw Ghetto Rabbi Shapira cried out not to God but to the Jewish people: "Before Amalek came to fight with you, there were among you servile people who esteemed the very thinking championed by Amalek. You were impressed with the superficial culture in which Amalek takes such pride. As a result, your response to Jewish culture and the wisdom of Torah was chilly. You were sure that Amalek was very cultured, that his philosophy was quite as good as anything. To be sure, it had its

---

[32] Emmanuel Levinas, *Totality and Infinity*, trans. Alphonso Lingis (Pittsburgh: Duquesne University Press, 1969), 75.
[33] *The Haggadah*, 115.
[34] Ibid., 67.
[35] Wiesel, *A Passover Haggadah*, 24.
[36] Levi, *Survival in Auschwitz*, 74.
[37] Ibid., 166.

ethics, and there is profit to be had from it in this world. What did God do? He brought you face to face with Amalek."[38]

Similarly, according to Rashi, only one in five of the Israelites who were enslaved in Egypt went forth from Egypt (Rashi, commentary on Exodus 13:18). Why did some many remain behind? Were they blind to their plight? The true horror of the Egyptian exile, as Adin Steinsaltz explains it, "was that the slaves gradually became more and more like their masters, thinking like them and even dreaming the same dreams. Their greatest sorrow, in fact, was that their masters would not let them fulfill the Egyptian dream."[39] And their greatest wretchedness was that they saw no harm in dreaming the Egyptian dream, a dream of power and possessions, of pleasure and prestige, a nightmare in which more is better but never enough. Their greatest wretchedness lay in the fact that their eyes had grown so used to the Egyptian darkness that they no longer noticed the darkness. What, exactly, is the nature of the Egyptian darkness?

"And there was a thick darkness throughout the land of Egypt for three days. And no man could see his brother" (Exodus 10:22–23). This is the Plague of Darkness invoked in the Haggadah.[40] It is a plague that befell humanity with the inception of the Kingdom of Night, the plague without which there would have been no Kingdom of Night. It was a Night in which every Jew was "ferociously alone," as Primo Levi states it,[41] a Night in which every Jew awoke at every instant "frozen with terror,"[42] an inescapable Night, as survivor Fania Fénelon suggests in her memoir, where writes, "I spend every night there—every night!"[43] Who is our brother, to whom this darkness blinds us? Our brother is our fellow human being, the *ben adam*, the child of Adam. Unable to behold the face of our brother, we are unable to behold the infinite dearness of our fellow human being and the infinite responsibility that devolves upon us with regard to our fellow human being.

The Plague of Darkness is the deadly plague of blindness not only to the soul that emanates from the face of the other but also to our own soul, the other that *is* our own soul, as Levinas has said: "The soul is the other in me."[44] The soul is the Torah in me. The soul is the outcry of the other who invades me and disturbs my sleep, like the barking dogs of Egypt on the night when the Holy One passed through the land and took the Egyptians'

---

[38] Shapira, *Sacred Fire*, 56.

[39] Adin Steinsaltz, *On Being Free* (Northvale, NJ: Jason Aronson, 1995), 22.

[40] *The Haggadah*, 129.

[41] Levi, *Survival in Auschwitz*, 88.

[42] Ibid., 62.

[43] Fania Fénelon, *Playing for Time*, trans. Judith Landry (New York: Atheneum, 1977), ix.

[44] Emmanuel Levinas, *Otherwise than Being or Beyond Essence*, trans. Alphonso Lingis (The Hague: Martinus Nijhoff, 1981), 193.

first born (Exodus 12:12; see *Shemot Rabbah* 31:9).[45] The Plague of Darkness articulates the evil of Egypt, the evil from which the Israelites were delivered: it was not the evil of slave labor but the evil of this blindness to the holiness of the other child of Adam, a blindness to the prohibition against murder revealed at Mount Sinai, the prohibition that came at the height of the Season of Our Liberation, that came with the Revelation of the very dimension of height.

The Ninth Plague was repeated in the blindness that came with the darkness that descended upon humanity with the advent of modernity and that culminated in the Third Reich. If modernity is characterized by a process of thinking God out of the picture, it is also marked by an increasing darkness that blinds us to the face of the other human being. Blind to the face, we grow deaf to the demand, to what Levinas calls "the exigency of the holy" revealed in the face of the other human being.[46]

At what hour in the morning, according to Jewish law, shall a Jew put on his *tefillin*, the leather straps around the arm and the head donned for prayer? When it is light enough for him to recognize the face of his neighbor (*Kitzur Shulchan Arukh* 10:2). Putting on *tefillin*, we affirm that there is no Torah without the face, no face without Torah, no higher relation without the human relation. Putting on *tefillin*, then, is no mere ritual; far more than that, it is, in the words of Levinas, the confirmation of "the conception of God in which He is welcomed in the face-to-face with the other, in the obligation towards the other."[47] Indeed, Levinas takes this welcome, this greeting, to constitute the very meaning of Judaism.[48] Therefore, before Jews pray each morning, many of them affirm, "I take upon myself the commandment to love your neighbor as yourself." Did they say this prayer in Auschwitz, in the midst of another darkness in which no man could see his brother?

And so we realize that at the core of the silence of the world invoked by Elie Wiesel's *Un di velt hot geshvign* is the blindness of humanity, the blindness of the Plague of Darkness. Here, too, humanity is contemporary with the tale of the first Passover related in the Haggadah—contemporary not only with the deliverance from Egypt but also with the Ninth Plague that swept over Egypt. In the time of the Shoah, was God, too, stricken with this blindness? In a Midrash on Exodus 15:11, where it is written, "*Mi k'mokhah b'elim?*, Who is Like You among the mighty?" we have "*Mi k'mokhah b'ilemim?*, Who is like You among the mute?" That is, how long will you stand by silently while Your children suffer? (*Mekilta*

---

[45] *The Haggadah*, 129.

[46] Levinas, *Ethics and Infinity*, 105.

[47] Emmanuel Levinas, "Revelation in the Jewish Tradition," trans. Sarah Richmond, in Sean Hand, ed., *The Levinas Reader* (Oxford: Basil Blackwell, 1989), 204.

[48] Emmanuel Levinas, *Difficult Freedom: Essays on Judaism*, trans. Sean Hand (Baltimore: Johns Hopkins University Press, 1990), 173.

Shirata 8). Wiesel reminds us that "'God is the shadow of man' was commented upon by the Baal Shem as follows: just as a shadow follows the gestures and motions of the body, God follows those of the soul. If man is charitable, God will be charitable too. The name of man's secret is God, and the name of God's secret is none other than the one initiated by man: love... Who loves, loves God."[49] The blindness of humanity, then, is the blindness of divinity.

This exchange between Eliezer and his father upon their arrival in Birkenau, from Elie Wiesel's *Night*, comes to mind:

> I told him [his father] that I could not believe that human beings were being burned in our times; the world would never tolerate such crimes......
>
> "The world? The world is not interested in us. Today, everything is possible, even the crematoria..." His voice broke.
>
> "Father," I said. "If that is true, then I don't want to wait. I'll run into the electrified barbed wire. That would be easier than the slow death in the flames."
>
> He didn't answer. He was weeping. His body was shaking. Everyone around us was weeping.[50]

The same question concerning a deaf and blind humanity plagued the Jews in the ghettos, during a time of another enslavement. Emmanuel Ringelblum wrote in his diary: "Does the world know about our suffering? And if it knows, *why is it silent?* Why is the world not stirred when tens of thousands of Jews are shot in Fonari [more commonly known as Ponary]? Why is the world silent when tens of thousands of Jews are poisoned in Chelmno? Why is the world silent when hundreds of thousands of Jews are massacred in Galicia and other newly occupied areas?"[51] This entry is dated 27 June 1942, by which time the leaders of the world knew what was transpiring in Europe: in May 1942 the Jewish Labor Bund sent a report to London estimating that over 350,000 Jews had been slaughtered and that the Nazis intended to exterminate all the Jews of Europe.[52]

---

[49] Wiesel, *Souls on Fire*, 31.

[50] Elie Wiesel, *Night*, trans. Marion Wiesel (New York: Hill & Wang, 2006), 33.

[51] Emmanuel Ringelblum, *Notes from the Warsaw Ghetto*, trans. and ed. Jacob Sloan (New York: Schocken Books, 1974), 296.

[52] Lucy Dawidowicz, *The War against the Jews: 1933–1945* (New York: Bantam Books, 1986), 128.

Nearly two years earlier, in an entry from Warsaw Ghetto diary dated 10 October 1940, Chaim Kaplan anticipated this silence: "The naive among the Jews and Poles ask: Can the world sit silent?"[53] A year after Ringelblum's entry—a year after the massive deportation of the Jews from Warsaw to Treblinka—Yitzhak Katznelson continued to raise the cry on 21 July 1943: "With us they were free to do exactly as their heart (a German heart!) desired because no onlooker would open his mouth, would utter a word, or would ask—'Murderer, what is this you are doing? Why this slaughter of a whole nation?'"[54] And two and a half months later he repeats, "Whilst we were the victims of genocide at the hands of these brute beasts of the nether world, the nations of the world kept silent."[55] Thus, millennia after the Ninth Plague swept through Egypt, humanity in its blindness remains contemporary with it.

What is the remedy for this blindness? What can overcome this darkness? We have a clue in the Haggadah's invocation of the Torah: "God remembered" (Exodus 2:24).[56] And so we have these lines from Elie Wiesel: "Let Him remember—for He alone can make us remember."[57] The light that belongs to memory is the light invoked in the Scripture: "The commandment is the candle and the Torah the light" (Proverbs 6:23). This is the light that overcomes the Plague of Darkness and that draws us out of our blindness. Inasmuch as the movement into freedom is a movement from the exile of Egypt to the Revelation at Mount Sinai, the movement into freedom is a movement into the commandment, into the *mitzvah*, the root of which is *tzavta*, which means "connection." Connection to what? To the commanding Voice that reverberates in the human outcry and shines in the human face, where the exigency of the holy reveals itself. Thus, we discover a link between the Haggadah and the Shoah.

Just one more thing: If the memory of God is our memory of Him and His memory of us, and if God is the shadow of man, then the "Our" in the Season of Our Liberation refers both to God and to humanity: if Israel is liberated from the narrow confines of *Mitzraim* (the Hebrew word for "Egypt," which means "narrowness"), God is liberated from the narrow confines of *Mistarim*. At Mount Sinai the two come together, God and Israel, as bride and groom, where, says the Midrash, a wedding ceremony was performed, with the two tablets signifying bride and groom—each bringing about the liberation of the other (*Shemot Rabbah* 41:6; *Tanchuma*,

---

[53] Chaim A. Kaplan, *Scroll of Agony: The Warsaw Diary of Chaim A. Kaplan*, trans. and ed. Abraham I. Katsh (New York: Collier, 1973), 213.

[54] Katznelson, *Vittel Diary*, 50–51.

[55] Ibid., 204.

[56] *The Haggadah*, 115–17; translations of the Hebrew Bible are my own.

[57] Elie Wiesel, *Against Silence: The Voice and Vision of Elie Wiesel*, Vol. 1, ed. Irving Abrahamson (New York: Holocaust Library, 1985), 114.

Ki Tisa 16). For both the bride and the groom the movement into freedom is a movement of remembrance, as a teaching from the Baal Shem Tov suggests: "Oblivion is at the root of exile the way memory is at the root of redemption,"[58] where oblivion lies not only in the absence of memory but also in the absence of light. And where does memory overcome blindness? Where does the movement from exile to redemption occur? In telling the tale of redemption: in the Haggadah.

---

[58] Wiesel, *Souls on Fire*, 227.

Passover, Holy Thursday, and Catholic Liturgy

Eugene Fisher

Catholic liturgy is rooted in Jewish liturgical practices. This can be seen most clearly in the Last Supper, which was a Passover seder celebrated by Jesus and his closest followers. Central to the seder is the consumption of unleavened bread, which evokes the food the Jews brought with them when they fled Egypt for the Promised Land, and wine, which evokes the blood swiped on their doors so that the Angel of Death would pass over their homes and save them from death. Central to Catholic liturgy is the Eucharist, unleavened bread and wine, representing for us the body and blood of Jesus, our Savior who enables us to pass over from sin into new life with the One God, the God of Israel. One can see this especially during Holy Week, which leads up to Easter, which celebrates the resurrection of Jesus, his passing over from death to life.

The Liturgical Cycle

It is important to set our understanding of how the Catholic Mass, the Eucharist, is rooted in Judaism and Jewish tradition in the larger context of the fact that the annual Christian liturgical cycle has its origins in the ancient Jewish liturgical calendar. This is to be found in the Hebrew Scriptures, specifically in its first five books, which we Christians call the Pentateuch (from the Latin for "five") and the Jews call the Torah (Teaching/Law). Here, one can find the origins of the Jewish liturgical festivals. Passover/Pesach is in the springtime, when the days become longer and the land becomes fertile and can be planted with the seeds of plants, the seeds of life that will nourish the People of God for the year. In the autumn, as the days become shorter and colder, the Jews commemorate the High Holy Days of repentance and Atonement for their sins of the year, committing themselves to renewed observance of the 613 commandments of the Torah.

Having repented and vowed to sin no more the Jews can celebrate the beginning of a new liturgical year of hope and commitment, vowing also to help all in need and work for freedom and justice, sufficient food and health, not only for themselves but for all humans. This is the goal toward which the Jewish People, as the Chosen People of God are oriented, *tikkun olam*, healing the world in preparation for the coming of the Messiah who will announce the coming of the End Time of universal peace, justice, health and harmony for all humanity.

Holy Thursday, Easter, and Passover

Passover/Pesach celebrates God's liberation of the Jews from slavery in Egypt to freedom in the Promised Land. The height of the Exodus was their stay at the base of Mount Sinai, which Moses climbed (twice) to receive the commandments which would guide the freed Israelites in the Way of God in their daily lives as individuals, as a community, and as a nation.

The word *Pesach* comes from the Hebrew for "passing over." When the Jews were still in slavery in Egypt and prayed to God for deliverance God sent ten "plagues" on the Egyptians to convince the Pharaoh to set them free. During the Passover Seder (which means "order" of service) a Jewish family will pour a drop of red wine, representing blood, onto their plates, both to memorialize God's divine mercy toward them and to pray for the Egyptians who were victimized by each "plague." The ten are: Blood, Frogs, Vermin, Beasts, Cattle Disease, Boils, Hail, Locusts, Darkness, and, finally, when the Pharaoh had rejected all these divine appeals, the Slaying of the First Born of every Egyptian family.

In each of these plagues, the Jews and their families were spared. And in the final one the Angel of Death literally "Passed Over" their houses. The Angel of Death knew the inhabitants of these houses were Jewish because they dabbed a smear of blood from a lamb on their doorposts. They were quite literally saved by the blood of a sacrificed lamb. One can see here the origin of the notion of Jesus, sacrificed on the Cross, as the Paschal Lamb (the Lamb of *Pesach*/Passover) saving all Christians and indeed all humanity from the death of the slavery of their sins. We are free to rise from our sins and follow the commandments God gave to Moses and the Jewish people at Mount Sinai, and through them to all of us Christians through the Hebrew Bible based teachings of the Jew, Jesus of Nazareth.

The story of the plagues and redemption from death is a warning to Jews and to all humanity. If countries or the groups in countries who exercise power over others they can and will be disciplined by God, perhaps by being plagued or destroyed. If those in power lack concern for others or do not work to alleviate the suffering of those in need they should be aware that harm may well come to them to the extent that they have ignored the needs of others or caused them harm. Peoples who want to prosper must, the

Torah commands, work for liberty and justice for all. "Proclaim liberty throughout the land for all its inhabitants."

The Last Supper as recounted in the gospels was celebrated by Jesus and his Jewish followers in an upper room, likely representing being on top of a mountain, Sinai. It was a seder, or "order" which indicates that there are strict rules for the meal: what is to be eaten, in what order, and what prayers are said as each portion is eaten. This was understood by the authors of the gospels as the first Eucharist, the day before his crucifixion, when he "suffered and died at the hands of Pontius Pilate," as our Creed clearly states. There may have been a few Jews involved. But these, the chief priest and his followers, were appointed by Pontius Pilate and served him in every way. They were, as most Jews in Jerusalem in Jesus' time knew well, quislings, traitors to their people who served the occupying power, Rome.

Thus, the ancient Christian antisemitic teaching that the Jews, all Jews, were responsible for the death of Jesus, and that all Jews ever afterword must carry this guilt on their shoulders, was and is totally false. Sadly, this ancient teaching of contempt for Jews and Judaism was upheld by most Christians for nearly two millennia, paving the way for the dehumanization of Jews which was used by the Nazis to "justify" their attempt to murder the entire people of Jesus, the Jews. Fortunately, after the Holocaust/Shoah, the Catholic Church during the Second Vatican Council took a deep look at this horrific ancient teaching and formally rejected it in the document, *Nostra Aetate* ("In Our Time").

The Last Supper was a Jewish Passover Seder, and the "order" of the Eucharistic Sacrifice/Meal follows the order of its origin. And what precedes the consecration of the Eucharist follows what takes place in Jewish synagogues to this day: readings from scriptures and commentaries (homilies) interpreting them and applying their lessons to our contemporary lives, needs and challenges. Our Mass thus brings to life the Jewish origin of our faith, a Passover Seder/Last Supper. It is our Passover/Pesach/Holy Thursday. And it is also our Good Friday, our death in slavery to sin, and our Resurrection into a new life of holiness with Jesus on Easter Sunday.

Jesus and his Jewish followers came together in community to say blessings over the unleavened bread and the red wine. To this day we Catholics gather each Sunday to bless bread and wine and share them lovingly, just as Jewish families to this day gather on *Pesach*/Passover do every year. On Holy Thursday Christians, following the liturgical practice of our Jewish older siblings hear the passage from the biblical book of Exodus of the original exodus of the People of God, the Jews, from slavery in Egypt to freedom, from death to life. This helps us understand what we celebrate in Holy Week, Holy Thursday, Good Friday, and Easter. This narrative defines our faith and, by acknowledging the validity of the Commandments given to the Jews and through them to us on Mount Sinai defines the heart of what our God, the One God of Israel, calls us to do with our lives.

In the early days of Christianity Christians, being mostly Jews, followed the Jewish calendar when commemorating the Last Supper. But as Christians, over time, became gentiles, especially during the time of the Fathers of the Church, roughly the 4th through the 6th centuries, practices and understanding of the year changed, influence by changing circumstances, such as becoming an officially recognized religion in the Roman Empire, and practices and understandings from the various religions of the period. The dating of Holy Week, it was argued, should follow the solar calendar rather than the biblical lunar calendar. The debate ended in a compromise, centering on the vernal equinox when the hours of daylight and darkness are equal, which was the biblical timing that Jews including Jesus and his disciples followed, and the solar calendar. To this day Holy Week and Passover/Pesach in effect circle one another, sometimes coinciding and sometimes weeks apart.

So there continues to be continuity but also discontinuity between the two sibling religions, Judaism and its younger sibling Christianity. The Jewish Passover is central to Judaism and Holy Week is central to Christianity.

Shavuot and Pentecost

It is ordered in the Hebrew Scriptures that God's People, the Jews, should celebrate a holy day seven weeks after *Pesach*. Seven times seven, 49 days. Seven Sabbaths. Shavuot in Hebrew is plural for "seven." The basis of this feast is biblical. After years wandering in the desert, the Jews came to Mount Sinai, where God called Moses to come to the top. There he received the gift of the Torah, the Law of Life, summarized as the Decalogue, the Ten Commandments. Moses came down and the people were worshiping an idol that they had made while he was conversing with God. He used the two stone tablets to destroy the idol and climbed up the mountain again, where he received a second set of tablets,

Fig. 16 Gustave Doré (1832-83), "Moses breaking the Tablets of the Law"

which the Jews vowed to observe and obey. The Law/Torah would guide them on the path of life, individually and as a people.

Jews sinned, were punished, repented, and were forgiven. Shavuoth is thus a celebration of God's love and mercy, of divine grace and human freedom. If the people know and understand the Way God has set for them to follow, they are free to choose to follow it and walk the way of life with God at their side and within their hearts. Observing the Law/Torah is what makes a Jew a Jew. Hence Jews can accept converts from any group in the world, and become a people reflecting all the peoples of the earth. One can become a Jew by being born of a Jewish mother, or one can join the Jewish people by accepting to follow the Torah/Law.

Shavuoth is the day of the founding of the Jewish People, the definitive coming together of the tribes into a single people with a single Way of Life under and with a single One God, Who is the One God of all humanity. God chose the Jewish People to gift with Her Will and the people became God's Chosen forever.

In Christian tradition, as recorded in the Book of Acts, it was on Shavuoth that the followers of Jesus gathered in prayer. On that day, the Spirit of God descended on and within them. The word for the Spirit of God in the Hebrew Scriptures is *Ruah*, breath or wind In Genesis it is the divine breath/wind that calmed the waters of creation and made all life, including human life. Just as the weekly Christian celebration of the death and life of Jesus is one day after the Jewish Shabbat so is the Christian celebration of new life in the Spirit of God celebrated one day after Shavuoth, on the fiftieth day after Easter. Pentecost means fifty. It is the day memorializing the founding of the Church as the People of God, the Chosen People.

In both cases it is likely not coincidental that the founding feasts of Easter and Pentecost are celebrated one day after the founding feasts in the Jewish liturgical calendar. This may well be an indication that the founders of Christianity did not in any way seek to "replace" Judaism but to stand alongside it liturgically and covenantally. We know that the early Christians well into the 4th and 5th centuries of the Common Era would attend synagogues on Shabbat and churches for mass on Sunday. We know this was a common practice because John Chrysostum devoted a series of sermons denouncing his congregants for doing this. In the process he brought together many of the anti-Jewish and anti-Judaism tropes that coalesced into what we today call the ancient Christian teaching of contempt for Jews and Judaism. This included such falsehoods as the collective responsibility of Jews for the death of Jesus, the notion that Jews would steal from Christians and, ultimately, that Jews would kidnap and kill Christian children in order to use their blood in their ritual meals such as *Pesach*. This last is known historically as the blood libel charge.

It is understandable and, in retrospect, inevitable, that the early Christians, being Jews, would use the narratives of the Hebrew Scriptures to describe the meaning of what happened to Jesus' followers on Pentecost.

Pentecost was/is understood by Christianity as its beginning just as Shavuoth was/is the beginning of Judaism. The descent of the Spirit seen as flames and clouds in the *upper* room (mountain top) reveal the sense of continuity between the events which defined the religion in which the Jewish Christians were raised and what was happening to them in their adulthood after the death and resurrection of Jesus.

One word to describe this continuity is that Christian sacred history is in some way not totally describabable in human words since God is involved "fulfilling" or repeating in a new way the central events of Jewish history as described the Torah/Pentateuch. The authors of the New Testament, as were Jesus and his followers, were Jews so drew on their own sacred history to understand their own.

"Fulfillment" for the New Testament authors did not in any sense mean "replacement." For them, the Judaism in which they were raised remained fully valid. God, the Hebrew Scriptures clearly teach, will never abandon the Jews, the Chosen People of God. But God could and did begin a new Chosen People, Christians, through the Jew Jesus, to reach out and proclaim and draw into a new covenant all humans graced with forgiveness by the sacrifice of Jesus on the Cross.

What Jesus' followers did after receiving the Holy Spirit in the upper room was to go immediately to the Temple in Jerusalem and offer sacrifices to the One God of Israel as commanded in the Hebrew Scriptures (cf. Acts of the Apostles, chapter 2). The good news proclaimed by Christians is new, open to all humanity. But it is not bad news for Jews, who are now and always required to adhere to the faith of Abraham and Sarah, Moses and the prophets. *Nostra Aetate* issued by the Second Vatican Council defined this well. We Christians and Jews together, side by side facing in the same direction, await the "perfect fulfillment" of God's promises for us all, for all humanity, when the Messiah will come or return to usher in the Messianic Age of universal justice, health and peace for all humanity. At that blessed time all humans will sing the praises of God with one voice, joined by love and happiness. If one delves into the mysteries of Christianity one will encounter the mysteries, and hopes of Judaism and the Jewish people, who will forever remain the Chosen People of God, just as we will.

Rosh Hashonah and Advent

The most sacred period of the year for Christianity takes place in the Spring, during Holy Week, as we have seen. While Passover/Pesach is the defining feast of Judaism and Jewish tradition, the most sacred period takes place in the Fall, on the day of the new moon. This is known as the Ten Days of Awe. It marks the beginning of the New Year, a time of hope and harvest,

Rosh Hashonah. Interestingly, on the tenth day Jews start out the new year with a day of repentance for the sins of the past year and a resolve to turn back to God and to the People of God in full observance of the 613 commandments of the Torah. This is Yom Kippur, the Day of Atonement. To truly repent and resolve to sin no more, Jews are mandated to go out to anyone they may have harmed, intentionally or inadvertently and do what they can to alleviate the harm and make the victims whole again. The Jewish greeting, *L'Shanah Tovah* (have a good year) is not just a pleasantry but a promise to do what is necessary to help those in need.

The Ten Days of Awe are marked by prayers and fasting, repentance and reconciliation, asking for the forgiveness of God and forgiving and reconciling with each other, whether Jews or non-Jews. It thus marks the beginning of a new life of observance of Torah and love for each other and all humanity. Jesus the Jew said it well when he summarized the Law/Torah/Commandments as "Love God with your whole heart, your whole soul and your whole mind" (Deut 6:5) and "Love your neighbor (i.e., other Jews and all humans) as yourself" (Lev 19:18). The *shofar* (Ram's Horn) is sounded in every synagogue call all Jews to come together in prayer and to act together for *tikkun olam*, the healing of the world, helping all those in need, in preparation for the coming of the Messianic Age of universal peace, health and harmony.

Jewish Christians, our founding mothers and fathers, saw these themes of repentance and reconciliation to be connected to the sacrificial death and triumphal resurrection of their Founder, Jesus/Yeshua of Nazareth. They went to the Temple in Jerusalem, as did other Jews, to offer sacrifice.

In 70 C.E. the Romans destroyed the Temple (as they had earlier murdered Jesus/Yeshua). This posed a central problem for both Jews and Jewish Christians. Both Jews and Jewish Christians reacted creatively. Indeed, it was the reaction of the two communities to the destruction of the Temple that came to define them as religious traditions.

For Jews, this reaction was lead by the Pharisees, particularly the Pharisaic followers of Hillel, who lived in the century before Jesus. The New Testament provides numerous examples of Jesus in dialogue/discussion/dispute with various Pharisees. If one reads rabbinic literature one comes to realize that there was a second major group of Pharisees, the followers of Shammai. Hillel emphasized the spirit of the law and going beyond the dictates of the law when it came to respecting and helping others. Shammai was more of a literalist, arguing that one only had to observe the letter of the law, a minimalist interpretation. If one reads the New Testament stories of Jesus' interactions with Pharisees, one soon comes to realize that Jesus did not disagree with "the" Pharisees.

In every case but one (if a man can divorce his wife) Jesus sides with the interpretation of Hillel rather than that of Shammai. Interestingly, the Hillelites prevailed in the internal Pharisaic discussion as well, so that Judaism and Christianity are remarkably similar in their understanding of what we would call social morality and ethics, how we as believers should interact with each other, help those in need, etc. Pharisaic/Hillelite Judaism interpreting observance of the Law/Torah as "replacing" the sacrifices of the Temple with lives of sacrifice and observance of the Torah.

Christianity "replaced" the sacrifices of the Temple by emphasizing the one, full sacrifice of Christ on the Cross, a sacrifice that served for the remission of the sins of all humanity. Jesus went to the Cross willingly and knowingly, so Jesus, as stated especially in the Epistle to the Hebrews, was/is both priest and sacrificial victim. He was/is the sacrificed lamb, whose blood remits the sins of all, so that we may pass over from the death/slavery of sin to the life/freedom of life with the Son of God, the Paschal Lamb.

For Christians, the Temple sacrifices were no longer needed. The Paschal Lamb had been sacrificed "once and for all." For Jews, the Temple sacrifices were replaced by *mitzvoth*, good deeds, prayer, and study of the Hebrew Scriptures, which in Hebrew is *TaNaKh*: Torah (the Pentateuch), Neviiim (the Prophets) and Ketuvim (Writings). Other Jewish groups that had existed before the destruction of the Temple merged into the Pharisees, who evolved into Rabbis, Sadducees, Essenes, Herodians, Jewish Christians. So only two Jewish groups survived the destruction: Pharisees/Rabbis and the followers of Jesus/Yeshua.

Since Jesus' sacrifice replaced the Temple sacrifices the feast of Atonement/Yom Kippur merged into Good Friday, commemorating the death of Jesus, so it no longer appears on the Fall Christian calendar. But we Christians do have a period in the Fall/Early Winter of prayer, repentance and reconciliation which corresponds to the period of time of the Days of Awe: Advent, preparing for the coming birth of Jesus/Yeshua of Nazareth. In four weeks, a month, Christians live lives of repentance. Our readings from books such as Jeremiah and Isaiah are the same as the readings in the synagogue, illustrating yet again how Christianity remains close to its elder sibling. We end the year and seek to begin the new year asking for the forgiveness of God and working for reconciliation with our neighbors of whatever faith, or none.

Sukkoth and Thanksgiving

Five days after *Yom Kippur* Jews have a joyous celebration of life. Sukkoth means "Booths." It is a festival celebrating the Fall harvest. In biblical times it was one of three "pilgrimages" to the Jerusalem temple to offer sacrifices of thanksgiving to God for the harvest which would provide food for the people throughout the coming Winter. For eight days Jews remember the forty years of wandering in the desert. During such a period, of course, the Jews would have to build temporary shelters called booths or tabernacles. Sukkoth are built the family's home and often next to synagogues for those who are homeless or who live, for example, in apartments where they cannot build a sukkah. The roof is of branches. From them are hung autumn fruits and vegetables. Jewish families pray and eat under open skies as did the Jews of the Exodus over two millennia ago.

Jews give thanks for the fact that their ancestors were able to reach, as God promised them, the Promised Land. Early American European settlers, such as the Pilgrims, believed deeply in the Bible and felt that they were following the path of Jews from poverty and oppression in Europe to a new life in America, the Promised Land for them. So, following the Bible, they developed their own day of thanksgiving for the harvest. Yet again Christians were following the Jewish liturgical cycle wrapped around the seasons of the year and evoking the history, as recorded in the Bible, of God's People, the Jews, in a way that they could see in their own lives a living embodiment of ancient Israel.

Sukkoth ends with a day of Rejoicing in the Torah, *Simhat Torah*, which in this case means the Pentateuch. During the year the entire Pentateuch is read, Shabbat to Shabbat, in the synagogue, the final reading being done on *Simhat Torah*. Our Catholic reading of the New Testament likewise follows, in the main with some exceptions, a cyclic reading of the Scriptures. Yet again we see Christian liturgical practice following that of our Jewish Christian ancestors, just as our Eucharist is a version of the Jewish *Pesach* Seder.

Hanukkah and Christmas

In mid-winter, the days are short and darkness hovers over the land. Jewish tradition celebrates light in the darkness and hope for the future with the festival of Hanukkah. Also, at the winter solstice Christians celebrate the birth of Jesus in Bethlehem (House of Bread), new life and the presence of God on earth in the midst of darkness.

Hannukah recalls a time when a foreign power had conquered the land, long before the time of Jesus. The occupying power dictated that Jews were to offer worship to an idol which had been set up in the Temple. It was declared illegal, on penalty of death, to observe the Jewish faith. Once again, as throughout their history, the Jews rejected idolatry and rose in rebellion. It took time and the sacrifice of many lives, but the pagans were driven from Jerusalem and the Temple cleansed and re-dedicated to the One God of Israel. In a very real sense this feast is an affirmation of the Exodus, freedom from slavery and the call to be with God in prayer and practice. It is essentially the same story celebrated in the seder at *Pesach*/Passover. And the lighting of candles, as in the seder, is central.

The story goes that as part of re-dedicating the Temple to God ("Hanukkah" means "dedication" in Hebrew) the Temple *Menorah* (candelabra) needed to be lit and kept burning for eight days. But there was only enough oil to keep it burning for one, and it would take a number of days to make enough oil to keep it burning. The priests lit it. A miracle took place and the menorah burned for eight days, giving sufficient time to produce more oil.

Hanukkah is celebrated for eight days. Each night a new candle is lit. Children play games and receive presents. The candles are not blown out but burn all night, in honor of God, the source of all light and hope. Today, Jews also recall on Hanukkah, the deadly nights of the Shoah/Holocaust, the deaths of six million, and the survival of some. Again, this is a Passover/Pesach, passing from the dark horrors of the death camps to new life and hope.

Christmas, too, celebrates the birth of the light of salvation. We put lights on a tree in our homes and lights around our doors and windows. Hanukkah and Christmas are affirmations of the light of faith and freedom of religion not only for Jews and Christians but for all humanity.

Purim and Mardi Gras

Purim and Mardi Gras are Spring festivals. Neither is a major religious festival. Both are more cultural and celebrational than liturgical or theological. Purim takes place, in the Jewish calendar, on the fourteenth day of Adar, which can occur at some point during the months of February and March. Purim is based on the biblical Book of Esther. It celebrates her victory over the evil minister of the Persian king Ahasueris, Haman, who was attempting to influence the king to order the execution of all Jews.

On Purim, Jews wear costumes representing the key figures in the Book of Esther. There are dances and re-enactments of the events, a carnival of joy and thanksgiving for having been passed over by death at the hands of the Persians, again much like the Exodus, freedom from death and rebirth in a new life. The Book of Esther is read in full and acted out. Children cheer at the name of Mordecai, who threw "lots" (purim) similar to dice to determine the date of the murder of the Jews, not allowing it to happen until that day, by which time Esther had taken out the evil Haman, at whose name the children boo. There are noisemakers and songs and stamping of feet, a joyous dance.

Purim is paralleled in the Christian calendar by the celebration of Mardi Gras ("Fat Tuesday"). As Jews dance and celebrate the victory of Esther so Christians dance and march, wear costumes, use noise and music makers. Mardi Gras is a celebration of springtime and renewed life the day before Ash Wednesday, the beginning of Lent, during which Catholics fast and do penance in preparation for Holy Week and the victory of Easter.

Sabbath, Sunday, and Conclusion

One of the ten commandments given to Moses and the Jewish People on Mount Sinai (again note the centrality of the Exodus in Jewish liturgical tradition) was the commandment to rest on the seventh day of the week, the Sabbath (which means seven) just as God rested on the seventh day of Creation in the Book of Genesis. The Sabbath meal begins with the mother of the family lighting a candle on a table set with a white tablecloth and adorned with flowers (if possible). Just as at the *Pesach*/Passover Seder wine is poured and blessed, unleavened bread is broken. The bread and the wine are shared around the table, evoking the coming-together of the Jewish people in the Exodus and the unity of the family with each other and with the whole People of God, the Jewish People. Every Sabbath meal therefore is a re-enactment of the Passover Haggadah, *Pesach*.

Shabbat, the Sabbath, which celebrates Passover every week, is the central Jewish liturgical experience. After or most probably before the Sabbath meal the family will go to the synagogue greeting each other with the phrase "Shabbat Shalom" (Have Peace on the Sabbath). This Jewish greeting is likely the origin of the Catholic Eucharistic greeting "Peace be with you." This small gesture once again illustrates the interwoven nature of the Jewish and Christian liturgical traditions.

In Jewish tradition the other six days of the week are understood to be bridesmaids. The Sabbath is the Bride of Israel when the Jewish People are chosen and wedded to the One God of Israel. It recalls Creation, God resting on the seventh day, a time every week when Jews live in peace with all. It is a moment lived in the End Time of universal peace, justice, and harmony. The family's time is spent in prayer and study of the Torah.

Christians, as has been noted, observe the Sabbath not on the seventh, last day of the week but on the first day of the week, understood as the day of the Resurrection, the beginning of a new Creation with the risen Christ. Catholics go to Mass and receive the unleavened bread and the wine, coming together a community, the People of God, centering the day around rest and the family. Again, this shows what we as Christians have learned from our elder sibling, the Jewish People. And, again, the Christian celebration of Easter every Sunday (just as the Jews celebrate Passover every Shabbat) is central to our lived faith life, as Shabbat/Pesach is central to Judaism.

Our liturgical traditions, Jewish and Christian, are intertwined. St. Paul evoked this in Romans 9–11. Judaism and Christianity are two

branches rooted in the same Tree of Life planted/created by the One God of us all.
    Amen.

Further Readings

Erst, Anna Marie, *Discovering Our Jewish Roots*. Paulist Press, 1996.

Fisher, Eugene, editor, *The Jewish Roots of Christian Liturgy*. Paulist Press, 1990.

Klenicki, Leon, *The Passover Celebration: A Haggadah for the Seder*. Archdiocese of Chicago. Liturgy Training Publications, 1990.

Klenicki, Leon, and Fisher, Eugene, *Root and Branches: Biblical Judaism, Rabbinic Judaism and Early Christianity*. Winona, Minn., St. Mary's Press, 1987.

Petuchowski, John, and Brocke, Michael, *The Lord's Prayer and Jewish Liturgy*. NY: Seabury Press, 1978.

Saldarini, Anthony J., *Jesus and Passover*. Paulist Press, 1984.

Townsend, John T., *A Liturgical Interpretation of the Passion of Jesus Christ*. NY: National Conference of Christians and Jews. 1990.

Setting Our Tables with Grace and Respect: Reformed Table Talk for Post-Shoah Times

Henry Knight

For Post-Shoah people of faith, the confluence of Passover and Holy Week presents challenging questions for how one lives with others along with one's own core traditions responsibly. For post-Holocaust Christians, these questions come to focused articulation in the story of the Upper Room and its subsequent impact on the Eucharist, a grounding sacramental expression of Christian identity. How Christians hear and tell their grounding narrative, particularly with regard to their covenantal Jewish cousins, is focused in this telling story. To complicate matters, Jews as well as Christians, face unsettling questions raised by the Holocaust regarding the fundamental assumptions of covenantal theism that both traditions embrace and on which they rely. This essay continues a reflection on this matter from a Protestant, Christian perspective that began with a series of lectures I gave at Atlantic School of Theology in Halifax, Nova Scotia in the spring of 2002 and now published as Celebrating Holy Week in a Post-Holocaust World (Westminster, 2005).

Here I focus on three sets of issues occasioned by reflecting on my place at a table prepared for Passover in a self-consciously post-Shoah setting and its implications for how I would host a Eucharistic table prepared for responsible post-Shoah sacramental life during Holy Week, more particularly one recalling what happened at the Seder remembered in the Upper Room. Both tables call forth my presence, asking me the confessional question, Where are you? as I take my place in a Post-Shoah world. My response represents only my personal sacramental identity as a self-consciously post-Holocaust Christian. Nonetheless, this is how I see myself at the table of life I share with others and how I take my place with them as guest and host.

A Guest at the Table

As a post-Shoah Christian seeking to repair my relationships with Jews and Judaism, what is my place at a Passover Seder? The answer to that question might seem obvious. Clearly, my place is that of a guest. When invited, I accept that invitation as respectfully as I can and then participate in that table celebration as responsibly as I am able. Pondering such an invitation, however, raises the issue of supersessionism in my relationship with Judaism as well as my relationship with friends who welcome me at their table.

Supersessionism refers to the logic of displacement that operates in classical Christian theology as well as in the popular Christian imagination with regard to Jews and Judaism. That is, supersessionism refers to the belief that Christianity has surpassed and replaced Judaism as the rightful heir of God's promises and the true representative people of God. The term, supersessionism is derived from the Latin *super sedere*, which literally means to take the place of another, typically their place at a table. Consequently, a Christian's place at a Seder table carries multivalent significance.

Supersessionism comes in overt and damning forms. And, in those cases, it is relatively easy to identify and to resist. But supersessionism can come in subtle and softer forms as well, not to mention structural forms that are embedded in classical Christian theological and liturgical traditions.[1] With this in mind, post-Shoah Christians may wish to ponder ways that supersessionary thinking can undermine otherwise intended expressions of solidarity and support for Jewish friends and traditions. For example, Christian adoption of Jewish ritual life could be viewed as a way to affirm Jewish life. Indeed, Christian congregations and individual families in the spirit of inter-faith respect have hosted Passover Seders as ways of educating their congregations with regard to Jewish faith and life, as well as understanding the Jewish background of their own Christian traditions.

---

[1] David Novak describes these options as two different forms of supersessionism: "hard supersessionism" and "soft supersessionism." Hard supersessionism operates with an overt replacement logic whereby Judaism is viewed as a failed embodiment to live as God's representative people and Christianity is viewed as that community that replaces Judaism in the divine economy of salvation history. Soft supersessionism allows for a positive view of Judaism as a community that has embodied God's expectations and served as a limited representation of God's ways with the world. Christianity, in turn, lives in witness to Christ's fulfillment of divine expectations and the full incarnation of what Israel only partially embodied. See his discussion of this matter in David Novak, "The Covenant in Rabbinic Thought" in *Two Faiths, One Covenant? Jewish and Christian Identity in the Presence of the Other*, Eugene B. Korn & John T. Pawlikowski, eds. (Lanham: Rowman & Littlefield Publishers, Inc.: 2005) 66.

At what point, however, does such an enterprise move from educating for understanding to a more subtle form of supersessionary thinking wherein valued comparisons encourage problematic replacement understandings and attitudes? *Our Haggadah*, a personal reflection by Cokie and Steve Roberts, recounts a genuinely respectful record of their interfaith family's tradition of honoring Passover in their mixed marriage and family traditions. Their story matches the ritualized narrative they relate in their idiosyncratic way—a way of preserving the story and Jewish identity that Passover proclaims while hoping for the coming of the Messiah and the subsequent messianic time of a fulfilled creation. Indeed, they point out in two separate introductions that their intention is to honor their distinctive religious identities with Cokie Roberts explaining,

> By saying all this, I don't want you to think that I'm in any way trying to 'Christianize' the Seder. Not at all. Even when Seders take place in churches, Catholic bishops discourage any attempt to 'baptize' Passover, advising, 'When Christians celebrate this sacred feast among themselves, the rites of the Haggadah for the Seder should be respected in all their integrity. The Seder…should be celebrated in a dignified manner and with sensitivity to those to whom the Seder truly belongs.' And the Seder belongs to the Jewish people.[2]

We should note that their reference to the statement by the Catholic Bishops is partial. The larger framework discourages Catholic adoption of the Seder in fear of the disrespect it guards against. The Roberts' situation is not typical, however. Inclusion and respect can take bold and adventurous form, as their example demonstrates.

At the same time, we must remain alert to naïve attempts to bridge the difficult history that lies behind and embedded in the distinctive traditions of Jewish and Christian identity. The Roberts offer an embodied example illustrating how a straightforward statement forbidding or promoting Christians hosting a Passover Seder is too simple a guideline. In their case, they are practicing respectful hospitality for one another's traditions within their own family bonds and those of their respective faith identities.

In my own case, I have grounded my attempts to place myself in this intersecting set of narratives in the biblical story of Jacob. His competitive relationship with his estranged brother required a lifetime of reflection. Indeed, that journey led to an intense encounter with his multifaceted, supersessionary history at the River Jabbok. That night of wrestling resulted in Jacob's emergence with a wounded hip and a resulting

---

[2] Cokie & Steve Roberts, *Our Haggadah, Uniting Traditions for Interfaith Families* (New York: Harper Collins, 2011) xlvi.

limp. At the risk of taking the story too far, I realize that my relationship to these matters is similar and requires acknowledgement of the wounding that comes from facing one's own dimensions of shame. But taking the story too far and adopting Jacob's identity as Israel would be a second theft. That path must be avoided. As a result, I have concluded that my place as a post-Shoah Christian at a Seder table is always as a respectful and limping guest. In other words, while I may limp, I am not Israel. In that capacity, I can learn as much as I can about my hosts and their traditions, participating with delight and respect when invited.

Limping Presence

Christians like me limp as a consequence of facing and facing up to the history of supersessionism and its consequences, which have often been dire for Jewish siblings in our family of Abraham. Those consequences stretch back to the origins of my faith family and include a full range of dehumanizing ways of treating the others who claim our shared Abrahamic legacy. From competition to polemic and blame, from polemic and blame to contempt and demonization, from there to dismissal and eventually murder, the journey followed a troubling path. Raul Hilberg captured this historical movement in haunting clarity:

> The missionaries of Christianity had said in effect: You have no right to live among us as Jews. The secular rulers who followed had proclaimed: You have no right to live among us. The German Nazis at last decreed: You have no right to live.[3]

For post-Shoah Christians like me this shadow history haunts our sense of credibility, integrity, *and* identity. We wrestle with all of that as Jacob wrestled with his own shadow history, recognizing that in his long night at the Jabbok he faced himself, his relationships with others—including his brother, his parents, his family and their future—and he wrestled with God. Hence, he named the place *Peniel*—the face of God. As a Protestant Christian I find in Martin Luther a haunting reminder that the pursuit of reform can embody a logic of purification that uses others as foils (Roman Catholics as well as Jews) in their quest for truth.

As much as I may owe Luther, I cannot embrace what Regina Schwartz calls a logic of scarcity[4] that funds his hermeneutical pursuit of a purified Christianity. Jews were particularly vilified by him in his later life

---

[3] Raul Hilberg, *The Destruction of the European Jews: Revised and Definitive Edition* (New York: Holmes & Meier, 1985) vol. 1, 9.

[4] Regina M. Schwartz, *The Curse of Cain: The Violent Legacy of Monotheism* (Chicago: The University of Chicago Press, 1997) xi, 7, 15ff.

and appear to be an exaggerated, albeit logical extension, of the purifying pursuit of truth that Luther embodied throughout his life, not simply in exaggerated fashion at the end. Instead, the limp of a lingering logic of scarcity shadows Protestant theological table talk.

The limp, then, is an embodied reminder of the wounded wholeness that includes the recognition that my relationships with Jews—as well as others—has a problematic, shadow history that I must acknowledge and seek to integrate into my identity and my relationships with others. I do that through an evolving theology of hospitality that grounds me critically in my own Christian tradition at the same time it provides me with a way of embracing others who understand and see the world (and themselves) differently than I do.[5] This hermeneutical awareness helps me understand my place at a Seder as being an invited guest. I welcome and celebrate it, knowing that my identity grows out of one that shares many of the qualities of the family extending their hospitality to me. Indeed, the limp I bring to their table reminds me that the extended, historical family that welcomes me is rooted in Jacob's story and that the hospitality they extend to me is an expression of its other-oriented embrace. Nonetheless, the shadow side of that relationship embodied by the supersessionary expressions of my tradition haunts every embrace of that larger, storied identity.

There is more to my limping embrace, however. Beyond the betrayals of my theological companions across the ages and the shadow history I have identified, there is the still problematic interventionist logic in covenantal theism that requires examination. And its problems are shared by Christians and Jews, Judaism and Christianity. As Jews and Christians address the divine source of all life in prayer, we typically ask God to act in our lives and within our histories. Indeed, the *Haggadot* for most Seders recount the overarching narrative of liberation from Egyptian slavery and the deliverance through the Sea of Reeds. The story continues, describing the journey into the wilderness where the people of Israel dwell under divine care feeding on manna from heaven provided by God for their survival. That is, in covenantal fidelity to the people God intervenes to assure their survival from the night of Passover through the long passage in the wilderness to the promised land. God faithfully accompanies the people Israel on their generation-long trek from slavery to freedom.

Christianity similarly understands God to be active in history and prays regularly for divine engagement within history. The interventionist assumptions that accompany such prayers and understandings reflect the structures of covenantal theism. That is, God has established created life and remains in covenantal relationship to created life expecting the human partners to live in similar relationship with one another and with God. God is

---

[5] See Henry F. Knight, *Confessing Christ in a Post-Holocaust World: A Midrashic Experiment* (Westport, CT: Greenwood Press, 2000).

both the witness and guarantor to this structure, promising fidelity to those in covenant with God and expecting fidelity among all partners. That structure can be represented with the following diagram:

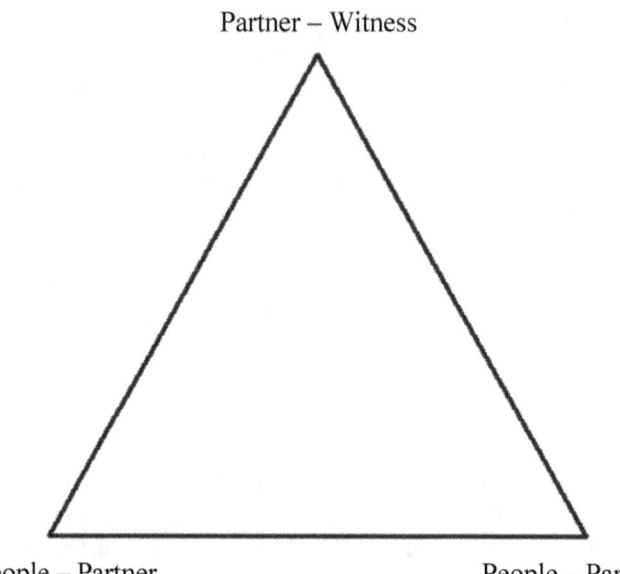

As the diagram represents, a theistic God is conceived apart from the created order and engages with creation, a separate reality from God, in discrete and ongoing actions. Nonetheless, God acts to engage creation from outside or beyond, guiding and infusing it with life. Human partners participate in and through covenantal bonds with one another and with God, their divine partner. Deliverance, like providential care, is viewed as God's response and faithful support of these covenantal bonds.

In similar fashion, violence, evil, and other horrible occurrences are viewed as alienation from covenant life and even as divine punishment. That is, the covenanting God of theism is active in history from outside or beyond history in interventional acts, inspiring, infusing, tending, and judging the human partners. This model of divinity is threatened, if not utterly shattered, by the radical suffering of the Shoah.

Richard Rubenstein gives a dramatic expression of this crisis in his work *After Auschwitz*. He explains that the Shoah exposes a fundamental flaw in the idea of God as an electing deity choosing the people Israel as a representative people. Functionally, the act of election becomes an act of targeting a people. The corresponding idea of an electing (read targeting) God, thereby, reveals such a divinity to be unworthy of trust or allegiance, much less substantive belief.[6] Emil Fackenheim offers a different perspective while recognizing the undermining character of the problems that arise for biblical faith after the Holocaust.

As an expression of faith, Fackenheim asserts the need for midrashic resistance to the biblical record and *its witness* to a covenanting God.[7] The biblical witness must now include the voices and experiences of those who have suffered because of their covenantal identity. To do otherwise, he asserts, risks giving Hitler a posthumous, post-Holocaust victory.[8] To that, he advanced his 614th command: "Thou shall not give Hitler a posthumous victory." Both thinkers disclose the limits of covenantal theism, which they both acknowledge are the imaginal frameworks most typically employed by the people of the Abrahamic traditions.

Their critiques are aimed at the models of faith and ways of configuring the divine-human relationship at work in them. While they do not advocate abandoning covenantal life, they do ask that we reconsider how we understand divinity within these frameworks. Rubenstein focuses on the understanding or idea of God at work in the doctrine of election and Fackenheim focuses on the logic of midrash to resist biblical faith's own limited boundaries of conceptualization. Both thinkers disclose the imaginal limits of the model of covenantal theism and push us to think about divinity anew with Fackenheim inviting us to retain the biblical, covenantal framework in doing so.

To be sure, other thinkers have explored different models of divinity for undertaking such a task, often in panentheistic fashion. One notable example is provided by Emmanuel Levinas who focuses on the power of the human face to call forth life in response to life, identifying the sacred with what happens in the interactions between persons. For Levinas, the sacred is dynamic and occurs in the interaction, in acts of hospitality, in life calling forth life. Covenantal theism gives way to covenantal panentheism with external transcendence replaced by immanent transcendence or some other process model of divinity.[9]

Another similarly oriented Jewish theologian, Michael Fishbane, focuses on living in *sacred attunement* with the God of creation, who has elected to be dependent on all of creation and needful of a people who can demonstrate how to live in partnership with that ongoing gift of life. In both

---

[6] Richard L. Rubenstein, *After Auschwitz: History, Theology, and Contemporary Judaism*, 2nd Edition (Baltimore: Johns Hopkins University Press, 1966, 1992) 13.

[7] Emil Fackenheim, *God's Presence in History: Jewish Affirmations and Philosophical Reflections* (New York: Harper Torchbooks, 1970) 20ff.

[8] Ibid. 84 ff.

[9] That is, however God "acts" within history, God acts in and through the agency of human partners and in and through the full evolutionary scope of natural processes.

cases, the Other of creation is manifest and encountered in acts of seeing (i.e., interpretation) which recognize the hidden wholeness of created life in which we live.[10]

There are hints offered in the narratives that are shared around the Seder and Eucharistic tables supporting this kind of reconceptualization. For example, divinity need not be understood as imperial, coming like edicts and interventions from Pharaoh. Instead, divinity can be encountered in acts of hospitality and generosity offered to friends, and particularly to strangers. Moses was given shelter and a new beginning through the hospitality and generosity of Jethro in Midian. Without Jethro's welcome and the generosity of his family the narrative we have come to revere would have been interrupted, perhaps fatally so.

Life began anew for Moses because of simple, but powerful gifts that offered room for him to begin again. And the gift of Sinai, while it happened in the wilderness on an isolated mountain top, had to be recovered and *mended in the making* among a fractured people in need of its guidance for survival. While such recognition matches the reflections of Emmanuel Levinas, they first arose in the midst of need and interdependence. Perhaps it is wise to reflect on the ways in which we meet an immanent transcendence during times of trial and need when acts of welcome reveal the power of hospitality to give and nurture life. They break the chains of oppression and death. If we are careful, we could call this the *power of between* that delivers liberating expressions of life even in the face of death.

Further reflection in this regard is beyond the scope of this essay. Nonetheless, the paradigms of covenant faith ritualized during these annual events are fundamentally challenged by the Shoah calling forth responses that resist their problematic dimensions while affirming their formative place in the identities of those who gather at table with one another. Midrash provides important theological space in this regard. Just as important, the space provided welcome guests demonstrates the power of hospitality to affirm and give life.

A Midrashic Host

This logic is also manifest for me at the Eucharistic table I host as a Protestant Christian clergy person. As I welcome others at my own confessional table, I do so aware of similar theological concerns about the language of divinity, sacrifice, and replacement thinking that I might embody and express. Hence, I take my place during Holy Week cognizant of

---

[10] Fishbane identifies this work as "hermeneutical theology." Michael Fishbane, *Sacred Attunement: A Jewish Theology* (Chicago: The University of Chicago Press, 2008) ix–xiv, 44, 62–64, 208.

how I recount the prayers I lead, the hymns I select, the prayers I offer, and the world I represent.

Also, I do so seeking to be responsible to the one whose table I represent. These combined concerns have led me to a midrashic orientation that I believe offers a faithful way of representing the one I confess to be the center of my life while welcoming others to the table he has placed before us and to which he continues to invite our presence. At the same time, the core values of hospitality frame my respect for those who find their place at other tables. That is confessional language, to be sure, but carefully chosen as my own post-Shoah Christian attempt to address these matters.

Post-Shoah Christians join post-Shoah Jews and Judaism in rethinking how we understand the holy, divinity, sacrifice, and their relationships to one another. Indeed, I hold and read the story of the Upper Room as a radical affirmation of the relationality of the holy. That is, the holy is recognized and honored in what Michael Fishbane calls acts of *sacred attunement*,[11] when we offer space for life to unfold with respect and mutual care. Therefore, how I set the tables I host and how I take my place at tables that welcome me are, themselves, sacramental concerns. Therefore, how I host any Eucharistic table, much less one that commemorates the meal at the Upper Room during Holy Week, becomes a sacred obligation to embody tables of hospitality "that establish, in relationships with others, room for the other to be other… and room for the holy, in its otherness, to be embraced and welcomed, as well."[12]

As I have explained in *Celebrating Holy Week in a Post Holocaust World*,

> Jesus saw in the gathering of a meal an occasion that could substitute for the sacrificial offerings (*korbanot*) of the Temple. The Table became a sanctuary for honoring and sharing the gracious generosity of God's ways with creation. The rule and realm of God was at hand in the gestalt of hospitality encountered in and around a meal. While Jesus had shared this message in parable and enacted it in other settings, on the occasion of his last meal and in the shadow of his encounter in the Temple courtyard, he moved to elevate the character of what happened in and through the meal to be equivalent to what was seen as present only at the Temple… [13]

The Upper Room…

---

[11] Fishbane, *Sacred Attunement: A Jewish Theology*, ix–xiv, 44, 62–64, 208.
[12] Knight, *Celebrating Holy Week in a Post Holocaust World* (Louisville, Kentucky: Westminster John Knox Press, 2005) 57.
[13] Knight, *Celebrating Holy Week in a Post Holocaust World*, 66.

... gathering is associated with Passover and ritualized either as a Seder (as in the Synoptics) or as a *havurah* meal just prior to Passover (as in John). Either way, the ritualization, if we are not careful, can obscure the more general framework of a meal that underlies the gathering. Jesus saw every meal as a parabolic occasion in which one could embody the dynamics of God's ways with creation. Through the hospitality practiced at table, those who shared meals with others touched the very dynamics of God's ways with creation. God, the host of life, made his children welcome by making room for them as guests in the created domain. Created in God's image, God's children were themselves asked to be hosts to others, welcoming them into God's garden of life. Indeed, the vulnerable character of such hospitality is demonstrated in the footwashing ceremonies that recall the setting in John's Gospel and by Jesus serving his disciples while telling them they would fail him either by denial or betrayal in the days ahead. The hospitality of the table was being extended and deepened to capture the hospitality behind the very gift of creation and expressive of God's ways with all of creation—a wager Jesus was willing to make in the face of impending disaster.[14]

There is replacement logic at work in the narrative, but that logic is not directed at Jews or the Jewish people. Rather, it is directed at the sacrificial system of the Temple and its supporting theology. Jesus was angered by what he had encountered when he approached the Temple earlier in the week. A clue left behind in the gospels, particularly the synoptic ones like *Matthew*, lies in the language from the Temple that Jesus adopted and adapted in the Upper Room. Matthew captures it succinctly:

> While they were eating, Jesus took a loaf of bread, and after blessing it he broke it, gave it to the disciples and said, "Take, eat; this is my body." Then he took a cup, and after giving thanks he gave it to them, saying, "Drink from it, all of you; for this is my blood of the covenant, which is poured out for many for the forgiveness of sins I tell you, I will never again drink of this fruit of the vine until that day when I drink it new with you in my Father's kingdom." (Matthew 26: 26–29 NRSV)

Jesus was using the words of the Temple priests when he took up the bread and the wine. Instead of holding a sacrificial lamb, Jesus took the bread, saying, "*This* is my body (*soma*, Greek for flesh or body)." Instead of pouring out a cup of the animal's blood on the altar, Jesus took a cup of wine, saying, "*This* is my cup." Jesus had taken the symbolic elements of thanksgiving at their Passover meal and refocused his followers'

---

[14] Knight, *Celebrating Holy Week in a Post Holocaust World*, 70.

understanding that their shared table was a temple—sacred space in sacred time—where the holy could be embodied and honored through acts of remembrance and hospitality.

For centuries these words have been read differently by the Church, echoing the theological understandings of John more than those embedded in the synoptics. They have projected the crucifixion of Jesus as the ultimate sacrificial act equating Jesus and his crucifixion with the sacrificial lamb offered for Passover. While his death (and life) may have been sacrificial in character, it need not have been a sacrifice required by and offered to God as an act of propitiation. Instead, Jesus, I maintain, is better seen and served by recognizing that what happened at the table in his presence at the Upper Room embodied the hospitality of God that undergirds the very gift of creation. The simple gifts of sustenance—bread and wine—become symbolic expressions of human interdependence capturing the sacrificial character of human relationships lived in hospitable respect one for the other—even in the face of impending death.

In this way, the acts of taking bread and wine transmute the sacrificial actions at the Temple to acts of shared sustenance with others. Symbolic elements of a meal become the offerings of sacrificial commitment in human relationships. The offering is embodied in interpersonal commitment to others with the focus shifting from the sacrifice of a ritually slaughtered animal (or human being) to the attitude of host to guest in the gift of hospitality of food and drink at a table of remembrance and shared commitment. Interdependence and hospitality are linked to deliverance, and deliverance is joined to mutual care in shared life with and on behalf of others.

After his cruel death at the hands of the Romans, Jesus' last meal took on added meaning and became a way of remembering the embodied gifts of his extraordinary life and of celebrating his continuing presence among and with his followers. In the face of Roman oppression this storied meal expressed the power of sacrificial freedom in the face of cruelty and overwhelming abuse: the offering of oneself to others and for others—a fully embodied story of deliverance from evil and its powers as well as a foretaste of the rule and realm of heaven expressed in the gifts of bread and wine. The holy happens at the table where guests can be welcomed with freely offered hospitality and respect even in the face of deadly power.

Tables that Liberate and Heal

We set our tables, especially on ritualized occasions, with special care. We do so in obvious as well as subtle ways with cups and plates and special foods; with words and gestures, toasts, and prayers; and with stories that frame our gatherings with one another. We even set aside reserved seats for special guests, whether that seat is reserved for a fellow traveler, Elijah, or a gentile friend.

In the shadows of incomprehensible violence, how we set our tables makes a difference of extraordinary proportion. For those who were the victims of that violence—or who identify with the victims as their children or partners in life—the practice of hospitality embodies a vulnerable expression of faith in others, especially others whose backgrounds shelter them from the vulnerability that such acts of hospitality embody. While that is a tangled grammatical phrase, the grace-filled trust it expresses is not. In the elegant simplicity of a meal, hospitality rebuilds the world by welcoming others who do not share the vulnerability of the night remembered at its table. This is true for Jews in starkly obvious ways. But it is also true for Christians as they rebuild a world that welcomes Jews as Jews. In the ritual context of a Passover Seder or the Eucharist, the gift of respect has the power to mend a broken world.

When we reset the ways that we talk about God and others as an ecology of respected relationships, we reconstitute the world as a gift shared by God with all of us, each having a place at the table of life. When we take our place in the world and do so with gratitude for those who have made a place for us, we enrich that gift by extending it to others. When we host our own tables with a similar grace by making room for others, especially others who have made room for us, we are also making room for the One who has made room for all of us. That, too, is a tangled phrase, but needed theology just the same. When we set our tables with the grace and respect of hospitality, we participate in the divine hospitality that has made room for all of life. And for that, we give our most profound thanks for the tables that include us and at which we sometimes take our place as host.

Setting our tables with grace and respect makes our tables bigger and stronger at the same time it renders all who gather there more vulnerable. That truth focuses our attention on the immanent transcendence we meet in our midst. That is true for Seder tables as well ones that commemorate the Upper Room. Indeed, when Christians gather at their tables, Eucharistic or otherwise, and respect those who gather at other tables, we enlarge and enrich our own. When we acknowledge and transform our lack of hospitality in the past, we embody the spirit of the ancient prayer (*Our Father...*) that acknowledges that the holy happens in our midst *as* we give it expression at our tables and in our lives.

Manna and Matsa: Nourishment for the Soul

Susan CM Lumière

Introduction

As I contemplated writing a personal memoir as my contribution to the Passover Haggadah, I came to realize that celebrating Passover represents the most Jewish activity that my extended family ever observed. I was raised by loving, secular, assimilated, American-born parents who exposed me to some facets of Jewishness.

Carving an independent path, I became the most culturally identified and Jewishly aware person in my entire family—of my generation, my parents' generation, and younger generations. This memoir will delve into my upbringing, discoveries, and journey, not toward religious observance per se, but the embracing of myriad aspects of our rich culture and how it has enhanced and impacted my life.

Memories of various Passover seders and their significance to me will accompany the stages of my development. Although many of my recollections will go far afield of the holiday itself and focus upon many elements of my consciousness and awakening, seders and thoughts I have about Passover will be interwoven among the vignettes. Caveat lector: there will be tangents.

Early Experiences

Born on a U.S. Army-Air Force base in Virginia during World War II, I had no opportunity to be surrounded by either of my parents' large, Jewish families in Pittsburgh, Pennsylvania, or Omaha, Nebraska. A year after the war ended, my mother and I traveled across the Atlantic Ocean on the British luxury liner, the Queen Elizabeth, to meet my father, a career army officer, in London. I was told that at the age of three, I went up to all persons I saw and asked them, in my very proper British accent, if they were Jewish. ("I say, old chap, d'you by any chance 'appen to be Jewish? Oh, then, pip pip and cheerio!")

In truth, it was a bit simpler: "I'M Jewish; are YOU Jewish?" Obviously, I had no idea what being Jewish meant, but it was a good, if invasive, beginning.

After England, we moved to Boyle Heights, in East Los Angeles, California, for a brief time, when it had a substantial Jewish population, and then to a Los Angeles neighborhood near the Carthay Circle, not far from Fairfax, another area inhabited by many Jewish families. I loved my surroundings, school, family, and friends. That was where I celebrated my first family seder in the duplex where my parents, aunt, uncle, cousins and I all lived. None except my Russian grandmother kept the traditions strictly, but we ate the two Passover meals and took turns reading from the Haggadah. Most of us ate "chametz," leavened grains, during the eight days of the holiday, in addition to *matsa*. My family was more concerned about coaxing skinny little Susan to eat than whether I could ask "The Four Questions."

When I was nine, I was abruptly plucked out of that cozy environment when my father, Hershel, was sent overseas to command troops during the Korean War. My mother, Gerry Pearl, and I relocated to a suburb of Pittsburgh. Her birthplace was Squirrel Hill, a Jewish area; but in the tiny town where we stayed, I experienced my first and most memorable encounter with anti-Semitism. There were two Jewish students in the entire school. I, the strange girl from California, had no friends or playmates. It was, as my professor (later to be mentioned) called it, "the dislike of the unlike." One day, as I walked home from school, a gang of boys hid in some bushes, threw rocks at me, and called me a "dirty Jew." There isn't a lot of entertainment in small towns. Ironically, one of my assailants was the only other Jewish child in the school, Billy Siegel. I doubt if any of them knew what a Jew was, or perhaps Billy was trying to gain acceptance for himself by joining the bullies. While in Pennsylvania, our one seder was informal and more centered on the food than on the rituals or significance of Passover.

After the Korean War, my family was almost flown to Cairo, Egypt, soon after Colonel Nasser had seized power. By a stroke of luck and "military intelligence," someone must have realized that stationing a Jewish family in Pharaoh's, I mean, Nasser's country wasn't a smart idea. Two days before our flight (to, not from, Egypt, the opposite of the story in *Exodus*,) we received orders to board a naval ship and sail in the opposite direction, across the Pacific Ocean to Yokohama, Japan. Had we somehow been in Egypt in 1956, we would have been very close to the Suez War when Israel, the United Kingdom, and France fought against Egypt.

I never met any Jewish children in Tokyo; but there was a small building with a chaplain where a few officers and enlisted men could attend Jewish services, a place we rarely visited. Sometimes, non-Jewish Japanese citizens would wander in; and we joked that they were there for the Jewish sushi—lox.

We lived very near Emperor Hirohito's Palace, and I was invited to take horseback riding lessons at the royal stables; because my father was the Chief Finance Officer of the entire U.S. Army Headquarters in Tokyo.

There were a few anti-Semitic remarks that my family overheard made by military personnel and, undoubtedly, plenty that we never heard. I believe that my brilliant, highly capable father, who was also an attorney and President of Court Martials, was denied a full colonelship (and turned down at West Point,) because he was Jewish; but, overall, we were treated with respect in Japan.

At school, being new and Jewish were not handicaps. All students were from military families, and all of us were accustomed to being uprooted and transferred. Because of the turnover in the student body, there were no cliques or snobbery that I observed, no overt bullying but, rather, a feeling of camaraderie.

Going to Yoyogi Elementary School put me into contact with children and teachers from many places and ethnic backgrounds. One day, I was surprised to see a prominent black dot on the forehead of my school chum, Arthur. He explained that it was because of Ash Wednesday. He wasn't ridiculed for being Catholic; just as no one at school cared about my Jewish background. There is certainly discrimination and prejudice in the military, but I never observed classmates of any race or creed being targeted or becoming friendless.

My family had two brief seders in Tokyo with just the three of us present—basically, nice meals with lit candles on the table. Even if my parents had been traditional, I'm fairly sure Passover items weren't available at the local PX or at stalls in the humble Ginza, now one of the most luxurious districts in the world. At that time, the Japanese were known for being able to ingeniously imitate just about any product. Apparently, there was no market for imitation *matsot*, no company named "Matzobishi." (To give you an example of the difference between life in Tokyo in 1955 and today, a complete, top-of-the-line Chateaubriand steak dinner from soup to dessert cost $1.50 at the Officers' Club. Fifty-five years later, a pound of steak in Tokyo averages $200 a pound—and doesn't include an ice cream sundae.) Had any Jews wished to order rabbinically approved meat, they would have been unsuccessful. Kobe beef was not kosher beef.

My parents had both come from Orthodox Jewish homes and were the only ones in their respective families to earn college degrees. Lucky me! Both were very interested in being modern and American. They wanted me to have all the advantages that their impoverished immigrant families could not provide for them. We celebrated Passover and Easter, (in a secular way) Chanukah and Christmas. We even had a Chanukah bush that resembled a Christmas tree in all but the star or angel at the top. Other Jewish families in my Los Angeles neighborhood did, too. It was the American thing to do. When I lived in Tokyo, my mom and dad asked me if I wanted one big present for Christmas or eight little presents for Chanukah. I chose eight, not for reasons of religion or loyalty, but for the number. It never occurred to me to ask for eight big presents!

Back in the States, my parents and I occasionally attended synagogue on the High Holy Days. My larger family was scattered and preoccupied, and celebrating Passover became less frequent. After my paternal grandmother, Bubbe Gittel, a valiant soul, died, there was even less interest in preserving the traditions. My maternal grandmother, Bubbe Goldie, raised six children, cared for an ailing husband before being widowed, and struggled financially. Yet, her compassion and commitment to "tzedakah," charity, were so strong that she would cook large baskets of food, get on the bus, and deliver them to people even poorer than she was. If I needed a role model who exemplified the finest Jewish qualities, Goldie was one. Gittel was another. Even if neither inspired adherence to religious customs in my parents or in any of the grandchildren, their generosity and goodness did not go unnoticed.

I was enrolled at the beautiful Wilshire Boulevard Temple when Rabbi Edgar Magnin was there. That synagogue is the oldest congregation in Los Angeles. I didn't like my Sunday School teacher, and my kind parents did the best possible thing for me—they allowed me to become a Sunday School dropout. (Ironically, my first teaching assignment was at a Sunday School.)

The reason I know their decision was wise and beneficial is because it engendered no resentment. Others I know rebelled and rejected Judaism when their families insisted, but I could have a basic sense of my Jewishness and embrace my heritage when I was ready, in my own way. My parents gave me an opportunity but trusted me enough to accept or refuse it.

Like their parents, Gerry and Hersh embodied the best Jewish values and traits. They were magnanimous, nurturing, very funny and witty, educated, open-minded, welcoming, trustworthy, down-to-earth, cosmopolitan, tolerant, hard-working, sincere, and honest. My mother was a gourmet cook who taught me how to prepare delicious Jewish dishes.

The state of Israel was born four years after I was. Yet, as odd as it seems, I don't remember the country ever being mentioned in my home or by anyone in my extended family. We had a "pushke," a charity tin; but the money went to local organizations, not to Israel. It's bizarre to admit, but more attention was given to the "Ed Solomon Show," as Bubbe Gittel called it, than to the existence of Israel, which had no relevance to any of us.

My first awareness of the Holocaust and of Israel came about when I was fourteen and read Leon Uris's novel, *Exodus*. It made a deep impression. No one I knew had ever discussed the Shoah, and I found out later that I had some relatives in Russia who had survived. I don't know what they went through; but my cousin, Sonya, married a Russian colonel and never told her children that she was Jewish. Her brother, Manye, a pilot, was shot down by the Germans. Both were to have been sent here before World War I but were cheated out of their visas. How I wish I had asked Sonya about her life when I finally met her.

Because I attended Beverly Hills High School and not Fairfax, I didn't encounter any openly observant Jewish students, even though the BHHS student body was 97% Jewish.

My ties to my culture were very weak during that time. I may have attended a Jewish wedding, danced the hora and eaten brunch at Nate 'n' Al's Delicatessen, but that was all. This was about to change dramatically.

Transformation

In a UCLA psychology class, in my freshman year, I met the son of an Orthodox rabbi, who became my first serious boyfriend. Our relationship lasted only a year and a half, but being exposed to his way of life impacted me permanently. He was one of those I mentioned who rebelled against Judaism. He balked at the restrictions and expectations imposed on him by his family and was a significantly wayward son.

His lovely parents, both survivors, welcomed me into their home, although I was never invited to their seder. One Shabbat afternoon, I drove over to visit, and the rebbetzin audibly gasped when she noticed that I had had my hair done professionally and was carrying a purse. Dangling from my guilty hand was a bunch of telltale car keys. I had no idea that what I had done was taboo or offensive. Since my family identified as Reform Jews, I wasn't familiar with Orthodox customs.

My parents did not meet my boyfriend's parents until the tail end of our relationship. Nor were mine pleased that I had become involved with a young man from an Orthodox background. They were very hospitable to my boyfriend and never asked me to stop seeing him, but they were worried that I'd be swept into his family's lifestyle and feared that I'd be trapped and unhappy. We didn't have detailed discussions about their attitude toward Orthodoxy; but I suspect that, in part, they may have associated it with superstition and at odds with the American way of life. As suggested before, Orthodoxy certainly wasn't compatible with a life spent in the US Army. Without heavily voicing their doubts, my parents were also perceptive enough to sense that my boyfriend was lacking in integrity and character. When I came to the same conclusion, I ended the connection.

Unexpectedly, on the night I said farewell, his parents drove to our home in desperation, met my parents for the first time and begged them to convince me to take their son back. I had always assumed that the rabbi and rebbetzin thought I wasn't good enough, because I wasn't observant. To my surprise, they saw me as a good influence who could keep their son away from trouble. My parents and I had the decency not to reveal to them the very egregious acts that caused me to initiate the separation, and I can only imagine what his parents knew that we didn't.

Rather than keep you in suspense, you deserve to know that one of my beau's offenses was trying to take credit for a paper I had written. Had my professor believed him, I could have been expelled from the university and deprived of my academic and teaching careers. I hadn't known that my beloved was flunking out of college and had decided to sacrifice my well-being to save himself with a misbegotten scheme.

Did I suddenly find religion and become devout after my breakup? Not at all. For me to have done that, I would have had to feel a calling from within. I was a free spirit and non-conformist. Following rigid rules and guidelines, religious or otherwise, was anathema to me and made no sense—but, despite that, my time with the miscreant's family led to a very positive outcome.

In my circle, being Jewish was about Judaism—religious beliefs and holidays. No one I knew was involved in the broader Jewish culture. My parents and relatives knew how to speak Yiddish; but, as was often the case, didn't teach it their children. All my cousins in LA were girls, so there were no bar mitzvahs until the next generation and no bat mitzvahs.

Had Henry, my baby brother, survived, his would have been my family's first and only bar mitzvah ceremony of his generation and would have been celebrated lavishly, unlike my father's, whose party took place in the basement of a small shul in Omaha in the winter of 1921, accompanied by herring and pumpernickel bread. Three years later, my dad became a founding member of Aleph Zadik Aleph, or AZA, a Jewish high school fraternity and service organization. Jews were excluded from the Greek letter clubs in those years, so from adversity came triumph. Soon adopted by B'nai B'rith, the AZA and BBG, B'nai B'rith Girls, grew exponentially; and chapters now exist in over forty countries.

Non-religious Jewish organizations and activities existed in Los Angeles, but we didn't take part or know about them. There were some options in the forties and fifties for girls and women, such as the BBG and Hadassah, but there are more now. My mom and I were active in the Brownies and the Girl Scouts, as were my friends. None of us even knew about the BBG, which had, ironically, been launched by my father and his Omaha fraternity.

So, how did meeting the rabbi's son change my life profoundly? In my sophomore year, I enrolled in a class that I thought had to do with music appreciation but turned out to be technical. Casting about for a substitute, I noticed a Hebrew literature class in translation offered at the same time. A kernel of curiosity had been planted by my association with my erstwhile boyfriend and his family. I enrolled in the esteemed Dr. David Lieber's class, became intrigued, met a sister student who was to become a lifelong, cherished friend, Harlene; and my journey was launched.

I was even invited to present a speech in a campus auditorium about the Golden Age of Jewish culture in Medieval Spain, something I never could have imagined myself doing a few months before.

The following year I signed up for a Jewish history class with an illustrious Israeli professor, Dr. Jacob Landau, master of eleven languages. One book that was assigned for the second semester was *The Course of Modern Jewish History* by Howard Morley Sachar. I devoured that book three times from cover to cover, the stories and events resonating deeply. To say that I was mesmerized would be an understatement. By that time, I had a double major, Near Eastern Studies and Social Psychology. The attraction to both Jewish and Middle Eastern studies shows that I was instinctively following my DNA all along. Half a century later, I discovered that I have 88% Ashkenazi, 6% non-Jewish Central European, 3% Turkish, and 3% Persian ancestry.

In most of the Near Eastern Studies classes that weren't part of the Jewish curriculum, the Arab and Jewish students self-segregated, choosing to sit on opposite sides of the room, divided by an invisible "mechitza," or screen. Thankfully, there was no evidence of the violence, boycotts, or overt hostility present on so many campuses today; but there was a measure of animosity, suspicion, and heated arguments between the two factions. Our Turkish professor of Middle Eastern sociology looked nervous and intimidated when he sensed rivalry in class and sat in his chair, fidgeting with his worry beads.

Most Americans remember where they were when they learned of President Kennedy's assassination. I was sitting in my Middle Eastern history class, waiting for our Iranian professor, who had never been late. At 11:10 a.m., he entered the room visibly shaken and pale. Many classes were dismissed, and we hurried to the main cafeteria to hear the devastating news. Whatever tension had been brewing between the Arab and Jewish students was quickly forgotten.

Another memory from UCLA involves a rally against the Shah of Iran. My friend from Hebrew literature convinced me to attend, and we were both chagrinned when we learned that the Shah had been good to the Jews of his country and that we had been naively hoodwinked into showing support for his detractors. This was a decade and a half before the Ayatollah Khomeini overthrew the Shah. From then on we concentrated on Jewish matters. I wonder how many of those protesters would have despised the Shah if they had known what the Ayatollah had in store for their homeland.

We were caught up in the dizzying zeitgeist of the sixties. All of a sudden, ethnic pride emerged. It was no longer necessary or desirable to conform to the White Anglo-Saxon Protestant image, at least on the coasts and campuses. Blacks sported Afros and dashikis; Jews sported Jewfros and had fewer nose jobs. I dyed my blond hair black, never went back, and emulated Geula Gil, a popular Israeli singer. "Fiddler on the Roof" came out in 1964 and was a smash hit. New dimensions were being added to my Jewish consciousness, and it was exhilarating.

Warren "Zev" Garber was the teaching assistant for the Jewish history class I had taken, but I wasn't to meet him until my senior year.

Zev was teaching a pilot Hebrew class, based on linguistics. I've always been interested in foreign languages. I've studied Spanish, Hebrew, Serbo-Croatian, Arabic, and Yiddish.

I had never taken Hebrew before college, but I fell madly in love with it. Zev's instruction inspired a great feeling for the language. I was able to communicate in Hebrew after four months, thanks to Zev and our Israeli conversation teacher. I ordered special grammar books from Israel and a beginner's newspaper with crossword puzzles in simple Hebrew. I sat under trees on campus, immersed in my studies. I even began to dream in Hebrew; and when I finally went to Israel, it was assumed that I was a returning Sabra.

When my parents asked me what I wanted as a college graduation gift, instead of a car or trip to Europe, I asked for an enormous, expensive English-Hebrew dictionary. They wondered how they had produced a daughter who was becoming "so Jewish." I loved dating and parties, but scholarship and exploring Jewish culture occupied a great deal of my time.

The summer after my graduation, I was fortunate enough to attend BCI, Brandeis Camp Institute—now known as Brandeis-Bardin Institute. Pioneering visionary, Shlomo Bardin, had created a remarkable retreat in the Santa Susana Mountains for college students and others. It was the first time I had gone to a camp. Dr. Bardin promised to give us an experience we would never forget, and he did. In the mornings, we performed agricultural chores, as if we were on a kibbutz. In the afternoons, we took classes in Israeli dance with Dani Dassa, which inspired my 50+ years of passion for international folk dancing. We also had classes in Jewish music, art, drama, Judaica, and other subjects. At night we participated in various Jewish activities and ceremonies. While there I created the script, lyrics, and choreography of a musical satire. Being at BCI brought out talent I didn't know I had. The drama teacher, a prominent Hollywood movie coach, liked my production and asked if I would like to study acting with him. It was an honor, but I knew I wanted to be a teacher and so declined.

Guess who was in residence at BCI for the month I was there? None other than the revered Rabbi Mordecai Kaplan, the co-founder of Reconstructionist Judaism, and his delightful wife. By the time I was at BCI, Reconstructionism was well-established; but I didn't become acquainted with it until later.

During my last year as an undergraduate, I became friendly with a group of Israelis. I frequented the Sabra Cafe in West Hollywood and practiced my Hebrew. That spring I made my own seder for my friends. I had inherited my mother's flair for cooking and even perfected a recipe for irresistible chicken soup and fluffy *matsa* balls, the quintessential dish of our people's cuisine. Why keep it a secret? In addition to organically grown chicken and spring water, the soup contains chicken bouillon cubes, a little black ground pepper, sliced carrots, a generous amount of Manischewitz wine (Concord grape or blackberry) and fresh lemon juice. Truly, no other soup can hold a "k'naydl" to it. I was so pleased that I could host a seder and read the Haggadah in Hebrew. It was a momentous occasion to mark how far I had come in my Jewish identity.

Israel at Last

My fervent goal was to visit Israel. Although unaffiliated with any organization, I had become a gung-ho Zionist. A big advantage to being a teacher was having summers off for travel. I had bought a ticket six months in advance for a charter flight to Israel, sponsored by the Israeli Maccabee Soccer Club. The plane was scheduled to take off on June 28th. The year was 1967. As silly as it sounds, my Ouija board had warned me that war would prevent me from going to Israel; but I was unshakably determined to go. As we know, the Six Day War broke out on June 5th. The travel restrictions for Americans were lifted three days before my flight. Thanks to Moshe Dayan and his invincible troops, my dream of going to Israel became a reality.

Although this part of the story is a bit tangential, it is so uncanny and unique that it must be included. I had planned to travel alone from Stuttgart, where the charter plane would land, by hopping onto the Orient Express through Germany, Austria, Yugoslavia, and Greece and then flying to Tel Aviv. I met two charming Israelis on the plane, and they convinced me to abandon my risky, harebrained plan and travel to Paris with them. Accepting their invitation probably saved my life. In Paris many of the French recognized that we were Jewish/Israeli and congratulated us on the stunning victory—that we had had nothing to do with. My new friends had their tickets for Israel, but my flight was from Athens.

Too late for that, I said "shalom" to Shmuel and Ilana and headed to the Orly Airport, barely surviving one of those infamous, heart-stopping taxicab rides. I sauntered into the El Al terminal only to be greeted by a sea of black. Hundreds of Orthodox Jewish families had been camping out for days, wall to wall, BECAUSE of the Wall, the Western Wall, on the floor of the terminal, waiting for a chance to fly to the Holy Land, now that the old city of Jerusalem had been liberated. My heart sank. All those years of saving, preparing, and yearning for Israel; and I was to be denied entrance to the Promised Land.

Still, I had chutzpah, so I gamely approached the ticket counter and asked if there were any chances of flying that day. The winsome clerk told me that there was one available seat on an already departing plane. My timing was spot on. The Chasidim had been waiting for a long time ahead of me, but they wanted to travel together. No one among them wanted a lone seat. The clerk radioed the pilot to stop for me. I threw my travelers' checks onto the counter, burst through the doors, and clambered down the steps to the tarmac in my wobbly sandals and miniskirt, clutching seven bulky suitcases. I chased after the moving El Al plane. The passengers suddenly spotted me and excitedly cheered me on. Finally, the plane stopped, I hurtled up the ramp, and the entire plane broke into a rousing cheer. I do like attention, but that was beyond thrilling—for me and for my well-wishers. I wish that my daring, madcap pursuit had been filmed. I'm certain it was "b'shert," destined, for me to be on that plane.

Imagine being allowed onto a plane headed for the Middle East with unchecked luggage and no identification check. There were no suicide bombers in those days, and security was much more relaxed.

As soon as I landed at Lod, now Ben-Gurion Airport, I felt a glorious sense of being home. The level of caring, welcome, empathy and connection I felt was like no other. Strangers invited me to their homes; and one lady literally gave me the shirt off her back, so I wouldn't get sunburned. I was only a tourist, but because I had arrived so soon after the war, I was treated as a "mitnadevet," a volunteer. The Israelis I met viewed a visit to their country as a show of support and acted accordingly.

HaKotel, the Wall, was so newly opened that there were no prayer notes inserted into cracks between the ancient stones. On another outing some kibbutzniks and I ignored the yellow tape in the newly captured Gaza Strip that warned trespassers to keep out. We jumped into the Red Sea with our clothes on, and the military guards laughed.

A friend I had known in Los Angeles had flown to Israel to join his IDF commander when he saw him on television, but the war had ended before he arrived. He offered to show me the land, and we toured for a while. One evening we climbed over a locked gate to an enclosure that was designed to display plants and trees from the biblical Garden of Eden. The guard, lonely for companionship, welcomed us and didn't complain about our illegal entry. I mention these experiences to describe the atmosphere of those days and to contrast it with all the changes that have happened since.

On another day, an IDF paratrooper and I were graciously served Arabic coffee in a cave by a sixteen-year-old Palestinian boy whose parents had fled and left him during the recent war. We also saw Arabs selling fresh bagels, which was an amusing and unexpected sight. There were white flags of surrender all over and bullet holes in my hotel room walls, but the entire country was celebrating the swift end to the war and the remarkable conquest. Never was there a safer or more joyful time to be in Israel, except perhaps in 1948. We civilians could walk anywhere day or night and hitch rides on army trucks with the handsome Israeli soldiers.

Toward the end of my visit, I was offered a job teaching English to 18-year-old delinquent Moroccan boys in the desert town of Dimona, 400 miles from nowhere; but I wisely declined and packed my bags for home. As much as I wanted to stay in Eretz Yisrael and absorb the magic, I owed more allegiance and love to my parents. I was their only child, and it would have broken all our hearts had I chosen to abandon them. They hadn't lost me to Orthodoxy, nor to Zionism. If I forget thee, O Mother; if I forget thee, O Father...May I never forget to honor you both AND Jerusalem.

Once back in Tel Aviv, I hitched a ride on a donkey cart, put my luggage next to the driver, and rode to the airport sitting on a load of watermelons, spitting out seeds all the way to Lod.

Back in America

The next part of this memoir will be a summary of the ways in which I've expanded my participation in Jewish life and a mention of some special seders. I briefly taught Hebrew at the Valley Beth Shalom Synagogue and became a folk singer for two traveling Israeli dance troupes, "Hadarim" and "Finjan." "Yerushalayim Shel Zahav" ("Jerusalem of Gold") had become the signature song of the Six Day War. Singing it on tour brought back memories of Israel, a place that I was missing.

Later, I took classes at Los Angeles Valley College in Jewish Studies with Professor Zev Garber and Rabbi Mark Goodman; studied at American Jewish University, the Skirball Cultural Center, and Chabad; read numerous books, saw films, painted pictures, wrote humorous and serious articles; and attended lectures, concerts, exhibits, and events with Jewish themes. I also introduced my students to Israeli songs and dances; briefly taught Israeli folk dance to adults; wrote Jewish jokes and satirical lyrics; took private Yiddish classes; and formed a Yiddish Culture Club; (known as the "Honorable Menschen" and the "Munchin' Menschen.") The purpose of the club was to learn and promote the Yiddish language, host social events, see films, and attend concerts and plays having to do with Yiddish themes.

At one point in my career, I became a professional Middle Eastern sword dancer. My very first performance was, of all places, at the childhood synagogue I had abandoned, the Wilshire Boulevard Temple. I also performed at weddings, bar mitzvahs, and a Jewish luau.

In addition to all this fun, I wrote and performed a one-woman musical parody called "East Side Story," featuring Leonard Bernstein and

Elvis, who was Jewish, as I hope you know. In his honor, I wrote "Heartbreak Kotel."

I keep in contact with treasured friends from the early years. One great advantage to being one of Zev's students, besides my fifty-seven-year friendship with him, is that when I took his exceptional Holocaust class, I met and formed friendships with a Polish survivor and a polio survivor. They were women of inestimable valor, resilience, and personality, Shifra and Min. The three of us became practically inseparable. I also met one of my most valued friends through Professor Zev, his wife, Susan.

Those of you who know Zev Garber, know that he does not simply show up in class, teach and go home. Since I've known him at UCLA, Zev has taken the time to know his students and socialize with them. He reaches out and has a genuine interest in including us in his circle and community, reinforcing our connection to Jewish life and studies.

Although I taught in Jewish temples, the main part of my career was spent in public schools, teaching art and academics. Because we had many festivals, musicals, and pageants, I often made costumes for my students and myself. Some of my costumes were Jewish-themed, and one was related specifically to Passover.

A party I attended in honor of Friday the Thirteenth centered upon "Unlucky Events." I wore an Egyptian gown, headdress, jewelry, and a large sandwich board with a map of Egypt and three-dimensional figures of frogs, insects, hail, etc., representing the ten plagues of Egypt. I wish I had saved the outfit for future seders, although my hosts might have questioned my choice.

Celebrations

As noted, my seder attendance was sporadic during my early years but gathered momentum later on. Thanks to connecting with longtime friends and new ones from classes, Israeli dancing, and the Yiddish Culture Club, I sometimes attended as many as four whirlwind seders in two days. Maybe I was turning into a Passover junkie. There was no warmer, more beautiful occasion for strengthening bonds of friendship, honoring hallowed traditions, reflecting upon the miracles of Jewish survival and existence, and sharing a feeling of unity.

It was and is a time of thanksgiving and renewal, becoming more meaningful as each year passes. I attended a marvelous Chabad seder; Orthodox seders; New Age seders; electronic seders—ones where we consulted our iPhones for guidance; streamlined, high-speed seders; an elegant Israeli seder with classical music; a vegan seder; a multiracial seder, which featured chocolate-covered *matsot* enjoyed in a Jacuzzi; and one hosted by a well-meaning but inept bachelor whose brisket was so hard and dry it could have stood for the bricks used by Hebrew slaves for Pharaoh's penthouse—(Rameses' Ramada Inn?). Some of the most meaningful seders were held at the home of the parents of a close friend, Esther, both of whom miraculously survived the Shoah.

In Conclusion

At the beginning of this essay, I mentioned my lack of belief in and observance of religious rituals. I did not claim to be an atheist or an agnostic, however. After a lot of thinking, reading and searching during my college years, I came to believe in a Supreme Being. By witnessing and participating in several unmistakable miracles and personally experiencing profound connections with the Divine, I have no doubt that a supernatural, incomprehensible intelligence exists and permeates our universe. Some of my ideas about HaShem have been influenced by Jewish thought, though not exclusively.

Until this point of my narrative, the hero of the Passover story has been alluded to only once and obliquely but not spoken of by name. I read a startling statement in a book called *A History of the Jews* by the distinguished Abram Leon Sachar, founding president of Brandeis University, award-winning historian, and father of the aforementioned Howard Morley Sachar.

Sachar writes that Moshe Rabbenu, Moses, our Rabbi, he who shaped the Mosaic faith, might be the greatest Hebrew leader who NEVER lived. There is skepticism and controversy about whether any events described in the Bible actually happened, including the Exodus, of course; but what Sachar wrote astonished me. Here's an excerpt: "Moses created the Hebrew people when he united them by the bonds of religion. His immense influence easily marks him as the outstanding character in Hebrew history, one of the moral giants of all time.

Yet, of his life, of his very existence, we have no conclusive proof. Not a contemporaneous document, not a stele, not a shred of evidence has been found to authenticate his historicity. Perhaps, someday his existence, too, will be scientifically demonstrated, as Hammurabi's was, when, in 1902, the tablets of his laws were discovered. Until then the paradox must remain that the most influential personality in Jewish history may be merely the product of Jewish imagination... It has been suggested that even if this picturesque account (of the Exodus) were purely mythical, even if there were no Moses, it would be necessary to create one to account for the developments which transformed the early history of the Hebrews."

Sachar goes on to say that most modern critics accept Moses as a definite historical figure and consider him to have been a magnificent nomad leader and powerful, highly effective tribal chieftain.

Obviously, the purpose of my essay is not to present arguments about the authenticity or lack thereof of the biblical account of Moses. That has no place in this account. It goes without saying that, though interested, I am absolutely unqualified. The reason I raise the issue at all is merely to show that I was floored by the idea that the existence of Moses, the towering pillar of three religions, could be questioned. Every time I attended a seder thereafter, I was reminded of Sachar's words.

There is a more personally compelling reason that I wanted to include the passage from Dr. Sachar's book, besides feeling that Moses must be a part of this story. If not Moses, then who? Abram Sachar was the father of the author who had written my favorite Jewish history book, the one that had fired my imagination and fueled my enthusiasm in my pursuit of Jewish studies when I was nineteen. Exactly fifty years later, a friend gave me A. Sachar's book. I felt connected to both authors and knew that they had enriched my life. I had come full circle.

A humorous encounter occurred regarding this subject. I was seated next to a Brazilian passenger on a flight. I spoke no Portuguese, and he spoke no English. Fortunately, Spanish saved the day. Coincidentally, my seatmate, a young scholar, was reading an article about the Bible. I told him about the speculation surrounding Moses. A lively discussion ensued. As the flight came to an end and we prepared to disembark, my companion politely introduced me to his friend, Moises. I shook his hand and said, "Quisiera saludarte, pero tu no existes." (I would like to greet you, but you do not exist.) We had a good laugh over that.

However, my comments were not so well-received at the next seder I attended. My hostess took umbrage at the suggestion that Moses might be imaginary, although she is more of a devotee of Hinduism than Judaism. Yet isn't it a time-honored tradition for Jews to question almost everything?

I cherish the custom of our people to argue, debate, challenge and explore all aspects of our faith and history unceasingly and not to slavishly submit to dogma. I love the fact that one can live a good and fulfilling Jewish life without being religious and that I can eclectically choose what holds meaning for me and discard what does not.

So, this is a tale of seven and a half decades which shows how a third-generation American, a military child, raised with just enough exposure to her people's customs to get a foothold, evolved and discovered a whole world, both tangible and intangible. Knowing what I do now, had I not been born Jewish, I would have longed to be a part of the most fascinating and diverse culture I've ever encountered, to partake of the spiritual manna that is offered. Fortunately, I didn't need to convert. So, symbolically, I lift my Passover goblet and simply say, "L'chaim." May we all have the opportunity to celebrate and honor the ancient holiday with loved ones and read our Haggadahs in peace and in safety.

Ziva: The Warrior of Light

Susan Garber

I grew up in a secular Jewish home. Until I was in my late twenties, I was unaware that for Jews the Sabbath began on Friday night and ended on Saturday evening. Shabbat was a word I had never heard of. Sunday was the day of rest as far as I knew, for at that time in the San Fernando Valley of California almost all private businesses would close on that day. I did go to synagogue with my parents on Yom Kippur and what I loved most about that was hearing the shofar blow when the first star appeared in the evening sky. And for me, Passover meant being happy to see my extended family (on one night—I didn't know Passover was an eight-day festival with not one, but two seders in the Diaspora).

However, what always stood out in my memory about this night was the readings from the haggadah, with its story of freedom made possible by God's intervention. And connected to this was my having seen Cecil B. DeMilles 1956 version of The Ten Commandments when I was an eight-year-old. I've never grown tired of reading the haggadah (now on two nights) and watching that film. They both inspired me to write a fantasy story many years ago and its main sequences take place during the time the Hebrews were in Egypt and when they left to begin their journey to the land promised to them by God. I have changed this story somewhat so that it will fit into a short-story format for the Annotated Passover Haggadah.

Prologue

"Are men to be ruled by God's law? Or are they to be ruled by the whims of a dictator, like Rameses? Are men the property of the state? Or are they free souls under God?"

Cecil B. DeMille
(from the introduction in his 1956 film, *The Ten Commandments*)

The Book of the Wars of the Lord is mentioned by name only once (Num. 21:14) in the Torah, the first five books of the Hebrew Bible. It also may be hinted at in two other biblical passages (Josh. 10:13 and 2 Sam. 1:18). If it still existed, I was determined to be the archaeologist who would find it.

When I was 10 years old, searching through a stack of books at Tel Tales, my parents' book shop, in Simi Valley, California, by chance I came across a small volume titled Halohemet Ziv. Because I read and spoke Hebrew, I knew the words roughly translated as The Warrior of Light. More specifically, a female warrior who was

Fig. 17

surrounded by an aura of natural light, just as the illumination from the sun, moon, and stars is natural. Its author was the leader of a sect known as hashomerim (the Guardians). The little book fascinated me. So much so that it set me upon the path to my chosen profession. It spoke about an ancient scroll that was a record of Israelite victories during their sojourn in the wilderness. And almost two decades later, a hint in that book led me to Ein Gedi on the western shore of the Dead Sea.

Beyond Ein Gedi were the high mountains of the Judean desert. I knew the area well, having explored numerous caves in those mountains. I also was very familiar with the ancient mosaic synagogue floor that had been discovered at Ein Gedi. Along with the beautiful and intricate artwork on this floor, in a corner next to where the entrance to the synagogue would have been, was a warning from the community that once called this desert oasis in Israel their home. It declared that if anyone revealed the secret of the community, they would be cursed. It is known that perfume was manufactured there and that even Cleopatra used this fragrance extracted from a species of balsam that only grew at Ein Gedi. Was it the formula of the famous perfume that was the secret? I was certain there was something more to it than that.

A few newspapers had heard of my intention to discover what the cryptic message of Ein Gedi referred to. When I was interviewed in Israel, I told the journalists nothing of the book that had inspired this quest. That is why I was very surprised to receive an email message from someone who wanted to speak to me in person about hashomerim. He claimed to be the son of the author of Halohemet Ziv. Upon his father's death, he became the leader of the clandestine group who had guarded a secret generation after generation. He wrote that his name was Rabbi Aryeh ha-Zaddik (the righteous lion). I normally would have ignored a request to meet a stranger in this way, but something intrigued me with the words he wrote. I responded that "yes," I would meet him at his home in Talpiot, a suburb of Jerusalem.

I arrived at the rabbi's residence late in the morning. The sky, brooding and gray, was almost ready to give way to a spring rainstorm. I parked my rental car in front of the modest two story detached house that was encompassed by a lovely, well-tended garden. The rabbi was at the front gate before I had a chance to ring the bell hanging from a wooden post next to it. Rabbi Aryeh was a much younger man than I had expected. His handsome face was partially hidden by a full beard and he had brown curly hair with payot (prayer curls) that cascaded down the sides of his cheeks. He was a tall man with a slim, yet muscular, body. I believed in the old cliché that a person's eyes were the mirror of their soul. And Rabbi Aryeh had gentle, soft brown eyes.

"I'm Margalit Ehrlich," I said to him as he smiled.

I recognized you immediately," he quickly replied with an answer that surprised me. Seeing the strange look on my face, he immediately explained. "I saw your photo in an archaeology magazine."

We sat down to talk at his kitchen table. He said he wanted to impart knowledge to me of a woman called Ziva, the daughter of Aaron ("exalted") and niece of Moses ("son"). I smiled to myself. What kind of tale was this going to be? The Bible referred only to the four sons of Aaron—Nadab (generous offering), Abihu ("he is my father"), Eleazar ("God has helped"), and Ithamar ("island of palms"). But hashomerim seemed to insist that Aaron and his wife Elisheba ("God is an oath") also had a daughter. I remembered her name from the little book written by Rabbi Aryeh's father. His story began:

In the Pastures of Goshen

It was *erev pesach*, just hours before the very first *Pesach* (Passover). In Egypt, it was the end of the season of *proyet (peret)*, the time of the emergence of crops. *Shemu (shumu)*, the season of low water and the harvest, was about to begin. The fields normally were bursting with barley and emmer as well as various other crops. But much of this had been devastated by blights that were said to have been brought upon Egypt by the God of the Hebrews. The fertile silt laden soil of the Nile's delta region normally produced the crops that fed most of Egypt. *Akhet,* the inundation season of The River (Nile), had promised a rich harvest, but that promise was now forgotten.

The village of Goshen ("drawing near"), located in this important area of Lower Egypt, had been the home of the *habiru* ("dusty ones") over several generations. Propelled by the hardships brought by drought and famine, they were forced to leave their homeland as many other peoples were. The *habiru* or Hebrews were a people comprised of several tribes that were joined together by a common thread—they were independent souls who did not bend to the will of any earthly king, only to the will of their god, Yahweh, alone.

One of these people was Joseph ("he will add"), the son of Jacob ("seize by the heel"). He gained favor with the Hyksos king of Egypt and became his chief advisor. A vast amount of fertile pastureland in the Nile delta was granted to Joseph and his family members. They prospered and grew in number and might. They left the life of the shepherd for that of the farmer and craftsman. For over two hundred years, they lived in relative peace with their Egyptian neighbors. They traded with them, shared in family celebrations, and, at times, some even intermarried and wandered after their gods.

Yet there always had been a great divide between the Egyptians and the foreigners. Not all these strangers had peaceful intentions as did the Hebrews. Long before the Hebrews sojourned into Egypt, there were those who saw the hold of the Egyptian pharaohs was weakening. And there came a time when Hyksos shepherd kings controlled Lower Egypt and eventually even territory within Upper Egypt.

The Egyptians waited, knowing that someday the time would arise when they would once again rule the Two Lands. Eventually this came to pass. They drove the Hyksos ruler from Avaris, his capital city. The Two Lands (Lower and Upper Egypt) were reunited. All reference to the Hyksos was removed. It was as if these kings had never lived, their existence cancelled. The Great Humiliation under these shepherd rulers was wiped clean from the memory of the Egyptians. Only a distrust of the stranger remained. Including the Hebrews, those foreigners who had not fled were largely enslaved. Taskmasters were set over them.

The Egyptian revival that followed was breathtaking in scope. There was a rebirth of culture. Military strength grew allowing imperial expansion abroad. At home, enormous building projects were found everywhere. These were made possible largely through the bitter bondage of slaves, some of whom had once been free men and women in this land.

The Hebrews, however, never forgot the covenant they had made with God. They knew that He would send a Deliverer who would lead them out of bondage and back to the land He had promised would be theirs. Yonatan and Ziva, a young man and woman, walking down a path in a barley field, just outside the village of Goshen, were speaking about an uncertain future that now faced them. It was a future that meant they might soon be leaving a place that their people had called home for generations. They were a handsome couple. She was tall and shapely, with long, wavy raven black hair and green eyes that tilted slightly upward at the outer corners. He, too, was tall, with a strong body. He viewed the world with a seriousness that was unnerving. Yet, when he was with Ziva, the serious look seemed to be overtaken by a softness that could not deny his love for her. Ziva was impetuous, rebellious, except when she was in Yonatan's company. He had a calming effect upon her. This had been so since they were children.

The families of Ziva and Yonatan, as well as a few others in Goshen, had retained some of their prior wealth. They were the exception because they were important to Pharaoh's house. They possessed superior skills in such things as metal working and masonry that pleased the king greatly. And they served him well because they knew if they did not, that they and their children might find themselves in chains. The men and older boys would be sent to toil in the mud of the brick pits, the fields, the mines, or on the ropes pulling the enormous stone blocks that went into building Pharaoh's treasure cities in such places as Pithom ("House of Atum") and Ramses ("House of Ra").

Ziva's father, Aaron, fashioned weapons for Pharaoh's army. Yonatan ("God has given"), like his father Simeon ("hearing"), was a mason and sculptor. From huge pillars of stone, with his skill and the skill of many others, the precise likeness of the king's image would emerge from the stone. But Yonatan was much more than a craftsman. He was a *navi*, a prophet, who was wise beyond his years.

Ziva confronted his wisdom on this bright, sunny morning that gave no hint of what terror the night's darkness would reveal. It was on this night that God was going to strike down the firstborn of Egypt. But He would pass over any house, protecting those within, if the doorposts and lintels had been sprinkled with lamb's blood.

"Yonatan, what of our dear companion Gahiji? We grew up together. When I finished my chores, I could not wait to join you, my brothers, and Gahiji in the fields beyond my father's shop. At first you and my brothers would tell me to go home to the women, but Gahiji accepted me immediately, even though I was a girl."

As a child, Ziva was different from other girls. Like them, she learned the skills of women. Her mother and aunts taught her the art of the loom, how to bake bread, and to brew the most wonderful honey beer. But once her chores and lessons were completed, usually by mid-day, she ran off to the barley fields that lie beyond her family's compound. There she played "war games" alongside her five handsome brothers and two of their friends. Gahiji ("hunter") was an Egyptian. His father was Bakari ("noble oath"), an advisor to the Pharaoh. Gahiji was short and stocky, but a "fierce warrior." Yonatan was the other friend who played at these "war games" with great skill, but who never really seemed to enjoy them as the others did.

Both Yonatan and Gahiji had no birth brothers or sisters, but the friendship they formed with Ziva and her brothers created an extended family for them. To the consternation of the boys, Ziva excelled at archery and spear throwing. She never missed a target, no matter how far it was placed in front of her. And Yonatan always was aware that she was special. Yes, she was beautiful and was free-spirited, but she was kind to those in need, both human and animal. He saw a worth in her that was yet to fully reveal itself.

Ziva continued speaking about their closeness to Gahiji. "We shared everything—happiness, sorrow, and pride in all our accomplishments. Don't you remember? And tonight, Gahiji will die for he is the firstborn of the Pharaoh's chief counselor. I cannot believe that our God, who is supposed to be just, would decree this. Or that you, the wisest of men, can accept what is to happen."

In a sad, but firm voice Yonatan answered her. "Have you forgotten the drowning of the infant sons of our people? A pharaoh, who had no memory of our forefather Joseph, decreed this horrific deed be done and it was so. We were defenseless, having no country of our own to flee to; no army that would drive our enemies away. Your uncle Moses escaped this fate because his mother placed him in a basket made of bulrushes, sealed with pitch and slime. She set it upon the waters of The River. Was it simply coincidence that the daughter of the king drew the basket from the water and reared him as her own son, a prince of Egypt? When he discovered his true heritage and killed an Egyptian who was beating a Hebrew slave, he fled to Midian. And it was there he spoke with God face to face. And God's words were that he must return to Egypt where he was to tell Pharaoh to let the Hebrews go. Ziva, with freedom, we will be able to shape our own destiny."

"But this is the only place we have ever known," Ziva responded. "How do we know what awaits us in the wilderness beyond this land? At least here we have food and shelter. As of now, the plagues Yahweh has brought upon Egypt have not changed Pharaoh's heart, only hardened it against us. And what if death of Egypt's firstborn does not soften it? Will he then carry out his own plan to slay our firstborn?"

Yonatan replied passionately, "Nine times Pharaoh has refused to let us go and nine times disaster has fallen upon Egypt. This was by Pharaoh's choice, not God's. And when he decreed that our firstborn would be slain, it was he who sealed the fate of the firstborn of Egypt. Each plague showed that the power of their supreme gods was nothing next to the will of Yahweh whose ways and thoughts are beyond ours. *Ehyeh asher Ehyeh – I will be that I will be.* This is what your uncle Moses said God wished to be called—a presence ever evolving in our minds, never limited, eternal."

Ziva was listening with intent to what Yonatan was saying. He hoped she could accept his words. He knew how worried she was about the days ahead. He continued to speak.

"When the waters of the Nile turned into blood for a week's time, did Hapi, the Nile god provide suitable drinking water? Did Heket, the frog-headed goddess of fertility and renewal, make the thousands of frogs, that crept up from The River and overran all living space on land, go back where they came from? When the dust from the earth was turned into lice to torment both man and beast, did the Egyptian god of the earth, Geb, make this stop? As flies swarmed all over the places where Egyptians gather, we were left unscathed. For them, their fly-headed god of creation, Khepri, provided no relief.

Ziva, with this, for the first time, Pharaoh felt he must bargain with our God. Yet once the flies departed, he reneged on his promise to let us go. Following this, as cattle and livestock died, was the cow-headed goddess of love and protection, Hathor, able to fulfill her purpose?

And then the sixth plague arrived, which was different than the preceding five. It was a direct attack upon the Egyptians themselves. Boils and sores formed when ashes began settling on their skin, as well as on the skin of their animals. Because of this, the Egyptians found themselves to be in a state of "uncleanness." Therefore, even Pharaoh's magicians and priests could not stand before him, for they, too, were "unclean." Pharaoh still would not listen. Hail, turning to fire as it hit the ground, caused great destruction to flax and barley crops as they were ripening in the fields.

The Egyptian people could not make their clothing without flax. And with no barley, they could not brew the beer that they needed for daily drink and religious libations. Then the plague of locusts hit. Those crops which the hail had not touched, the locusts devoured. Still Pharaoh would not free us from bondage. God then, unannounced, caused darkness that lasted for three days to descend upon Egypt. Ra, the greatest of their gods, could not banish the darkness. Our God was destroying all they believed their gods had created! Yahweh will prevail. We will be free by tomorrow."

The sun was about to set as they approached Ziva's home. Her family, including her uncle Moses, his wife Zipporah ("bird") and son Gershom ("a stranger there") were already inside the house. Yonatan's father Simeon was there also. They were waiting with great dread for what was to occur at midnight. This would be when God's hand, in the form of a destroying angel, moved over Egypt. He would only spare those inside dwellings where bunches of hyssops had been used to sprinkle lamb's blood on the doorposts and lintel.

The evening meal was different this night. Lamb was eaten to recall their past heritage as shepherds. Herbs consisting of lettuce, watercress and endive were consumed to symbolize their bondage in the present moment, as well as the plagues that had befallen the Egyptians because of Pharaoh's unwise decisions. As symbols of the journey they would be embarking upon and the land that the Lord promised would be theirs in the future - a land flowing with milk and honey—they partook of the unleavened bread of haste and they drank sweet honey wine.

Vengeance

At midnight, the Destroyer arrived and took the lives of the firstborn of Egypt. And after this, the word reached the Hebrews of Goshen that Pharaoh had finally set them free. He told Moses that the Hebrews could take any spoils they wished, but they should just leave. Over the next few days, they, as well as many others who had sought God's protection as His spirit passed over Egypt, prepared for the journey. Yonatan and Ziva decided to take a last walk through the fields that they had played upon as children and had strolled through as young lovers.

Yonatan spoke softly, but solemnly, to Ziva." Before your uncle returned from Midian, do you remember my telling you of the dream I had? In it, the Deliverer took us out of Egypt, as if we were borne upon the wings of an eagle, God's wings. But I've had other dreams about the journey to the land promised to us. The concerns you expressed were not wrong. The land will not simply fall into our hands. We will struggle with our own faith and fight many battles with others before proving ourselves worthy to enter the land of promise."

"What about us? Ziva replied. Will we marry in the wilderness or in the land that God will take us to? Will we be safe and happy there?"

Yonatan's eyes grew sad for an instant. He turned away from Ziva so she would not notice. He then knelt on the ground and in the soft soil he wrote with his fingertips these words: One body, one soul. "And remember this Ziva. God will keep us from evil. He will protect our souls, the going out and the coming in. Forever."

He stood up and took Ziva's hand. They walked back home as the darkness of evening began to overtake the sky. They were at the edge of the meadow, when, as if out of nowhere, someone was standing beside them. It was an Egyptian nobleman—Gahiji's father! With a quick movement, he plunged a knife deep into Yonatan's chest. "My son's death is avenged!" he cried out. He then disappeared into the night.

Ziva fell on her knees, next to where Yonatan lay dying. She cradled him in her arms, as he spoke his last words "Follow after God, forever!" She kissed his lips and then rocked his body back and forth. She could not let him go. They found her like this hours later, having to pry her away from Yonatan's body. Simeon, his father and only family, was there, sobbing uncontrollably. Despite his grief, he tried to console Ziva, but something in her mind had snapped. She had not even cried. Simeon looked up to heaven: "God of Abraham, why?" Ziva, on her feet now, stared at him blankly. She knew where the guilt was to be found. If the first born of the Egyptians had not died, Yonatan would still be alive. And when Yonatan was buried, she could barely look at Moses, her uncle. In her tormented mind, she blamed Moses and God for what had happened. And she knew what must be done. She would seek revenge.

The Exodus and Dreams

The shofars sounded from all directions, signaling that the tribes of Israel should assemble. The six hundred thousand Israelites, as well as the mixed multitude who had joined them, listened to the words of God's servant and their leader, Moses, "Hear, O Israel, the Lord, our God, the Lord is One." The Hebrews repeated his words, thus, confirming their faith in God alone, denying any other god or gods. They were ready to leave Egypt, not knowing what tomorrow would bring nor caring. They were free. And they now saw themselves as a nation—Israel—not simply a loose confederation of different tribes.

Amongst those who had known Yonatan, all but one remembered the vision he had for his people. A vision of freedom that was about to materialize. They would honor his memory by bravely venturing into this new reality, where they would shape their own future. Ziva had forgotten Yonatan's dreams, or at least had blocked them from her thoughts. She left Egypt with her people, but her heart, her joy in life, was buried in memories of her time in Goshen with Yonatan. All that propelled her now was her need to avenge his death. His murderer had vanished into the night, but to her, the true culprit resided in the minds of the Israelites, in their belief in the One God. And who but her uncle was most responsible for fanning the passions for this God.

When night came upon the encampment at Succoth, they rested. The sky above was covered by clouds that appeared to be on fire. For the people, this was proof of God's protective presence. Perhaps, it was this sight that caused Ziva to dream. A woman appeared to her. She was beautiful, with fiery red hair and fair skin.

Her voice was strong and compelling. "I am Lilith." she said.

In folklore and mysticism, Lilith ("*lailah* [night]") is seen as Adam's first wife. She was strong-willed and would not give in to any of her husband's desires. She fled from him. Adam pleaded with God to bring her back to Eden. God sent angels to find her, but she could not be captured. One of the angels, Samael, curious about humans as all angels are, was fascinated by Lilith. So much so, that he fell from God's grace and was banished from heaven. Lilith transformed into a demoness, a succubus, who stole men's seed and took the breath of life from babies in the night. She hated both man and God. Her goal was to destroy God's creation and replace it with her own.

"I have heard tales of you. Some say you are a demoness, others see you as a goddess. What do you want of me?" Ziva said with both awe and puzzlement.

"I am seen differently by each person, but once, I was a woman, like you, Ziva. I only wanted women to be respected. And we can be, when we take control of our own destiny and depend on nothing, but our own wits. You could help me accomplish so much. I have vowed not to let God or man stand in my way."

Ziva felt that in Lilith she had found a kindred spirit. Yet, Yonathan had great reverence for God. Perhaps it would be wrong to ally herself with this woman. But on the other hand...

Lilith spoke once more, reading Ziva's thoughts. "I know of Yonatan. He was not like most men, yet this mighty God ended his life. There was so much he could have done for his people. And the happiness he brought to you. It was taken away by Yahweh. Who but the foolish could put their faith in such a god?"

Ziva's sentiments exactly. Lilith spoke the truth. "I will follow you. Tell me what I must do." Ziva looked to Lilith for instruction.

"When you awaken, you will know what needs to be done," said Lilith with a sly smile. She disappeared and Ziva woke up with a start.

Men had always looked with yearning at Ziva. Yet in the past, she had never returned any of their glances. She had only sought to catch the eye of Yonatan. Now, all was different. She looked at men seductively, both the Israelite and those of the mixed multitude. As the days passed, her indiscretions were becoming the talk of the camp. Her own family was growing ashamed of her. And many of the other young women were beginning to follow her lead.

Faith in God was beginning to falter, as the hardships of the journey increased. An occasional pleasure was becoming a regular diversion for many of the men, both young and old alike. Yes. Lilith was absolutely correct when she said Ziva would know what needed to be done. And Ziva did it well.

At the Foot of the Holy Mountain

Over and over again, the Lord proved His greatness and might to the people. It was most evident when Pharaoh decided he had acted too hastily, in allowing the slaves to leave Egypt. He sent his chariots after the Hebrews who were camped at the edge of the Red or Reed Sea. They would have been trapped if God had not parted the waters so that the Hebrews were able to pass safely between the walls of water that now raged on either side. When everyone was on the opposite shore, the waters suddenly crashed down upon the Egyptians who came to pursue them. All of Pharaoh's charioteers died. Such a feat would prove the Lord is God, but the people grew restless as each day went by. God produced food for them, when they hungered, and water, when they thirsted. They still doubted Him. And Ziva, with helpful suggestions from Lilith, who continued to appear in her dreams, used these doubts to further drive a wedge between the people and their God.

Moses led the people to the foot of Sinai, the holy mountain in Midian. He had gone up upon it to receive God's law and had been away for many days. One afternoon, Ziva brought water and a smile to Issachar ("reward"), the son of Jahath ("He will deplete"). The men of the camp respected him and listened to his words, especially now that Moses was not in sight. Ziva saw in him a very useful tool in achieving her goal—destroying the people's faith.

She plied him with her words, "The God of Our Fathers toys with us, do you not agree Issachar? He leads us into the barren desert. In Egypt, our labors were difficult, but we knew what each day would bring. Not this uncertainty that we face now. Where is my uncle? Could any man look upon a god and live?"

"Moses will return to us, with the Law, as he promised," Issachar responded with a tinge of doubt in his voice.

Ziva sensed his uncertainty. "And if he doesn't, what will become of us all? Would it not be better to return to Egypt?"

"We would be slaughtered." was his response.

"Not if we built a god of gold and worshipped it in their way. Then they would accept us. The dislike and distrust they feel for us would vanish. We would be like them, not the strange and hated people who believe in a god that cannot be seen," Ziva said convincingly.

More time passed and Moses still did not return from the mountain. Issachar and others began to echo Ziva's words. They argued with Aaron, her father, who had been anointed High Priest, that he must build a golden calf for them. At first Aaron refused, but the people were growing more and more restless. Anger coupled with fear was beginning to cloud their judgment. Finally, he gave in to their demands. He asked that the people break the golden rings in their ears and then bring them to him. Many, willingly, did so. And Aaron melted the rings and used the molten liquid to fashion the Golden Calf.

And the next day, which Aaron had proclaimed a feast day, the people danced and sang before the idol. Any sense of morality had vanished, and perversity was rampant in the camp. Ziva was at the center of it, reveling in her triumph. She danced lasciviously before the men. She paused and climbed up upon the altar. There, she loudly proclaimed that this golden idol was their new god who would lead them back to Goshen, where they belonged.

Then they heard him. It was Moses. He had come down from the holy mountain. A strange light shone from his face. The two stone tablets, upon which God's laws were written thereon by His own fingers, were held in each of his arms. From his vantage point, he could see the corruption that had overtaken the camp. "Since you choose not to live by God's law, you will die by it." At this, he hurled the tablets at the altar of the Golden Calf, where his niece, Ziva, had perched herself. She perished in an instant, but in that instant every cell in her body was alive with agonizing pain.

From Darkness into Light

Somehow, Ziva was aware of the darkness. She was a soul without a body. She knew other souls were present in this place beyond time and space. She had no physical attributes, yet she sensed their sadness, which was her sadness. In this forsaken realm, they were lost to all, forever. Forever! She was to be with Yonatan, forever. But he was not here. How could he be? Those who resided at this level of Sheol had committed the most grievous sins. Their souls could not be redeemed.

Slowly, a sound began to manifest itself in the darkness. It was a still, silent voice. She thought she could hear her name being called. "Ziva," it whispered.

"*Hineni (*Here I am)," she replied.

"You know why you are here, don't you?"

At this, Ziva recalled all the evil she had wrought in her last days. It was as if she was revisiting that terrible time, moment by moment.

The still, silent voice continued to reveal itself to Ziva. "You sought to destroy all that held your people together—the *Ikkar*, the Principle. There must be a moral order in which humans deal fairly with each other and act as caretakers of the Earth. The evil that filled your soul, and that of so many others, continues on, even when life ends. When evil far outweighs good, all worlds feel its negative effect. To make sure balance is maintained, souls such as yours are kept in the Dark Place. However, a Righteous One has interceded on your behalf.

You will be able to leave Sheol, if you so choose. Yes, even here a soul has free will. Yours will have a new purpose, a new path to travel. It will transmigrate numerous times in an attempt to restore the balance of energy that was upset by your transgressions. You will lead many battles against those, such as Lilith, who appeal to the evil impulse of human nature—the *yetzer hara*. And the Holy Ark containing My laws will be carried before you. You are being given a chance to redeem yourself. Your name has been erased from all memory, but you can restore it. You can make it honorable by following your *yetzer hatov*—impulse to do good. Do you wish this to be so?"

Ziva pictured Yonatan in front of her. Was he with her, even in the darkness? And the Righteous One who pleaded for her – was it he? His image faded, but she was sure she knew the answers to her questions. And by her own choice, she decided to embark upon the holy mission that had been offered to her.

And then, a dark flame came forth form the depths of the darkness. The colorless, amorphous fog began to take shape and radiant colors began to issue forth. A supernal point of light shone forth through the colors and overtook all. At the center of this brightness, something was beginning to form.

It is a woman. Her skirt is made with wide strips of leather. Her bodice is leather, also, with sleeves made from narrower strips of leather crisscrossed and held together with metal rivets. A golden eagle comprises the greater part of her breastplate, but at its center is a grid. Within each square of the grid is a jewel, twelve in all, each different, representing the tribes of Israel. On either side of the grid stands a lion. From her braided leather belt, studded with brass rivets, hangs a ram's horn on the left and a hamsa, representing the hand of God, on the right. Her feet are clad in leather sandals with straps that crisscross well above the knees. A sword in a scabbard is strapped to her back. Her gauntlets, again of leather, contain inscriptions. On the right—*acharai ya (*follow God). On the left "—Ein Sof (no end)," the mystical name for God.

Other than her clothing, what does she look like? She is somewhat taller than most women. Her build is strong, yet shapely. She has black wavy hair that cascades down her back to her waist. Her eyes are green and brilliant. Her lips are full and sensuous. She is surrounded by a golden aura, the color of the barley field in Goshen, where two lovers once walked. Her name, itself, implies brightness, brilliance, the splendor of natural illumination. She is *halohemet ziv*—the warrior woman of light. She once was known as Ziva.

Epilogue

Rabbi Aryeh completed his story. I knew he sincerely believed all he had said. However, it would take a lot more to convince me that any part of it could be supported by evidence. But I knew there was more he was not saying. His father's little book led me to believe the secret of Ein Gedi was not about perfume, but about a scroll that had been hidden for over 3000 years. It told of the battles the Hebrews had fought during their wandering through the desert. I needed to ask him a question concerning the very thing that had convinced me to speak with him in the first place.

"The Book of the Wars of the Lord. You know where it is hidden, don't you?" I asked him.

His reply was direct and startling. "You will find it near Ein Gedi in an area you once explored. Look for the cave with the jagged delta shaped opening. Once inside, the four letters of the Holy Name will guide you. Be prepared to find more than you initially sought. I can say no more. It is up to you now."

A week later, I returned to his home. I had found the scroll. It was remarkably well preserved. I did not want to remove it from the large stone chest it rested in. However, I was able to open it a bit, just enough to see some of the writing. Next to it was another scroll, smaller in size and not as well preserved.

From the amount I could read from the smaller scroll, I saw that it spoke of events from a time hundreds of years following events in The Book of the Wars of the Lord. Strangely, it was written by the same hand. How could this be? Then I was able to decipher words that took my breath away—"aron kodesh" (Holy Ark). And "Look for it where the "tannin" (dragon/serpent) sleeps under the city of Jerusalem."

"Rabbi Aryeh, why have you allowed me to discover what you and others have kept as esoteric knowledge from generation to generation? The Ark of the Covenant! This is beyond anything I could ever have imagined. I did not remove the scrolls from the cave, but now I am almost certain that the dragon well (Neh 2:13) will lead to the most important archaeological find in history."

He responded "No one else needs to know about the scrolls. You were right to leave them in the cave. They will remain safe there. The Israel Antiquities Authority would collect them immediately, if they knew about them. You know that. And there are many who would use the Ark, if they had it in their possession, to bring forth more evil upon an already corrupt world. It must be you alone who finds the Holy Ark. Are you aware of the origin of your surname?"

I was puzzled by his question, but answered him. "It is said that the surname 'Ehrlich' was taken by those Jews living in German lands who were directly descended from Aaron, the High Priest and brother of Moses." I paused for a second. "Are you suggesting that somehow I am connected to Ziva, the woman in your story and in Halohemet Ziv?"

I saw him smile. And I began to understand. I closed my eyes and for an instant I saw myself walking with him, long ago, in a field of golden barley."

The Virtual Seder:
15 Nissan, 5780

Kenneth Hanson

Why is this Passover different from all others? Why will the seder of the year 5780 be remembered for all time as the most challenging commemoration of the Exodus from Egypt ever undertaken? When, long ago, the Israelites were liberated from the grasp of a despotic pharaoh, Egypt had been ravaged by ten dreadful plagues, and the shadow of death brooded over the landscape, claiming Egypt's firstborn sons. In our own day, another plague has visited households across the globe, indiscriminately taking the lives of countless innocents. No one is spared, nor will any sign on our door posts and lentils be effectual against an unseen foe, in the form of the virus known as COVID-19.

It is customary at every seder to make an announcement that all those who are hungry or in need are invited to come and partake of this feast. This year, however, the announcement lacked not only sincerity, but veracity, since the bulk of the world's population had been directed to shelter in place. In fact, a counter order was issued. No one was to be invited to this commemoration. This Passover was intended for no gatherings larger than the nuclear family, while an enormous number of Jews were left to observe the seder in lonely solitude.

I am a *ger tzedek*, a Jew by choice, whose wife, a Russian physician with a medical practice in Siberia, and our adopted eight-year-old girl girl, were in Novosibirsk, Russia's third largest city, experiencing a similar lockdown as in other parts of the world. One year previously, we applied for a U.S. Green Card for our little girl, but due to the international health emergency, its processing was delayed, with no information as to when it might be processed. Given the eleven-hour time difference between Siberia and America's East Coast, there would be no Passover Seder for our family. I do, however, have a grown son by a previous marriage, also a *ger tzedek*, who lives in the same city as I.

We had been exploring the possibility of having a virtual Seder, and I had been carefully gathering the required elements of the meal. I had done a little grocery shopping, wearing a face mask, at the kosher section of my local supermarket. Both my son in his downtown apartment and I in my empty house busied ourselves that afternoon cooking and preparing *matsa* ball soup.

My mood, however, was somewhat melancholy, considering the absence of my wife and daughter and the reality of the ongoing global pandemic. Conducting my own seder in solitude was unthinkable, and even joining my son via an iPad was a prospect laden with sullen resignation. Would our seder be an expression of joy on any level? Would it resonate with the ancient sentiments of the Israelites upon their release from bondage, or would it be a reflection of our own "house arrest" in a modern nightmare, evincing no signs of deliverance from a new angel of death, stretching hidden tentacles across the globe?

Later that afternoon, as I sat alone in my study, I grabbed my iPad and opened the app I use regularly to watch Israel television news, to find the live streaming of what was being called "The Great Israeli Seder." A large rectangular table in the television studio was decoratively arrayed with sumptuous culinary delights, complementing the traditional Seder plate. Half a dozen guests sat around its perimeter, speaking to the television audience, and sharing personal stories and reflections on the meaning of the feast. They were by no means alone, however. The walls of the studio were literally alive, with scores of video screens, displaying the images of individuals from across the country, who had, through their own computers and devices, magically joined this Seder.

On a personal level I felt mystically connected with them all, sitting mesmerized in front of my own tablet for over two hours. Various Israeli officials and dignitaries, from Bibi Netanyahu to Beni Gantz, to Reuven Rivlin, joined the celebration on their own screens, taking turns reading portions of the Haggadah, putting aside political differences. Most gripping were the live interviews with elderly survivors of the Shoah, who shared memories of previous Passovers, where extended families were gathered together and all seemed well in the land of Israel. The loneliness of the season was expressed as a stark contrast to better days of years gone by. Yet, everyone knew, viscerally, that is Seder was historically unique.

A technological *nes gadol* had transformed isolation into a shared experience unlike any other. The state of Israel had been strictly shut down during this Passover. Police cars cruised the streets and highways throughout the country, making sure the people stayed indoors and refrained from the large gatherings typically associated with Passover. While this horrifying eleventh plague was loose in the land, all who remained within were as secure as if their doorposts and lintels had been dabbed with lamb's blood. As Israel's great virtual Seder concluded, attention returned to the wall of video screens, as an assortment of Israeli citizens took turns singing "Ekhad Mi Yodea?" The amazing harmonies they created, each from his or her own device, were undoubtedly the high point of the evening. Without question the people of Israel, even in isolation, had found a way to come together in the most extraordinary of circumstances.

For me this was a moment of inspiration that changed my attitude toward my own virtual Seder, which I proceeded to arrange with newfound enthusiasm. I covered my dining room table with a fine linen cloth, in the center of which I placed the large silver passover plate that I had purchased in Jerusalem. I established one place-setting for myself and another for Elijah, whose mystical presence would be more appreciated on this particular Pesach. The festival candles, in crystal glass holders I had acquired in Tsfat, were ready for lighting, and the *matsa* ball soup was simmering on the stovetop. I quickly exchanged my T-shirt for a bright white shirt, and covered my head with an intricately designed kippah, also from Tsfat. When the appropriate time came, just prior to sundown, I propped up my iPad on the far end of the table, to provide a full view of what I was doing as I conducted the Seder.

Swiping upward from the home screen, I launched the Facebook app and navigated to a video chat with my son. His image instantly appeared, via his iPad, and he greeted me from his kitchen, spoon in hand, as he finished preparing his own pot of *matsa* ball soup. I rushed back to my kitchen, to shut off the stove, which was warming the other parts of my meal, and hastily returned to commence the candle lighting. Acknowledging that there were no women present to kindle the festival lights, I struck the match myself and proceeded to recite the blessing.

Haggadah in hand, with my son following along in his own apartment, I filled my wine cup and intoned the blessing, not mechanically, but with a sense of *kavannah* ("intention") that I had rarely felt before. Ceremonially washing hands also seemed special on this night, given the degree to which hand washing had become manic, during the pandemic. It was oddly refreshing to wash hands, not from fear of the virus, but simply to attain ritual purity as an element of a higher religious observance.

Linked from iPad to iPad, my son and I continued through the Haggadah. I broke the *matsa*, hid the Afikoman, and my son, being the youngest present, proceeded to recite the four questions. Raising the wine cup, we toasted our endurance as a people, noting that in every generation there have been those who rise against us to annihilate us.

During this Passover season, the annihilating enemy was of course the pandemic. We took turns reciting the story of the Exodus, dipping a finger in the wine cup as we jointly recited the ten plagues. I momentarily paused from my reading of the Haggadah, to replay on my iPhone the recording I had made of the Great Israeli Seder, in which the participants, just hours before, had themselves recited the plagues. We were mindful that we were members of a larger family, united with Jews around the world, performing the same rituals from generation to generation. Continuing our own ceremony, we chanted Dayenu together, with such spirit that we almost forgot the fact that we were quite alone.

We ate the *maror* and Hillel's Sandwich, finally elevating the cup of Elijah. Retreating momentarily from the table, I opened the front door of my home. Alas, Elijah had not come this night, though I found, hanging from the door handle, the weekly service notice from my lawn care team. A poor substitute for the celebrated prophet, they were among those considered an essential service during the lockdown, and I felt that I had, at the very least, been "visited." After drinking the fourth cup of wine, we sang together Chad Gadya and ate the festive meal, separately, yet together.

At the end we made the joint pronouncement, "Next year in Jerusalem!" The traditional declaration carried with it a shared hope, that in the time to come, we should all be free of pestilence and dread, that the meaning of this Passover, faithfully conducted despite every obstacle, will resonate long into the future, that the memory of this unique and special time, virtually experienced through the miracle of technology, will always be present in our hearts.

Contributors

Editors

Zev Garber is Emeritus Professor and Chair of Jewish Studies and Philosophy at Los Angeles Valley College, and he has also served as Visiting Professor of Religious Studies at the University of California at Riverside, Visiting Rosenthal Professor of Judaic Studies at Case Western Reserve University, and as President of the National Association of Professors of Hebrew. As Emeritus Editor of *Shofar* and founding Editor of *Shofat Supplements in Jewish Studies* and *Studies in the Shoah* series, he has presented and/or written hundreds of articles and reviews (academic and popular) in the areas of Judaica, Shoah, Jewish Jesus, and interfaith dialogue. He has authored and edited 15 academic books, including, *Mel Gibson's Passion: The Film, the Controversy, and Its Implications*; *The Jewish Jesus: Revelation, Reflection, Reclamation*; *Teaching the Historical Jesus*; and *Judaism and Jesus* (co-author, Ken Hanson). Colleagues and scholars acknowledge his academic scholarship and leadership in *The Maven in Blue Jeans: A Festschrift in Honor of Zev Garber* (Purdue University Press, 2009).

Kenneth Hanson is an Associate Professor and Coordinator of the University of Central Florida Judaic Studies Program. He earned a Ph.D. in Hebrew Studies from the University of Texas at Austin in 1991. His many scholarly articles focus on the Second Jewish Commonwealth, the Dead Sea Scrolls, the historical Jesus, and Jewish Christianity. He has also published several books of popular scholarship, including: *Dead Sea Scrolls: The Untold Story*; *Kabbalah: Three Thousand Years of Mystic Tradition*; and *Secrets from the Lost Bible*. He has been interviewed multiple times on nationally syndicated radio, and his research was featured on the History Channel documentary, "Banned from the Bible." He teaches a wide range of Judaic Studies courses, including the Hebrew language, the Hebrew Bible, Jewish history and culture, and the history of the Holocaust. He recently produced and narrated an award-winning documentary entitled "The Druze: An Ethnic Minority in the Holy Land."

Contributors

Jonathan Arnold, Esq. is an Oxford-educated attorney versed in the academic, commercial, insurance, multimedia, outside counsel, publishing/podcasting, technology, and UCC law fields. Select and recent articles include *Development of New Approaches in Int'l Trade Law*, (2018, Cal. Int'l. Law Journal) and *The Emerging Locality of International Law*, (2016, Valley Lawyer). He was cited by the California Court of Appeal on the proper application of Specific Jurisdiction, *VirtualMagic Asia, Inc. v. Fil-Cartoons, Inc.* (2002) 99 Cal.App.4th 228, 121 Cal.Rptr.2d 1, 9-11.

Annette Boeckler is Assistant Professor of Jewish Studies at Johannes Gutenberg University of Mayence and rabbinical student at the Levisson Instituut in Amsterdam. She was department leader at the former "Zurich Lehrhaus." Before Brexit, she worked as lecturer and head librarian at the rabbinical seminary Leo Baeck College in London. Her research field is the theology of Jewish prayer, especially the development of German liberal liturgy. She is an internationally acclaimed lecturer and has taught in Brazil, the Netherlands, England, the U.S., Portugal, France, Germany, and Switzerland.

Eugene J. Fisher is Distinguished Professor of Theology at Saint Leo University. He has worked tirelessly for the reconciliation between Catholics and Jews. Ahead of his time, he affected change as Director of Catholic-Jewish relations for the U. S. Conference of Catholic Bishops beginning in 1977; he has also authored numerous works in the field of Catholic-Jewish relations. He has been a Consultor to the Holy See and a member of the International Catholic-Jewish Liaison Committee. Dr. Fisher is an active member of learned and professional societies, such as the Catholic Biblical Association, the National Association of Professors of Hebrew, and the Society of Biblical Literature (SBL). He has lectured widely throughout the United States, Canada, Europe, Latin America, and Australia. He has published over twenty-five books and monographs, and some 300 articles in major religious journals, many of which have been translated into French, Spanish, Italian, Portuguese, Polish and German for publication in Latin America and Europe. See: *"Nostra Aetate*: A Personal Reflection," *Journal of Ecumenical Studies* (Fall 2015, Vol 50, no 4) pages 529-538 and *A Life in Dialogue, Building Bridges between Catholics and Jews: A Memoir*, St. Petersburg, FL: Mr. Media Books, 2017.

Susan Garber, wife of Zev Garber, is a homemaker. She is a gardener and lover of animals who cares for two dogs, a cat, and a parrot, who has been with her for over fifty years. She has proofread several books and is a writer of fantasy and science fiction stories.

Leonard J. Greenspoon holds the Philip M. and Ethel Klutznick Chair in Jewish Civilization at Creighton University, where he is also Professor of Theology and of Classical and Near Eastern Studies. Greenspoon is editor of the 32-volume Studies in Jewish Civilization series. His latest book, *Jewish Bible Translations: Personalities, Passions, Politics, and Progress*, was published by the Jewish Publication Society in November 2020. This is the first ever book-length study of Jewish Bible versions. In 2018, Greenspoon was the recipient of a Festschrift at the 2019 annual meeting of the Society of Biblical Literature, and he was the featured scholar in a section titled "Wisdom of the Ages." For 2020, Greenspoon has also been named researcher of the year at Creighton.

Nathan Harpaz is an art historian and a museum professional. He earned degrees in Psychology and Art History from Tel Aviv University and a doctoral degree in Interdisciplinary Studies from Union Institute and University in Cincinnati, OH. He is a former art museum director in Tel Aviv, Israel and the author of the book published by Purdue University Press *Zionist Architecture and Town Planning: The Building of Tel Aviv (1919–1929)*. Dr. Harpaz is currently the director of the Koehnline Museum of Art near Chicago and he teaches art history, Jewish art, and museum studies at Oakton College.

Yitzchak Kerem is an historian of Greek and Sephardic Jewry, as well as the Holocaust, at the Hebrew University of Jerusalem. He is a researcher at the Institute of Jewish Languages, and a lecturer at the Mekor Sephardic Studies Program and the Jewish History Department. Since 1992 he has also served as editor of the academic e-mail publication "Sefarad vehaMizrah," formerly at Aristotle University, Thessaloniki, Greece. He has also served as director of the Institute of Hellenic-Jewish Relations at the University of Denver and as visiting Israeli scholar in Sephardic Studies at the American Jewish University, Los Angeles (2008–2009). He has been a researcher on Greek Jewry in the Holocaust at Yad Vashem, Jerusalem and has been a contributor to Pinkas Kehilot Yavan (1999), as well as editor of the Greek section in the *New Encyclopedia Judaica*. He has previously served as sub-editor of the *Encyclopedia of the Holocaust* (Balkans section). He has nominated over 1,000 "Righteous Gentiles" for Yad Vashem and coordinated a summer workshop project for researchers on Sephardic Jewry in the Holocaust (1999), at the U.S. Holocaust Memorial Museum. He is a documentary filmmaker on Greek and Sephardic Jewry and the Holocaust, as well as a contributor of articles in the *Larousse Encyclopedia of the Holocaust*, along with publications of the Ben-Zvi Institute. He is an expert in Sephardic and Eastern Jewish Genealogy.

Henry Knight is Professor Emeritus of Holocaust and Genocide Studies and the former Director of the Cohen Center for Holocaust and Genocide Studies at Keene State College in Keene, New Hampshire. Dr. Knight directed the Cohen Center from July 2007 through his retirement in June 2019 and taught in the College's academic program, which offers the nation's first undergraduate major in Holocaust and Genocide Studies. Knight continues to serve as the co-chair of the biennial Steven S. Weinstein Holocaust Symposium (formerly the Pastora Goldner Holocaust Symposium) that he and Prof. Leonard Grob of Fairleigh Dickenson University co-founded in 1996. Prof. Knight is the recipient of two teaching awards for excellence in the classroom from The University of Tulsa and a similar honor from Keene State College. He is the author or editor of several books and numerous articles on post-Holocaust theology and ethics. A past president of the Annual Scholars Conference on the Holocaust and the Churches, Knight continues to serve as a Reader for the Elie Wiesel Foundation for Humanity's *Prize in Ethics* essay contest.

William H. Krieger is Department Chair and Associate Professor of Philosophy at the University of Rhode Island and URI Program Director and Archaeologist with the Tell es-Safi Archaeological Project. He was educated at Columbia University, The Jewish Theological Seminary of America, and Claremont Graduate University. Prof Krieger specializes in issues surrounding Archaeological Theory and Methods, as well as the Philosophy of Science and Technology. His recent publications include, "When Are Medical Apps Medical? Off-Label Use and the FDA" (*Digital Health*, 2016), "Marketing Archaeology" (*Ethical Theory and Moral Practice*, 2014), "Theory, Locality, and Methodology in Archaeology: Just Add Water" (*HOPOS*, 2012*),* and an edited volume that won the *CHOICE* Outstanding Academic Title for 2011, *Science at the Frontiers: Perspectives in the History and Philosophy of Science.*

Susan CM Lumiere is retired from her career as a mentor and teacher of art and academics for the Los Angeles Unified School District, specializing in multicultural and interdisciplinary studies. She also taught Sunday School at Westwood Temple and Hebrew at the Valley Beth Shalom Synagogue. Susan is an artist and former professional dancer and sang for two traveling Israeli dance troupes. Currently, she writes commentaries and satire. She was educated at UCLA, Los Angeles Valley College, American Jewish

University, and Chabad of North Hollywood. She was also the founder of a Yiddish Culture Club in the Los Angeles area.

Diane Mizrachi is the librarian for Jewish and Israel Studies in addition to other Social Sciences at the University of California, Los Angeles. She received her Masters degree in Library Science from Bar Ilan University, Israel, and a Ph.D. in Information Studies at UCLA. She worked as a librarian at Beit Berl College in Kfar Saba, Israel, before coming to UCLA. Her professional research and publications primarily cover college students' library and information behaviors, including library anxiety, and academic reading format (print and electronic) preferences and behaviors. Her passions are Jewish history and philosophy.

Norman Simms was born in Borough Park, Brooklyn in 1940 and went to public school, eventually ending up at Stuyvesant High. He went to Machzike Talmud Torah in the 1940s. He gained a BA at Alfred University in upstate New York and then an MA and PhD from Washington University in St Louis. After four years in Canada at the University of Manitoba, he went to New Zealand with his wife and two children, and stayed there until he retired in 2010 spending his career at the University of Waikato. He had various study leaves abroad (Folklore Institute in Bucharest; Folklife Institute in Leeds, UK; Jewish Studies Center in Brown University in the USA). He has taught in France (Université de Pau and La Nouvelle Sorbonne in Paris) and in Israel (Ben Gurion University). In Hamilton, New Zealand he and his wife ran the local Jewish Studies Association for about twenty-five years, with Jewish Studies weekend seminars regularly. He retired in 2010 and has been at home writing articles, books, and reviews.

David Patterson holds the Hillel A. Feinberg Distinguished Chair in Holocaust Studies at the Ackerman Center for Holocaust Studies, University of Texas at Dallas and a Senior Research Fellow at the Institute for the Study of Global Antisemitsm and Policy (ISGAP). He is a commissioner on the Texas Holocaust and Genocide Commission, a member of the Executive Board of Academic Advisors for ISGAP, and a member of the Executive Board of the Annual Scholars' Conference on the Holocaust and the Churches. He has lectured at universities on six continents and throughout the United States. A winner of the National Jewish Book Award, the Koret Jewish Book Award, and the Holocaust Scholars' Conference Eternal Flame Award, he has published more than 35 books and more than 240 articles, essays, and book chapters on topics in literature, philosophy, the Holocaust, and Jewish studies. His most recent books are *Shoah and Torah* (SUNY, forthcoming); *Elie Wiesel's Hasidic Legacy* (SUNY, forthcoming); *The Holocaust and the Non-Representable* (SUNY, 2018); *Anti-Semitism and Its*

Metaphysical Origins (Cambridge, 2015); *Genocide in Jewish Thought* (Cambridge, 2012); and *A Genealogy of Evil: Anti-Semitism from Nazism to Islamic Jihad* (Cambridge, 2010).

Roberta Sabbath earned her Ph.D. in Comparative Literature from the University of California, Riverside. As Religious Studies Coordinator and Visiting Assistant Professor in the English Department, Dr. Sabbath publishes and speaks frequently in the religious studies and culture fields. Editor of *Sacred Tropes: Tanakh, New Testament, and Qur'an as Literature and Culture* (Brill Press 2009) and *Troubling Topics, Sacred Texts: Readings in Hebrew Bible, New Testament, and Qur'an* (De Gruyter Press 2021), she also teaches both religious studies and literature classes including Bible (Hebrew Bible, New Testament, Qur'an) as Literature, mythology, world literature, and Judaism and Jewish Identities. Her monograph-in-progress is *Sacred Body: Readings in Jewish Literary Illumination*. Dr. Sabbath created the Hate Uncycled: 4 Conversations series for UNLV Townhall events (Spring 2021) and is collaborating with the UNLV Dance Department for Holocaust Survivor Choreographic Collaboration, which is a video, dance, and oral history project developed from earlier collaborations for World Literature and UNLV Veterans Administration.

Peter S. Zaas is Professor of Biblical Studies and Director of the Kieval Institute for Jewish-Christian Studies at Siena College in Loudonville, NY. He was educated at the Cleveland College of Jewish Studies, Oberlin College, and the University of Chicago, where he earned a Ph.D. in New Testament and Early Christian Studies. He is the author of a number of articles in the fields of New Testament, Jewish theology, and the religious history of the Second Temple period, including contributions to A. Cohen and P. Mendes-Flohr, eds. *Contemporary Jewish Religious Thought* (1987), A.-J. Levine and M. Brettler, ed. *Jewish Annotated New Testament* (2011, 2nd rev. ed., 2017), and Zev Garber, ed. *Teaching the Historical Jesus* (2014).

Image Credits

Fig. 1. Image in public domain; Fig. 2. Photo from collection of Douglas Stone. Fig. 3. https://www.aish.com/h/pes/l/48969586.html. Fig. 4. Licensed under the Creative Commons Attribution-Share Alike 2.0 Generic license. Fig. 5. Image in public domain. Fig. 6. Licensed under the Creative Commons Attribution-Share Alike 4.0 International license. Fig. 7. Image in public domain. Fig. 8. Licensed under the Creative Commons Attribution-Share Alike 1.0 Generic license. Fig. 9. Image in public domain. Fig. 10. Image in public domain. Fig. 11. Image in public domain. Fig. 12. Image in public domain. Fig. 13. Image in public domain. Fig. 14. Image in public domain. Fig. 15. Image in public domain. Fig. 16. Image in public domain. Fig. 17. Image created by Susan Lumière.